SIGNIFYING ANIMALS

ONE WORLD ARCHAEOLOGY
Series Editor: P. J. Ucko

SIGNIFYING ANIMALS

Human meaning in the natural world

Edited by Roy Willis

Department of Social Anthropology, University of Edinburgh

London and New York

First published by Unwin Hyman Ltd in 1990

First published in paperback 1994
by Routledge
11 New Fetter Lane, London EC4P 4EE

Simultaneously published in the USA and Canada
by Routledge
29 West 35th Street, New York, NY 10001

Typeset in 10 on 11 point Bembo by Computape (Pickering) Ltd, Pickering,
North Yorkshire

Printed and bound in Great Britain at the University Press Cambridge

British Library Cataloguing in Publication Data
A catalogue record for this book is available from the British Library

Library of Congress Cataloging in Publication Data
   Signifying animals: human meaning in the natural world / edited by Roy Willis.
      p.   cm. (One world archaeology: 16)
   Includes bibliographical references.
   1. Animals – Symbolic aspects. 2. Animals – Folklore.
3. Hunting and gathering societies. I. Willis, Roy G.
GR705.S57 1989
398.2'45-dc20 89–16644

ISBN 0–415–09555–7

List of contributors

Atholl Anderson, Department of Anthropology, University of Otago, Dunedin, New Zealand.

Mark Tomas Bahti, Independent Researcher, Tucson, Arizona, USA.

G. Koolemans Beynen, Library, Ohio State University, Columbus, USA.

Mary Douglas, Department of Anthropology, University College London, UK.

Jawaharlal Handoo, Folklore Unit, Central Institute of Indian Languages, Mysore, India.

David C. Hyndman, Department of Anthropology and Sociology, University of Queensland, St Lucia, Australia.

Anthony Jackson, Department of Social Anthropology, University of Edinburgh.

Wendy James, Institute of Social Anthropology, Oxford University, UK.

Ian Keen, Department of Anthropology, Australian National University, Canberra, ACT, Australia.

Elizabeth A. Lawrence, Independent Researcher, Adamsville, Rhode Island, USA.

J. Olowo Ojoade, Centre for Development Studies, University of Jos, Jos, Nigeria.

Ann Osborn,★ Fundación de Investigaciones Arqueológicas Nacionales, Bogotá, Colombia.

Gísli Pálsson, Department of Sociology, University of Iceland, Reykjavik, Iceland.

Bernard Saladin d'Anglure, Department of Anthropology, Université Laval, Québec, Canada.

Nicholas J. Saunders, Department of Archaeology, University of Southampton, UK.

Eugenia Shanklin, Trenton State College, Trenton, New Jersey, USA.

Slawoj Szynkiewicz, Department of Ethnology, University of Warsaw, Poland.

Roy Willis, Department of Social Anthropology, University of Edinburgh, UK.

Pablo G. Wright, Argentine Centre of American Ethnology, Bueños Aires, Argentina.

★ Deceased

Foreword

This book is one of a major series of more than 20 volumes resulting from the World Archaeological Congress held in Southampton, England, in September 1986. The series reflects the enormous academic impact of the Congress, which was attended by 850 people from more than 70 countries, and attracted many additional contributions from others who were unable to attend in person.

The *One World Archaeology* series is the result of a determined and highly successful attempt to bring together for the first time not only archaeologists and anthropologists from many different parts of the world, as well as academics from a host of contingent disciplines, but also non-academics from a wide range of cultural backgrounds, who could lend their own expertise to the discussions at the Congress. Many of the latter, accustomed to being treated as the 'subjects' of archaeological and anthropological observation, had never before been admitted as equal participants in the discussion of their own (cultural) past or present, with their own particularly vital contribution to make towards global, cross-cultural understanding.

The Congress therefore really addressed world archaeology in its widest sense. Central to a world archaeological approach is the investigation not only of how people lived in the past but also of how, and why, changes took place resulting in the forms of society and culture which exist today. Contrary to popular belief, and the archaeology of some 20 years ago, world archaeology is much more than the mere recording of specific historical events, embracing as it does the study of social and cultural change in its entirety. All the books in the *One World Archaeology* series are the result of meetings and discussions which took place within a context that encouraged a feeling of self-criticism and humility in the participants about their own interpretations and concepts of the past. Many participants experienced a new self-awareness, as well as a degree of awe about past and present human endeavours, all of which is reflected in this unique series.

The Congress was organized around major themes. Several of these themes were based on the discussion of full-length papers which had been circulated some months previously to all who had indicated a special interest in them. Other sessions, including some dealing with areas of specialization defined by period or geographical region, were based on oral addresses, or a combination of precirculated papers and lectures. In all cases, the entire sessions were recorded on cassette, and all contributors were presented with the recordings of the discussion of their papers. A major part of the thinking behind the Congress was that such a meeting of many hundreds of participants that did not leave behind a published record of its academic discussions would be little more than an exercise in tourism.

Thus, from the very beginning of the detailed planning for the World Archaeological Congress in 1982, the intention was to produce post-Congress books containing a selection only of the contributions, revised in the light of discussions during the sessions themselves as well as during subsequent consultations with the academic editors appointed for each book. From the outset, contributors to the Congress knew that if their papers were selected for publication, they would have only a few months to revise them according to editorial specifications, and that they would become authors in an important academic volume scheduled to appear within a reasonable period following the Southampton meeting.

The publication of the series reflects the intense planning which took place before the Congress. Not only were all contributors aware of the subsequent production schedules, but also session organizers were already planning their books before and during the Congress. The editors were entitled to commission additional chapters for their books when they felt that there were significant gaps in the coverage of a topic during the Congress, or where discussion at the Congress indicated a need for additional contributions.

One of the main themes of the Congress was devoted to 'Cultural Attitudes to Animals, including Birds, Fish and Invertebrates'. The theme was based on discussion of precirculated full-length papers, covering four and a half days, and was under the overall control of Tim Ingold, Senior Lecturer in the Department of Social Anthropology, University of Manchester, and Mark Maltby, Research Fellow in the Faunal Remains Unit of the Department of Archaeology, University of Southampton. The choice of this topic for a major theme arose from a desire to explore, from an interdisciplinary perspective, the many facets of the varying relationships that have developed between humans and animals, as these are reflected by the historical diversity of cultural traditions.

Discussions during the Congress were grouped around four main headings, each of which has led to the publication of a book. The first, organized by Tim Ingold, was concerned with 'What is an Animal?', leading to the book of the same title. The second subtheme, on 'The Appropriation, Domination and Exploitation of Animals', lasted for over a day and a half and was under the control of Juliet Clutton-Brock, editor of the volume *The walking larder: patterns of domestication, pastoralism, and predation*. A day was devoted to discussion of the 'Semantics of Animal Symbolism' and the co-ordinator, Roy Willis, is also the editor of this resulting book. Howard Morphy was in charge of the fourth subtheme on 'Learning from Art about the Cultural Relationships between Humans and Animals', and has edited the volume entitled *Animals into art*.

The overall theme took as its starting point the assumption that there is no *one* human attitude consistently maintained towards a particular species of animal, and that similar human sentiments have been attached to a huge variety of different animals at different times and in different places. It set out to investigate the similarities and differences in practices and beliefs connected with animals, including birds, fish, and invertebrates, across both time and space.

Prior to this century, in the West, animal behaviour was usually portrayed and interpreted in terms of a contrast with human behaviour. Darwin was not alone in his frequent adoption of an anthropocentric perspective in formulating questions and in presenting hypotheses and interpretations. It has often been claimed that people of non-Western cultures generally view animals quite differently. Another aim of the Congress theme was to explore such contrasts and to suggest some of the factors underlying both anthropomorphic and anthropocentric perceptions of animals which are currently prevalent, at least in Western society.

Ecological, psychological, cultural, and utilitarian considerations are all involved in peoples' attitudes to, and treatment of, other species. These factors were considered not only from a wide, interdisciplinary point of view but also, as befits a world archaeological context, especially in an historical perspective, giving due emphasis to their changes over time.

For example, in the West when those of us who live in towns and cities think of dogs and cats we usually think of them as companions, although dogs are also, in other contexts, considered essential for herding, guarding, and hunting other animals. In ancient Egypt, cats were often shown in artwork as pets, but they were possibly also used to hunt and catch birds. In many present-day cultures across the world people think of quite different animals, such as cattle and pigs, as friends or companions. On the other hand, the hyaena is normally considered by the layman today to be wild and untrainable, yet an ancient Egyptian representation appears to show one being handled. Once we move beyond the normal level of trying to ascertain from any excavation simply what animals were eaten or used for transportation, we are bound to look again at the nature of the relationships and interactions between human groups and the animals in their environments. Another aim of this theme, therefore, was to investigate how different people think, and thought, about different classes of animals, to discover the principles of classification involved, and to show how these principles constituted logical systems of belief and action. The presence of so many Congress participants from the so-called Third and Fourth Worlds made it possible to embrace a truly cross-cultural perspective on these issues.

One point of interest lies in the investigation, on a worldwide basis, of the reason why particular animals have been domesticated by humans – whether for food, such as meat or milk, or for other reasons, such as for ritual purposes.

Contributors to the theme on 'Cultural Attitudes to Animals' adopted a variety of perspectives for looking at the complex ways in which past and present humans have interrelated with beings they classify as animals. Some of these perspectives were predominantly economic and ecological, others were symbolic, concerned with the classification of both the physical and the social environment, and still others were primarily philosophical or theological. All these different perspectives are required for a full interpretation of the artworks of the past, which in their representations of humans and animals reveal some of the foci and inspirations of cultural attitudes to animals.

In focusing on the nature of the varying relationships that can develop between human and animals, one is led inevitably to the question: what actually is an animal or a human? By asking such a question, archaeologists and others are forced to become aware of their own individual and cultural preconceptions, and to pay attention to a set of problems concerning attitudes.

In this book Roy Willis and his contributors are concerned with the 'special' relationships, some of which have been grouped together under the term 'totemism', that may exist between humans and animals. The main themes in *Signifying animals* are discussed in its Introduction. My aim in this Foreword is to examine those aspects of the book that have struck me personally as being of particular fascination, and to draw attention to the possible implications of these aspects for archaeological enquiry.

As the Introduction points out, totemism is a concept that has played an enormously important part in the historical development of social anthropology. Of course, in the latter part of the 19th century there was no disciplinary division between archaeology and anthropology, and various kinds of totemic interpretation were also quite commonly applied to past societies. The concept of totemism acquired a central place, particularly in the works of psychologists (Wundt 1916, Freud 1950 (1912–13), Neumann 1974, pp. 269–70) as they grappled with the supposed prehistoric development of the human psyche. In some cases, totemism even became the title of a supposed stage in human development.

Although the concept of totemism did not retain a central place in archaeological theory in general, it is often forgotten that it has continued to be associated with certain classes of archaeological evidence, not least the mobile, and particularly the parietal, art of Upper Palaeolithic Europe (Ucko & Rosenfeld 1967, pp. 123–37, 174–95; *Animals into art*, edited by H. Morphy) as well as some prehistoric figurine complements (Clark 1961, p. 103). In addition, it still lurks today in the secondary literature dealing with a very wide variety of cultures, from the Lower and Upper Palaeolithic (Maringer 1960), to predynastic Egypt, with supposed totemic 'nomes' (districts) (James 1957, p. 235).

By and large, it must be admitted that the continued use of the term totemism within certain specialist archaeological circles has not been accompanied by any great sophistication or refinement of the concept itself. Indeed, it is striking that one of the supposed signs of prehistoric totemic practice has been taken to be a taboo on the eating of the animal species with which a special relationship has been presumed to exist in the culture concerned. Archaeologists have ignored, or been ignorant of much, if not all, of the complexity of totemic relationship(s) as they are revealed in this book (and see Ingold 1988, Tapper 1988). As outlined in the Introduction, it is almost as if archaeology has remained fixed at the point of Rivers's (1914) third element of totemism – a ritual prohibition on the eating of a totemic species – without even realizing that such a practice was, in any case, just one of three supposedly conjoined aspects of totemism. In some cases, archaeological disregard of anthropological attempts to refine and define the term appears to be almost a matter of some pride (Giedion 1962, p. 283):

> The many shades of meaning that totemism can assume are not directly important in our context: whether it represented direct descent from an animal, a close relationship between one's primeval ancestor and a revered animal, interchange of forms (the animal becoming a man or a man taking on the form of an animal); or whether the major emphasis lies with the tribal totem or the individual totem.

Thus, totemism, in archaeological interpretation, has been seen as the end result of a postulated practice vaguely assumed to reflect an ancient close relationship between the animal and human world, whether that close relationship was derived primarily from economic considerations (*The walking larder*, edited by J. Clutton-Brock), or from some supposed early psychological interdependence between the two (*What is an animal?*, edited by T. Ingold). Only in very exceptional cases (e.g. Cook & Ranere in *The walking larder*) has the archaeologist recognized differential animal–human relations as either the reflection of particular forms of social organization or of emblems representing social or cultural groupings.

Still less does archaeology appear to have entered the debate about totemic practices being an essential part of the ongoing interdependence between human beings and Nature (see Introduction, and Shennan in *What's new?*, edited by S. E. van der Leeuw & R. Torrence). *Signifying animals* is a book that should place a reconsideration of the prehistoric evidence for human–animal relationships high on the agenda of future research. All too often such relationships continue to be expressed solely in terms of presumed 'cult' animals (e.g. Ross 1967, pp. 306, 308, 310 for the Celts), even by those who do not assume an evolutionary stage of totemism with an automatic development from a zoomorphic to an anthropomorphic cult (Ross 1967, pp. 297–8).

The walking larder examined and stressed the critically important ecological balance between human beings and their animal foods in a variety of different situations in time and place. Even in this context *attitudes* to the animals concerned were found to be of the utmost importance. *What is an animal?* emphasized that a clear-cut division of the world into humans and animals, on the basis of simple economic or attitudinal criteria, was likely to be a serious oversimplification of the actual situations to be found in any cultural system in the world. The complex nature of the human/animal world is also clearly exposed in *Animals into art*, a book that examines the special characteristics of expression through art of some of the considerations developed in detail in *Signifying animals*.

Many of the lessons in the following pages may not be easy for archaeologists to assimilate and accommodate. Indeed, several essential parts of the
now historical anthropological debate have yet to be considered by archaeologists, no doubt only to be rejected, in many cases, in favour of new
possibilities for interpretation of archaeological material. For example,
much of the archaeological interest in the postulated existence of totemism
in the past arose from a little-understood claim by Lévy-Bruhl (1966) (see
Introduction) that totemism was part of the world-view that characterized
the 'primitive', and thus was one of the elements that differentiated primitive thought from the thought-processes of more 'complex' human cultures.
Archaeologists must come to terms with the fact that the relationship
between humans and animals remains both intimate and anything but rigid
in all societies, including contemporary Western ones, and is thus neither a
thing of the past nor limited to 'other peoples'. As the above books in the
One World Archaeology series exemplify (and see also *Who needs the past?* and
Conflict in the archaeology of living traditions, both edited by R. Layton), to
attempt to diagnose a totemic relationship between human and animal
simply on the basis of an assumption of a different mode of thought in
ancient times would be insupportable. If totemism were present in previous
societal groupings it would undoubtedly have played an essential part, as it
does today, in the definition of what constituted such a society. As a result,
its presence (or absence) may provide extremely important information
about the nature of possible past social organization, information of a kind
not normally thought to be available to the archaeologist.

Before the 1960s the study of prehistory was grossly influenced by a
classic reluctance to believe that archaeological data could reveal any information beyond the level of technology, subsistence patterns, and ecology.
Recently (*The meanings of things*, edited by I. Hodder), there has been a
strong move towards considering archaeological information as relevant to
and indicative of the ideational sphere. There has also been a growing
realization that exclusive emphasis on group identity and processes
inevitably denigrates the social role of the individual within any given
society (*What's new?*, edited by S. E. van der Leeuw & R. Torrence).
Signifying animals presents a range of new information about the significance
of human–animal (totemic) attitudes and practices, information that is
relevant to both levels of analysis and that challenges archaeologists to
reconsider their material in the context of these parameters of explanation.

To take just one example, attempts have been made (Ucko & Rosenfeld
1967, 1972) to introduce some rigour into the methods whereby archaeologists identify (and thus record) what should be regarded as an anthropo-
morph, a human representation, an amalgam of human and animal features,
and so on. These attempts were undertaken in the context of trying to
decide, for example, the validity of assumptions about the worship of a
single Mother Goddess throughout some 4000 or more years of prehistory
in the Near East, or the relative frequencies of humans, signs, and animals in
Palaeolithic cave art. In some ways the application of such a rigorous

approach was in conflict with the realization that distinctive characteristics of much, if not all, art are not only its symbolic mode but also its inherent quality of ambiguity (*Animals into art*, edited by H. Morphy). Many of the chapters in *Signifying animals* reveal the complexities of concepts about the human form and human nature and their supposed relatedness to nonhuman forms and characteristics. Such complexities are often made explicit in myth and through ritual. *Signifying animals*, therefore, demands that archaeologists clearly recognize the distinction between rigour in their analytical methodologies of classification and typology – which must, almost inevitably, focus on the narrow and 'evident' (e.g. vertical stance, frontal facial features, primary and secondary sexual characteristics, etc., to define the intended human depiction) – and the intricacies and complexities of the indigenous classificatory systems of the cultures that they study. I myself have argued (Ucko & Rosenfeld 1972) for a strict minimal definition for the identification, and sexing, of humans within the Palaeolithic canon of representations, but Rosenfeld (1977) and Khan (1988) have pointed out that to do so risks oversimplification of a culture's repertoire (European Palaeolithic in Rosenfeld's case and Saudi Arabian rock art of several dates in Khan's case), to the extent of possibly grave distortion (see chapters by Clottes and Lorblanchet in *Animals into art*, edited by H. Morphy). Such distortions could be of exactly the kind to obfuscate the sophisticated symbolism adopted by any society to express a complex, and deeply thought-out, philosophy about the nature of the world around, the relationship of humans (however defined) to the non-humans (however defined) surrounding them, and expressing the identity and distinctiveness of the membership of the group to which the 'artist'/practitioner belonged and with which she or he 'identified'.

In a compelling way, therefore, *Signifying animals* challenges one to think again about the possible intentions of those who created such representations as the Hornos de la Peña 'sorcerer' (Ucko 1987, 1989), to think again, not because early interpretations of the depiction, by Luquet (1910) or Breuil (1952), as a 'sorcerer', which rely simply on evidence such as its apparent aslant stance or apparent animal-tail, had any particular virtue, but because the self-evident difference in stylistic convention of such representations from others, which appear to the modern observer to be naturalistic, almost portrait-like, may have been (intended or not as) statements about social identity of a kind barely suspected in the archaeological record until now. Such implications suggest that renewed attention to matters of style *and content* would be profitable, and lead away from currently fashionable approaches (Conkey 1980, Gamble 1982) that ignore content in their search for delimitation of prehistoric groupings, and their possible interactions.

It must be clearly recognized that this book offers no easy remedy for past archaeological sins of omission. On the contrary, even some apparently learnt lessons may have to be reinvestigated. It is true that some recent archaeological analyses of material culture (e.g. *The meanings of things*, edited by I. Hodder) incorporate many approaches deriving from anthropological

symbolic analysis. These include the recognition that the ascription of
special significance to a particular category of object or animal species is not
likely to be due to economic factors alone but to the particular belief system
of the culture concerned, whereby what was classified (i.e. understood
and/or seen) by the particular culture as 'anomalous' is likely to be assigned
special significance. In this book Douglas (Ch. 1) develops this argument
further and warns against the possibility of dangerous oversimplifications.
She suggests that the identification of the anomalous within any classificatory system cannot be accomplished with reference to any assumed *actual*
biological (or other) deviancy; the recognition of anomaly is culture specific.
Just as important is Douglas's self-critical claim that similarity is also a
culture-specific act of classification and therefore cannot, of itself, be
adopted as explanation. It is quite clear that we have until now tended to
accept mere assertions that the practices or products of one society or group
resemble those of another, without making any in-depth analysis of the
phenomena and their social contexts. In the context of social anthropology,
any claim for metaphorical usage must be substantiated by evidence for the
institutionalized (i.e. regular) acceptance of the metaphor within the society
concerned. Without this, Douglas claims, 'the searcher will always find
what he seeks'. In the sphere of archaeology, and most particularly in
prehistoric investigation, the secure identification of similarity and metaphorical usage will have to depend on detailed analysis of use, habit, and
practice. In so recommending, Douglas's advice is strikingly close to that
given by Chase in *Foraging and farming* (edited by D. R. Harris & G. C.
Hillman). Chase investigates the complexity of activity surrounding
the restrictions imposed by Australian Aborigines in the Cape York
Peninsula on

> eating certain plants or animals through their affiliation to certain
> 'dreamings', and the consumption of others . . . only in certain ritual
> contexts, and then only by adult males of a certain ritual status.
> Examples of the latter include the total prohibition of use upon plants
> and animals at certain sites where dreaming ancestors came to rest, and
> the graded restriction of use for various social categories (age, sex,
> mourning relatives, etc.) at specific locations, and for various sizes of
> species.   (*Foraging and farming*, pp. 48–9)

For the archaeologist, therefore, the challenge to be met may well be the
need for even greater detail of description and analysis than is normally
attempted with faunal (and other) remains.
    One of the consequences of attempting to unravel complex social
phenomena is the need to clarify terminology and to elucidate semantic
meanings. Totemism, within the archaeological literature, has become a
somewhat vague term for an undifferentiated complex of practices and ideas.
The situation is somewhat similar to that regarding the term 'complementarity' – which is often used by anthropologists to express the concept that an

entity is at one and the same time both unitary and dual. Whereas anthropologists have recently recognized (Willis, Introduction; Needham 1987) the critical need for a clear definition of terms such as 'totemism' and 'complementarity' before they are further employed, archaeologists have continued to make use of them without being aware, apparently, of the implications of so doing. In the case of 'complementarity' Needham (1987, p. 101) concludes that the term as commonly used by anthropologists 'has no intrinsic logical form'; nonetheless, it has been persistently selected as meaningful and appropriate on a purely intuitive basis (Willis pers. comm.). It formed (and for many scholars still forms) the key concept in attempts to unravel the symbolic (and possibly totemic) meaning of Palaeolithic cave art; just as for many anthropologists it has seemed indispensable in the analysis of schemes of dualistic symbolic classification.

Despite criticisms (Ucko & Rosenfeld 1967, pp. 214, 218) of the term 'complementary opposition' as used by Leroi-Gourhan (1968) in his then revolutionary reinterpretation of Palaeolithic metaphorical and metaphysical expression, the term has continued in vogue in much French and Spanish literature on prehistoric art. Indeed, the whole of the postulated relationship between bovid and horse, and between men and women, as well as between these two categories, as is revealed by analysis of cave art, depends on what is essentially an undefined concept. Now Needham (1987, p. 101) has exposed both 'complementarity' and 'complementary opposition' as devoid of ascertainable meaning, the former in particular 'possess-[ing] no formal properties such as might be defined in the notation of symbolic logic'. Unless archaeologists attempt to recognize the *regular* in their evidence, they have no hope of discerning the code of any past system. In other words, if an anthropologist postulates (Willis pers. comm.) that a particular cosmology, for example, may be based on *anti*-logic ('duality-unity'), it will often be possible to examine this theory in the light of that society's own verbal explanations and statements. In archaeology, however, such a postulation cannot legitimately be made *a priori* with regard to such things as the distribution of parietal motifs within cave areas, nor about consequent symbolic equivalences of animal, abstract, or human depictions there. Similarly, methodological rigour, together with a much greater depth of analysis than is normally carried out, must be the basis for any subsequent sensitive investigation of possible metaphorical meaning within archaeological remains. Failure to clarify the concepts involved and too-ready acceptance of the possibly exceptional as the norm, has led to the unsatisfactory nature of much of the current literature on prehistoric religions (e.g. Gimbutas 1986).

Challenges such as these demand that archaeologists should also rethink their traditional interpretations of the nature of apparent sacrifices, whether of animals or humans. In the past the sacrifice of humans around Archaic Egyptian tombs has been taken (Emery 1961, pp. 135–9) to represent a 'primitive' stage in Egyptian cultural evolution before models of humans were substituted for the real thing. In Kerma, on the contrary, sacrifice of

humans has been assumed (Chaix 1986) to be a particular phase of cultural
expression during which humans took the place of animals. The central
importance of sacrifice, both actual and metaphorical, in many societies – of
whatever degree of so-called social complexity – demands reanalysis of
archaeological evidence of various kinds (e.g. Ross 1967). To fail to appreciate evidence of sacrifice involves failure to recognize evidence for cultural
equivalences between animal (or other) and human. To ignore the sacrificial
as one possible level of interpretation of animal (and other) debris may lead
to all kinds of unwarranted economic assumptions about the society concerned (*The walking larder*, edited by J. Clutton-Brock).

Another of the striking contributions of *Signifying animals* to archaeological interpretation should be the realization of the complexity of devices
adopted by cultures to accommodate the incorporation of belief systems
derived (in whatever way) from other societies. Some of the generally
accepted archaeological statements about changes to the nature of deities
such as Isis, Horus, and many others, under the supposed influence of
Greece and Rome seem wholly unsatisfactory when one reads in this book
about the complex nature of mythical rationalizations for deity incorpor-
ations within the belief systems of many societies. Equally indicative of the
need to rethink much of traditional archaeological interpretation of this kind
of evidence is the realization that economic incorporation of a new plant or
animal species into the normal diet may not be matched, at least for a
considerable period of time, by incorporation also into the belief and
categorization systems of the societies concerned (*Foraging and farming*,
edited by D. R. Harris & G. C. Hillman).

Incorporation of elements from one society by another is a statement
about the nature of change. Conventionally, change – through a diachronic
perspective – is supposed to be the preserve of archaeological and historical
enquiry. This book suggests some of the kinds of influences that may
restrain and then reorientate explanatory models of human–animal interaction, in one case at least such changes being derived from changed
economic activity. The apparent longevity of certain symbolic equivalences
in the past, for example, the falcon with kingship in ancient Egypt (Podgorski 1986), despite frequent political fluctuations and numerous experiments and changes in economic practices, suggests that archaeological data,
with their exceptional depth of enquiry, may be able to shed additional light
on factors of change, incorporation, and innovation (*What's new?*, edited by
S. E. van der Leeuw & R. Torrence). Symbolic equivalences between status
and animal symbolism need to be reinvestigated in terms of effective
changes in control of power within a society – without any necessary
assumption that such changes will have immediate and self-evident visible
effects. Ancient Egypt, with its wealth of literary and artistic evidence
(Kemp 1989), would appear a prime area for reconsideration.

Signifying animals is, therefore, a book that challenges a whole sphere of
archaeological enquiry and interpretation. Quite fundamentally it also questions whether archaeology has been concentrating on the appropriate ques-

tions in its analysis of past remains of animal and human interactions. It may be difficult, in practice, to rid the archaeological literature of the assumption that the special kinship and/or ritual relationship between humans and animals ('totemic') necessarily involves a taboo on the killing and especially on the eating of the animals in question. This is not the case. There may sometimes be such a taboo, but it is in any case not restricted to totemic relationships. After all, as Serpell has already made abundantly clear in *The walking larder* (edited by J. Clutton-Brock), the relationship between humans and their pets often involves a taboo on the killing and eating of the animal concerned.

Much less straightforward is the possibility that reanalysis of existing archaeological data might reveal evidence of cultural contacts previously ignored, but vitally important to most kinds of archaeological interpretation. Interesting possibilities exist in so-called works of art; thus, incorporation of new ideologies may lead to apparently strange equivalences whereby, for example, the horse, cow and/or pig may be equated with humans, while other introduced species are not (*The walking larder*, edited by J. Clutton-Brock). Considerations of stylistic elements of pig and horse representations in contexts such as Laura rock art (Cape York, Australia) should now attempt to confront ideational questions about possible human–animal relations, building on existing analyses of the apparently new stylistic elements in the representations that have so far been interpreted (Rosenfeld *et al.* 1981) only within the context of how these depictions could have acted as successful communication mechanisms. What is at least as challenging is the realization that for however long a particular society may have been involved with animal husbandry (or, presumably, farming), it may still be preoccupied in a major way with expressing its relationship(s) to fauna (and, presumably, flora) through ritual, dance, art, or special dietary preferences or avoidances, etc.

All such considerations take the reader back to the essential question as to whether, or to what degree, archaeology can hope to recover evidence of the 'mental maps' of past cultures. As has become clear over the past few years, and as is made explicit in the books within the *One World Archaeology* series, all archaeology is a matter of interpretation, whether it be concerned with technology, subsistence activities, or social organization. This should not discourage archaeologists from proposing models of past activity in order to explain the archaeological evidence of the past. To do so may well result in complex theoretical analysis and description (*Domination and resistance*, edited by D. Miller, M. Rowlands & C. Tilley; *State and society*, edited by J. Gledhill, B. Bender & M. T. Larsen; *Centre and periphery*, edited by T. Champion), as well as competing alternative theories of explanation, but this is the nature of all healthy social enquiry.

The public at large, and formal educational structures in particular (*The excluded past*, edited by P. Stone & R. MacKenzie), may legitimately demand simplicity and clarity of explanation. However, *Signifying animals* is a most important corrective to any assumptions deriving from the domain of public education that an approach to the study of the past based solely on historical and explanatory narrative can really be appropriate. To ignore the evidence, presented in these pages, for the complexity and sophistication of metaphor between human and animal, for the ingenuity of explanation to account for apparent similarities and dissimilarities between categories of Natural and Cultural elements that are part and parcel of all human activity, whatever its time or place, would be to denigrate the potential richness of the evidence with which the archaeologist is confronted.

Equally, this book challenges archaeology, in an unprecedented way, to deny its Western inheritance, that is, the assumption that the complexity of belief systems, and the actions resulting from such beliefs, are beyond its reach. It challenges reanalysis of this category of archaeological material and demands that all archaeologists be as daring as those who have already moved into the sphere of attempting to deduce social organizations and social structures from static material cultures. These enlightened archaeologists have transformed our expectations about what may have existed in prehistoric periods, infinitely enriching what were previously assumed to be cultural waste lands. It is necessary now to make people aware of the kinds of conceptual complexities that presumably coexisted with the kinship, territorial, and power structures that archaeologists nowadays believe to have existed in past societies.

Many chapters in this book are controversial. Some will undoubtedly convince by their revelations about the nature of the particular archaeological evidence concerned; for example, that it is no longer satisfactory to accept a level of explanation that simply categorizes material – without further analysis of symbolism – as funerary goods. Other chapters may not convince, but they certainly demonstrate the kinds of complex explanatory frameworks that need to be applied to the archaeological material concerned. It is the nature of complexity, and the kinds of parameters that may have been employed to make explicit the fundamental complexity of the human–animal relationship by all of the societies with which archaeologists and anthropologists are concerned, that is the fundamental point at issue; as Geertz puts it, 'the sort of piled up structures of inference and implication' through which the archaeologist, just like the ethnographer, 'is continually trying to pick his way' (quoted by Douglas, Ch. 1).

The Introduction to this book reports that totemism was 'officially pronounced dead nearly 30 years ago, [but] obstinately refuses to "lie down"'. Uncomfortably for archaeology, but undoubtedly to the benefit of its future development, 'it presently exhibits a vitality recalling the great days [of the past]'. Part of any vitality within future archaeological investigation will depend on the outcome of future discussions as to whether totemism can be accepted as the means through which humans have categorized the world around them in terms of their own human societal principles of classification, as well as by the success or otherwise of archaeological attempts to develop rigorous methods by which to pick up the indications of totemic practices, let alone systems, from the evidence of past societal debris.

Should these two elements come together in archaeological enquiry, *Signifying animals* will be seen as a major landmark in such future developments.

P. J. Ucko
Southampton

References

Breuil, H. 1952. *Four hundred centuries of cave art.* Montignac: Centre d'Etudes et de Documentation Préhistoriques.

Chaix, L. 1986. Animals in the sacred world at Kerma (Sudan, East Africa). In *Cultural attitudes to animals including birds, fish and invertebrates.* World Archaeological Congress, Vol. 2 (mimeo).

Clark G. 1961. *World prehistory: an outline.* Cambridge: Cambridge University Press.

Conkey, M. W. 1980. The identification of prehistoric hunter-gatherer aggregation sites: the case of Altamira. *Current Anthropology* **21**(5), 609–30.

Emery, W. B. 1961. *Archaic Egypt.* Harmondsworth: Penguin.

Freud, S. 1950 (1912–13). *Totem and taboo.* London: Routledge & Kegan Paul.

Gamble, C. 1982. Interaction and alliance in Palaeolithic society. *Man* **17**, 92–107.

Giedion, S. 1962. *The eternal present: the beginnings of art.* London: Oxford University Press.

Gimbutas, M. 1986. Birds, animals, amphibians and insects of the old European Goddess of Death and Regeneration. In *Final Papers.* World Archaeological Congress, Vol. 2 (mimeo).

Ingold, T. 1988. Introduction. In *What is an animal?* T. Ingold (ed.) 1–16. London: Unwin Hyman.

James, E. O. 1957. *Prehistoric religion.* London: Thames & Hudson.

Kemp, B. J. 1989. *Ancient Egypt: anatomy of a civilization.* London & New York: Routledge.

Khan, M. 1988. The prehistoric rock art of northern Saudi Arabia: a synthetic approach to the study of rock art from Wadi Damm, northeast of Tobruk. Unpublished PhD thesis, University of Southampton.

Leroi-Gourhan, A. 1968 (1964). *The art of prehistoric man in Western Europe.* London: Thames & Hudson.

Lévy-Bruhl, L. 1966 (1922). *Primitive mentality.* New York: Beacon Press.

Luquet, G. H. 1910. Les caractères des figures humaines dans l'art paléolithique, *L'Anthropologie* **21**, 409–23.

Maringer, J. 1960. *The gods of prehistoric man.* London: Weidenfeld & Nicolson.

Needham, R. 1987. *Counterpoints.* Berkeley: University of California Press.

Neumann, E. 1974. *The great mother: an analysis of the archetype.* Princeton: Princeton University Press.

Podgorski, T. 1986. The semantics of relation between King and Falcon to the end of the New Kingdom of Egypt. In *Cultural attitudes to animals including birds, fish and invertebrates.* World Archaeological Congress, Vol. 2 (mimeo).

Rivers, W. H. 1914. *A history of Melanesian society.* Cambridge: Cambridge University Press.

Rosenfeld, A. 1977. Profile figures: schematization of the human figure in the Magdalenian Culture of Europe. In *Form in indigenous art,* P. J. Ucko (ed.), 90–109. London: Duckworth.

Rosenfeld, A., D. Horton & J. Winter 1981. *Early man in north Queensland*. Canberra: Department of Prehistory, Australian National University.

Ross, A. 1967. *Pagan Celtic Britain: studies in iconography and tradition*. London: Routledge & Kegan Paul.

Tapper, R. 1988. Animality, humanity, morality, society. In *What is an animal?* T. Ingold (ed.), 47–62. London: Unwin Hyman.

Ucko, P. J. 1987. Débuts illusoires dans l'étude de la tradition artistique. *Préhistoire Ariegeoise* **42**, 15–81.

Ucko, P. J. 1989. Subjectivity and the recording of palaeolithic cave art. In *Un Siglio despues de Sautuola*, M. R. Gonzales Morales (ed.), Santander: Disputación Regional de Cantabria.

Ucko, P. J. & A. Rosenfeld 1967. *Palaeolithic cave art*. London: Weidenfeld & Nicolson.

Ucko, P. J. & A. Rosenfeld 1972. Anthropomorphic representations in palaeolithic art. In *Santander symposium 1970*, M. B. Almagro & M. A. Garcia (eds) 149–211. Santander: Patronata de las cuevas prehistóricas de Santander.

Wundt, W. M. 1916. *The elements of folk psychology*. London: Allen & Unwin.

Contents

Preface

In September 1986 a number of scholars with special knowledge of small-scale human societies in every inhabited continent met for a day and a half during the World Archaeological Congress in Southampton, England. The purpose of this gathering was to discuss human understanding of the world of animate nature, under the general title of Semantics of Animal Symbolism. It is a tribute to the comradely good humour and civilized forbearance of the participants that it was somehow possible to hear and discuss some 30 presentations in a relatively brief space of time. This volume is derived from those discussions, and the papers presented there.

The gathering in Southampton was distinguished by the participation of a substantial number of contributors from what has come to be called the Third World, many of them comparatively young and virtually unknown outside their own countries. Their presence was of special significance to social anthropology, since their societies of origin had traditionally and conventionally provided the ethnographic raw material that was processed into learned texts by metropolitan scholarship.

Ann Osborn, the gifted author of Chapter 11, died from cancer in Bogotá in August 1988. An obituary appeared in 1989 in *Anthropology Today* 5(1), p. 28. Her chapter is based on her dissertation at Oxford University. She was unable to complete the final revision of the chapter before she died. Where some amplification was required, additional material has been inserted, taken, almost verbatim, from the original dissertation. The selection was undertaken by Dr Warwick Bray, Dr Marianne Cardala de Schrimpff and Professor Peter Ucko, to whom I am very grateful. The ideas and wording of the additions (except for minimal changes to ensure coherence) are Osborn's own.

The chapters by Wendy James (Ch. 14) and Nicholas Saunders (Ch. 12) were received after the Congress meeting in 1986. The chapter by Bernard Saladin d'Anglure (Ch. 13) is a slightly abridged version of a text originally published in 1980 in *Etudes Mongoles et Sibériennes* **11**, pp. 63–94. I have inserted into the chapter by Slawoj Szynkiewicz (Ch. 6) an illustration from *Development of the Mongolian national style painting 'Mongol Zurag' in brief* by N. Tsultem (Ulan Bator: State Publishing House, 1986).

I would like to thank Joanna Overing, Les Hiatt, and David Parkin who shared the job of chairing sessions at the Congress and expertly maintained a friendly but firm control over the proceedings. I would also like to thank Tim Ingold and Peter Ucko for their indispensable help and encouragement during the preparation of this volume and Jane Hubert for expert assistance with the editorial work.

Roy Willis
Edinburgh

Preface to the paperback edition

This is a book about the different ways human beings around the world have imagined themselves in relation to those other animate creatures that invariably inhabit each particular group's cultural domain. Western readers and those familiar with that tradition of systematic inquiry readily perceive in these exotic accounts of beasts, visible and invisible, the lineaments of mythological thought: a way of construing patterns of meaning that, while comprehensible and even logical in its own peculiar terms, is also plainly at variance with the way things 'really' are. Which is to say, at variance with the account of matters delivered by the detached and remorselessly cumulative methods of scientific investigation, experiment and proof.

By 1986, when the great international Congress was held that provided the diverse contributions to *Signifying animals*, it was already suspected by certain anthropologists with global intuitions, perhaps picking up on earlier suggestions by Jaspers or Tillich, that there was more than a hint of the mythological in the modern scientific world-view. I refer to that account of reality first given canonical formulation in the seventeenth-century works of Bacon and, most particularly, Descartes, and exemplified and expanded by Galileo and Newton and, in our own time, by Monod, Watson and Crick. In the world-view so constructed by Western Scientific Man during the past three-and-a-half centuries, the Scientist as Hero confronts as his object and prey a world of nature from which all traces of mind or spirit have disappeared, leaving in their place what is understood to be nothing more than a vast and immensely complex machine. Mastery and possession of this enormous object, Descartes proposed in the *Discourse on method*, was the proper destiny of scientific humanity. The unending quest for knowledge, and the limitless power that comes with it, took mythological form in the legend of the heroic and damned Dr Faustus, the crazed *savant* who sold his soul to the Devil in exchange for total domination of nature.

Since 1986, another quest with the enchanting resonances of myth has increasingly competed with the still enormously potent Faustian idea for possession of the Western scientific, as well as popular, imagination. Rooted in the Celtic and Arthurian search for the Holy Grail, it promises, instead of the domination of nature, the restoration of a lost wholeness and plenitude with humanity's reincorporation in the natural commonwealth.

What both these mythologically charged projects have in common is their pre-eminent concern with 'Nature', or, as it is now more usually called, 'the environment'. The mythological divide reflects a fundamental schism in the formerly monolithic House of Science itself. In *The rebirth of nature* (1990), Rupert Sheldrake traces the beginning of the abandonment of the Cartesian–mechanistic world-view in physics to Faraday's introduction of the 'field' concept early in the nineteenth century on the basis of his experiments in electromagnetism. The 'field' concept as developed in modern physics and adopted in other branches of science has, as Sheldrake points out, many of the characteristics of the scientifically discredited notions of 'soul' or 'spirit' as typically found in the cosmologies of pre-scientific cultures (Sheldrake 1990: p. 106). For physics the final break with the 'nature as mindless machine' model of reality came in 1927 with the formal adoption of Heisenberg's Uncertainty Principle. This principle recognized that the absolute Cartesian division between observer and observed, between mind and nature, could no longer be maintained; that human beings were themselves part of nature; and that nature at the most elementary level, that of the atomic particle, was possessed of a kind of consciousness (Capra 1982: p. 77). Sheldrake goes so far as to claim that present-day science has reconstituted animism, the derogatory term coined by the nineteenth-century British anthropologist J. B. Tylor to denote the 'illusory' imputation by many 'primitive' peoples of a 'spirit' or 'soul' to everything that existed.

But by no means all branches of Western science have gone this far. Molecular biology, to take a prominent example, continues with notable success to follow the Cartesian programme of seeking to understand and master nature by identifying its smallest component parts and ascertaining their interrelationship. Crick and Watson's discovery of the DNA chain and the consequent development of genetic engineering represent a triumphant reaffirmation of the Cartesian vision as science takes control of the newly revealed 'machinery' of all animate life, including human life. These latest technological moves towards human domination of nature have led the anthropologist Marilyn Strathern to reflect on the apparent 'disappearance' of the natural ground of human kinship as human culture, in the form of the new post-Watson/Crick technological intervention in human reproduction, 'consumes' nature (Strathern 1992: p. 3). Another commentator, citing the climatic changes, including 'global warming', occasioned by the industrial transformation of the planet, writes of the 'end of Nature' (McGibben, 1990).

The concept of 'kinship' invoked by Strathern illustrates the emergent struggle I discern between the propagators of the Faustian and Arthurian visions for possession of the mind and soul of Western science. As Strathern shows us, that science's new power over human reproduction can be represented as a deprivation for human beings themselves – the loss of a sense, within the diminished but emotionally potent area of life defined in Western society as the domain of 'kinship', of being 'anchored' in nature. An opposing view that also takes up the 'kinship' theme is to be found in the work of the ecological philosopher Arne Naess. Pointing to the new science of ecology's discovery of the bonds of symbiotic interdependence between all species on the planet, Naess asserts that there now exists 'a cognitive basis for a sense of belonging', indeed of kinship, between all forms of life on this Earth (Naess 1989: p. 168). Such a planetary sense of kinship 'was not possible earlier' – that is, before the accumulation of global knowledge achieved by Faustian science (ibid.).

Thus we currently have in the Western scientific community one school of thought that equates the advance of knowledge with human spiritual impoverishment and the diminution, even 'death', of nature, while another school hails nature's 'rebirth' and the prospect of humanity's spiritual enrichment through acceptance of its proper place in the natural world. We can recognize here, in the oppositional contrast between the holistic vision of Sheldrake and Naess and the poignant sense of human isolation in an alien universe inherent in the Cartesian model of nature as a mindless machine, an affinity with the duality of continuity and separation that, as we shall see, pervades cosmological thought in tribal cultures. And within anthropology itself, a related controversy opposes holistic postmodernism to the traditionally objectivist self-concept of the 'modern' discipline (Clifford & Marcus 1984). Against the background of these grand and not-so-grand debates, these voices from diverse planetary regions and distinct historical epochs speak to our present concerns with undeniable relevance.

Roy Willis
Edinburgh

References

Capra, F. 1982. *The turning point: society and the rising culture*. London: Fontana.

Clifford, J. & G. E. Marcus (eds) 1984. *Writing culture: the poetics and politics of ethnography*. Berkeley: University of California Press.

McGibben, B. 1990. *The end of nature*. London: Penguin.

Naess, A. 1989. *Ecology, community and lifestyle*. D. Rothenberg (trans). Cambridge: Cambridge University Press.

Sheldrake, R. 1990. *The rebirth of nature*. London: Century.

Strathern, M. 1992. *After nature: English kinship in the late twentieth century*. Cambridge: Cambridge University Press.

Introduction

ROY WILLIS

The general topic of this volume, the human–animal relation, returns us to the complex of ideas that provided modern anthropology with its distinctive subject matter more than a century ago under the label of 'totemism'. This approach provides a context, at once sociological and historical, within which to situate *Signifying animals*, and it merits further consideration before account can properly be taken of particular contributions.

Let us begin by looking at the frequently deplored sociological phenomenon of anthropology's increasing compartmentalization into effectively autonomous subdisciplines. This process of disciplinary specialization clearly reflects the evolution of science's division of labour in the wider societies of Euro-America and Australasia. But anthropology is also not exempt from the converse and dialectical process of knowledge construction, through which the accumulation of detailed information is matched and subsumed through the discovery of deeper and more inclusive connections between previously separate theoretical domains. Anthropology in the later 20th century has not lacked exemplary figures who, in their reassertion of the subject's historic mission, recall the giants of the later 19th century, particularly Tylor and Morgan who, in bringing together for the first time a coherent and distinctive set of theories and a specific body of empirical data, can be said to have founded the modern science of anthropology.

But to refer to latter-day generalists of anthropology – to names such as Bateson, Lévi-Strauss, Turner, Harris, Dumont, and Douglas – is also to call attention to the existence of an immense gulf of understanding and consciousness between all these scholars – who themselves represent diverse and often mutually inconsistent theoretical positions – and those other thinkers we are accustomed to regard as our intellectual ancestors, the founding fathers of our discipline. The divide between 'ancestors' and 'moderns' in anthropology is analogous to the gulf that separated pre-Copernican from Newtonian cosmologists in Europe. Modern anthropology cannot help being aware, in a way that Tylor, Frazer, and Morgan, and even Boas and Malinowski were not, of the incurable *relativity*, in a world of cultural difference, of their own, Western-scientific civilization.

In contrast, the giants of the past wrote out of a shared sense of unshakeable intellectual and moral superiority to those they studied. In the words of Stocking (1987, p. 47), a learned American historian of anthropology, there was a consensus among the Victorian founding fathers that their discipline was focused on the customs and social institutions of 'dark-skinned, non-European, "uncivilized" peoples'.

This primarily visual image of stark 'otherness' encouraged the Victorians to believe that anthropology had the potential to become a genuinely scientific discipline, with the relation between anthropologist and 'primitive' being seen as analogous to that between natural science and nature. In the introduction to his *Primitive culture*, Tylor (1871, p. 2) stated that his paradigm for anthropology was drawn not from the sociological evolutionism of Spencer or the zoological evolutionism of Darwin, but rather from the science of inorganic nature – what today is called physics. As Tylor understood it, this was a subject devoted to understanding the workings of a natural domain that was construed as a complex machine.

But it was also apparent to Tylor and his coevals that, pursuing the analogy with physics, anthropology's conception of its subject matter could not remain at the purely phenomenal level of description: some underlying though still hidden reality, of a sociological kind, must surely exist to account for the blatant otherness of the dark-hued primitive. That sociological peculiarity was duly discovered in the institution of totemism.

Though the term was first coined by McLennan in an 1869 article, its full theoretical potential was not realized until 20 years later, when McLennan's disciple W. Robertson Smith asked J. G. Frazer to write an article on totemism for the *Encyclopaedia Britannica*.

According to McLennan's original definition:

> tribes in the totem stage believed themselves descended from, or of the same breed, as some species of animal or plant, which was their 'symbol and emblem', and 'religiously regarded' or 'taboo'; recognizing kinship only through the mother, they also followed 'exogamy as their marriage law' – so that one could not marry a member of the same totem. (Stocking 1987, p. 297)

Frazer's magisterial statement dropped the diagnostic specification of descent through the mother, which belonged to McLennan's long-running and, by then, obsolete dispute with Maine on the evolutionary priority of matrilineal as against patrilineal descent. Otherwise, apart from what now strikes us as the embarrassingly 'ethnocentric' tone, Frazer's description of totemistic society could still appear valid to the present-day anthropologist:

> A Totem is a class of material objects which a savage regards with superstitious respect, believing that there exists between him and every member of the class an intimate and altogether special relation . . .

> The clan totem is reverenced by a body of men and women who call themselves by the name of the totem, believe themselves to be of one blood, descendants of a common ancestor, and are bound together by common obligations to each other and by a common faith in the totem. *Totemism is thus both a religious and a social system.* (Frazer 1910: pp. 3, 4; emphasis added)

With the 'discovery' of totemism as the characteristic social form of primitive humanity, anthropology could consider itself a fully fledged science with its own specific subject matter. What distinguished primitive from modern society was that whereas in the latter there was an absolute distinction between the secular and the religious domains, between the cultural and the natural, between the present and the past, with the former the converse was true. For the primitive, it was increasingly apparent, human kinship, marriage and descent were aspects of the natural world, and vice versa; and in the totemic animal, man beheld both his living brother and his remote, godlike ancestor. It seemed, indeed, as if in the primitive world *all* the fundamental discriminations that structured modern civilization, even the basic categories of logical thought, were strangely compromised. The special nature of savagedom was succinctly encapsulated in Frazer's assertion that totemism was both a *religious* and a *social* institution.

Durkheim's classic interpretation of Australian totemism ingeniously sought to explain the religious aspect as an illusory projection of the social: society itself, Durkheim argued (1912), was the *real* object of worship in totemistic religion, though this fact was hidden from the worshippers themselves. But Durkheim's interpretation of totemism as unconsciously sociocentric religion differed from that of Frazer only in that Durkheim sought to derive a general theory of both religion and society from the Australian ethnography; his assumption that the apparently bizarre convictions of primitive humanity were understandable errors arrived at on the basis of inadequate evidence was no different from that of Tylor and Frazer and, later, of the classic British school of fieldwork-based interpretive anthropology that began with the Torres Straits Expedition of 1898 and achieved its greatest efflorescence between the First World War and the Second World War.

The first notable field study of totemism by a British anthropologist was that of Rivers (1914) who characterized totemism on the basis of his Melanesian data as consisting of three elements in combination: the *social*, the association of human group and natural phenomenon; the *psychological*, the belief in human kinship with nature, typically taking the form of a concept of human descent from a nonhuman species, and *ritual*, often involving a prohibition against eating members of the totemic species. Rivers's dissection of the totemic phenomenon appeared only two years after Durkheim's monumental attempt to 'explain' totemism and only a year after the appearance of Freud's (1913) thesis, which saw it as a projection on to animals of infantile emotions generated within the family. In the United States Boas (1916) saw the association between human groups and nonhuman species supposedly characteristic of totemism as just one possible way of marking the separate identity of groups defined by exogamy (out-marriage). Boas's contribution was part of what was to become an American tradition of scepticism about the reality of totemism as a distinctively 'primitive' form of society, a tradition inaugurated by Goldenweiser (1910) and continued by Lowie (1920) and Murdock (1949).

In Europe, however, the French folklorist van Gennep (1920) was able to list no less than 41 competing theories of totemism. It was mainly anthropologists of the British school who, during the four decades after van Gennep's survey, continued to speculate on the origins of totemism. For Malinowski, the prominence of animals and plants in totemic religion arose from the value of these species as human food, while totemic rituals were attempts to achieve magical 'control' over these food resources (Malinowski 1948). Radcliffe-Brown (1929) saw totemism as a development of an earlier 'ritual' attitude towards game animals and all natural food resources, supposedly characteristic of hunter-gatherer societies. More sophisticated than these simplistic attempts to 'explain away' totemism were the less theoretically ambitious empirical studies of totemic systems of Firth (1930–1) in Polynesia and Elkin (1933–4) in Australia. While avoiding causal explanations, both of these studies emphasized the complexity of totemic beliefs and practices.

In Africa anthropologists have tended to use the term 'totem' as a convenient label for commonly occurring associations in 'tribal' cosmologies between objects of the natural environment, both animate and inanimate, and human individuals and groups. But rather than speculating about the origins of such beliefs in the tradition of the founding fathers of modern anthropology, scholars such as Fortes (1945), Evans-Pritchard (1956), and Lienhardt (1961) have treated 'totemic' objects, animate or inanimate, as signs or, to use Lienhardt's (1961) term, 'emblems', of enduring relations between human individuals or groups and agencies belonging to an invisible world. Thus the members of many Nuer clans explain their 'totemic' relations with particular wild species with a standard account of their clan ancestor being born twin to a member of that species (Evans-Pritchard 1956).

But with the contribution of Lévi-Strauss (1962a, 1962b) the whole 'totemic debate' was raised to a new level of generality, from the level of 'primitive' society and culture to that of universal human thought processes. According to Lévi-Strauss, what had been called totemism was nothing more alien to our understanding than the operation, in conditions where human communities found themselves intimately involved with natural phenomena, of the familiar panhuman faculty of analogical reasoning. Comparative study of natural species, both their morphology and their behaviour, provided nonliterate and prescientific humanity with a ready-to-hand means of conceptualizing relations between human groups. It was the analogical resemblances between these two 'systems of differences', the one natural and the other cultural, that had been misinterpreted by anthropology as signifying a peculiar mode of social experience. Nearly three decades have passed since the double appearance in 1962 of *Le totémisme aujourd'hui* and *La pensée sauvage* (*The savage mind*), two books that together constituted Lévi-Strauss's magisterial dismissal of the 'totemic illusion'. During that time the structuralist principle that social phenomena are to be treated as elements in total systems of signs – semantic units that exist only in their oppositional and associational relations to each other – has been incorporated into the mainstream of anthropological thought and adopted even by those most hostile to Lévi-Strauss's philosophical position. It is hardly possible, for example, to conceive of the well-known studies of animal categories by Douglas (1957), Leach (1964), Bulmer (1967), and Tambiah (1969), without the pre-existent and underlying Lévi-Straussian conceptual framework.

The post-Lévi-Straussian approach is typified in Worsley's prefatory comments (1967, pp. 141–2) to his account of totemism among the Groote Eylandt people of northern Australia, an account that draws on the theories of cognitive development of Vygotsky:

> The analysis here develops, not in negative opposition to [Lévi-Strauss's] approach, but in apposition to it. Any discussion of totemism must be conditioned by his significant contribution to our understanding of the phenomenon: it must extend his insights.

But as Worsley also observes, Lévi-Strauss's intention was not to *understand* totemism, but to abolish it as a possible topic of anthropological discourse (Worsley 1967). However, this effect, which should have been a logical consequence of the argument of *Le totémisme aujourd'hui* and *La pensée sauvage*, has patently not come about. Though officially pronounced dead nearly 30 years ago, totemism obstinately refuses to 'lie down'. Indeed, it presently exhibits a vitality recalling the great days of Frazer and Durkheim.

As well as Worsley's contribution, it is evident that Australia, *locus classicus* of totemic studies, continues to generate fresh material and new interpretations through the work of Strehlow (1970), Meggitt (1962), Peterson (1972), Munn (1973), Newsome (1980), Morton (1987), Keen (Ch. 7 of this volume and elsewhere), and others. From Papua New Guinea have come the influential studies of animal symbolism of Bulmer (1967), Rappoport (1968), and Gell (1973), and the country is represented in this volume with work by Hyndman (Ch. 5). From Amazonia, Lévi-Strauss's own anthropological terrain, have come notable studies, rich in the symbolism of animals, by Reichel-Dolmatoff (1971), Overing (1975), and Crocker (1985), while from montane South America we have contributions to this volume by Osborn (Ch. 11) and Wright (Ch. 4), and for North America by Bahti (Ch. 10). Africa has produced in the past 30 years a plethora of studies focused on human relations with the world of nature, ranging from the now near-classic monographs of Lienhardt (1961), Griaule (1965), and Douglas (1966), to the recent and exemplary work of Jackson (1982) and James (1988), the last-named being also represented in this volume (Ch. 14).

Whence comes this renewed surge of interest in an anthropological debate that a generation ago had been written off as grounded in an error belonging to the turbulent infancy of our discipline? Two currents of thought, one originating within anthropological theory and the other in the wider society outside academic anthropology, appear to be combining to bring about this rather surprising result, a veritable 'totemic revival'.

Within anthropology itself, the major advance has consisted in drawing attention to what could be called a missing dimension in what has generally been recognized as Lévi-Strauss's landmark contribution to our understanding of humankind's relation with nonhuman nature. Thus Tambiah (1969), drawing on his field data from Thailand, concluded that

> the Thai villagers' relation to the animal world shows neither a sense of affinity with animals alone nor a clear-cut distinction and separation from them, but rather a co-existence of both attitudes in varying intensities which create a perpetual tension.

Since the mid-1970s, the academic debate about humanity's relation with the natural world has, in a sense, been overtaken by a remarkable upsurge in social concern with what is generally called ecology (cf. Ingold 1988).

This social movement in Euro-America, broadly focused on the relation between human society and the nonhuman material environment, or 'nature', has grown from a tiny group of concerned individuals from different countries and walks of life who came together in Rome in 1968. This group was convinced that industrialism's perceived profligate exploitation of the world's natural resources portended global catastrophe unless brought under control (Meadows 1972).

This once novel perception has since developed into a broad-based popular movement with religious, political, and philosophical aspects. Some theorists trace the origins of what is perceived as an unbalanced view of humanity's place in nature to the assertion in the origin myth of Judaeo-Christianity, the biblical Book of Genesis, that God has given man 'dominion over the fish of the sea, and over the fowl of the air, and over the cattle and over all the earth' (cf. Shanklin 1985, pp. 375–6). This religious legitimation of human domination and exploitation of the world of nature is now frequently contrasted with a nonhierarchic relation of interdependence between human beings and nature that is held to characterize the worldviews of many small-scale, 'tribal' societies. For many ecological theorists, such societies are seen as providing appropriate models for postindustrial Western civilization. The sense of interconnection between nature and culture, between human and animal, social and religious institutions, which Victorian anthropology saw as a fascinating error of primitive man, a view that Lévi-Strauss in turn dismissed as an erroneous misreading of primitive protoscience, has now been rehabilitated in Western scholarly thought as an accurate reflection of existential reality: in this view humankind *is* part of nature and everything in the universe is connected with everything else, or so the physicists assure us. Western culture, it seems, is now in a phase that might almost be called neototemistic.

Anthropologists, as social beings, are inevitably influenced by such large-scale shifts in academic and popular consciousness. In this volume James (Ch. 14) draws our attention to how structuralist interpretations of animal symbolism, such as those of Douglas (1957, 1966) and the present writer (Willis 1974) presented human relations with animate nature in dichotomous, 'confrontational' terms. In contrast, James tells us, what we have just described as the ecological or neototemistic sensibility in Western thought has made anthropologists aware of 'indigenous themes of continuity, of integration, and of interaction between the various species of the living world, including ourselves' (p. 198).

The same idea is apparent in Osborn's (Ch. 11) comment on the U'wa people of montane Colombia that they 'do not make a rigid distinction between themselves and nature' (p. 157). It is explicit in the mythology of Australian, Amerindian and Inuit peoples as described by various contributors to this volume (Chs 4, 7, 10, 11, 13). Douglas, in her programmatic contribution to this volume (Ch. 1) makes a similar point to James when she urges that 'attention be paid to how animals interact with humans and to the interests that humans pursue when they chase or eat or tame animals or harness them to work' (pp. 34–5).

This new sensitivity to indigenous ideas of continuity between human and nonhuman nature is interesting and important. Studies informed by it, like James's fascinating account (Ch. 14) of the antelope as an image of the Uduk notion of 'self', not only illuminate the connections between humanity and nature but also tend to dissolve the dichotomy, intrinsic to all earlier anthropology, whether Lévi-Straussian, Frazerian, or Tylorian, between observer and observed. But it is equally important, and necessary, to note that all human cultures, including our own, *simultaneously* recognize a *duality* that divides each cultural group's world-view or cosmology while *also recognizing some underlying commonality or continuity* between the opposed constituents. As to the content of the dual demiworlds, the nature of the unifying principle, and the location of the cosmological divide, these of course vary widely between one human group and another. But underlying the extraordinary variety of cultural forms there is, I maintain, a common conceptual framework, based on the opposed but complementary principles of separation and continuity, which seems diagnostic of human cultural constructions. It is interesting to find the fruitful tension between these two principles running through the learned controversies in Ingold's companion volume to this, entitled *What is an animal?* (1988). Here there was evident disagreement on where the boundary between human and nonhuman lay, how much continuity and how much difference there is between *Homo Sapiens sapiens* and other animate species. The representatives of what Ingold describes as different 'systems of thought', analogous in some ways to distinct tribal cosmologies, return unsurprisingly conflicting answers to these fundamental questions. But what is equally interesting, as Ingold also recognizes, is that these questions are all framed in the same way, along opposed but complementary axes of continuity and difference (see Ingold 1988, p. 4, Fig. 1.1)

At this stage of the discussion it is appropriate to note the close formal resemblance between these scientists' conception of humankind as being *both* part of, continuous with, the world of nonhuman nature, *and* separate from it – so that we have here a coexistent unity and duality, which is a

logical contradiction – and the French philosopher Lévy-Bruhl's summation
of the world-view that he saw as characteristic of 'primitive' thought. For
Lévy-Bruhl that world-view embodied a contradiction which he designated
'duality–unity' and described as follows:

> As far as we are permitted to go back into observable primitive societies
> . . . man has had the revelation that reality is such as he sees it and at the
> same time there exists another reality, or better said, that the reality
> given to him is *at one and the same time what it is and other than what it is*.
> (Lévy-Bruhl 1975, p. 103; emphasis added)

I want provisionally to accept this observation of Lévy-Bruhl's as valid,
though for the moment unexplained (I attempt that below), and also to
suggest that his generalization applies to *all* human cosmologies, so-called
'primitive' and so-called 'modern' alike. In *all* cosmological systems, I
suggest, we find an oppositional complementarity, which involves a logical
contradiction, between what we have been calling the principles of separation and continuity.[1] Human beings are of course not exempt from that
inherent contradiction. Characteristically, indeed, they exemplify it and are
defined as those beings that are both part of, and continuous with, the rest of
creation (or nature), and radically separate from it. In Uduk thinking, as we
have already seen (Ch. 14), a once-unitary world of animate beings became
divided into two opposed yet related kinds, the domesticated and the wild.
The U'wa Indian people of montane Colombia, described by Osborn
(Ch. 11), see the great division of the world as that between mortal beings –
a category that includes people, nonhuman animals, and plants – and the
immortal beings, the deities. Mortal beings are all made of the same
materials, and the ancestry of humans includes animal, tree, and plant
forebears. It is only the conscious control exercised over the cosmos by
mortal human beings, through ritual chanting, that prevents human identity
as a separate mortal community from being lost through return to these
nonhuman ancestral forms.

If we turn to the historical structure of Western cosmology we encounter
again the familiar theme of a primordial unity riven into a stark division
between creator and creation, spirit and matter. Since Descartes, nonhuman
animals have been conventionally classified as belonging entirely to the
material side of that grand cosmological divide, and only humans participate in it, by virtue of their possession of material and mortal bodies, as
well as immortal spirits. But as with the Uduk, the inner or spiritual self of
the human being mirrors the outward cosmological divide. Here what is
often called the 'beast within' – the 'Id' in Freud's schema – confronts, again
in Freud's (1939) influential portrayal, the 'higher', cultural self.

But it is when we examine the cosmology of the Hopi Indians of the
North American Southwest, described by Bahti (Ch. 10), that we encounter
what is not only the simplest but also the most subtle and – by outsiders –
most easily misunderstood example of what I am suggesting here is a

universal human world-making propensity. Evidently, the Hopi world is dual. The division is all-embracing, as is the duality: everything in the tangible, material world – people, animals, and things – has a counterpart in the other, spiritual world. But though separated in one sense, these two worlds – as Bahti calls them – are also intimately interrelated, existing in the same time and space. Moreover, as Bahti insists, these two worlds are equally 'real', since, it would seem, the Hopi concept translated here as 'spirit' or 'essence' does not have the implications of 'unreality' that it does in English. One recalls here that an earlier commentator on Hopi cosmology, Whorf, that 'armchair anthropologist' of genius, preferred to entitle the two aspects of Hopi duality as manifest and unmanifest or, alternatively, as objective and subjective (Whorf 1956). According to Bahti, relations between human beings and other animals in the material world have to be understood as drawing their meaning from such relations in the immaterial world, where there is apparently less distinction made between these two categories, animals readily becoming people, and vice versa.

Another example of complementary dualism from a people related to the Hopi is provided by Saunders in his discussion of the jaguar as metaphor in the pre-Columbian Aztec empire (Ch. 12). Saunders shows how the jaguar served as a symbol of shamanic and royal power. Material images of this animal were invested with reflective eyes of obsidian that mirrored the duplicate world of spirit.

In the case of the Hopi cosmos, there is clearly a profound ontological distinction, a duality as Bahti calls it, between two juxtaposed aspects of reality. Yet the connection between those two worlds could hardly be more intimate and total, a connection envisaged symbolically as a 'threshold' through which the Hopi pass during their religious ceremonies. It would be hard to imagine a more perfect representation of the *complementarity* which, I have suggested, invariably exists between the two grand cosmogonic principles of separation and continuity. It is this structural complementarity that is peculiarly obscured by the disjunctive bias of Cartesian-mechanistic philosophy, the cosmology that engendered modern anthropology in the later 19th century (see Willis, Ch. 19). Because it proposes an alternative world-view with such exemplary clarity, the Hopi cosmos has been presented by a number of observers, from Whorf onwards, as virtually unparalleled among human cultural creations. As against this widely held opinion, the direction of my argument would suggest that, on the contrary, the 'complementary dualism' of the Hopi world is typical of many, perhaps most tribal cosmologies around the globe, whether they be found in Australasia, the Pacific, the Arctic, Asia, Africa, or the Americas.

What I mean can best be approached by considering what happens if we attempt, against Bahti's advice, to interpret Hopi ideas in English. Immediately we are drawn to express the grand Hopi cosmological dualism in terms of the two fundamental categories of English and Euro-American cosmology: spirit (or 'mind') and matter. But these categories carry with them an implicit 'metaphysics', to use Whorf's expression, a metaphysics of ontological disjunction. In the Hopi cosmos, on the contrary, the corresponding dualistic categories exist in a relation of complementarity. It follows that our attempt to translate Hopi cosmological concepts accurately into ordinary English is doomed to failure.

It is interesting that sensitive ethnographers of other non-Western societies and cultures that are quite unrelated to the Hopi report very similar problems. As Turner (1975, p. 21) has observed, 'African thought embeds itself from the outset in materiality, but demonstrates that materiality is not inert but vital'. Keen, in his discussion of the religious symbolism of the Yolngu people of northern Australia (Ch. 7), stresses

> the apparent *immediacy* of these [mythological] events in Yolngu discourse about the beings. People will casually point out a feature and say something like 'that's where the Djang'kawu sat', as though it were sometime the year before. (author's emphasis)

Such statements disconcert the Western observer because they imply a relation of complementarity between two other categories of his cosmology that seem to mirror, though at a lower, less inclusive level, the disjunctive dualism of spirit and matter, and that is the duality of time and space.[2] Evidently, these *natural* categories, which form the worlds of all living creatures, are differentially perceived in human societies in accordance with the fundamental *cultural* dualism peculiar to each group. In Hopi culture the dual worlds occupy the same *space*, whereas for the Yolngu, who in this respect appear to typify Australian Aboriginal cosmology, the Dreaming and the present (the two aspects of the primary duality) exist together in the same *time*. The basic principles ordering the construction of these two cosmologies, Hopi and Yolngu, are, however, the same.

To make meaningful comparisons across the entire range of such 'alternative' cosmologies, we evidently need concepts that are more abstract than the culturally loaded terms of ordinary language. It is relevant to our purpose that there exists in linguistics, the science of language, a semantic analogue to the universal principles we have posited. In linguistics, what we have called the structural complementarity of the principles of separation and continuity is recognized as the relation between the *paradigmatic* (oppositional and contrastive) and *syntagmatic* (combinatorial and connective) axes of meaning. According to the linguist Lyons (1968, pp. 70–81), these fundamental semantic dimensions exist in a relation of complementarity at every level of linguistic analysis from the phoneme to such higher-order units as words and sentences. I suggest that this observation is equally valid for those inclusive semantic constructs anthropologists call cosmologies.[3]

This inquiry into the nature of human experience of the animate non-human world cannot, however, remain at the level of linguistic semantics. Since all we know of cosmological constructs is contained in their formulation in local languages, to resort to linguistic factors or models in attempting to account for common features in those constructs would be merely tautological. To account for the observed presence of universal structural regularities in human world-making, regularities that are, I suggest, reflected in the empirically established linguistic and semantic fact of paradigmatic/syntagmatic complementarity, we need to identify an extra-linguistic basis for this seemingly universal world-making faculty in *Homo sapiens*. Such a basis, I also suggest, can be found in the biologist von Uexküll's concept of *Umwelt-Lehre*, invoked by Sebeok and Ingold (1988).

According to von Uexküll (1982), every natural organism 'constructs' its own 'world' from the flux of events constituting its natural environment. This characteristic, species-specific *Umwelt*, is built out of the working together of each creature's receptor and effector organs, its perception of the 'outer' world, as filtered through its sensory equipment, and its reaction to those perceptions. Thus the members of each natural species inhabit different, organically constructed 'worlds' that vary in content and complexity according to the range and relative sophistication of the creature's 'world-making' equipment. Human beings, as natural organisms, also have their characteristic *Umwelt*, which is broadly similar to that of the other primates. For example, *Homo sapiens* can naturally perceive, and react to, only a small 'slice' of the total range of naturally occurring electromagnetic energy in the universe. They are similarly restricted in their perception of time, being unable to discriminate units of astronomical time less than an eighteenth of a second.

Here, in the *Umwelt* concept of von Uexküll, we seem to have the evolutionary precursor and analogue of human world-making. There is a parallel here, too, with Lenneberg's (1967) demonstration of the correspondence between the classificatory ability innate in many nonhuman animals and the classificatory principle characteristic of all known human languages.

There is an interesting formal resemblance between the *naturally* constructed *Umwelten* of all animate species and the *culturally* constructed cosmologies of all human groups. The founder of general systems theory, von Bertalanffy, appears to have been the first commentator to notice the remarkable congruence between these two kinds of construct as presented in the works of von Uexküll, on the one hand, and of Whorf, on the other (von Bertalanffy 1955). One obvious difference between the *Umwelten* of nonhuman animals and of human beings is that humankind has managed, through the invention of technology, immensely to increase the range and power of its naturally given receptor and effector organs through which the species both perceives and reacts to its environment. That is a *quantitative* difference between an imagined human being in his 'natural' state and *Homo faber*, which is most evident in modern industrial civilization but which is also a universal characteristic of all human societies, however 'primitive' their technological equipment in comparative terms.

However, there is a far more important, *qualitative* difference between the natural *Umwelten* of nonhuman species and the – to varying degrees – technological *Umwelten* of human societies, and it is a difference that appears to have escaped von Bertalanffy's notice. Whereas with nonhuman animals the natural *Umwelt* is constructed by the individual organism, a human, cultural cosmology is the product of an interactive process between individuals. Only a single individual is required to perceive and react to an environment or make a tool, but the making of a human 'culture' requires the cooperative interaction of two or more individuals. In other words, while the individual organism is the generator of its species-specific *Umwelt*, human world-making is a transorganic phenomenon.

Thus, if the irreducible 'unit' of world-making (*Umwelt* construction) among nonhuman animals is the single organism, the corresponding irreducible 'unit' in human society is the dyad of self-and-other. This conclusion is supported by recent experimental discoveries in the cognitive psychology of human infants. This important work, which has been pioneered in the United States by Stern (1985) and others, and in Britain by Bower (1977) and Trevarthen, has demolished the long-held theory of infant cognition and behaviour associated with William James and the behaviourists, according to which the human newborn experiences a chaos of 'blooming and buzzing confusion' that it eventually learns to order through the categories of language. From the moment of birth, it is now evident, the normal human infant experiences itself as an entity existing *in relation with* other entities, and in particular, with that other who is, typically, its mother. In Bower's words (1977, p. 36), the newborn infant 'knows it is a human being'.

This startling inference from experimental observations has been notably developed in recent research by two other Edinburgh University psychologists, Trevarthen & Logotheti, who have coined the term 'innate intersubjectivity' to describe the cognitive and experiential world characteristic of human beings from earliest infancy. This term (Trevarthen & Logotheti 1989) 'is intended to convey the idea of a universal motivation, present in the newborn and peculiar to our species, for active participation in the exchange of collective meanings of culture'.

Carrithers (1989), a social anthropologist, has referred to the same peculiarly human world-making propensity as 'innate sociality', arguing that this faculty is more fundamental than any given, concrete manifestation of 'culture', being a precondition of it. At the same time, and given the universality of this culture-constructing faculty in human beings, the immense variety of human cultures as revealed by a century of anthropological field research, is exactly what the theory would predict. Such a theory of innate 'sociality' or 'inter-subjectivity' in human beings simultaneously explains both the evident universality of the world-making propensity in humankind and the astonishing range of variation between human cultures.

As has just been implied, we can now return with renewed insight to the problem encountered earlier, which was how to explain the provenance of the basic structuring principle, the complementarity of separation and continuity (in semantics, the complementarity of paradigmatic and syntagmatic dimensions of meaning) which, I have argued, is discernible in all known cosmological systems. This combination of contrary principles manifests in

its most basic form as a duality which, against all logic, is also a unity, as
Lévy-Bruhl (1975) maintained.

Now if, as has already been suggested, the fundamental 'unit' that generates human experience is the dyadic relation of organismic self-and-other,
this 'system' can also be thought of as a duality which is also a unity. And
since there is no reason to doubt that all cosmologies are human constructs
and all, despite immense variation in content, are structured by the same
basic principles, I would hypothesize that the basic motivation for cosmology construction is to be found in the primal human experience of the
self-and-other dyad.

From another direction, through a poststructuralist critique of the claim
to 'objectivity' in field research of orthodox anthropology, Wagner (1975)
has arrived at a remarkably similar theory of human world-making to the
one I am presenting here. Wagner argues that the typical anthropological
monograph is the outcome of a *dialogue* between anthropologist and indigenous colleague, in which the pre-existent social understandings of both
parties to the dialogue are mediated in terms of a third, interactive construction. The triadic form of this constructive enterprise, Wagner maintains, is
identical with that by which, in any and every culture, the system of cultural
meanings (exemplified in what we are here calling the cosmology) is
continually constructed, and deconstructed, through a process of reciprocal
interaction between group members.

Wagner maintains that all cosmologies divide the world into two domains
which he calls the 'innate', or 'given', and the 'artificial', or 'cultural'
(Wagner, 1975, pp. 71–102, 1978, p. 23). While one may have reservations
as to the universality of these particular English-language concepts, the rest
of Wagner's analysis, including his contention that these two cosmological
domains (or 'aspects') exist in a relation of mutuality (Wagner 1975, p. 25),
can be accepted.

Again according to Wagner (1975, p. 23), this universal cosmological
dualism is created out of the common human faculty of symbolization,
which 'defines and precipitates a sharp distinction between its own symbols
and orders on one hand and the world of their reference and ordering on the
other'. The continuing process of cultural 'invention' (a process that Wagner
calls 'obviation' – see Shanklin's comments in Ch. 15) is one in which 'the
realm of human responsibility must forever be created out of the innate, and
the realm of the innate must be constituted out of that of the artificial'
(Wagner 1978, p. 31). World-making is thus a triadic process in which
human cultural invention mediates between two opposed but complementary aspects of 'reality' that are also the product of social invention. Here, in
the process of cultural creation as described by Wagner, we encounter again
the complementarity of self-and-other which, I have suggested, is the
primordial experience that generates all human cultural forms.

An example of this world-making process in action is to be found in
Hyndman's description (Ch. 5) of the construction by the men of the
Wopkaimin people of montane New Guinea of an elaborately schematic

representation of the landscape, using trophies of the hunt. The trophy array, Hyndman tells us, conveys meaning 'in its own right'. It is a complex representation of a physical environment that is also 'wholly a cultural artefact', perceived through the organizing filter of Wopkaimin cultural values. Perceived environment and trophy array are metaphors of each other, their meaningful similarity mediated by the daily activities of the men as they collectively go about their daily task of making a living, for themselves and their families, as hunters. The 'mental map' (Hyndman's term) thus constructed includes a temporal dimension which has the same kind of reciprocally metaphoric relation with space as obtains between trophy array and culturally perceived landscape.

Handoo's analysis of cultural attitudes to birds and animals in Indian folklore (Ch. 2) provides another example of the dialectic of social metaphor. Here the world-making process occurs in the privileged arena of 'play', distanced by convention from the 'real' world of purposive interaction. The process relates two cultural constructs: the world of animals, which is consciously modelled on human society, and an imaginary world 'peopled' with animal actors. This imaginary world of the folktale is differentiated from the 'real' world by the simple device of inverting the characteristics of its animal inhabitants in relation to their real-world counterparts. So large beasts such as the elephant that are supposedly powerful and wise are portrayed as weak and foolish, while small creatures that seem of little account are credited in folktales with wisdom and courage. It then becomes possible, by reversing the play of metaphor, to imagine a differently constructed human society.

Shanklin's analysis (Ch. 15) of the origin myth of the Kom people of Cameroon, West Africa, explicitly invokes Wagner's 'obviation' model of mythological world-making. Shanklin's diagram (Fig. 15.1), which is formally identical with that proposed by Wagner (1975), represents both a cosmology (in this case that of the Kom) and also the universal process by which cosmologies, as inclusive systems of cultural meaning, are everywhere generated. Shanklin's representation of dual structure and the process by which the opposition between the two complementary aspects of the Kom universe is mediated by the python-king (Ch. 15, Fig. 15.1) is congruent with the general theory of world-making I am putting forward. In the accompanying diagram (Fig.1) I attempt to illustrate Shanklin's interpretation.

The central, vertical dotted line that transects the triangles in both Figure 1 and Figure 15.1 is identical with the division between the two basic domains or aspects of the Kom universe and also follows what I have called the axis of continuity, while the horizontal lines in both triangles follow the axis of separation. The two cosmological domains or aspects could be called those of the given and the potential, the visible and the invisible, or even of 'life' and 'death'.

In Kom cosmology, as expressed in their origin myth, the python is the prime mediator between the opposed and complementary domains of the

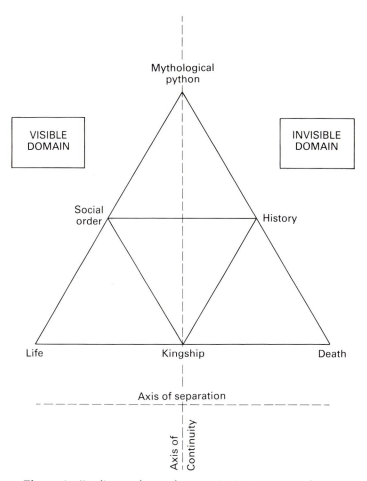

Figure 1 Dualism and complementarity in Kom cosmology.

visible and invisible. It is also a representation of kingship: the *Fon*, or king, can appear as a python or he can represent the destructive, as opposed to the constructive, aspects of kingship by appearing as a leopard. A king assumes animal form – either python or leopard – when he dies and passes into the invisible world.

A notable feature of the Kom myth is that the world-making python does not appear in its corporeal form but as an 'absent presence' denoted by its track. Unlike the tracks of other terrestrial creatures, the track of a snake peculiarly resembles the animal itself. Here the track, the 'natural sign' of the snake, presents a mirror image of a being that is itself both king and python (or, alternatively, leopard). The 'track' motif can thus be seen as a complex reference to the dual nature of Kom reality and to the mediative – both world-making and world-destroying – role of kingship.

The python symbol thus unites in itself a complex cluster of contrasts and associations that together define the structure of the Kom universe. In semantic terms it is patently and potently *paradigmatic*: it signifies the major, dualistic categories of that universe. But the python track, emblem of the royal beast itself, also serves in the origin myth as a syntagmatic, lineal chain that sets out and defines the spatial extent of Kom society and culture, while the successive appearances and disappearances of the track establish and interrelate the crucial events of Kom history.

In comparison with the Kom python, which is so thoroughly enmeshed in the structure and dynamics of local cosmology, the New Zealand moa offers an instructive contrast. Here is another huge beast, which has been extinct since at least the 17th century, but which has left its 'track' in Maori traditions and, most significantly for a scientifically oriented culture like that of white New Zealand, in numerous and massive skeletal remains. There is no reason to doubt that *Dinornithiformes*, called moa by the Maori, became extinct well before the colonial period began in the late 18th century.

Anderson (Ch. 18) invites us to consider the significance of persistent reports of moa sightings from the 1830s onwards. He notes that the reports only began after news of the giant bird's former existence, as evidenced by the skeletal relics and Maori tradition, had become common knowledge among the white immigrant population; that the reports always came from whites living at the edges of colonial settlement; and that the descriptions emphasized the exaggeratedly humanoid features of the alleged beast, such as its extreme tallness and upright, bipedal gait. Anderson also notes the generic similarity between these alleged moa sightings and reports of 'wild men' from other parts of the world, with the Himalayan yeti and the North American 'bigfoot' as well-known instances.[4]

Anderson's discussion of the anomalous 'sightings' of an extinct animal interprets the colonial moa as a psychological transformation, in a stressful situation (impoverished colonists facing the wilderness) of the traditional European image of 'the beast within'. This interpretation deserves comment, as an example of what I want to call the disconnected or disjunctive significance of the symbolic animal in modern Western thought, a disconnection that reflects the absolute division or dichotomy between the two domains of superior mind/spirit and inferior matter, referred to earlier. This dichotomy, which appears to be peculiar to Western cosmology, was originally formulated by Descartes, who is generally regarded as the founder of modern philosophy, in the early 17th century (see Willis, Ch. 19). In the imaginary but powerful symbolic animal described by Anderson, we see the fundamental split in Western cosmology reflected in the dual and disconnected conceptions of the feared 'beast within' the human person and the no less feared wild humanoid, the 'beast without', that supposedly lives just beyond the frontiers of Western civilization.

Wright's account (Ch. 4) of the symbolic ideas of the Toba people of northeast Argentina affords another dimension to the comparison between non-Western and Western cosmologies. Wright's contribution is mainly concerned with the meaning of mythical animals for the Toba. In Toba cosmology, where the fundamental dualism is glossed by Wright as 'male' and 'female', mythical animals belong to a time when all beings, human and nonhuman, were able to change their forms at will. But access to these ambiguous beings, described as having immense 'power', is open to human dwellers in the present, mundane world of fixed categories. Such access is conferred through the medium of the shaman, the ritual specialist who confers success in the hunt and healing of sickness. Similar relations between a mythical domain of primal, shape-shifting beings and the mundane world are described in Saladin d'Anglure's vivid account (Ch. 13) of Inuit cosmology. Here the polar bear, like his human analogue, the shaman, mediates between the mundane world and the living world of myth where primal beings of power have the gift of shape-shifting. But whereas in the non-Western world the 'real' beast typically appears as a mythological being, in the Western world mythological concepts occasionally assume the form of monstrous entities, ambiguously combining human and bestial attributes.

A noteworthy example of such a potently symbolic representation which, like Anderson's, occurs in a 'frontier' context, is Lawrence's discussion (Ch. 17) of rodeo horses. Here we have a ritual drama focused on the composite, animate image of a man on a wild horse, the man struggling to subdue the beast, which is struggling to unseat the man. Lawrence shows how this image of two antithetical modes of being, the domesticated and the wild, symbolizes the cosmological drama enacted historically on the western frontier of the United States: modern civilization's conquest of nature. Significantly, the moment when the man succeeds in subduing his mount is called 'breaking the bronc': the integrity of wild beasthood is destroyed and the animal participates in the dichotomous existence of his master, divided between 'natural' and 'cultural' modes of being.

Pálsson's account (Ch. 9) of changing Icelandic perceptions of fish shows how the transformation from nonindustrial to industrial cosmology in this European culture has radically altered the perceived relation between humankind and the natural world. In the preindustrial era relations between human and nonhuman beings were filtered through a dualistic cosmology that divided the universe between the domains of land and sea, as graphically portrayed in the Sagas. In this dual world humans were relatively powerless and their success, or otherwise, in catching fish was decided by certain ambiguous aquatic beings who mediated between the two cosmic domains.

In contrast, with the development of modern capitalism in Iceland in this century, the preindustrial cosmology broke down, along with the precapitalist peasant society and culture that sustained it. In the modern cosmology humankind confronts and dominates nature, and the fishing industry is simply one instance of that cosmic dominance.

In the preindustrial Icelandic universe, according to Pálsson, the power to catch fish was inherent in a quality of 'fishiness' in the fisherman: to the extent that he himself participated in 'fishhood' his prey were drawn to him, and caught. Other contributions, particularly chapters 12 and 13, suggest that human participation in nonhuman animality is the mark of social pre-eminence and power. These are individuals whose power, like that of the Inuit, Amerindian, and Siberian shaman (cf. Eliade 1968) derives from his ability to mediate between ordinary and extraordinary domains and whose zoomorphic attributes symbolize the ability to transcend the categories of ordinary existence.

The python-king of the Kom people is an example, common in Africa, of intimate association between kingship and a feral species. Many ethnographic examples indicate that ambiguously zoomorphic and anthropomorphic images readily occur as representations of world-making power in non-Western societies. A famous instance in the literature of anthropology is the pangolin or scaly anteater, a humanoid emblem of royalty among the Lele people of Central Africa (Douglas 1966 and Ch. 1). Where these societies are relatively unstratified and egalitarian, such power is typically vested in the mediative figure of the shaman, master of animals and vehicle of healing efficacy. In hierarchical non-Western societies, such as the pre-Columbian Aztec (Ch. 12), the mediative role is focused in the person of the king, as supreme world-maker.

In contrast with the centrality of such ambiguous images in non-Western societies, modern, scientific culture relegates them to the periphery of its dominion, to that liminal space where the empire of rationality confronts the as yet unsubdued forces of chaos.

Qualified achievements, future prospects

Douglas (Ch. 1), in her cautionary remarks on the dangers attending the unguarded use of the concepts of 'anomaly' and 'metaphor', also invites us to look ahead to the possibilities for new research and theoretical advance in the area of animal symbolism. By taking account of indigenous concepts of human–animal interaction in particular cultural contexts, Douglas tells us, we can avoid the structuralist error of unwarrantably imposing our own perceptions of metaphorical relation on the field data. Douglas's argument is akin to James's (Ch. 14) drawing of our attention to the neglected indigenous themes of continuity, integration, and interaction 'between the various species of the living world, including ourselves'. In turn, these pertinent observations join up with my own insistence on the need, while preserving the insights and achievements of Lévi-Straussian structuralism, to reinstate the repressed dimension of continuity in our interpretations of animal symbolism.

As for new research, the scope is clearly enormous and strikingly attested by the vast range of interests and approaches represented in this volume by contributions from every inhabited continent. A broad though not exclusive distinction is apparent between those analyses that are universal in their implications for understanding of human relations with the nonhuman world of nature, and those focused more narrowly on local systems of relations. But here too there are frequent insights of wider import. Thus Saladin d'Anglure (Ch. 13) in the course of his description of the dialectics of humans and animals among the Inuit of the Canadian Arctic, draws attention to the erotic relation between human and beast, a recurrent theme of ancient religion and magic. The image evoked, of commingled human and bestial being that is also an act of generation, may well be the most archaic of all metaphors of cultural world-making, to judge by its worldwide distribution in tribal origin myths. Closely related to that sacred and taboo-laden image is that of the composite human and animal entity of which there are several examples in this book.

The possibility that certain ancient and widely distributed images of nonhuman life-forms may be genetically programmed in *Homo sapiens* has been raised in the context of ophidian imagery by a contributor to the companion volume *What is an animal?* (Ingold 1988). In this volume Willis (Ch. 19) considers, in the light of Mundkur's well-documented survey (Mundkur 1983, 1988), the cross-cultural significance of the serpent as a focal image of the 'otherness' of nonhuman animality. Willis's discussion is complemented by Beynen's analysis (Ch. 3) of the meaning of this animal as a component of a triadic relation between serpent, man, and woman in the mythology of the Semitic cultural region.

Most of the contributions to this book however, in the tradition of post-Boasian and post-Malinowskian anthropology, are studies of ongoing symbolic relations within specific cultural groups rather than attempts to examine universal themes. But here too the range is large and includes several readily apparent subcategories. One such division includes Jackson's Lévi-Straussian analysis (Ch. 8) of animal symbolism in Pictish society, drawn mainly from archaeological evidence.

In contrast to the studies concerned with total systems of relations where animal classification performs a semantic function akin to that of grammatical categories in natural languages, Ojoade's contribution (Ch. 16) focuses on the multiple significances of a single animal species, the domestic dog, in the cultures of modern Nigeria. More specialized still, but of no less interest, is Slawoj Szynkiewicz's analysis (Ch. 6) of the complex symbolism invested in the tibial bone of the sheep in Mongol culture.

To name a symbolic animal, or animal part (for example, as a Wopkaimin trophy, or a Mongol sheep tibia) is to name a *relation*. I have argued that this relation is always problematic, in the sense that unlike social relations, which always imply each other (as, for example, wife–husband, or patron–client) the animal symbol conveys two opposed sets of meanings, signifying both separation and continuity, being both paradigm and syntagm. (In English the very term 'animal' has this double sense, being opposed to 'human' in common usage but embracing the human species in scientific parlance.[5])

I have further argued that this problematic duality of the animal symbol

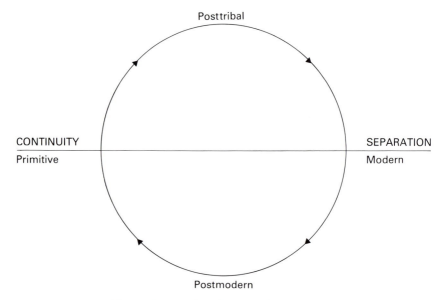

Figure 2   Social evolution and involution.

reflects its implication in a cosmogonic or world-making process that always and everywhere has the form of a continuing mediation between two juxtaposed domains or aspects of a unitary reality; and that the living source of this universal schema is to be found in what I have called the transorganismic dyad of self-and-other, a mode of being peculiar to *Homo sapiens* and diagnostic of the species.

The analysis has distinguished two polar types of cultural universe or cosmology, one being primarily oriented towards the world-making dimension of continuity and the syntagmatic, and the other primarily oriented towards separation and the paradigmatic. The first type has customarily and variously been called 'primitive', 'archaic', 'tribal', or 'premodern', the second simply 'modern'. This crude typology reflects the fixedly Eurocentric anthropology of a century ago with its underlying premise of unidirectional social evolution, and is inappropriate in the light of current knowledge. With the collapse of Eurocentrism and unidirectional evolutionism in the early 20th century, and the consequent relativization of 'Western' culture, our global perception of societal change could perhaps better be represented as one of oscillation between the two poles of continuity (or 'primitiveness') and separation (or 'modernization'). We could then distinguish between the *evolution* of modernizing, posttribal societies oriented towards separation, and the *involution* of postmodern, ecologically conscious societies increasingly oriented towards continuity (see Fig. 2).

These relatively different cultural worlds are not, of course, isolated one from another. Through an exchange of information mediated by radio, television, books, and newspapers, through personal travel and tourism, and sometimes through the work of anthropologists, the fruits of diverse kinds of social experience are diffused among the local collectivities of humankind to create, amid diversity, the evident beginnings of a novel sense of global community: the present volume may, perhaps, be seen as a contribution to that emergent sense of community.

Acknowledgements

I thank Wendy James and Peter Ucko for helpful comments on an earlier draft of this Introduction.

Notes

1   To forestall possible misunderstanding, I am not asserting that *all* non-Western cosmologies are dualistic in form – many are patently not – but that a perception of 'reality' as a duality which is also a unity is widespread and probably universal, as Lévy-Bruhl maintained. For a particularly striking, recently described example of complementary dualism in a non-Western cosmology see Crocker (1985). See also Jackson's comments in Chapter 8.
2   It is noteworthy that modern Western physics has 'rediscovered' the primitively given complementarity of time and space, as also of 'observer' and 'observed', 'mind' and 'matter' (see also Willis, Ch. 20).
3   It is well known that Lévi-Strauss derived his model of mythological thought, including his reading of totemism, from the structural linguistics of Saussure and Jakobson. Post-structuralist critics of Lévi-Strauss such as Turner (1977), Greimas (1966), and Dundes (1968) have all noted the tendency of Lévi-Strauss to privilege the *paradigmatic* (oppositional and contrastive) dimension of meaning in his interpretations of mythological and 'totemic' thought, and an associated suppression of the *syntagmatic* (connective and combinatorial) dimension of meaning, as these terms are understood in structural linguistics. How this alleged defect should be remedied is less clear, though both Greimas and Dundes see a model for syntagmatic interpretation in the work of the Russian folklorist Propp (cf. Willis 1984).
4   Popular interest is currently being aroused in Western countries by descriptions of purported human encounters with humanoid beings from outer space, the 'last frontier'. Strieber (1987) is an excellent example of this genre.
5   The king of the Kuba people of Zaïre is said by de Heusch (1985, p. 98) to have the attributes of wild-beasthood in Kuba cosmology.
6   As Ingold observes in his Introduction to *What is an animal?* (1988), the meaning of this relation in English differs from that of a social relation in being transitively asymmetric: whereas a human being can be thought of as a kind of animal, it makes no sense to speak of the 'humanity' of a non-human animal. In contrast, the Kom king not only 'is' a python, but the mythological python is also a king.

References

von Bertalannfy, L. 1955. An essay on the relativity of categories. *Philosophy of Science* **22**(4), 243–63.

Boas, F. 1916. The origin of totemism. *American Anthropologist* **18**, 319–26.

Bower, T. G. R. 1977. *A primer of infant development*. San Francisco: Freeman.

Bulmer, R. 1967. Why the cassowary is not a bird. *Man* **2**(1), 5–25.

Carrithers, M. 1989. Sociality, not aggression, is the prime human trait. In *Societies at peace*, S. Howell and R. Willis (eds), 187–211. London: Routledge.

Crocker, J. C. 1985. *Vital souls: Bororo cosmology, natural symbols, and shamanism.* Tucson: University of Arizona Press.

Douglas, M. 1957. Animals in Lele religious thought. *Africa* **27**(1), 46–58.

Douglas, M. 1966. *Purity and danger*. London: Routledge & Kegan Paul.

Dundes, A. 1968. Introduction to second English edition of V. Propp, *Morphology of the folktale*, xi–xvii. Austin, Texas: University of Texas Press.

Durkheim, E. 1912. *Les formes élémentaires de la vie religieuse*. Paris: Presses Universitaires de France.

Eliade, M. 1968. *Le chamanisme et les techniques archaïques de l'extase*. Paris: Bibliothèque Scientifique.

Elkin, A. P. 1933–4. Studies in Australian totemism. *Oceania* **4**(1 & 2), 65–90, 113–31.

Evans-Pritchard, E. E. 1956. Zande clan names. *Man* **62**, 69–71.

Firth, R. 1930–1. Totemism in Polynesia. *Oceania* **1** (3 & 4), 251–321, 378–98.

Fortes, M. 1945. *The dynamics of clanship among the Tallensi*. London: Oxford University Press.

Frazer, J. G. 1910. *Totemism and exogamy: a treatise on certain early forms of religion and society*. 4 vols. London: Macmillan.

Freud, S. 1913. *Totem und Tabu*. Leipzig & Vienna: Heller.

Freud, S. 1939. Civilization and its discontents. In *Civilization, war and death*, J. Richardson (ed.). London: Hogarth.

Gell, A. 1973. *The metamorphosis of the cassowaries: Umeda society, language and ritual*. London: Athlone Press.

van Gennep, A. 1920. *L'état actuel du problème totémique*. Paris: Leroux.

Goldenweiser, A. 1910. Totemism, an analytical study. *Journal of American Folklore* **23**, 179–293.

Greimas, A. J. 1966. *Sémantique structurale*. Paris: Larousse.

Griaule, M. 1965. *Conversations with Ogotommêli: an introduction to Dogon religious ideas*. London: Oxford University Press.

de Heusch, L. 1985. *Sacrifice in Africa: a structuralist approach*. Manchester: Manchester University Press.

Ingold, T. 1988. Introduction. In *What is an animal?* T. Ingold (ed.), 1–16. London: Unwin Hyman.

Jackson, M. 1982. *Allegories of the wilderness: ethics and ambiguities in Kuranko narratives*. Bloomington: Indiana University Press.

James, W. 1988. *The listening ebony: moral knowledge, religion and power among the Uduk of the Sudan*. Oxford: Clarendon Press.

Leach, E. R. 1964. Anthropological aspects of language: animal categories and verbal abuse. In *New directions in the study of language*, E. H. Lenneberg (ed.), 23–63. Cambridge, Mass.: MIT Press.

Lenneberg, E. H. 1967. *Biological foundations of language*. New York: Wiley.

Lévi-Strauss, C. 1962a. *Le totémisme aujourd'hui*. Paris: Presses Universitaires de France.

Lévi-Strauss, C. 1962b. *La pensée sauvage*. Paris: Plon.

Lévy-Bruhl, L. 1975. *The notebooks on primitive mentality*. Oxford: Blackwell.

Lienhardt, R. G. 1961. *Divinity and experience: the religion of the Dinka*. Oxford: Clarendon Press.

Lowie, R. H. 1920. *Primitive society*. New York: Liveright.

Lyons, J. 1968. *Introduction to theoretical linguistics*. Cambridge: Cambridge University Press.

Malinowski, B. 1948. *Magic, science and religion*. Boston: Beacon Press.

McLennan, J. F. 1869, 1870. The worship of animals and plants. *Fortnightly Review*, **6** (1869); 407–27, 562–82; **7** (1870), 194–216.

Meadows, D. H. 1972. *The limits to growth: a report for the Club of Rome's project on the predicament of mankind*. New York: Universe Books.

Meggitt, M. J. 1962. *Desert people: a study of the Walbiri Aborigines of Central Australia*. Sydney: Angus & Robertson.

Morton, J. 1987. The effectiveness of totemism: 'increase ritual' and resource control in central Australia. *Man* **22**, 453–74.

Mundkur, B. 1983. *The cult of the serpent: an interdisciplinary survey of its manifestations and origins*. New York: State University of New York Press.

Mundkur, B. 1988. Human animality: the mental imagery of fear, and religiosity. In *What is an animal?* T. Ingold (ed.), 141–84. London: Unwin Hyman.

Munn, N. 1973. *Walbiri iconography: graphic representation and cultural symbolism in a central Australian society*. Ithaca, NY: Cornell University Press.

Murdock, G. P. 1949. *Social structure*. New York: Macmillan.

Newsome, A. E. 1980. The eco-mythology of the red kangaroo in Central Australia. *Mankind* **12**, 327–33.

Overing, J. 1975. *The Piaroa, a people of the Orinoco Basin*. Oxford: Clarendon Press.

Peterson, N. 1972. Totemism yesterday: sentiment and local organization among the Australian Aborigines. *Man* **7**, 12–32.

Radcliffe-Brown, A. R. 1929. The sociological theory of totemism. In *Structure and function in primitive society*, A. R. Radcliffe-Brown, 117–32. London: Cohen & West. (Reprinted from *Proceedings of the Fourth Pacific Science Congress*, Batavia.)

Rappoport, R. A. 1968. *Pigs for the ancestors: ritual in the ecology of a New Guinea people*. New Haven: Yale University Press.

Reichel-Dolmatoff, G. 1971. *Amazonian cosmos: the sexual and religious symbolism of the Tukano Indians*. Chicago: University of Chicago Press.

Rivers, W. H. R. 1914. *The history of Melanesian society*. 2 vols. Cambridge: Cambridge University Press.

Sebeok, T. A. 1988. 'Animal' in biological and semiotic perspective. In *What is an animal?* T. Ingold (ed.), 63–76. London: Unwin Hyman.

Shanklin, E. 1985. Sustenance and symbol: anthropological studies of domesticated animals. *Annual Review of Anthropology* 14, 375–403.

Stern, D. 1985. *The interpersonal world of the infant*. New York: Basic Books.

Stocking, George W., Jr. 1987. *Victorian anthropology*. New York: Free Press.

Strehlow, T. G. H. 1970. Geography and the totemic landscape in Central Australia: a functional study. In *Australian Aboriginal anthropology: modern studies in the social anthropology of the Australian Aborigines*, R. M. Berndt (ed.), 92–140. Perth: University of Western Australia Press.

Strieber, W. 1987. *Communion: a true story*. New York: Wilson & Neff.

Tambiah, S. J. 1969. Animals are good to think and good to prohibit. *Ethnology* 8(4), 424–59.

Trevarthen, C. and Logotheti, K. 1989. Child in society and society in children: the nature of basic trust. In *Societies at peace*, S. Howell & R. Willis (eds), 165–86. London: Routledge.

Turner, T. S. 1977. Narrative structure and mythopoesis: a critique and reformulation of structuralist concepts of myth, narrative and poetics. *Arethusa* **10**(1), 103–63.

Turner, V. W. 1975. *Revelation and divination in Ndembu ritual*. Ithaca, NY: Cornell University Press.

Tylor, E. B. 1871. *Primitive culture*. 2 vols. London: John Murray.

von Uexküll, J. 1982. The theory of meaning. *Semiotica* **42**(1), 25–82.

Wagner, R. 1975. *The invention of culture*. Englewood Cliffs, NJ: Prentice-Hall.

Wagner, R. 1978. *Lethal speech: Daribi myth as symbolic obviation*. Ithaca, NY: Cornell University Press.

Whorf, B. L. 1956. *Language, thought and reality*. New York: Wiley.

Willis, R. G. 1974. *Man and beast*. London: Hart-Davis, MacGibbon.

Willis, R. G. 1984. Strukturale Analyse von Mythen und Oraler Literatur. *Kölner Zeitschrift für Soziologie und Sozialpsychologie* **26**, 141–57.

Worsley, P. 1967. Groote Eylandt totemism and *Le Totémisme aujourd'hui*. In *The Structural study of myth and totemism*, E. Leach (ed.), 141–59. London: Tavistock.

1 *The pangolin revisited: a new approach to animal symbolism*

MARY DOUGLAS

This chapter is a warning against two common ideas about animal symbolism. One is against the unwary use of anomaly. The other is the same warning against metaphor. When I have explained the traps I will suggest a way of avoiding them.

The idea that perception of an anomalous animal kind comes to us out of the nature of biological orders can be firmly laid aside. Animal anomalies are not installed in nature but emerge from particular features of classificatory schemes. In *Purity and danger* (1966) I thought that this was to say enough. I focused on the 'nonfit'. Since no scheme of classification can cover the infinite variety of experience there will always be elements that do not fit. Then it is a matter of cultural idiosyncrasy as to which elements escape through the meshes of the classifications, and of cultural bias as to whether they are noticed at all, and whether, if they are noticed as anomalous, this provokes any special interest, either of approval or distaste. The programme that then seemed to lie ahead was to examine the social conditions that demand very concise and exhaustive classifications and those that encourage a lax attitude to fit and misfit. Questions about classification, rather than questions about the identification of particular anomalies or metaphors, have been the centre of my interests, starting with *Natural symbols* (1970) and going on to the present. The programme does not help to interpret metaphors or to recognize anomalies since it focuses only on features of classification that are sustained by practical use, so at first sight it is not easy for me to have something to say about animal symbolism. But there are many things that have to be said about the justification of interpretations of metaphors and anomalies in general that could perhaps be helpful.

It is obviously wrong to say that a thing is anomalous by using our own categories. It is not even enough to argue from our idea of nature to natural anomalies, such as flightless birds, flying fish, or barkless dogs. We should not expect that what we regard as deviant subspecies widely distributed across oceans and deserts would be accorded special taxonomic status in all cultures. Bulmer (1986) tested this in trying to trace the prohibited birds in Leviticus 11 and Deuteronomy 13, but was forced to conclude that the evidence did not stand up. He was very attached to the idea that a panhuman cognitive disquiet arises in response to deviant subspecies, so the negative result, though disappointing to him, is a valuable contribution to scholarship. The idea rests on the assumption that species are natural kinds, a thesis that Hull (1978) has effectively questioned. With the doubt that perhaps species are not separated by natural boundaries, other doubts arise.

An anthropologist who claims to know that a particular animal or human kind is perceived as an anomaly in the foreign culture needs to justify the claim. But how? Asserting that foreigners recognize an anomaly is a more complex form of the problem raised when asserting that the foreigners see one thing as a metaphor of another. The right way for the anthropologist to deal with suspected anomalies will be the same right way to deal with metaphors. Most of the analyses of the symbolism of animals show the animal kingdom as a projection or metaphor of social life; the analysis depends implicitly on resemblance or picturing. It may be directly, as when the animal is said to depict particular human feelings, such as compassion or cruelty. Or more indirectly, as when by their industry or unruliness, for instance, they are taken to represent certain kinds of human behaviour. All metaphorical identifications depend on making a match. The exercise is to identify some sameness in both fields. However, there is no limit to the power of the imagination for seeing patterns and finding resemblances. So there is no limit to the scope for finding similarity between any sets of objects.

Similarity is not a quality of things in themselves, as Goodman (1972) points out. He makes seven strictures against treating similarity as explanation. The first stricture relates to his concern for a better understanding of the nature of abstraction and realism in art:

> Similarity does not distinguish any symbols as peculiarly 'iconic', or account for the grading of pictures as more or less realistic or conventional.
>   Representation does not depend on resemblance alone.

Similarity is relative, variable and culture-dependent.

The second stricture is that similarity does not pick out replicas. The third applies the second to events; two performances of the same work may be very different, repetitions of the same behaviour may involve widely varying sequences of motions. What makes sameness certain in scientific work?

> If we experiment twice, do the differences between the two occasions make them different experiments or only different instances of the same experiment, the answer . . . is always relative to a theory – we cannot repeat an experiment and look for a covering theory; we must have at least a partial theory before we know whether we have a repetition of the experiment (Goodman 1972, p. 439)

The fourth stricture is that similarity does not explain metaphor or metaphorical truth. Rather the other way round, the practice of referring to two objects metaphorically constitutes their similarity.

Metaphorical use may serve to explain the similarity better than – or at
least as well as – the similarity explains the metaphor (Goodman 1972,
p. 440)

The fifth and sixth strictures are to do with induction and although they
are very relevant to the inductions we make as anthropologists about the
principles governing other cultures, I make bold to leave them aside in the
present context. Already to accept the first four strictures would be for
anthropologists a severe curtailment of our usual interpretive activities. The
only comfort is that similarity depends on use, on a habit, a practice, a
theory however small or a hypothesis however implicit, that picks out the
common properties that are held to constitute similarity. If the anthropologist can locate the foreign theory that entrenches a foreign metaphor, and if
the theory can be shown to be actually used by the foreigners for prediction,
production or remedy, then his interpretation is on safe ground. Otherwise
he is probably abusing similarity by making it do more work than it can
perform.

This adds up to saying that an interpretation based on discerning a match
between one set of things and its representation needs some further guarantee. Metaphors are no more natural phenomena than anomalies. To escape
the reproach of having been too imaginative, the anthropologist needs to do
more. First, the foreign metaphor has to have local testimony that this is
what it means to the foreigner. Then there is the quality of that testimony: is
it just one person who said so, or is there some evidence for the wider use of
the metaphor; and is the usage a one-off lyrical moment in a poet's rhap-
sody, or is it institutionalized as part of the regular habits of the people, a
resemblance picked out by their theories of the world and their hypotheses?

All three requirements were met by Turner's (1962) analysis of
whiteness metaphors in Ndembu culture. Why can we believe him when
he says that for the Ndembu the whiteness of milk resembles the white sap
of a certain tree, and that whiteness of both and whiteness in general
means matrilineal descent and continuity? We accept these metaphors not
merely because he can quote and name his Ndembu instructors. He
witnessed the uses to which the metaphors were put in ceremonies that
deployed the redness of blood and of red saps of trees, and the blackness of
charcoal and of bile. But important evidence of the institutionalizing of the
meanings of the colours is in his account of the social alignments in clans
and villages. His interpretations of the metaphors depends upon their use
in ceremonies that act the part of theories in upholding perceptions of
similarity. Their explanations of the causes of barrenness, sickness and
death are indeed theories in which the metaphors are entrenched with
consistency at many different levels.

The example is all the better for my purpose because Turner did
incautiously let go of these safeguards of his interpretation and tried to find
Ndembu meanings of whiteness in other cultures (1962) and, needless to say,
found them and got to be duly criticized for it. In situations where there are

no guarantees against subjective recognition of similarity, the searcher will always find what he seeks.

I freely confess that in *Natural Symbols* (1970) I wrote as if the interpretation of the metaphor must be right if it can be shown to correspond to the social structure. But my perception of the social structure as being like that of the symbolic order is a resemblance that I have picked out. It also needs anchorage. Goodman says that correspondence never carries its own guarantee; the match between the symbolic system and the social system is a similarity that I perceive, but of itself it cannot confirm the interpretation that matches them up. Alas, Goodman's strictures on the abuse of similarity undo this interpretive complacency. First, they apply to the recognition of any pattern as being similar to something else, since similarity is not a quality that inheres in things. When we recognize the social system as the same from one year to the next, we are again invoking similarity; but now we know that similarity is not a quality of things. The matching features of the social system between one visit and the next have to be selected by the viewer as in any other similarity case. Just to see the same social arrangements continuing between two visits involves backgrounding the changes or overlooking them altogether.

Ignorant of these snares, I have attributed to the ancient Israelites a metaphorical construction that makes table, altar, and marriage bed into analogies one with another, and also temple, nation, and human body, and used the larger structure of analogy to explain animal categories prohibited in the Mosaic dietary code (Douglas 1975a). If all these interpretations have to be sent back to the drawing board because we start to take Goodman seriously, so also must be many other interpretations of animal symbols. No names, no pack drill: I name no names, but remark only that I am in good company. The case for animal metaphors is no weaker and no stronger than the case for metaphors found in hair, food, and sex.

Another favourite interpretive ploy is an even worse case: that is the promise to show that symbolic forms are inverted images of social reality. First there is the questionable identifying of enduring images in the symbolism; second, there is the challengeable identifying of enduring patterns in social behaviour; third, there is the dubious alleged resemblance between the symbolic pattern and the pattern of society. Fourth, there is the even more difficult identifying of an inverse pattern of an image; then the alleged enduring inverse pattern of social reality, and last, there is more trouble with the claimed match between the two inverted images.

One attempt to escape from the similarity strictures and other doubts is to throw all the metaphors into the air at once; set the wheel of lights turning, and make such a virtuoso dazzle that everyone will succumb to the irresistible pattern of patterns reflecting one another. This method is used brilliantly by Geertz (1973) in his account of Balinese cockfighting. Reading it, criticism is seduced by each new facet of resemblance that is brought into the play of matching metaphors. For example the cock which the man watching the cockfight is holding between his knees is a metaphorical penis. In themselves umpteen extra facets of metaphor do not improve the analysis of the cockfight's meaning; their alleged coherence, because it depends on notions of similarity, comes under the strictures like the rest. Claimed coherence between metaphors is a good sign of the investigator's perseverance and ingenuity; trying to demonstrate it is a spur to improve the evidence. But of itself coherence between numerous metaphors cannot justify an argument. Something more is needed.

Following Ryle (1949), Geertz has called this method of pursuing the ethnographer's avocation 'thick description', an attempt to get at 'the sort of piled up structures of inference and implication through which an ethnographer is continually trying to pick his way' (Geertz 1973, p. 7). As the meanings of the people being studied are thickly interleaved, so does the ethnographer's skill have to be as subtle in uncovering the various layers. The power of this form of reporting to carry conviction depends on showing coherence between multiple contexts.

There is a difference between Ryle's and Geertz's use of the idea of thick description. For Ryle it is used critically in a philosophical argument about what the everyday processes of interpretation involve. Geertz is using it prescriptively to help ethnographers to describe what other people's meanings are. Both are wary of imputing too much intellectual theorizing to the agents who are the subject of study. Geertz is deeply wary of the kind of theorizing that codifies abstract regularities and seeks to generalize even to the point of creating a fantasy world of academic satisfaction that has no correspondence with ethnographic realities. For him the essential task of theory-building is to make thick description possible, generalizing within cases and not across them (Geertz 1973, p. 26) and then gradually to build up an understanding about how cultural processes work. He is not trying to do without theory, but he likes it to be modest and secure in its micro-foundations.

Geertz is very explicit that he is not recommending thick description as a method to replace established techniques of gathering information. It is rather an outcome or objective. If he were proffering the rich concatenation of metaphors that he deploys as a method of ethnography he would be vulnerable to the charge of resting explanation on similarity. The strictures do not apply if thickness of description be sought with enough attention to the intentions that have been framed by institutional supports that co-ordinate and steady the meanings, but we the observers have to catalogue them and assess them. We also have to justify our interpretations of the metaphors, and here again, similarity does not pick out replicas or icons. We also depend on theories and institutional habits for our interpretations. Though I fully share Geertz's preference for small theories tried and working at microlevels, I am sure that it is much better that they be made explicit.

The temptation to let resemblance do the work of explanation is strong because coherence of metaphors works very well as an interpretive rule within one culture. Remember that similarity is culture-dependent. Similarity has explanatory power within our own culture, based as it has to be upon shared similarity perceptions. Statements of similarity 'are still ser-viceable in the streets' (Goodman 1972, p. 446), but they do not help us to go from one culture to another.

On this line of argument, if fieldwork reports have problems with metaphors, so much the more does mythology. Nothing can stave off doubt about the interpretation of metaphor in purely literary uses. In some genres there are verbal equivalents to the supporting institutional structures that safeguard Turner's Ndembu interpretations. For example, though there is plenty of cause for scepticism about my interpretation of the Mosaic dietary rules, this is in fact much more secure just because it is about rules to be observed and therefore about concepts and theories expected to be in use in a more practical way than stories can ever be. Narrative has problems about symbolization and literary solutions of its own that do not help with interpreting anthropological materials about symbols in use and I regret to say that I do not think that the literary analysis, bound as it is to representa-tional models of interpretation, can be helped by the viewpoint that I am developing here.

Returning to Goodman's strictures, since similarity is culture-bound, our need is to develop our culture of anthropological interpretation. And since similarity does not pick out icons, since similarity of itself gives no guaran-tees of interpretation, no method based solely on representational theory will help. The theory has to be one that systematically links behaviour to interpretation; it has to be a theory of behaviour.

For lack of discussion of method and theory the materials that are collected in Central African fieldwork about animal symbolism remain very disparate. The Lele take a special interest in the lesser scaly anteater or tree pangolin (Figure 1.1). They used to make it the object of a fertility cult. I have described it (1957, p. 50) as anomalous in their system of classification on the basis of their descriptions of its habits and habitat, supplemented by knowledge of the rites they perform when they catch one and eat it, and by their theories of sickness and health. I would like to know whether neigh-bouring peoples whose forest it inhabits also regard it as a fish-like, mam-malian tree-climber, one of the most powerful nature spirits in their world, giver of fertility and good hunting.

Roberts (1986) and Thomas Blakeley (pers. comm.) have worked for a long time among the Tabwa, who live north and east of the Lele. The Tabwa also know of the pangolin and use its scales in medicine, but they pay less attention to the animal than they do to another ant-eating animal, the aardvark. In their mythology they are said to treat the aardvark as a heroic human surrogate, but I have explained why mythological material unsup-ported by practice and theory is a poor support for interpretation. Tabwa practice clearly does support the claim that the aardvark is regarded by the Tabwa as an anomalous beast: its long sensitive snout reminds them of a penis; when they kill it the hunters try not to let the women see it, because of their derisive laughter at the obscenely excessive sexuality of a creature with a penis at each end. Tabwa are reported to have no rituals at all about the

Figure 1.1 Tree pangolins.

aardvark. Most of my information about Lele attitudes to pangolins comes from dietary rules and behaviour, and I have no Lele myths about either pangolin or aardvark. To the best of my knowledge the Lele regard the aardvark as a rather unimpressive burrowing animal, of timid disposition, with hind legs too weak to run and a funny snout. It could be that there is much more similarity between the Lele and the Tabwa animal symbolism, but the very different interests of the various investigators make attempts at comparison pointless.

I am left with no comparable materials about animal symbolism in other parts of Central Africa, since my closest colleagues working in the vicinity are, respectively, specialists in history, mythology, ethnoscience and symbolism, but none is really interested in food habits and dietary regulations. It is possible, but I think implausible, that the Lele are unique in their complex of rules prohibiting different kinds of animal meats to different social categories. Goody (1982, pp. 38, 97) plays down the social symbolism of food in Africa compared with Europe and Asia, but among the Lele it expresses category distinctions of a more specialized kind, between male and female, child and adult, living and dead, religious initiates and lay folk. By mapping out the human categories and the animal categories, and noting the rules that connected them, I was able to draw diagrams that showed the animal kinds as projections of human society (1975b, p. 299). It was really quite easy and to me aesthetically satisfying. I expected the similarity of the two pictures to compel assent. But now that I know that similarity of itself does not pick out icons or replicas I have to think through the knowledge that resemblance does not guarantee interpretation. Taking aboard the full lesson that similarity cannot bear explanatory weight, I try to look at the material again.

In the summer of 1988 I returned to Zaire and revisited the Lele after a very long absence. Everything was changed. Christianization had driven the old religion underground; intense animosity between Christians and the rest was manifested in reciprocal accusations of sorcery; the pangolin cult was outlawed, its prohibitions a matter of fun for the Christians and of embarrassment for the believers. Furthermore, the depletion of the forest and of its fauna meant that no one now saw many of the animals that formerly figured on the regular menu. Consequently I was able to be told things about the animals that were initiates' secrets before. For example, I learnt that the pangolin's long ant-eating tongue is rooted at the top of the spine and holds the ribs in place. This gives it a tremendous advantage against sorcery, which attacks the lungs of victims, for its tongue anchors its ribs so that they can never come adrift from the spine as human ribs are thought to do, causing chest pains and coughing and death. A longer visit would elicit more of such wonderful information about individual animals. I learnt that the initiated diviners are forbidden to eat the Nile monitor because of its spotted skin and, as I began to get a list of prohibitions on other spotted animals, I found a whole theoretical field about the nature spirits and their interest in spottedness and a class of skin diseases that includes smallpox. Inevitably a concern with the classification of animals and humans leads to local theories about life and death whose outcome are shown in the menus and food rules. The theories sustain the classification and give meaning to the metaphors. Getting at their theories allows the investigator to bypass representational theories of cognition and so to avoid the strictures on misuse of similarity. But how do we get at their theories? Not by deducing them from the metaphors.

My argument is that the animal categories come up in the same patterns of relations as those of humans because the said humans understand the animal kinds to be acting according to the same principles as they themselves. On this approach the humans, that is the foreigners whom anthropologists report in ethnography, are using cognitive economy. They are not using animals for drawing elaborate pictures of themselves, nor are they neces-sarily using them for posing and answering profound metaphysical prob-lems. The argument is that they have practical reasons for trying to under-stand and predict the animals' ways, reasons to do with health and hygiene and sickness. The principles of seniority, marriage exchange, territory, and political hegemony that they use for explaining their own behaviour they also use for predictions about animal behaviour. It is a very economical argument depending on low-level micro-observation and modest theory, and more plausible than the theory of a projection of human society upon nature. In the late 1980s, after numerous philosophers have insisted that sameness is not a property of things, the idea that animal categories serve primarily as an abstract model of human society appears to be very questionable.

We can accept the idea that humans need to think out their difference from animals and that animal differentiations are a splendidly apt source of metaphors for thinking about human differentiation without accepting the idea that a well-matched differentiated animal world is essentially a resource for thinking about ourselves. Rather the other way round, how could we think about how animals relate to one another except on the basis of our own relationships?

This is not to question the iconicity of an animal model of the human world. We can question that mirroring society is its primary use. And we can be interested in how it gets to be constructed. I suggest that there is a more fundamental, nonmetaphorical kind of connection between the way humans think of themselves and how they think of animals. Once this other way is established, metaphors flourish upon its basis. The argument does not question Lévi-Strauss's (1962) idea that 'animals are good to think'. It merely supposes that totemic schemes are not essentially metaphoric con-structions, or rather that, insofar as they are interpretable as mirror images of human society, this will be because their categories have already been set up in the same patterns as the categories of human social relations. This is a variant of Horton's (1967) idea that in African traditional thought 'the mind in quest of explanatory analogies turns naturally to people and their relations'.

The similarity that we observe between the two spheres, human and animal, would result from the fact that both spheres are constructed upon the same principles. That the model of the animal world turns out to look so like that of the human world would be a byproduct of native theory about how animal society is constituted. The liberating idea that comes from taking Goodman and the other philosophers on similarity seriously is that there has not been so much picture-making in primitive thought as theorizing and not so much philosophy as reflection on practical issues; the models are derived from an immediate concern to figure out how the world works and concern to frame the classifications that work best with acceptable theory.

Briefly, Lele categorize humans and teach them how to behave with equals, seniors and juniors according to whether the relations come under the principles that govern the friendship or enmity of equals, or the principles of seniority and patronage. Equals, that is friends or enemies, recognize no territorial or property constraints. Patron–client relations have a strong territorial aspect. Client–client relations under the same patron entail mutual honour and respect, the practical issue is to know what is safe to eat.

If they want to understand why some animals of very different species share the same habitat peacefully, they apply their ideas of patron–client relations because it is a case of shared territory: if they want to understand the aggressive behaviour of carnivores they apply their ideas of enmity. By the same token, animals which cohabit in the territory of nature spirits are assumed to be clients of the spirits. The peaceful cohabitation of fish, lizards, water snakes and wild boar in the streams implies that they have secured the protection of the water spirits and have become their clients; on the human model this means that the spirits will avenge aggression against their clients, so it will not be safe to eat them if one is in alliance with a water spirit.

The model they use assumes a common set of intentions and reactions, as between humans and spirits, and between spirits and animals. If a Lele enters a clientship relation with a water spirit or if, as often happens, the spirit has made a pact of friendship with a human, the usual mutual respect from co-clients or towards friends' clients will be exacted. When humans enter into relations of clientship with various animals and spirits they do not prey on their nonhuman co-clients any more than they would on co-clients of a human overlord. To prey on co-clients would incur the anger of the patron. So it is not safe to eat animals indicated by rules that govern their own daily social life as co-clients of a common patron. Observing the intricate rules about what an individual human can eat or not eat with safety among animal species has a strong practical interest. The daily menu, which differentiates categories of humans by their diet sheet, is the surface appearance of deep theory about life and death and health and sickness.

If this is a plausible explanation of how Lele think about animal kinds, it is also a small but powerful theory about how other people think about the animal kinds that they have constructed. As a method it suggests that minute attention be paid to how animals interact with humans and to the interests that humans pursue when they chase or eat or tame animals or harness them to work. It is a method for establishing meanings that escapes the strictures on similarity. It explains the theorizing by which the classes of animal kinds are put together, but I should emphasize that it does not necessarily undermine extant analyses of animal symbols based on attributed metaphorical meanings. These always have to contend with the strictures on similarity unless a purely literary, even fictional, account is required.

The difficulties inherent in arguments based on similarity provide plenty of reason for worry for the structural analysis of myth and for the quantities of symbolic similarities that have been perceived in anthropology since Lévi-Strauss's publication in 1962 of *La pensée sauvage*. My own emphasis on practical reasoning about society as the basis for the systems of metaphors called totemism is actually anticipated very specifically in Radliffe-Brown (1952, p. 130) when he said that:

> For the primitive the universe as a whole is a moral or social order governed not by what we call natural law but rather by what we must call moral or ritual law ... In Australia, for example, there are innumerable ways in which the natives have built up between them-selves and the phenomena of nature a system of relations which are essentially similar to the relations that they have built up in their social structure between one human being and another.

In the last few pages of *The savage mind* Lévi-Strauss emphasizes the under-lying practical basis of primitive thought and its use of marriage relations for models (1966, p. 265). The difference that he sees between savage thought and ours does not lie in greater mystical or contemplative propensities on their side, but in our practice of disengaging our various metaphors from the matrix of social relations and dealing with them in fragments.

What I am proposing, then, is very much in the mainstream, with the only difference that this time it is not an idea but a method of research. My method is proposed as a remedy, a supplement, a way of establishing meanings by reference to use, a control on the imagination of the researcher. However, nothing much more can be said about proving or disproving the argument I am making unless ethnographic material is gathered with this theory in mind. Its merit is to answer a peculiarly Anglo-Saxon curiosity about the mechanisms of symbolic thinking. Lévi-Strauss's theory of totemism is sometimes presented as humanity brooding on itself and its place in nature. His emphasis on the contemplative interests is certainly there: 'This reciprocity of perspectives, in which man and the world mirror each other and which seems to us the only possible explanation of the properties and capacities of the savage mind' (Lévi-Strauss 1966, p. 222).

But the whole strategy of his argument was to relate the classifications of nature to the classifications of kinship and marriage. The mirror effect that we discern is the result of the process that I am writing about, a process whose study I suggest is an appropriate method for research on animal symbolism. It may be lack of imagination, but for some it is difficult to imagine humanity brooding on its identity and on its separation from animality or to accept the love of philosophic contemplation as the explanation of the consistency of so-called savage thought. In Genesis we have no special difficulty with the idea that God brooded over the waters because everything to do with divinity is mysterious, but how does humanity contemplate or consider? What mysterious mechanism sets up the initial categories?

According to the method I propose, we do not have to assume any such thing. Animals are brought into human social categories by a simple extension to them of the principles that serve for ordering human relationships. The method is to do the painstaking work of tracking how the categories are used.

References

Bulmer, R. 1986. *The unsolved problems of the birds of Leviticus.* Auckland: University of Auckland Working Papers in Anthropology.

Douglas, M. 1957. Animals in Lele religious symbolism. *Africa* **27**(1), 46–58.

Douglas, M. 1966. *Purity and danger: an analysis of concepts of pollution and taboo.* London: Routledge & Kegan Paul.

Douglas, M. 1970. *Natural symbols, explorations in cosmology.* London: Penguin.

Douglas, M. 1975a. Deciphering a meal. In M. Douglas, *Implicit meanings*, 249–75. London: Routledge & Kegan Paul.

Douglas, M. 1975b. Self-evidence. In M. Douglas, *Implicit meanings*, 276–318. London: Routledge & Kegan Paul.

Geertz, 1973. *The interpretation of cultures.* New York: Basic Books.

Goodman, N. 1972. *Problems and projects.* New York: Bobbs Merrill.

Goody, J. 1982. *Cooking, cuisine and class: a study in comparative sociology.* Cambridge: Cambridge University Press.

Horton, R. 1967. African traditional thought and Western science. *Africa* **37**(1 & 2), 50–7, 155–87.

Hull, D. 1978. Are species really individuals? *Systematic Zoology* **25**, 174–99.

Lévi-Strauss, C. 1962 (1964 trans. R. Needham) *Totemism.* London: Merlin Press.

Lévi-Strauss, C. 1966 [1962] *The savage mind.* London: Weidenfeld & Nicolson.

Radcliffe-Brown, A. R. 1952. The sociological theory of totemism [1929] In A. R. Radcliffe-Brown, *Structure and function in primitive society*, 117–32. London: Cohen & West.

Roberts, A. 1986. Social and historical contexts of Tabwa art. In *The rising of a new moon: a century of Tabwa art*, A. Roberts & E. Maurer (eds), 1–48. Seattle: University of Washington Press.

Ryle, G. 1949. *The concept of mind.* New York: Barnes & Noble.

Turner, V. W. 1962. *Chichamba, the white spirit.* Rhodes-Livingstone Paper 33. Manchester: Manchester University Press.

Turner, V. W. 1967. *The forest of symbols: Aspects of Ndembu ritual*, Ithaca, NY: Cornell University Press.

Turner, V. W. 1968. *The drums of affliction: a study of religious processes among the Ndembu of Zambia.* Oxford: Clarendon Press.

2 Cultural attitudes to birds and animals in folklore

JAWAHARLAL HANDOO

Human attitudes to birds, animals, and reptiles in different societies have been described by certain anthropologists in connection with other theoretical objectives. For example, the central concern of the exemplary studies of Leach and Lévi-Strauss devoted to animal classification has not been with the attitudes of human cultures to natural species. Rather, these works are by and large primarily concerned with the logic of cultural classifications, and to identify the relevant categories some attention had to be paid to the conventional attitudes associated with those categories, in both myth and reality. For instance, the main concern of Leach's (1964) study is animal categories and verbal abuse. Here Leach reveals the semantic relations between animal categories and their connections with kinship, edibility, taboo, and ritual.

According to Leach (1964, p. 37), animal categories in English culture (and he extends this scheme to the Kachins of Burma and believes that this kind of cultural categorization might be universal) seem to be identical with kinship categories and the categories of space, so much so that 'the way we employ words [about] animals allows us to make statements about the human relationships which belong to a [different] set'. Leach did not, however, examine these categories and the issues related with them in respect of the folklore and mythology of either the English or the Kachins.

Lévi-Strauss (1969, p. 1), on the other hand, shows 'how empirical categories – such as the categories of the raw and the cooked, the fresh and the decayed, the moist and the burned etc. ... can nonetheless be used as conceptual tools with which to elaborate abstract ideas and combine them in the form of propositions'. He therefore sets as his goal the discovery of these empirical categories and uses them as conceptual tools with which to explain the complex abstract ideas of human cultures. He uses myths for this kind of scientific exploration. In this manner he claims to show 'not how men think in myths, but how myths operate in men's minds without their being aware of the fact'. However, in the final analysis Lévi-Strauss is also concerned, just like Leach, with the mental structures that organize human societies. Both these scholars are interested in animal semantics not in relation to cultural attitudes, but as expressions of what they see as the working of the human mind.

In folklore proper a few lexicons and inventories of oral narratives and other major genres deal with animals, birds, insects, and reptiles, but these have been studied as 'motifs' or 'types', and the scope of these semantic units has never been related to the promising and potential area of cultural attitudes. For instance, besides treating animals or birds as motifs or sub-motifs within the general frame of the narrative lexicons such as the *Motif index of folk literature* (Thompson 1955–8), no attempt was made to find out animal patterns and their occurrence in folklore. Folklorists seem to have been content with the identification of animal motifs, and the indexing and archiving of them whenever possible. The only achievement of such collections has been to trace animal or bird motifs across cultures, more particularly Indo-European cultures.

In this chapter my main concern is to outline cultural attitudes as they are expressed in animal tales. These attitudes, as I try to show, are not the same as one finds in the real world. For it appears that the attitudes of human societies towards animals or birds in the real world are inverted in folklore. However, it is important to admit at the outset that there is no single general model that applies to attitudes to animals or birds in folklore. For instance, besides weak–strong, kind–unkind, just–unjust, and sacred–nonsacred, many other oppositions may have to be taken into consideration when describing this vast semantic field, such as animals of earth versus animals of water and sky, and the belief systems of cultures that feature such classifications.

The model I am proposing is as follows:

Animals in real world
Small/weak = unwise = defeat   Big/strong = wise = victory

Animals in folklore
Small/weak = wise = victory   Big/strong = unwise = defeat

In the real world the attitude to animals generally is that a big animal or bird or even a reptile is strong physically and is usually victorious in any kind of task or struggle. For example, a lion, elephant, or wolf is reckoned to be superior when compared with a fox, monkey, or jackal. However, in folklore, particularly narrative folklore, this attitude is inverted, and small, tiny, and physically weak animals or birds are shown as wiser than the big animals or birds and essentially victorious in their tasks and struggles against them. In this reversed model a lion is defeated by a fox, an elephant tricked by a hare, and a wolf completely destroyed by a clever monkey.

It is interesting to deviate from the animal world and delve into the world of fairy tales and the attitudes it represents in respect of the characters (kings, queens, princes, princesses, peasants, animals and supernatural creatures) that occur frequently in these tales. More often than not, we notice that the humble hero (without any acquired magical powers in the beginning) usually wins in the end. We also notice that the villainous characters or antagonists in these tales are depicted as strong or big beings but are usually unwise and even foolish, and hence prone to defeat or failure. However, whatever wisdom or strength they show during struggles or combats with the hero in the course of advancement of the structure of the tale is because of the special magical powers or agents they wield. The moment they lose or are deprived of these powers they fall dead or are beaten by the humble hero in struggles, despite their size and superior strength. The hero in the fairy tales, just like the small (weak) character in folktales about animals, is usually shown as physically weak and powerless, but wiser than his antagonist. It is due to this last attribute, which occurs as a constant element in fairy tales, that the hero overpowers his antagonist and gains victory over him. The logic of the power struggle in fairy tales can thus be reduced to two main formulas that show clearly the attitudes the cultures have towards fairy tale characters and also supports our argument about the attitudes to animals in folklore, more particularly popular animal tales. These two formulas are:

(a)   The protagonist increases his powers with the help of a donor (cf. Propp 1968) or by other means to equal his antagonist.
(b)   The protagonist simply decreases the extra powers of the antagonist with the help of a donor or by other means, making the antagonist equal to himself.

The logic of the fairy tale, as far as this particular model is concerned, does not therefore seem to be different in essence from the logic of the animal tales. It follows that this logic is sustained by a particular cultural attitude that may be universal. Let us now look at a few examples of animal tales, all taken from the collection of Bødker (1957):

(a)   Hare, claiming to be the ambassador of the Moon, shows the King of Elephants the Moon agitated in a lake. Elephant is persuaded that the Moon is angry and withdraws with his subjects. (546, p. 62).
(b)   Monkey, caught by Crocodile who wants to use Monkey's heart as a remedy for his sick wife, makes his captor believe that he has left his heart at home. Crocodile returns to the shore where Monkey escapes. (678, p. 71)
(c)   A swimming contest across a river between Lion and Tortoise is won by Tortoise, who places a relation to help on the opposite bank. (381, p. 47)
(d)   Hare promises to take Tiger to a much bigger animal. Making a noise in the dark as if eating something very nice, he says he is eating his own eyes, and thereby tricks Tiger into clawing out his own eyes and eating them. (200, p. 30)
(e)   Fox persuades Wolf to fish with his tail through a hole in the ice. In the morning the tail is frozen on to the ice, and is broken in Wolf's endeavours to get free. (187, p. 29)
(f)   A bird whose young ones are eaten by a snake steals a necklace and drops it into the Snake's nest. Pursuers find the snake and kill him. (24, p. 13)

(g) A pigeon living in a kitchen is joined by a crow, who one day, refusing to fly in search of food, stays at home and steals food in the kitchen. Found out, he is tortured to death. (460, p. 54)

(h) A crane places himself near a pond and looks vacantly at the fish, waiting until they are off their guard. The wise fish finds out his trick, and drives the crane away. (405, p. 49)

One of the important results of examining these examples is that the cultural attitudes to animals and birds in folklore do not seem to be guided by a fixed stereotype-scheme as regards the concepts of small (weak) and big (strong). These concepts, by and large, are dependent on a given relation in a given situation. For example, a monkey is weak but wise in relation to a crocodile in a given situation. The same animal may become big, strong and unwise in relation to a rat or a goat in a different situation. This is also true in the case of fairy tales. For example, the seventh or the youngest brother's killing of the dragon and winning the battle, the hand of the princess and the throne should be viewed in relation to the acts of elder brothers in such tales. In those tales where only a son or a brother–sister pair occur as main characters, the question of the younger brother being finally victorious does not arise. Surprisingly enough the pattern younger (weak, small) and wise and victorious seems to hold not only with heroes or protagonists but also donors and even antagonists (Handoo 1978). However, this superiority of the young even in the realm of antagonists is also based on relations and situations rather than on fixed concepts.

Of equal importance are the means employed in folktales by which the weak win the struggles or complete the tasks assigned to them. In many genres of folklore, such as fairy tales, where humans play very dominant roles, donors' actions are crucial in making means or magical agents available to the protagonist that help him overcome the obstacles and return victorious. This donation or help invariably transforms the small and weak protagonist into a strong, powerful and victorious hero. However, in the case of animal tales, as a special genre, one notices that the role of donor does not seem to be so important. There are some animal tales in which helping donors appear who extend help to animal heroes or bird heroines in completing their respective tasks. But such examples are rare; moreover, the functions of donors in such examples occur so sporadically that they do not have the same morphological status as in fairy tales. This means that protagonists in animal tales – by contrast with those in fairy tales – are characterized by self-help, self-confidence, and independence. The above examples, by and large, show these important characteristics.

Another interesting characteristic of the animal tale that reflects the attitudes cultures have to animals or birds and their behaviour is that this genre does not seem to be surrounded by the kind of strange or fantastic atmosphere generally noticed in fairy tales. Apart from the fact that animals are shown behaving like humans in many ways (talking, for instance), there seems to be nothing significantly unfamiliar. The animals and birds in these tales eat, drink, walk, run, fly, fight, snatch (steal?) food as one finds them doing in real life. However, what is interesting is that these animals and birds are arranged in categories and hierarchies that only human groups have in the real world. So in these tales animals have families, kinship structures, kings, wars and every other category human cultures have devised. If this kind of 'unfamiliar' has anything to do with human attitudes to animals, then this seems to be an important element of symbolism in animal tales.

An animal tale is a symbolic act (Zipes 1983, pp. 6–8) in which motifs, characters, themes, functions, and configurations are arranged in such a manner that they address the concerns of the cultures that create them. In India, animal tales, particularly the famous *Panchantantra* tales, are said to have been collected and used for educating children and young princes. Strangely enough, this symbolic function of animal tales and the cultural attitudes that they uphold seem not to have changed. In fact, even in the modern world this symbolism seems very popular with children everywhere and has been extended to suit new situations. For example, the heroes of popular culture, such as Donald Duck and Spiderman, seem to be extensions of traditional symbolism and conform to the model of the animal tale in which this symbolism finds expression. This clearly shows that in this symbolic act, through the medium of inversion, through the combination of the familiar and the slightly unfamiliar, children and adults are taught to recognize certain basic truths of life and existence. And in this way perhaps the impossible was made possible, at least temporarily.

Bruno Bettelheim (1976) has mentioned that the fairy tale estranges the child from the real world and allows him or her to deal with deep-rooted psychological problems and anxiety-provoking incidents to achieve autonomy. However, in the animal tale the search for autonomy does not seem to be so important. The symbolic inversion of the real world through the actions and behaviour of animals and birds seems to be the basic attitude of human societies to animal tales. That this inversion is based on psychological and sociological compulsions is something that deserves the attention of scholars.

References

Aarne, A. & Thompson, S. 1961. The types of the folktale. Helsinki: Folklore Fellows Communications 184.
Bettelheim, B. 1976. *The uses of enchantment: the meaning and importance of fairy tales.* New York: Knopf.
Bødker, L. 1957. Indian animal tales: a preliminary survey. Helsinki: Folklore Fellows Communications 170.
Handoo, J. 1978. *Current trends in folklore.* Mysore: University of Mysore Press.
Handoo, J. 1979. The world of Tayyam: myth and the message. *Journal of Indian Folkloristics* **2**(34), 65–88.
Handoo, J. 1984. Meaning in folklore: theory and practice. Bergen: Department of Folklore and Ethnology, University of Bergen, ISFNR Congress Papers 3.

42   CULTURAL ATTITUDES TO BIRDS AND ANIMALS

Leach, E. R. 1964. Anthropological aspects of language: animal categories and verbal abuse. In *New directions in the study of language*, E. H. Lenneberg (ed.), 23–63. Cambridge, Mass.: MIT Press
Lévi-Strauss, C. 1962. *The savage mind*. London: Weidenfeld & Nicolson.
Lévi-Strauss, C. 1969. *The raw and the cooked*. New York: Harper Colophone Press.
Propp, V. 1968. *Morphology of the folktale*. Austin: University of Texas Press.
Schwartz, E. K. 1956. A psychoanalytic study of the fairy tale. *American Journal of Psychotherapy* **10**, 740–62.
Thompson, S. 1955–58. *Motif-index of folk literature*. 6 vols. Bloomington: Indiana University Press.
Zipes, J. 1983. *Fairy tales and the art of subversion*. New York: Wildman.

3 Animal language in the Garden of Eden: folktale elements in Genesis

G. KOOLEMANS BEYNEN

The story of mankind's temptation, seduction, and Fall in the Garden of Eden is puzzling: Yahweh creates a paradise for His children and then adds something that can be best characterized as a time bomb: the Tree of Knowledge of Good and Evil. Along with the Tree we find, for good measure, an animal 'more cunning than the other animals' (Genesis 3, 1), which will make sure the bomb goes off. The inevitable explosion leaves mankind homeless and mortal; yet at least two major contemporary religions count this story among their basic myths.

All this seems to defy reason, and Westermann (1984, p. 239), whose series of books form the standard work on Genesis, says as much: 'The temptation ... stands as something absolutely inexplicable; it appears suddenly amid the good that Yahweh has created. It will remain there as a riddle.'

In my analysis of the dangerous reward in the so-called Animal Language tales, at 670 in the Aarne-Thompson classification (Thompson 1961, p. 233, 1974, pp. 303–4), I suggested (Beynen 1982, p. 174) that the solution proposed there had significance for an analysis of the dangerous proposed there had significance for an analysis of the dangerous gift in the Genesis narrative: the Tree of Knowledge of Good and Evil. This chapter takes up this suggestion and, concentrating on the narrative in Genesis 2 and 3, first uses the explanation for the dangerous reward to elucidate the dangerous nature of the Tree in the Garden of Eden; and, second, discusses the unassertive behaviour of Adam, who on the whole does what Eve and the serpent tell him to do.

Few interpret the story of mankind's Fall as a test, no matter how obvious such an interpretation may seem. Aalders (1981, p. 93) sees before mankind a 'clear-cut choice' between submission to Yahweh and independence resulting in death. One can object that such an important test so soon after the Creation was not fair, that mankind was too inexperienced for it, and that Yahweh should have known so. Aalders counters these objections by noting that mankind had earlier been ordered to work and guard the Garden (1981, p. 92; Genesis 2, 9), which he sees as an indication that mankind had the experience necessary to survive the temptation. This, however, is merely moving the problem to an earlier point in the narrative: one cannot justify unrealistic demands by pointing out that they had already been made previously. Also, even if Adam and Eve had carried out the command to 'work and guard' satisfactorily, it would still have been much more difficult to face the serpent's temptations than to 'work and guard', so that Adam and Eve's success in an earlier test does not make their exposure to the serpent and its arguments a fair test.

Jewish scholars, too, consider that the test was fair since Adam and Eve, like all the Ancients, 'were so great that their actions were measured by standards far above our own' (Bereishis/Genesis 1977, p. 13), which amounts to saying that Yahweh did mankind's first couple an honour by exposing them to a strong temptation. But nowhere in Genesis is it stated that Adam and Eve were so 'great', or how 'great' they were, whereas the serpent is characterized as 'the most cunning of the animals', so that we are still left with the possibility that Adam and Eve faced a superior adversary and that Yahweh's expectations, if any, that they would not yield to the serpent's arguments, were unfounded. It could be argued that Yahweh would certainly create man as even more cunning than any animal He had created, but the Genesis narrative does not support this argument. Blaming the serpent or Satan for the Fall was at one time an accepted theory, but has no adherents nowadays (Westerman 1984, p. 236).

Discussing the fairness of the test or of the punishment leads sooner or later to a discussion of whether or not Yahweh shares in the responsibility for mankind's Fall. Most writers find such a discussion rather fruitless; instead, they interpret the Genesis narrative as a depiction of life as it is and do not search for the reason why. Westermann (1974, p. 236) calls it 'a story of crime and punishment, for which a motivation is not required'. Sarna (1970, p. 24) concludes that the point of the narrative is (a) that evil exists, though as a human product not inherent in the Creation; and (b) that we should be thinking about what we can do about evil, rather than worrying about how it originated. The importance of the Genesis narrative, he continues, is in its difference from earlier creation accounts, which portrayed evil as a category associated with the gods and hence outside the sphere of human influence. In Genesis, however, evil is brought into the world by human actions, which implies that mankind can eliminate it as well. The Pandora legend in Greek mythology, Friedman (1987) points out, has the same implications.

Yet the suspicion remains that if mankind had been created stronger, it would have resisted the temptation (Bereishis/Genesis 1977, p. 100), and the rejoinder that the Knowledge of Good and Evil is a quality that cannot be created but that has to be acquired in a process of trial and error (Bereishis/Genesis 1977, p. 101), does not put our suspicions to rest since there is no *a priori* reason why Yahweh could not create such a quality, all the more since he did so rather successfully in creating the serpent. Our experience, however, teaches us that such a quality has indeed to be learned through mistakes, which leads us back to the point of view quoted above: the Genesis narrative depicts 'the world as human beings know it' (Fox 1983, p. 15), no matter whether this is fair or not or how this originated.

Interpreting Genesis as an analysis of human life comes close to Lévi-Strauss's thesis (1958, p. 237) that myths analyse life by explaining apparent contradictions. There are three analyses of Genesis inspired by his work, all of which concentrate on the overall structure of Genesis, though, and devote little attention to the puzzling nature of the Tree.

Leach discusses the structure of the first several chapters of Genesis and interprets the Fall as a becoming aware of sexual differences (1969, p. 15). Such a sexual interpretation, as Fox notices (1983, p. 15), is rejected as unwarranted by most scholars, as the problems treated in Genesis clearly go beyond sexual differences. Lévi-Strauss, too (1969, p. 50), has shown that oppositions such as the one of production versus management – which in Genesis and the AT 670 tales are associated with the female versus male opposition – are found in other societies in association with oppositions between, for example, moieties. We take this observation to mean that the management–production opposition, which we will identify later in this chapter as basic in the narrative's course of action, is apparently not necessarily connected with the male–female opposition, which is also how we interpret Fox's statement (1983, p. 15).

Freilich, too, analyses Genesis on the basis of Lévi-Strauss's writings, and his conclusion that Eve represents creativity while the serpent stands for the doubt that must accompany creativity (1975, p. 215) comes close to our analysis of the relation between Adam, Eve, and the serpent.

Genesis as a folktale

The narrative of mankind's Fall in Genesis 2–3 begins like a folktale: a parental figure, Yahweh, pronounces an interdiction and leaves. Then the interdiction is violated, which, as Propp (1968, pp. 26–7) pointed out, is the typical beginning of the folktale. The folktale flavour of the narrative, and especially of its beginning, has been noticed by several scholars (Gunkel 1922, pp. 15–18, Gaster 1975, pp. 29–48) but none produced an actual folktale from which the Genesis narrative could have been derived.

The continuation of the Genesis narrative lacks features typical of a folktale. First, there is no hero; Adam, the logical candidate, turns out to be an antihero. Second, there is no happy ending. Third, and most important, is the fact that the interdiction in Genesis is specific. Such interdictions are typical of the middle of a tale. For example, at the beginning of a tale we find a general command not to open the door, for example, in the tale of the Wolf and the Kids, AT 123 (Thompson 1961, p. 50), whereas in the middle we find – for example, in the Bluebeard tales, AT 312 (Thompson 1961, p. 103) – a command not to open one specific door, while all others may be opened. In Genesis we find an interdiction of the latter type: you may eat from any tree except one (Genesis 2, 16–17). This could mean that an inversion has taken place: the interdiction we find at the beginning of the Genesis narrative may originally have come from the middle of the story.

The original of the Genesis narrative would contain two elements: (a) an interrelation between a man, a woman, a serpent, and, possibly, a supernatural being; and (b) a gift connected with an interdiction, possibly in the middle of the tale rather than at the outset. We propose, hence, that the Genesis narrative was an inversion of an existing one, whereas Gaster (1975, vol. 1, p. 33), for example, considers it 'a conflation of ... originally alternative versions'.

The Animal Language tales

In an analysis of such a tale (AT 670), though without a supernatural being and with a dangerous reward instead of a gift,[1] I compared it with the AT 155 tales (Beynen 1982, p. 167). Both types have the same beginning: a shepherd saves a serpent from a fire in spite of his fear that it may bite and kill him.

In the AT 155 tales the shepherd's fears turn out to be justified: the serpent intends to kill him. The shepherd protests that he does not deserve such a fate, but the serpent answers that life is not just, and that one good turn does not deserve another. The shepherd proposes to ask opinions of others. However, they are domestic animals who expect to be slaughtered when they stop being of use to their masters. They therefore wholeheartedly agree with the serpent: life is not just and the shepherd has no right to expect thankfulness.

Finally the shepherd asks the fox. The fox pretends not to understand and asks that the original situation be restored so that it can better visualize what has happened. Its request is granted and the serpent is put back into the fire. The shepherd then leaves it there on the advice of the fox and the serpent perishes. The thankful shepherd promises the fox a bag of chickens, but when the fox opens the bag he finds that the shepherd has changed his mind and filled it with fierce dogs instead. The fox barely escapes and realizes belatedly that the serpent was right: life is not just.

In the AT 670 tales, on the other hand, the shepherd's fears turn out not to be justified. The serpent rewards him and he eventually lives happily ever after. The AT 670 tales affirm that life is just, that one good turn does deserve another, and that life is hence predictable and manageable. The AT 155 tales, however, state that life is without justice; it is unpredictable and chaotic (see Fig. 3.1).

A shepherd rescues a serpent and receives...

1) a reward (The AT 670 tales.
   Meaning: Life is just, predictable, and manageable.)

2) a punishment (The AT 155 tales.
   Meaning: Life is neither just, predictable, nor manageable.)

Figure 3.1 The meaning of the AT 670 and AT 155 tales.

The dangerous reward

The meaning of the AT 670 tales is more complicated, mostly because the shepherd's reward – the ability to understand Animal Language – is dangerous: it will make him rich but it is also potentially fatal since revealing his reward to anyone will cause him to die.

This dangerous reward is of interest because of its similarity to the Tree of Knowledge of Good and Evil. Both the reward and the Tree raise similar questions, respectively: 'Why would the serpent give a dangerous reward to its rescuer?' and: 'Why would Yahweh give His children a dangerous gift?'

The dangerous nature of the reward in the AT 670 tales becomes understandable when we examine the event that led to the reward being granted. Beynen (1982, p. 170) analysed the relation between man, woman, and the serpent in the AT 670 tales as a triangular relationship in which man preserves life while woman and the serpent change life, the former by creating it and the latter by destroying it (see Fig. 3.2).[2]

Man, in other words, is more or less like a manager or steward, and his role is aptly symbolized in his profession: a shepherd. A shepherd produces neither offspring, milk, nor wool but his primary responsibility is to keep the participants in the production process alive and to keep the process itself functioning.[3]

When the shepherd rescues the serpent, a contradiction results: in preserving life he has also preserved death, since the serpent symbolizes death. The reason for the danger inherent in the reward is then that the event which gave rise to the reward is also dangerous.[4]

Hence we find in the AT 670 tales tales a causal relation: a dangerous action results in an equally dangerous reward. This reward is in its inherent danger similar to the Tree of Knowledge of Good and Evil.

But there is a difference: in the AT 670 tales the dangerous reward *follows*

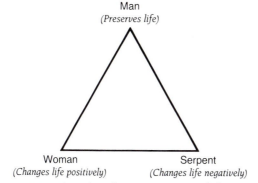

Figure 3.2   The roles of man, woman, and the serpent.

Figure 3.3   The functions of the dangerous events in the AT 670 tales and the
Genesis creation story.

the dangerous rescue in a causal relation; in the Genesis story the dangerous
gift *precedes* the Fall (see Fig. 3.3).

Life and death are intermixed in the Fall as they are in the rescue: Adam
and Eve do not die 'the same day' (Genesis 2, 17) but merely become mortal.
But they become fertile as well, since they do not have offspring until after
the Fall. Hence in their Fall, as in the rescue, life and death find themselves
inextricably intertwined and will henceforth coexist forever in mankind,
which will die as individuals but will live on as a race (Ahlström 1986).

Though both the Fall and the rescue are similar in their mixture of life and
death, they are also each other's opposites: a man saving a serpent is the
opposite of a serpent making a couple mortal. Hence the Genesis creation
story is the opposite of the AT 670 tales. In the Genesis narrative the gift or
reward precedes the opposite of what causes the gift in the AT 670 tales.[5]

Their meanings are also opposite: the AT 670 tales state that there is a
system in life, and that events have consequences that are similar to their
antecedents. The Genesis story states that there is no system in life by
showing that events precede the opposite of what normally would be their
own causes. The dangerous gift or reward occurs *with* a reason in the
AT 670 tales but *without* one in the Genesis creation story.

In the AT 670 tales man is shown as having control over his fate: he
controls the future since his actions will have results which are similar to
these actions. This is the same conception of life upon which a salvation by
works is based: mankind is saved – or condemned – as a result of its previous
actions. The Genesis narrative, on the other hand, shares its assumptions
with a salvation by mercy: mankind cannot influence the future, including
its eventual salvation; salvation is the outcome of Yahweh's mercy and not
the result of mankind's actions.

'Passive' Adam

The AT 670 tales (a) present life as rational and manageable, and (b) provide
an analysis of the roles of man, the serpent, and the woman. The Genesis
narrative reverses the course of action of the AT 670 tales but retains the
triangular role analysis. But presenting life as unpredictable undermines the
role of the man, since a managerial role presupposes that life is predictable
and manageable. The Genesis narrative contains therefore a new element:

the position of the manager is open. Hence the transformation of the AT 670 tales into the Genesis narrative entails man's inability to manage life: the triangular role model creates a slot, the inversion ensures that man cannot fill it.

Our interpretation explains Adam's strangely passive role: the serpent and Eve determine the course of action in Genesis 2–3 while Adam offers excuses and blames Eve (Genesis 3, 10–12). The Genesis story's conception of life makes Adam's role less important than those of the serpent and Eve, who are important enough to be singled out for a special enmity between their offspring; Adam is left out completely, although Eve's offspring would be his too (Genesis 3, 15).

The AT 670 tales offer on the one hand a model of roles in which the woman adds to life, the serpent destroys it, while the man tries to control and manage the overall process. On the other hand, however, the roles of the three participants are not so clear, but merge. First, when the serpent gives the man his reward, it thereby helps the man to preserve life, as is especially clear in variants quoted by Aarne (1914, p. 4) and Frazer (1931, pp. 121–2) where the reward is used to cure the sick. Second, the woman is not only the producer of life, she is also a potential bringer of death, because the man almost dies by telling the secret of the reward to his wife.[6] Third, man has to defend his managerial position in the AT 670 tales against his wife – who tries to tell him what to do, that is, tell her his secret – and in Genesis against the serpent, who tells Eve and Adam what to do.

In the AT 670 tales woman's potentially fatal nagging is stopped at the last moment when the man disciplines her. In Genesis 3, however, the assault on Adam's managerial position is successful. First the serpent usurps Adam's role when it tells Eve what to do, and then Eve exchanges roles with Adam by telling him what to do. In the AT 670 tales the man asserts his managerial position at the last moment and so separates life and death, which had become confused during the rescue at the beginning of the tale; in the Genesis 2–3 narrative Adam does not defend his managerial function, which results in a merger of life with death.

In the AT 670 tales tales man is typically represented as a shepherd, which brings to one's mind the biblical image of the Good Shepherd. There is a difference, though: in the AT 670 tales the shepherd is an average person who is poor at first but becomes rich later. In the Bible, on the other hand, the expression 'Good Shepherd' is applied to Yahweh or the Messiah only (e.g. Genesis 49, 24, Psalms 23, 1, Isaiah 40, 11, Ezekiel 34, John 10, 11, 14, 15), although Moses, Jeremiah, Daniel or Solomon, for example, could certainly be considered 'good shepherds' of the Israelites. The exclusive usage of the biblical expression 'Good Shepherd' is yet another indication that in the ideology of Genesis only Yahweh is the ruler, manager, or Good Shepherd.

The above analysis provides an explanation for Adam's unheroic behaviour: Yahweh is the real hero of the Genesis narrative. This does not explain, however, why Eve and even the serpent have a more active part than Adam.

Skaftymov (1924, pp. 127–8) discussed a similar problem: the overly negative portrayal of the Russian prince Vladimir in the Russian epic songs, the so-called *byliny*. Early Soviet folklorists saw in Vladimir's sorry picture an expression of the democratic and antimonarchistic nature of Russian folk art. Skaftymov disagreed and points out that artistic efficiency dictated a maximal difference between the hero and whoever else the audience could mistake for a hero. A princess, an opponent, or the hero's servant could not possibly be mistaken for the hero, hence they could be portrayed as intelligent or cunning. But a king like Vladimir could be taken for a hero, hence a strong signal has to be sent to the audience that he is not. His silly and loquacious behaviour is such a signal.

An audience listening to the Genesis story could take Adam for the hero and expect him to eventually outwit the serpent or even – God forbid! – Yahweh, for instance through the common fairy tale transformation of the fool into the handsome and clever prince. Whoever wrote Genesis wanted to avoid such misunderstandings and saw to it that it was clear that Adam was not the hero. A 20th-century audience may get the impression that this goal was not only reached but also surpassed and that Adam receives unnecessarily negative treatment, but this is because the Genesis story was originally told. What was merely efficient when telling the story may seem exaggerated to us, who read it.

Ideology in Genesis

In spite of its folktale flavour, the story of mankind's Fall cannot be traced to a tale that has served as its prototype. The AT 670 tales could have served as such, but the Genesis narrative is shown to be the opposite of its supposed model: the order of the tale has been inverted and one of its elements – the rescue – has been changed into its opposite: the Fall. The result of this inversion – the Genesis narrative – is so 'inexplicable' (Westermann 1984, p. 239), that one must rule out the possibility that it was originally a folktale. Instead, we propose that the inversion was a deliberate act that was part of an ideological controversy.

The Old Testament contains many traces of such controversies; for example, the various ways of referring to the divinity has resulted in identifying scribes as the 'Yahwist', the 'Elohist', or the 'Priestly author-editor' (Ellis 1968, p. 6, Gaster 1975, vol. 1, p. 8, Van Seters 1987, pp. 10, 116). The controversy behind the usage of these names is unknown but must have been crucial at one time, since the proper way of addressing the divinity is of the utmost importance in all religions.

More is known about the struggle between the Israelite religion and various other less well known Canaanite religions. At the arrival of the Israelites in Canaan these latter religions began to influence the Israelite religion. At first this was accepted; later, however, traditionalist or conservative movements began to try to eliminate Canaanite practices (Ahlström 1963, pp. 9, 10, 17, 22). Westermann (1984, p. 237) also refers to this struggle when he interprets Genesis 3, 15 as a condemnation of 'an oriental-heathen pattern of thought that claims to have a higher knowledge of life'.

The Canaanite religions shared with most religions of the Middle East practices such as temple prostitution and orgies, which the Old Testament condemned as morally repugnant, although they were actually efforts to increase agricultural fertility. They were based on homeopathic magic: acts connected with fertility would result in more fertility.

Temple prostitution and orgies have the same assumption as the AT 670 tales: life is predictable and hence manageable because actions and their results share some similarities; for example, a dangerous action has a danger-ous result, an orgy results in a good harvest. One can see the objection from the side of the Israelite religion: both the Canaanite religions and the AT 670 tales portray man as a reasonably successful manager who has little need for a god or gods.

In short, orgies and temple prostitution imply, like the AT 670 tales, that man is a competent manager and can take care of at least some of his problems – in this case the fertility of the soil – without having to rely on Yahweh. The adherents of the Israelite religion selected a tale that in its original form – like the Canaanite religions – assumed that mankind could solve its own problems. They then rewrote it to prove their point: mankind cannot solve its problems. The rewriting of the tale is part of an ideological attack by the Israelite religion on other ideological systems.

Ahlström (1963, p. 33) describes such an attack where a Canaanite term is used 'in a meaning precise[ly] opposite of that normal ... in the Syro-Palestinian area'. In this chapter we submit a tale that has been changed to express a meaning opposite to the meaning of the original tale. This latter change, like the one described by Ahlström, was ideologically motivated.

As a result, the Genesis narrative contains a polemic against a portrayal of man as a winner, if a vicarious one, in the battle of life. Instead, it asserts that man is an incompetent manager: he can manage neither the serpent nor Eve. His salvation will depend not on his works, but on Yahweh's mercy only.

Towards a typology of man–woman–serpent tales

In AT 670 tales male and female are accepted as separate categories, but with the assumption that the female category will turn destructive if not con-trolled by the male category. The Genesis narrative asserts that the male category cannot control the female category, only the Good Shepherd, Yahweh, can do so. Both the Genesis narrative and Mundkur (1988) see the problem of the man–woman relation as a religious problem. Shanklin (Ch. 15, this volume) analyses a different solution to the man–woman–serpent relation: she presents a case where man and the serpent form one category, while the woman belongs to a second one.

In both the AT 670 tales and in the Genesis creation story we see a similar distribution of roles: woman produces, the serpent kills, and the man is the manager and preserver of life. The AT 670 tales present life as predictable, manageable, and logical through the logical order of cause and result and the similarity of these events. In such a conception of life the role of man, as the manager, is prominent. In the Genesis narrative, life is presented as unpredictable and unmanageable, and this is accompanied by a decrease in the importance of Adam as the manager. Instead, Eve, the serpent, and, above all, Yahweh are the important figures in Genesis. One of man's managerial tasks is to keep life and death separated. In the AT 670 tales he is successful, though at the last moment. In the Genesis narrative man fails as a manager, and life and death merge forever.[7]

The Genesis narrative is a fairy tale gone wrong. It begins like a fairy tale, but then the harsh reality of life intrudes. And that is, after all, 'the world as [we] know it' (Fox 1983, p. 15): we begin life in the arms of parents who love us more than anyone, but after a longer or shorter period of paradisiacal bliss we have to face grim reality and 'work hard and sweat to make the soil produce anything' and then we 'go back to the soil from which [we] were formed' (Genesis 3, 19), and neither the most loving parent nor the Good Shepherd will rescue us from that fate.

Acknowledgements

The author wishes to express his appreciation to the Reverend Weldon Schloneger of the Bethel Mennonite Church, West Liberty, Ohio; the Reverend Don Nofziger of the Neil Avenue Mennonite Church, Columbus, Ohio; and the participants in the Menno Lunches at Ohio State University for their help in writing this chapter. The author assumes, of course, full responsibility for the views expressed.

Notes

1 In our analysis we make no distinction between a gift and a reward. Both are voluntary expressions of good will and as such are opposed to obligatory actions, for example, the payment of a price or the transfer of an inheritance. Whether or not there was a cause for the good will is unimportant for our analysis.

2 One of the AT 155 tales clearly shows that the nature of the serpent is to kill. In it the serpent is replaced by a scorpion, who asks a frog to carry it across the Nile. The frog objects that the scorpion will sting and kill it, whereupon the scorpion answers that that would be extremely unwise as it would drown if the frog died. The frog is convinced, takes the scorpion on its back, and when they are midway on their swim across the Nile the scorpion stings the frog. While the dying frog sinks, it still manages to ask the scorpion why it stung after it had been explained how unwise stinging would be. 'What do you expect?' the scorpion answers, 'This is the Middle East!'.

3 This is well brought out in a tale recorded by Cepenkov (1891, pp. 186–7), where a shepherd returns to his flock after having received his reward. He hears his animals say that it is a good thing he came back, because they would surely have perished without him.

4   The presence of the serpent in the fire has placed before the shepherd a difficult problem: how life and death are interrelated. The shepherd solves this problem in the AT 670 tales at the last moment by disciplining his wife (see note 7), but one can easily see how the serpent would have been blamed if the shepherd had not solved it. In the Genesis story Adam is confronted with a problem he does not solve, and, indeed, some scholars blame the serpent (Westermann 1984, p. 236).

5   It is quite possible that the chain of events in the AT 670 tales, that is, a rescue followed by a reward, is still present in the Genesis narrative, although in a disguised form. In the Genesis narrative a gift precedes a Fall; or a gift non-follows a nonrescue; or – when the two negatives cancel each other out – a gift or reward follows a rescue, which is the chain of events in the AT 670 tales (see Fig. 3.3). All that is important for the purpose of this chapter is that in the Genesis narrative elements occur in an irrational ordering while these same elements occur in the AT 670 tales in a rational one. The above narrative mathematics may seem far-fetched; however, a similar calculation occurs in a tale recorded by Beynen (1982, p. 171). While in most tales the man is a shepherd, he is a woodcutter in at least one other tale. A woodcutter, we propose, is someone who nonpreserves nonlife, hence he is someone who preserves life, when again the two negatives cancel each other. For contemporary Americans plants may be living items, but we assume that such a point of view is only a recent phenom-enon and that for the majority of the storytellers plants were not alive.

6   At one point in the AT 670 tales the wife finds out that her husband has some secret. When she asks him about it, he sooner or later answers her that he will die if he reveals the secret to her. She doesn't believe him and begins or continues to nag him. After some time the man decides it is better to die than continue to be nagged and prepares to tell and die, but before doing so he makes some prepar-ation for his death, for example, he organizes a funeral dinner or lies down in a coffin. While doing so he hears one of his domestic animals reproach the rooster for being unaffected by the master's impending death. The rooster then expresses his disrespect for someone who cannot even keep one wife under control, while roosters routinely rule over a much larger number. The husband then interrupts his funeral preparations, disciplines his wife by beating or scolding her, and all live happily ever after.

7   The Genesis narrative is not unique; Gaster (1975, pp. 31–2) gives instances of similar stories among the Efe and the Djaga. Further study will indicate whether these stories invalidate or corroborate our analysis.

References

Aalders, G. C. 1981. *The Bible student's commentary*: Vol. I, *Genesis*. Tr. by William Henen. Grand Rapids, Michigan: Zondervan.

Aarne, A. 1914. Der Tiersprachkundige Mann und seine neugierige Frau. *Folklore Fellows Communications* **2**(15) Hamina: Finnish Academy of Sciences.

Ahlström, G. W. 1963. *Aspects of syncretism in Israelite religion*. Horae Soederblom-inianae (Travaux publiés par la Société Nathan Soederblom) Vol. V. Lund: Gleerup.

Ahlström, G. W. 1986. Personal communication at the Joint Meeting of the Midwest Region of the Society of Biblical Literature, the Middle West Branch of the American Oriental Society, and the American Schools of Oriental Research, Midwest, Andrews University, Berrien Springs, Michigan, 11 February 1986.

Bereishis/Genesis 1977. *A new translation with a commentary anthologized from Talmudic, Midrastic, and Rabbinic sources.* New York: Mesorah.

Beynen, G. K. 1982. The Bulgarian Animal Language Tales. In *Bulgaria past and present*: Proceedings of the Second International Conference on Bulgarian Studies held at Druzhba, Varna, June 13–17 1978, D. Kosev (ed.), pp. 167–74. Sofia: Bulgarian Academy of Sciences.

Cepenkov, M. K. 1891. Durvarot sto razbirase jazicite na zivotinkite. *Shornik za narodni umotvorenija, nauka, i kniznina* 4(2), 186–7.

Ellis, P. F. 1968. *The Yahwist: the Bible's first theologian.* Notre Dame: Fides.

Fox, E. 1983. *In the beginning: a new English rendition of the Book of Genesis.* New York: Schocken.

Frazer, J. G. 1931. The Language of animals. In J. G. Frazer, *Garnered sheaves: essays, addresses, and reviews*, 93–127. London: Macmillan.

Freilich, M. 1975. Myth, method, and madness. *Current Anthropology* **16**, 207–26.

Friedman, V. 1987. Personal communication at the Fourth Bulgaro-American Conference in Smoljan, 24 June 1987.

Gaster, T. H. 1975. *Myth, legend and custom in the Old Testament: a comparative study with chapters from Sir James G. Frazer's Folklore in the Old Testament*, 2 vols. New York: Harper & Row.

Genesis. Genesis, in *Good News Bible: the Bible in today's English version*, 1–55. New York: Thomas Nelson.

Gunkel, H. 1922. *Genesis.* 5th edn, Göttingen:Vandenhoeck & Ruprecht.

Leach, E. R. 1961. Lévi-Strauss in the Garden of Eden; an examination of some recent developments in the analysis of Myth. In *Claude Lévi-Strauss: the anthropologist as hero*, E. Nelson & T. Hayes (eds.), 47–60. Cambridge, Mass.: MIT Press.

Leach, E. R. 1969. Genesis as Myth. In E. Leach, *Genesis as myth and other essays*, Jonathan Cape.

Lévi-Strauss, C. 1958. La structure des mythes. In C. Lévi-Strauss, *Anthropologie structurale*. Paris: Plon.

Lévi-Strauss, C. 1969. *The raw and the cooked.* New York: Harper & Row.

Mundkur, B. 1988. Human animality, the mental imagery of fear, and religiosity. In *What is an animal?* T. Ingold (ed.). 141–84. London: Unwin Hyman.

Propp, V. 1968. *The morphology of the folktale.* Austin: University of Texas Press.

Sarna, N. M. 1970. *Understanding Genesis.* New York: Schocken.

Shanklin, E. 1990. The track of the python: a West African origin story. In *Signifying animals: human meaning in the natural world*, R. Willis (ed.), Ch. 15. London: Unwin Hyman.

Skaftymov, A. P. 1924. *Poetika i genezis bylin* [The Poetics and origin of the *Byliny*] Moscow Saratov: Jaksanov.

Thompson, S. 1974. *One hundred favorite folktales.* Bloomington, Indiana: Indiana University Press.

Thompson, S. 1961. *The types of the folktales.* Folklore Fellows Communications 184. Hamina: Finnish Academy of Sciences.

Van Seters, J. 1987. Moses. In Vol. 10 of *The Encyclopaedia of Religion*. Mircea Eliade (ed.) pp. 115–21. New York: Macmillan.

Westermann, C. 1984. *Genesis 1–11: a commentary.* Minneapolis: Augsburg Publishing House.

4 A semantic analysis of the symbolism of Toba mythical animals

PABLO G. WRIGHT

A series of drawings of Toba mythical beings, made in 1983, gave rise to an inquiry involving the people of two communities, La Primavera and Misión Tecaaglé, both in Formosa Province, Argentina, to test their identification or recognition of these mythical beings (see Fig. 4.1).[1] The resulting information exceeded the limits of the original project, and this chapter presents preliminary results of the analysis of the data. These have both cognitive and symbolic aspects.[2]

The mythical beings of Toba universe configure a more or less defined category possessing characteristics that are special and distinctive from those of human and other living beings. Generically the expression that refers to this distinction is *jaqa'a* (another, strange, unknown, nonhuman) versus *jaqaja* (brother, friend, human) (Wright 1988b).

Metamorphosis

Among the nonhuman beings a clear distinction is observed between those that appear in the principal mythical narratives and those that inhabit the daily Toba world. The former are termed *nanoiknagaik* (powerful, transformers that may be transformed at will), and this refers to their capacity for changing their morphology or otherwise demonstrating the magnitude of their powers. Their activity is documented in the 'stories of the old' that deal with the age in which the world started, inhabited by dangerous wild animals, when human beings owned no cultural goods, and when the world did not have its present conformation. The ability to transform the shape at will is a characteristic feature of that era. Thus the animal–man distinction is labile, and most of the characters in the old stories have human form but possess the names or attitudes of animals.

A series of mythical catastrophes indicate the end of mythical time and the appearance of the present world, with its distinct categories of men, animals and geography, with norms and cultural goods, and with the negative effect of disease, witchcraft and death, which are counteracted by shamans.

Among the second group of nonhuman beings there exists a large sphere

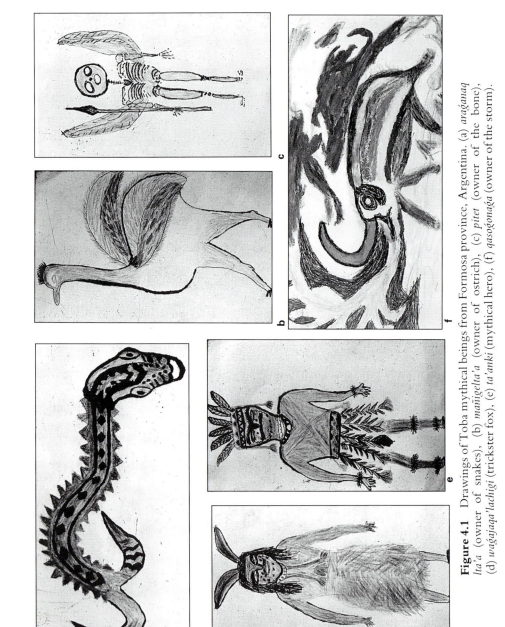

Figure 4.1 Drawings of Toba mythical beings from Formosa province, Argentina. (a) *araɣanaq lta'a* (owner of snakes), (b) *mañiqelta'a* (owner of ostrich), (c) *pitet* (owner of the bone), (d) *waɣajaqa'lachigi* (trickster fox), (e) *ta'anki* (mythical hero), (f) *qasoɣonaɣa* (owner of the storm).

that corresponds to the owners (*loogot*, *lta'a*, or *late'e*) of species of the natural world, to empirical phenomena (such as wind and rain), and to activities and diseases. These owners control them and bear a close relationship with human beings throughout their lives.

Among the *jaqa'a* beings of the second group is the category of auxiliary spirits (*ltagaiagawa*). Any nonhuman entity that communicates with a person and 'converses' with him, providing certain services in a more or less stable association, is a *ltagaiagawa*. In this traditional scheme the Christian deity appears as a nonhuman entity more powerful than the older ones, capable of fighting new diseases introduced by white men (such as smallpox, tuberculosis, and influenza), and also of providing teachings appropriate to the moral, social, and economic order of contemporary society. The Bible is interpreted as a repository of real and effective traditions capable of being read with an original hermeneutics and adapted to the particular circumstances of the lives of individuals or of the whole community.

The totality of the living beings of the Toba world, whether natural or supernatural, are organized according to a system of classification that involves a more or less explicit idea of hierarchies, although the most significant feature appears to be the spatial orientation, since this appears in the language in very specific forms. Every entity belongs to a defined sector of space. The regions which the Toba distinguish are the following:

heaven or above	(*pigem*)
earth	(*'alwa*)
village	(*lawo'*)
country	(*ne'enaga*)
forest	(*hawiaq*)
palm-grove	(*chaesat*)
swamp	(*qajim*)
water, ponds and brooks	(*'etagat*)
below or in the depths	(*ka'ageñi*)
night	(*pe*)

This sequence of categories appears also in Toba cosmology, which includes five cosmic levels, three of them fundamental: the earth, the sky, and the depths. The sky has three subdivisions that express an increasing distance from earth towards the 'more above'.

In the taxonomy of the animal kingdom (which extends to the sphere of nonhuman entities that have animal appearance), the principal terms are:

shiağawa	form of a human person
shigiak	generic for animal form

The *shiağawa* includes human as well as nonhuman beings. Since the proper habitat of men is the village or community, the term *shiağawa hawiağal'ek*, which means 'man inhabiting the forest', therefore alludes to a nonhuman entity, a being that does not live in the habitat proper to human beings.

Among the *shigiak* the main subcategories are:

shigiak	animals of regular size, or of wild habits
gojo	flying animals
araĝanaq	snakes
njaq	water animals
hil-lo	domestic animals (fowl and mammals)

The morphology of these animals in most cases fluctuates between animal and human or may combine traits of both categories. There are certain features that indicate to the Toba whether it is an 'empirical' animal or a nonhuman being. The following account exemplifies this:

He was going to the field and found ostrich (*Rhea americana*). They had told him to kill moderately, two or three, and to take care of the meat, so that it would not be wasted. Once he killed and threw away the meat, and when he went to hunt again he found nothing. The next time he also found nothing. The third time he met *mañigelta'a* (owner of the ostrich) and he told him that he had found nothing because he had thrown away a lot of meat. Its shape was that of a person but he had white feathers in his hand. There is a *mañigelta'a* that is like a person, but also one with the form of an ostrich but white, and is different from the rest because it does not have the feather colour mixed: it is all white. *'Mañigelta'a hichoĝoden na shiaĝawa hichoĝoden de nepé* ('The owner of the ostrich felt pity for the person and gave him something to hunt').

Here appear two descriptions of the owner of the ostrich. In both, the monochromatic characteristics of the feathers are shared, and are of special significance in determining the condition of the owner. The last phrase in the Toba account refers to the relation established by the person with the nonhuman entity and sums up the concepts already referred to, in the sense that there is the formation of a type of link (*hichoĝóden*) where the owner voluntarily donates certain benefits.

It is characteristic of the Toba tradition that the definition of certain animals as nonhuman is based on cognitive aspects that mark the essential difference from the 'normal' morphology attributed to animals (which includes not only the external features but also their etiology), or from the human one (which is differentiated by possessing elements proper to the species that it supposedly represents, such as size and skin). Apart from these differences, the possibility of 'speaking' with nonhuman beings indicates a degree of relationship that implies not only a positive volition of the nonhuman being towards man, but also the granting to man of an esoteric knowledge that results, for instance, in the comprehension of language, song and behaviour of the earthly species whose power had been bestowed on him.

Owner of the snakes

The descriptive aspects of the cognition of mythical animals encompasses a wide array of symbolic associations with many sectors of the culture. In the case of the owners of species the symbolism is related to social and economic norms, cosmological ideas, shamanism and others. The normative import-ance of the owner of the ostrich in hunting practice has already been shown. Another example will elaborate further on what has been said.

The *araǵanaqlta'a*, the owner or 'father' of the snakes is an entity described as a snake-like being of large size, polychromous skin with scales and a sort of saw on both sides of the body which serves it as locomotive apparatus. The body ends in a tail with two hooks with which it holds its prey. The head is like that of a *yarará* (*Lachesis* sp., Bothrops So.), and the mouth may hold victims of quite large size. Other versions of this entity exist and it will vary according to the peculiarities it assumes when it comes into contact with different people. Thus, some characterize it as a large snake with a bifurcated tail, others as a four-legged snake, others as a sort of *ñandú* (ostrich) with beak and multicoloured scaly neck.

In each version certain common features are present, which indicate that it is an *araǵanaqlta'a*, however much its shape or behaviour may vary. The Toba say this owner has its 'sign' (*ndage*) in the upper part of the head, in the form of a sort of red crest. This colour is frequently observed in nonhuman entities that have power. The sign is the symbolic element that identifies it as a mythical being.

According to the owner of the snake involved it may live in the country, or in the forest, varying its morphology accordingly.

The home of *araǵanaqlta'a* is located for preference in deep underground caves and, sometimes, in burrows near water. The association of this being with the aquatic domain and with other entities such as the rainbow encompasses a chain of interesting references. The atmospheric phenomena of rain and wind have a close relationship with them, as well as the storm (*qasoǵonaǵa*) that pertains to the celestial sphere. Water, as an element of the symbolic universe, has connections with notions of purity, therapy and, in a certain sense, are connected with female spheres (cf. Miller 1975). Men-struating women are prohibited from approaching water since this would anger the rainbow, causing earthquakes and diseases in all the community.

The link between the owner of the snakes, the terrestrial and/or aquatic plane, and the storm, in the celestial sphere, raises the question of the nature of the relationship between the mythic beings of the different sectors of the universe, so well classified spatially by the Toba. The three principal planes within the cosmic framework, namely earth, sky and depths, appear with different symbolic connotations. It is evident that the *sky* is the most powerful plane and its sign is positive. *Earth* appears to imply less power than the sky and its influence could become either positive or negative. A similar ambiguity is observed with regard to the third plane, that of the *depths*, and in this context would partake of some of the characteristics of the earth. Traditional deities that had great power derived from the celestial plane, such as, for example, the constellation of the Pleiades. Others of the earth level, however, such as *no'wet*, *ta'anki* or the Trickster Fox, seem to have as much relevance as the celestial ones and their importance in the mythic discourse of the culture is indeed central (cf. Wilbert & Simoneau 1982; Wright 1988c).

The effect of Christian preaching has caused the Toba symbolic system to vary somewhat in its spatial values, since God, Jesus, the Holy Spirit and the Virgin Mary have been reinterpreted as inhabitants of the sky, i.e. as *pigeml'ek* or *pigemlashi*.

An example of an encounter with the owner of the snakes illustrates the concepts that we are analysing:

> When you go hunting, *araġanaqlta'a* appears to be an ostrich since it holds up and lowers its head, but slower than the ostrich. When the hunters see the *ndage* (sign) they know then it is the owner of the snake and flee. In those days they were hunting and two *araġanaqlta'a*, a male and a female, came close and said: 'Ehhh! don't go, come home!' Then they left and they saw a man appear: it formed like a person, *ñigi shiaġawa salliaganek* (was transformed into a rich person). 'All right, I shall take you home and tomorrow you shall return home,' it said. They answered 'Yes', and then *araġanaqlta'a* returned to its original form of a large snake and said, 'Get up on my back!' Then they went to its house. When it was a person it had trousers, a suit, tie, shoes and its face was that of a Toba but the dress was white, its tongue was Toba. The house was I do not know how many metres deep, and when they arrived it formed again as a person, and there was no more *araġanaqlta'a* as a *bicho* (animal). Then he said: 'Now I shall give you all you need to hunt and I shall see that you lack nothing: *guasuncho*, honey, ostrich, everything. This is all mine but I shall give it to you. Now your family is crying, but tomorrow you shall go'. This offering was for a lifetime, to be able to reach old age, and to hunt; it was like a present. When the sun rose, they returned in the morning to the same place where the man had encountered *araġanaqlta'a*; then they taught him all that was necessary to save sick people. Power was granted upon him from heaven to pray, and to heal, with words, not suction. Then he returned home.

Sexual polarity

Changes may be observed in the morphology of the owner of the snakes, a characteristic that seems to be general with mythical animals. The subject of the encounter with a nonhuman being that takes humans to his abode and bestows its power on them is archetypical of the Toba initiation processes. Acting as an auxiliary spirit, the owner of the snakes bestows power on the individual so that he may secure food during his hunting and initiates him as a *dannaǵanaǵaik* (healer), a class of medicine-men distinguished from the traditional shamans that imply, also, other techniques, such as suction and blowing.

Generally the owners of species are symbols of abundance as large accumulators of goods. Their function is to see that food resources are not annihilated and to redistribute them among men. Thus the symbolism of their human appearance in the form of *salliaganek* (rich, chief), with occidental clothing although communicating in the vernacular language. The apparition of two owners, masculine and feminine, represents the basic sexual polarity with which the Toba classify all the beings of the universe.

The owners of species consist of a class of nonhuman beings that are linked symbolically with basic definitions of the Toba cosmology and axiology. Based on the different contexts of the myths, their role is constantly redefined according to the existential circumstances of the men with whom they come into contact. However, their presence legitimates the relationships of men with the 'natural' and 'social' environment, and introduces cultural elements that warrant obedience to the rules. One of them is the disease produced each time the established taboos are infringed. The role of the nonhuman beings as redistributors of foodstuffs and power has now been modified by the presence of the Christian deity which appears as the most powerful being and one that offers benefits free of the ambiguities that characterize those of the traditional nonhuman entities.

In the world of myths a Manichaean division between 'good' and 'evil' does not exist; all characters and beings combine both features. Christian preaching has placed in the positive and celestial pole all biblical supernatural beings, and, in opposition to these, placed in the negative pole, terrestrial and subterranean entities of ambivalent sign, that is, those that could be either benevolent or malevolent.

Mythical animals, which are all beings of nonhuman nature, are subject to mythopoetic and pragmatic elaborations that make them vary their cognitive and symbolic expressivity. The case of the owners of species offers an example of the viability of a sociocultural schema that has great functionality and adaptability to the variable historic conditions that affect the existence of this aboriginal group.

Notes

1 A collection of 14 illustrations made with coloured pencils on hardboard cards. I express my gratitude to Angel Achilai (*pitiǵat*) whose drawings were utilized as an information source, and to the La Primavera and Misión Tacaaglé communities. I also thank Jorge Wright who helped with the English translation of the original Spanish version of this chapter.

La Primavera and Misión Tacaaglé are two agricultural communities where formerly nomadic hunting and gathering Tobas lived grouped together. They are located to the northeast of the province of Formosa (Argentina), which borders on Paraguay. The investigation in relation to the drawings was undertaken in both communities in 1983 and 1985, and was sponsored by CONICET.

2   The cognitive and symbolic focus follows the general orientations of the works of Colby *et al.* (1981), Turner (1980), and Miller (1975). My emphasis stresses the need to undertake within a semantic approximation to linguistic and observational data a reading both of the cognitive and symbolic aspects. Both types of evidence combine to cover the interrelationship that the collected information possesses within a specific sociocultural context.

References

Buckwalter, A. 1980. *Vocabulario Toba*. Bueños Aires: Alleres Grancharoff.

Colby, B. *et al.* 1981. Towards a convergence of cognitive and symbolic anthropology. *American Ethnologist* (special issue) **8**(3), 422–50.

Klein, H. M. 1981. Location and direction in Toba: verbal morphology. *International Journal of American Linguistics* **48**(3), 422–50.

Klein, H. M. 1981. Location and direction in Toba: verbal morphology. *International Journal of American Linguistics* **8**(3), 227–35.

Loewen, J. *et al.* 1965. Shamanism, illness and power in Toba church life. *Practical Anthropology* **12**, 250–80.

Messineo, C. & Wright, P. G. 1988. Deixis and sociocultural context in Toba. Unpublished manuscript.

Miller, E. S. 1967. Pentecostalism among Argentine Toba. PhD. dissertation, University of Pittsburgh.

Miller, E. S. 1975. Shamans, power symbols and change in Argentine Toba culture. *American Ethnologist* **2**(3), 477–96.

Miller, E. S. 1979. *Los tobas argentinos: armonía y disonancia en una sociedad*. México: Siglo XXI editores.

Reyburn, W. 1954. *The Toba Indians of the Argentine Chaco. An interpretive essay*. Elkhart, Indiana: Mennonite Board of Missions and Charities.

Turner, V. 1980. *La selva de los símbolos*. Madrid: Siglo XXI de España editores. (English edition 1967).

Wilbert, J. & Simoneau, K. 1982. *Folk literature of the Toba Indians*. Los Angeles, Latin American Center, UCLA.

Vuoto, L. 1981. La fauna entre los toba taksek. *Entregas del IT*, **10**, 77–138. Tilcara.

Wright, P. G. 1981. Presencia protestante entre aborígenes del Chaco argentino. *Scripta Ethnologica* **7**, 73–84.

Wright, P. G. 1984. Análisis semántico preliminar de algunas ideas básicas en la morfología nominal y verbal toba. *III Congreso Nacional de Lingüística*, Universidad de Morón, octubre.

Wright, P. G. 1988a. Tradición y Aculturación en una organización socio-religiosa Toba contemporánea. *Cristianismo y Sociedad*, México **26**(95), 71–87.

Wright, P. G. 1988b. El tema del árbol cósmico en la comología y shamanismo de los Toba de la provincia de Formosa (Argentina). In *Languajes y palabras chamánicas*, P. Bidou & M. Perrin (eds). Quito: Ediciones Abya-Yala.

Wright, P. G. 1988c. Fox steals the catch from tiger. *Latin American Indian Literature Journal* **4**(1), 22–41.

5 *Back to the future: trophy arrays as mental maps in the Wopkaimin's culture of place*

DAVID C. HYNDMAN

Introduction

Between 500 and 3000 m on the southern slopes of the Hindenburg Mountains in central New Guinea is the homeland of some 700 Wopkaimin people (Fig. 5.1) They are hunter-horticulturalists culturally affiliated with over 33 000 other Mountain Ok-speakers (Fig. 5.1) who, by an unfortunate colonial legacy, are politically separated into West Papuans and Papua New Guineans. Subsistence ecology essentially revolves around the joint work of men and women cultivating *Colocasia* taro in shifting, slash-mulch, aggregate gardens and the exclusive work of men in hunting large terrestrial and arboreal game animals.

   Throughout the New Guinea mid-altitude fringe and Highlands, men retain game animal bones for a variety of technological, ornamental, decorative, and ritual purposes (Bulmer 1976). Mountain Ok hunters place game animal bones on display on the rear wall of men's houses (Barth 1975, Pernetta & Hyndman 1982). Such bone displays are commonly referred to as 'trophy collections' (Bulmer 1976) or 'trophy arrays' (Craig 1983). However, these labels are multidimensional and are indicative of more than decorative function. The Wopkaimin are not only decorating the men's house when they accumulate trophy arrays, they are also creating mental maps that convey meaning in their own right.

Mental maps

The perceived environment, according to Brookfield (1969, p. 74), 'is complex, monistic, distorted and discontinuous, unstable and full of interwoven irrelevancies; its complexity may in sum be less than that of the real environment, but it is far less easy to separate into discrete parts for analysis'. Wopkaimin behaviour is highly affected by that portion of their environment they actually perceive. They cannot absorb and retain the virtually infinite amount of environmental information that impinges on them daily. Their culture acts as a perceptual filter screening out most

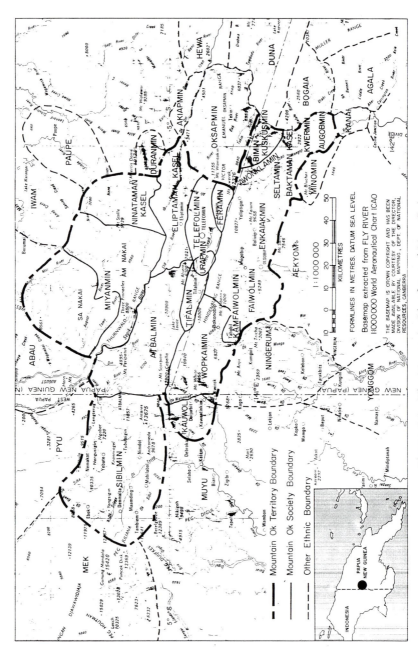

Figure 5.1 The Mountain Ok of central New Guinea.

information in a very selective manner. Culture informs the perception they
have of place and the mental maps they form from filtered information flow.
Mental maps are abstracted, simplified and compressed reality. The perceived environment is always and wholly a cultural artefact (Brookfield
1969). By collecting, organizing, storing, recalling and manipulating information, the Wopkaimin transform environmental complexity into a single
unified sense of place.

Mental (Gould & White 1974), or cognitive (Downs & Stea 1977) maps
are cultural models of place constructed by a simplifying process of many to
one, homomorphic transformations. Mental mapping is a process, an
activity of coming to grips with and comprehending the spatial environment. A mental map is a product, an organized representation 'that stands
for the environment, that portrays it, that is both a likeness and a simplified
model, something that is, above all, a mental image' (Downs & Stea 1977).
The process of mental mapping is directed purposeful behaviour that is
controlled and determined by cultural rules. Through mental mapping
the Wopkaimin create a sense of place by acquiring and storing essential
information about their everyday spatial environment and using it to decide
where to go, how to get there and what to do with it.

Mental maps are stored internally in the memory and externally as
concrete, material forms. Trophy arrays are the mode of representation of
Wopkaimin mental maps; they are as important as experience in providing
the basis of perception. Assembling trophy arrays comprises the two
processes of mapping: mapmaking or encoding and mapreading or decoding,
while the product of mapmaking is the assembled trophy array. Trophy
arrays are mental maps that communicate a sense of place. They are the
cultural product of acquiring, organizing and storing spatial information in
such a way as to be functional when required.

Mapmaking: the process of encoding

Trophy arrays are mental map responses to the culture of place. Place is
central to mental mapping because it introduces specificity and difference.
The Kam Basin is homeland to the Wopkaimin and their mental maps of this
specific, local place put things on the level of everyday living. Culture can be
seen working in what people do and in the tactics they employ. When the
Wopkaimin display animal bones on the rear wall of the men's house they
are materially representing something in the real world. No single person is
the sole source of these mental maps. Rather, they are contrapuntal poly-
phonic expressions of the initiated men residing together and collectively
producing a trophy array through the results of their combined hunting
efforts.

The Wopkaimin use things already around them but not especially concerned with symbolizing that for which they are to be used. Mental
mapping is an interactive, information feedback process in which learning

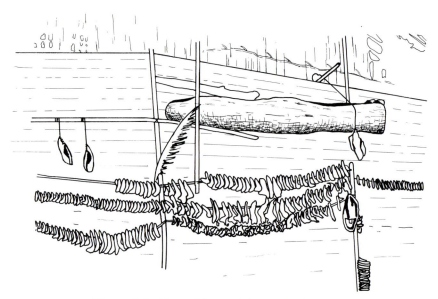

Figure 5.2 Kavorabip men's house trophy array.

by doing is crucial (Downs & Stea 1977). Direct interaction with the environment is a vital feature affecting both the type of spatial information obtained and the sources through which it is obtained. Mental mapping is a highly selective encoding process involving decisions about types of information stored, how it is symbolized, arranged and ordered and how relative importance or value is attached to it (Downs & Stea 1977). It is bricolage, 'the activity of roaming in the ruins of a culture, picking up useful bits and pieces to keep things going or even make them function better' (Benterrak *et al.* 1984, p. 148). Trophy arrays are visible bricolage. It is possible to trace the origins of the different bones and relics making up the mental map.

The two major selectivity criteria of Wopkaimin bricoleurs are functional importance and imageability. Mental maps depend on functional importance and closely mirror the spatial patterns of regular activity. There is a direct link between territory, ethnobiology, resource use and trophy arrays. Access to the locally diverse range of game animals is limited by time, space and ethnobiological classification (Hyndman 1984). Bones available from hunting returns already reflect the imposition of cultural selectivity and, as, apointed out by Wheatcroft (1975:, p. 408):

> throughout the Mountain Ok, only fully-initiated, senior men may eat the head of the pig from which mandible and skull is preserved ... Marsupials that women and children may eat never end up as preserved trophies in the men's house; and both cassowary and wild pig are foods only men eat. Thus, everything that ends up as a trophy in the men's house is masculine *par extraordinaire*.

Figure 5.3 Bakonabip men's house trophy array.

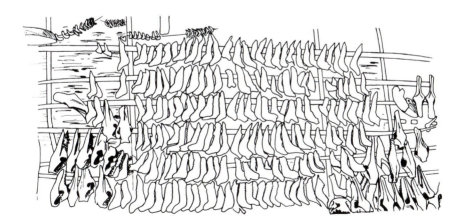

Figure 5.4 Bolang men's house trophy array

A sense of functional importance as selectivity criteria is illustrated by the bones the Wopkaimin choose to represent graphically their knowledge of the environment. That which is familiar and positively valued is graphically represented in proportions larger than normal expectation. Thus in the Kavorabip trophy array (Fig. 5.2) tree kangaroos predominate, in the Bakonabip trophy array (Fig. 5.3) cuscus and ringtails predominate and in the Bolang trophy array (Fig. 5.4) pigs predominate.

Table 5.1 shows that additional criteria of cultural selection are applied to the bones selected for use in trophy arrays. In the Bakonabip trophy array (Fig. 5.3) nearly three-quarters of the bones displayed come from only four species: the cuscus *Phalanger vestitus* 21 per cent, the ringtail *Pseudocheirus cupreus* 33 per cent, the domestic pig *Sus scrofa* 12 per cent, and the cassowary *Casuarius benetti* 6 per cent. In terms of hunting, the cuscus returned 8 per cent by weight and 11 per cent by number, and the ringtail 10 per cent by weight and 17 per cent by number, whereas the cassowary returned 25 per cent by weight but only 6 per cent by number. The same four species constitute less than 50 per cent of the number of bones used in the Migalsimabip trophy array; whereas the tree kangaroo *Dendrolagus dorianus* (42 per cent) and the bat *Pteropus neohibernicus* (7 per cent) are half of the bones displayed and they do not even appear in the Bakonabip trophy array.

Imageability is clearly a criterion for selecting bones for display in trophy arrays. The distinctiveness of the Kavorabip, Bakonabip and Bolang arrays reflects the contrasts in and the arrangements of the spatial environment around each hamlet. Form, visibility and use are the three characteristics of imageability (Downs & Stea 1977). Use reflects the functional role of local game animals, the greater their importance the greater the likelihood of their being selected. Form and visibility become criteria of selection through exposure time to wild and domestic animals and the potential animals' bones have for visual dominance when displayed. Mandibles, femurs and long bones of wild and domestic animals are culturally selected for inclusion in trophy arrays. Wopkaimin bricoleurs homomorphically transform residue bones from hunting and pig raising into mental maps.

Mapreading: the process of decoding

Mapreading is an organizing process. It is the capacity to reorganize culturally encoded bits of information on whatness, whereness and whenness and reduce them into meaningful, useful forms of ordered knowledge (Downs & Stea 1977). Trophy arrays encode and store spatial information. Reading these mental maps involves strategically retrieving and manipulating the information. The decoding process of mapreading is so charged with cultural meaning that there is nothing natural about it.

Mapreading is a means of communication. Encoding mental maps is culturally specific and so is the training in decoding them. Although different cultures produce different readings of the same landscape, it is not

Table 5.1 Bones selected for use in trophy arrays.

Game animals	Hunting returns[a]				Migalsimabip array[b]		Bakonabip array[c]	
	wt	%	no.	%	no.	%	no.	%
Echidnas								
Zaglossus bruijnii							1	0
Dasyurids								
Neophascogale lorentzi	0.2	0	2	3				
Bandicoots								
Echymipera kalubu					11	5		
Echymipera clara							2	1
Peroryctes longicuada								
Cuscus								
Phalanger rufoniger	5.5	4	1	1				
Phalanger gymnotis	4.1	3	2	3			1	0
Phalanger vestitus	11.2	8	8	11	16	8	35	21
Phalanger interpositus	4.6	3	3	4	5	2	17	
Phalanger carmelitae	5.7	4	3	4			2	1
Ringtails								
Pseudocheirus corinnae	1.02	0	1	1			4	2
Pseudocheirus cupreus	14.5	10	12	17	23	11	54	33
Pseudocheirus forbesii?	0.6	0	1	1				
Dactylonax palpator	0.2	0	1	1				
Wallabies								
Dorcopsulus vanheurni					85	42	7	4
Tree kangaroos								
Denrolagus dorianus					4	2	7	4
Bats								
Pteropus neghibernicus					14	7		
Dobsonia moluccensis	6.6	4	24	34				
Giant rats								
Mallomys rothschildi	1.8	1	2	3				
Rats								
Melomys rubex	0.06	0	2	3				
Cassowaries								
Casuarius bennetti	38.2	25	4	6	23	11	9	6
Domestic pigs								
Sus scrofa							19	12
Feral pigs								
Sus scrofa	36.3	24	3	4	18	9	2	1
Dogs								
Canis familiaris							1	0

Sources: [a] Hyndman 1984, [b] Pernetta & Hyndman 1982, [c] Fieldwork January 1985

necessary to imagine yourself as a Wopkaimin and then see what you think of their mental maps. I agree with Geertz (1983: p. 58) that ethnographers largely do not perceive what their informants perceive but they can search out and analyse the images – the symbolic forms people actually use to represent themselves to themselves. It is possible to read Wopkaimin trophy arrays because they are the mental maps they perceive with, or by means of, or through. Each reading 'produces a partial knowledge of the country, and using the reading is the only way to gain access to that knowledge; the country does not offer up the fullness of its meaning to the perceptive individual as some romantics and spiritualists would have us believe' (Benterrak *et al.* 1984, p. 67).

Trophy arrays as culturally shared, graphic representations have been read by several Mountain Ok ethnographers. Wheatcroft's reading of the trophy array in the major cult house (*am-awok*) of Bulolengabip, a Bufulmin parish hamlet of the Tifalmin (Fig. 5.1; for photos see Wheatcroft 1975, plates 21, 22; Craig 1983, plate 14) is as follows:

> The mandibles number just over 700, arranged in 12 horizontal rows ... Here and there at the top, but mainly at the top sides, the men have suspended about 60 pig skulls. Some skulls and mandibles were painted with red ochre contrasted by white limestone paint ... On both sides of the back wall, the men have arranged about 25 cassowary sacra (portion of the pelvis). Along the sides advancing towards the front of the house were items used in warfare, such as ancient disc clubs (of which there was one on each side), and a few arrows used to hunt marsupials during initiation ceremonies. Still farther to the front, along the sides, were about 30 pig shoulder blades that the men use during one part of the Kayuban initiation ... Along each side wall near the rear were the mandibles of *nuk kabano* and *nuk tifol* marsupials. (Wheatcroft 1975, pp. 401–4)

Jorgensen (1981, p. 70) reads the trophy array of the Telefolmin (Fig. 5.1) *yolam* cult house as being 'covered with symmetrically-disposed rows of domestic pig jawbones, often painted in white and red bands. At eye level are hung the blackened net bags (*manamem*) containing the skulls of the *usong* (ancestral spirits). Wild pig skulls and jawbones may be lined up along the floor at the base of the wall – perhaps with a crocodile skull traded from the Atbalmin'.

Barth (1975, pp. 247–8) provides the following reading of the Baktamanmin (Fig. 5.1) trophy arrays in the taro (*katiam*) and war (*yolam*) cult houses:

> The *katiam* ... sacra themselves include mandibles, collar-bones and fingerbones, not skulls or long-bones. The hunting trophies are cassowary pelvises, wild pig mandibles and a few skulls. Both male and female wild pig are found ... The *yolam*, by contrast ... is constituted around two central relics: the skull and mandible of an ancestor, and the

ancestral long-bones and brush turkey foot of the firepost shrine ... It also contains trophies of female wild pig killed in secret hunts.

Mountain Ok trophy arrays are art forms in the reading provided by Craig (1983, pp. 22–3):

> First of all, the arrays are accessible for criticism by an audience – admittedly, in most cases, an audience of initiated men, but nevertheless an audience ... Secondly there is the notion of the arrays as unspecific experimental models ... they do model certain relationships among the conceived entities in the Mountain Ok universe. Certainly, aspects of the model appear to relate to things as they are; but from the point of view of any individual relics curator, the models are also speculative, since no one model is a copy of another.

There is a distinction between identity categories refering to forms of the same thing and equivalence categories discriminating different things as the same kind of thing (Downs & Stea 1977). Telefolmin, Tifalmin and Baktamanmin trophy arrays are identity categories of the same thing but they are not equivalence categories. The process of bricolage has encoded bones from dissimilar animals into each mental map. Jorgensen (1981) reads the Telefolmin arrays as models of order versus entropy that distinguish between nurturing and killing, gardening and hunting. Barth (1975) reads Baktamanmin arrays as models of the relations between man, land and the ancestors. Neither culture is contiguous with the Wopkaimin; the Telefolmin lack cassowary and marsupial trophies nor, apparently, do the Baktamanmin retain marsupial bones. Because of cultural and ecological differences these trophy arrays are not equivalence categories.

The Tifalmin and Wopkaimin occupy contiguous territories and they display pig, cassowary and marsupial bones in their trophy arrays. Wheatcroft (1975, p. 410) reads the smoke-preserved bones of the Tifalmin array as a 'permanent link through time between the beginning and the present [that] become – in both real and magical ways – history itself, encoded in venerated relics'. A temporal message is also conveyed by Wopkaimin trophy arrays. Both cultures employ a vocabulary of shared categories in their mental maps which are generalized and simplified reconstructions of similar environmental experience.

Trophy arrays are structures that can be generated and reconstructed on demand. They act as mental map triggers to recall the characteristics of place, the specific set of information that gives the homeland a unique identity. Bones symbolize place and it is possible to fill in the necessary detail. Whatness demands a sense of place (Downs & Stea 1977). There is no single, objective characteristic of placeness. For the Wopkaimin it is the consequence of their mental maps agreed upon and made use of in their everyday life.

In the Bakonabip trophy array (Fig. 5.3) bones are grouped together on the basis of shared characteristics. They are identity categories for a range of places and equivalence categories for the wide variations of the local environment (Hyndman 1982). The Wopkaimin make a tripartite division of their homeland into an inner circle of hamlets (*abip*), bordered by gardens (*yon*) and encircled by rainforests (*sak*). Ancestral relics (*menamem*) are stored in string bags centrally at eye level on the trophy array. They belong to the *abip* realm in the relatively long-term hamlet sites placed centrally in the homeland. Domestic pigs are fostered to select families residing a short distance from hamlets, and mandibles from these animals are displayed beneath the ancestral relics. They are always slaughtered and butchered in the hamlet and sacrificed to the ancestors for continued success in pig raising. Wild pig bones are placed lower than domestic ones; they come from *gipsak*, the lowest zone of rainforest encircling the inner garden and hamlet zones. Wild boars are necessary for impregnating domestic sows and they threaten gardens. Marsupial mandibles are displayed highest off the floor, they primarily come from the mid to highest rainforests. Cassowary pelvis and thigh bones are placed in association with the wild pigs and marsupials representing the coexistence of these animals in the outer rainforests.

The Kavorabip (Fig. 5.2), Bakonabip (Fig. 5.3) and Bolang (Fig. 5.4) trophy arrays are all located in the men's houses of southern Mountain Ok people. Kavorabip and Bakonabip are Wopkaimin hamlets, Bolang is the westernmost of all Faiwolmin (Fig. 5.1) hamlets adjacent to the Wopkaimin Migalsim parish. Craig (1983, p. 4) reads from the Bolang trophy array that it also acts 'as an ecological model of animal resources in relation to human settlement and gardens'. It takes many years to complete a trophy array, maintenance is often sporadic and identity of trophies is often masked by heavy coats of sooted cobwebs. Eventually the temporal expansion of mental maps can lead to trophy arrays occupying the entire rear wall of men's houses.

Trophy arrays incorporate knowledge of the complex interrelationships between places and time. They can serve as a basis for interpretation and prediction because the kind of information they transmit is 'cyclical, leading to a steady state in the perceived environment and resources sub-system' (Brookfield 1969, p. 65). Trophy arrays are mental maps that carry the past forward in order to interpret present conditions. With them the Wopkaimin are able to look ahead in both space and time to cope with what is likely to happen. By generating reasonable expectations that relate time to space, they make appropriate decisions about resource use. The resources of a place depend on an evaluation of the perceived environment at a particular time (Brookfield 1969), and trophy arrays produce a mental map of the real environment by using the stock of information available. For the Wopkaimin the most obvious use for such prediction is in hunting. Trophies of successfully hunted animals are displayed as mnemonics to their future location.

The ecosystem the Wopkaimin perceive as homeland is restricted by the spatial range of their senses and the culture in which they live. Mental mapping is functional, but is specific to their homeland. They use their mental maps for relating resources and making sense out of the world. They connect together and condense the stream of experience to solve spatial problems, and the resource use of the past is displayed in the present to solve future problems. An understanding of Wopkaimin trophy arrays as a mode of expression depends on reading their mental maps.

Acknowledgements

Funding for the research on which this study is based has been provided variously by the University of Queensland, Australian National University, Natural Systems Research and Australian Research Grants Scheme No. 461 and research affiliation has been provided by the University of Papua New Guinea and the Papua New Guinea National Museum. I particularly wish to thank Bini and the other Wopkaimin for the learning experience, patience and hospitality they have extended to me over the years.

References

Barth, F. 1975. *Ritual and knowledge among the Baktaman of New Guinea*. New Haven, Conn.: Yale University Press.
Benterrak, K., S. Muecke & P. Roe 1984. *Reading the country*. Freemantle: Freemantle Arts Centre Press.
Brookfield, H. 1969. On the environment as perceived. *Progress in Geography* **1**, 51–80.
Bulmer, R. 1976. Selectivity in hunting and in disposal of animal bone by the Kalam of the New Guinea Highlands. In *Problems in economic and social archaeology*, G. Sieveking, I. Longworth and K. Wilson (eds). London: Duckworth.
Craig, B. 1983. *Relic and trophy arrays as art among the Mountain Ok, central New Guinea*, New York: 1982 Pacific Arts Symposium.
Downs, R. & D. Stea 1977. *Maps in minds: reflections on cognitive mapping*. New York: Harper & Row.
Geertz, C. 1983. *Local knowledge: further essays in interpretive anthropology*. New York: Basic Books.
Gould, P. & R. White 1974. *Mental maps*. London: Penguin.
Hyndman, D. 1982. Biotope gradient in a diversified New Guinea subsistence system. *Human Ecology* **10**, 219–59.
Hyndman, D. 1984. Hunting and the classification of game animals among the Wopkaimin. *Oceania* **54**, 289–309.
Pernetta, J. & D. Hyndman 1982. *Ethnozoology of the Ok Tedi drainage*. Working Paper 13. In Ok Tedi Environmental Study. Melbourne: Maunsell and Partners.

6 Sheep bone as a sign of human descent: tibial symbolism among the Mongols

SLAWOJ SZYNKIEWICZ

Animals typically play an important role in the symbolic culture of pastoral peoples, and also provide signs, which may be parts of an animal's body, such as bones, flesh, skin, or hair, to represent ideas or principles of social structure.

Among the pastoral Mongols of Soviet Mongolia the tibial bone of a sheep had many ceremonial and ritual uses until these customs were abandoned after forced atheization in the 1930s and 1940s. It would seem that these made up a complex whole that had a definite pattern. Although no longer discernible in its totality, it is possible to reconstruct it among the conservative Western Mongols, especially the Khoshuts and the Torguts of the Mongol Altai where my studies were conducted.[1]

Although individual instances may suggest that there are some very specific unconnected functions of the tibia bone as an independent sign, the tibia symbol is important in life crises, as well as in myths of origin. Thus I assume that it is a symbol related to an essential category of the social order.

To state my conclusion at the beginning, I suggest that the sheep tibia of the Mongols represents patrilineal descent or genealogical lineage, while its particular functions in various family ceremonies ensure communication with the ancestors. Hence its applications during rites of passage, especially births and weddings, as well as its appearance in narratives concerning the origin of a group.

The sheep tibia, with its flesh, constitutes one of several important meat dishes, each associated with specific ceremonies and having its own connotation. Tibia is the most frequently used of these meat dishes, but is not offered to matrilateral guests, who are given shoulder-blade meat. Neither consanguineal nor affinal women are supposed to partake of tibial meat, although men may share their portions with women if they wish.[2]

Tibias left after meals must be disposed of 'in a clean way', according to the traditional rules of conduct, which require the bones to be burned, deposited on a hill top or at any other supposedly 'pure' place. The rules are not strictly adhered to nowadays, but even now the tibia is not regarded as refuse and cannot just be thrown away. Many of the elders I spoke to felt that any tibia found in the steppe must be taken home, otherwise children would not be born in the family. Thus the tibia is the converse of the 'devilish' pelvis, which must be kicked and left when found.

The tibia is indeed a 'divine' bone, as it is called in a fragmentary creation myth that is recounted in the context of discussions about tibia among the Western Mongols. In this story it is said that the Buddha held a sheep tibia in his hand while creating animate beings, and particularly mankind. The same idea is found in stories about the origins of the Torgut tribe. It is said that Galdamba, the Torgut ancestor, was born with a sheep tibia in his hand, as well as clotted blood: a well-known attribute of Mongol heroes in their infancy, related to their future deeds rather than to their kinship affiliation. These two instances of the association of tibia bones with the beginnings of humanity and of ethnic groups seem to establish the collective inheritance of the groups concerned.

Another example occurs in the Khoshut account of their hero Mamaatan, whose ancestral status is accepted by the Altai section of the Koshuts. He was revered during annual sacrifices formerly held by the whole group, and his portrait was the central point of the ceremony. The use of the term 'portrait' here is apt, for depictions of historical personages were made by nomadic Mongols, as Figure 6.1 shows. According to one recollection of Mamaatan's portrait, which was lost in the 1930s, a tibia was depicted as a personal attribute of Mamaatan, while another recalled it resting in a ceremonial bucket shown in the lower section of the portrait.

This ceremonial bucket was normally used during familial offerings to the hearth as a receptacle for blessings and prosperity. The blessings were collected pending offerings by the family head who circumambulated the vessel in a ceremony called *dallag*. The items deposited in the bucket always included the fresh tibia of a sheep sacrificed for the occasion.

The fact that the ceremonial bucket is pictured in the Khoshut ancestor's portrait suggests that it was he who was supposed to fill the vessel with blessings. It was probably the ancestors who were addressed during these offerings to the hearth, until the Lamaist church took over and transformed this ritual of folk religion. The transformation had formally taken place by the end of the 17th century, though in conservative Western Mongolia it happened later, thus allowing the preservation of the initial association of the ritual with the ancestors as reflected in the 'semantics' of the portrait. The association suggests that the tibia mediated between the living and the ancestors.

At this level the symbolism of the tibia pertains to the origin of the people, its history and the beginnings of the descent system. This could be called the phylogenetic plane, as opposed to the ontogenetic plane, which refers to the individual life cycle. This level is more elaborated and links individuals with their past or the source of their existence, through the tradition of kinship. It is expressed in ritual behaviour and anchored in the phylogenetic level which serves to establish a mythological point of reference for this ritual behaviour.

The tibia is ritually important at all stages of the life cycle. It is prominent

Figure 6.1 Abadai-kaan portrayed by an unknown Mongolian artist. (Fine Arts Museum, Ulan Bator.)

at the beginning of each individual's life, thus evoking the beginnings of humankind and of the tribe. The bone ritually received at birth is a sign that represents the institution already established symbolically at the mythological level.

On the third day after delivery the child is ceremonially washed in a broth made from the tibias and associated meat of a specially killed sheep. The meat is eaten by the mother, and this is the only circumstance in which a woman is allowed to do this. The right-hand tibia is used in the ritual of calling for prosperity and blessing, the *dallag*. It is performed by an agnatic kinsman of the newborn, usually of the third ascending generation. Afterwards the bone is tied to the cradle for a while and then preserved in the chest where family valuables are kept and on which the family altar is placed. Beforehand, a *khadag* (ceremonial silk scarf), a sign of the highest honour, is attached to the bone. Each of the tibias stored in the chest should have a name, which is that of the associated child. These tibias must always be the bone of a right hindleg, as in all other cases discussed here.

Parents may invoke the tibia if the child becomes ill, and particularly when the illness concern the ears or the nose. For this purpose the child's 'own' bone is taken out, presented to the divinities at the family altar and again the *dallag* ritual is performed. The child's mother then carries the bone around the *yurt* (tent) while simultaneously making offerings of sprinkled milk to guardian spirits of the locality. The procedure may be followed by heating the bone and extracting some marrow in order to put a drop in the affected organ.

Tibias associated with children are often unintentionaly lost in the process of nomadic movement. There is no clear rule on how long they should be preserved; according to some opinions there are no limits. Some women said that the bones must be disposed of after seven years, the age at which a child is supposedly less vulnerable to external malignant influences. Another opinion, and the most interesting one, was that all the bones were removed from the chest when the mother's procreative ability was declining. In both cases the bones are then supposed to be deposited at a hill-top sanctuary or *ovoo*, a stone cairn or a light wooden structure, which is a central altar for the annual communal sacrifices to the guardian spirits of a locality.

The tibia as a personal asset of an individual is specific to this particular age group only (from birth to seven years old) and constitutes a distinct part of the tibia symbolic complex. There is a strong association between the tibia and the child, the bone being kept at the place where the child is born, and its absence is seen as a sign of nonprocreation. This can be compared with the method of disposal of the bone, and with the custom of picking up a discarded tibia bone to ensure fertility.

The ritual of *dallag* performed with the tibia symbolizes a child's relationship to its ancestors. Traditionally the ritual was addressed to the ancestors, as shown on Mamaatan's portrait, but in the context of Lamaism it is directed towards certain holy beings represented by Buddhist deities on the family altar. The power of the ancestors expressed in the folk religion has been transferred to the new deities in a process of syncretization. Therefore placing the tibia in front of the altar, as in the case of curing, can be interpreted as an equivalent of the *dallag*, or ceremonial recourse to the ancestors.

When a person begins adult life, a new tibia is given ritual prominence as the counterpart of the child's bone that has been disposed of. It is no longer a sign held by an individual, irrespective of sex, but an asset of a married couple. The bone loses its personal character and, at the same time, its agnatic connotations become more pronounced.

The replacement takes effect at the wedding. At the initial party, held in the bride's *yurt*, each side presents a sheep carcass with a full complement of meat, including tibias. Both tibias, which belong to opposite sides of the marriage alliance, become objects of specific competitions that display features of symbolic behaviour. The tibia belonging to the bride's family is handed to the bridegroom, who is supposed to break it, although it is sufficient to disconnect the tibia and the ankle bone, which is attached to the former by strong tendons. The task is laborious and therefore regarded as a proof of the young man's skill, and considered a festive part of the ceremony. On the other hand, it can be looked upon as a sign of separation of the girl from her family and descent group. This is supported by the fact that ankle bones among the Mongols connote offspring and fertility (Kabzinska-Stawarz 1985).

The tibia brought by the groom stays untouched until the whole wedding cortege, including the bride, has started on its way. A man of the groom's party has taken it secretly and now brings it into sight adorned with a *khadag*, thus starting a competition over the bone. Riders of both parties compete on horseback with the aim of getting hold of the tibia. Youths of the girl's side try to deprive their opponents of the bone, though the general expectation is that it should finally stay with the groom's party. If the latter are unable to safeguard it effectively, they are supposed to buy it from the winners. The competition is unanimously claimed to be a purely sporting event. However, its symbolic language suggests that it is an equivalent of another archaic wedding rite, the mock fight over the bride.

Having kept their own bone, the groom's kin carry it to the new *yurt* prepared for the newly wed couple. The method of introducing the bone into the *yurt* is peculiar: it is thrown into the tent through the smokehole in the centre of the roof. The custom is parallel to another, that of throwing a sheep's head out of the *yurt*. The latter custom is explicitly explained as 'clearing the path for the hearth smoke'. The practice of flinging the tibia through the smokehole does not appear to be interpreted by the actors. However, there is a clue in the Torgut belief that the souls of children to be born descend from the Pole Star to the family *yurt* through the smokehole (the familiar *Axis Mundi*). It might be suggested then that the tibia paves the way for the souls by taking the same path as the smoke, but goes in the opposite direction, corresponding to the direction of the flow of the results of the union.

Now comes the crucial moment in the ceremony, which is a sort of wedding oath. The young couple kneel and grasp the tibia by its ends[3] and recite a prayer of devotion to the sun (the moon is sometimes mentioned also), to the parental protective spirits (*zaya saxius*), and to the tibia itself. Placing the tibia in the context of celestial bodies and divine beings in this way strongly supports the interpretation of it as representing extra-mundane qualities.

The tibia is then placed behind the *yurt*'s roof strut, the one that has been brought from the groom's parental *yurt* as a sign of continuity, and situated precisely on the spot where in the past the Mongols kept the *onggons* (anthropomorphic representations of familial protective deities). After three days of the wedding ceremony the bone is placed in the pillow of the couple's bed (where it remains for years), a custom that is said to promote the birth of children. Thus the association between matrimonial procreation and the family and descent group is initiated.

A slightly different ceremony in connection with the wedding tibia has been recorded among the Torgut immigrants from the Xinjiang Tarbagatay. This conforms to the operation of the joint family system. A group of brothers use the same bone for their weddings, each taking it from the previously married older brother, so that the youngest preserves it in his pillow in accordance with the rule of succession to the family hearth by the youngest son. The idea of continuity and succession within the descent group (compare also association of the tibia with the hereditary roof strut) conforms to the proposition that the bone is a sign of the descent line based on succession.

Though the bone in the pillow is a common asset of the couple, it can be used individually as well. The only case of such a usage known to me is a rite of bringing back the supposedly departed soul of a sick adult. A procession around the sick person's *yurt*, carrying his tibia taken from the pillow, used to be a part of the performance. Dangerous circumstances such as these evoke recourse to the ancestors, as they do in the case of children's illnesses.

The tibia is supposed to be preserved until the final rite of passage, the death ritual. It then accompanies the corpse when it is on display in the *yurt* and is deposited with the dead at the burial site. It is said that this practice is carried out when the first of the married couple dies, irrespective of sex. That would seem to go against the tibia's property as the sign of the agnatic bond, since women do not change their descent affiliation on marriage. However, information about this procedure is very imprecise because it is only rarely practised by the present generation. Also, since men are usually the first to die, the recollection of the practice may follow from this, and not in fact apply in cases where the woman dies first.

Depositing the tibia with the dead perhaps represents a symbolic dispatch of the sign to its source, the ancestors, just as children's bones are deposited at a mountain sanctuary. At the same time, analogically, burial of the bone can be viewed as dispatching the accompanying soul to the same source. Such an interpretation is supported by the reported former custom of killing

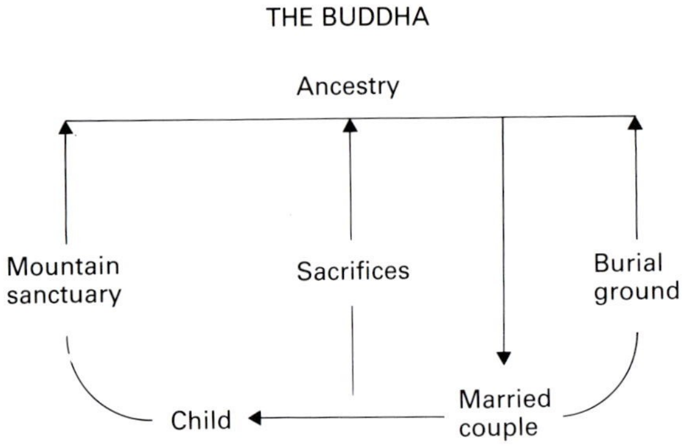

THE BUDDHA

Ancestry

Figure 6.2 The tibia stream.

senescent elders. According to legend, old people who wished to die were entertained with the most palatable dish, a sheep's tail. At the end of the meal a tibia was pushed into the man's mouth to suffocate him. Although some other bones would have been just as effective, a tibia had to be used for the killing.

Bronze Age burial sites in Mongalia and adjacent territories frequently contain sheep or goat tibias,[4] usually interpreted as remains of food offerings or provisions for the deceased. One cannot, however, rule out the possibility that the tibial complex already existed among the early Altaic peoples. If so, the bones would have had a more substantial symbolic meaning than merely catering for the last journey.

The social movement of tibias, their mythological significance, and their symbolic role in mediation and communication with the ancestors, are depicted in Figure 6.2. Although this chapter began with an account of mythological origins and the association of the tibia with birth, Figure 6.2 demonstrates that the process in fact begins with the ancestors, continues through parents, and then passes to the child. Parents produce the tibia sign for their children, while their own is associated with the ancestors and is dispatched conventionally during their wedding. The hereditary order of succession is preserved, in conformity with the kinship model through which the tibial complex works.

In conclusion, we consider whether mediation between individuals and the ancestors is the only function of the tibia. A person is, or used to be, a member of a descent group – a clan or lineage in the case of the Western Mongols of the first half of this century. It would thus be logical to hypothesize about possible clan communication with the ancestors through the tibia.

There is no definite data supporting such an hypothesis though some of the information suggests it indirectly. First, there is the tibia in the ceremonial bucket painted on the Khoshut ancestor's portrait, as described earlier. Its equivalent was used for the *dallag* in an annual ritual of venerating the ancestor. Both tibias represented extreme ends of a single line of communication. The ritual, however, was common for the whole Khoshut community in the Altai and had a tribal character. One may assume then that the tibia used in the ritual had been used symbolically by the ethnic group as a whole.

The second instance was the *ovoo* sacrifice, a communal event uniting respectively the Khoshuts and tribal subunits within the Torguts. The ritual consisted *inter alia* of an offering of a tibia from an immolated sheep. It is not known for sure whether the sacrifice was addressed to the ancestors in parallel with the *genius loci*, who was the main recipient. We are thus unable to determine whether that particular tibia mediated between a group of clans and their founder.

There is also a third instance, that of New Year's Day offerings within a camp. Camp member families belong in some cases to one lineage, which was the rule in the past. The offering is executed on a special altar, also called an *ovoo*, and consists of burning a tibia. The recipient is not specified, although an understanding prevails that it should be the powers of nature.

On the basis of the available data it is not possible to identify a 'group tibia', equivalent to the individual tibia, which might have mediated between a descent group as a whole and its ancestors. Nor is it possible to assume the existence of a symbolic link, via a tibia, between an individual and his descent group.

The apparent prevalence of personal or familial symbolic communication with the ancestors, rather than group communication with them, emphasizes individual freedom and familial independence in the maintenance of private bonds with the sacred. As far as the Mongols are concerned, descent and life crises appear to be individual matters. On the other hand, it might be merely that private interests have survived longer than collective ones.

To summarize the data, I present a componential chart of correlations between the tibia's occurrence or nonoccurrence and other properties discussed in this chapter (see Table 6.1). There is a total positive correlation in all cases, with one exception, shown in the final line of Table 6.1, which relates to the entertaining of the guests to whom tibial meat can be served provided they are aged and male, but irrespective of their kin affiliation.

The last column of Table 6.1 is defined as 'agnatic link'. This includes what is often referred to in the text as 'communication with the ancestors' and the same applies to some cases in the column headed 'supernatural protection'. The term 'ancestors' has been excluded from the headings because it was not used by those who gave me the information. Terms that can be translated as 'ancestors' refer to a social or genealogical category rather than a spiritual one. On the other hand, there exist beings definitely placed in the area of the sacred, called *zaya* and *onggon*, which by historical inference can be closely associated with the ancestors. Worship of the *zaya* (who determine fortune) is in decline, while *onggons* (protectors) are practically forgotten as a result of the Lamaist influence, which erases most

Table 6.1   The chart of correlations.

	Tibia	First man or ancestor	Child appears	Supernatural protection	Agnatic link
Buddha's act of creation	+	+			
Galdamba's birth	+	+			+
Mamaatan's image	+	+			+
Childbirth	+		+		
Curative action	+			+	
Disposal of child's bone	−		−		
Waste tibia	−(+)		−(+)		
Wedding complex					
Destruction	−				−
Competition	+(−)				+(−)
Throwing into the yurt	+		+		
Oath	+				+
Rest by strut	+				+
Pillow insert	+		+		
Brothers' share	+				+
Soul recalling	+			+	
Death, burial	+				+
Legendary death	+				+
Mamaatan sacrifice	+			+	+
Hearth sacrifice	+			+	+
Ovoo sacrifice	+			+	
New Year offerings	+			+	
Entertaining					
Agnatic kin	+				+
Matrilateral kin	−				−
Women, any	−				−
Non-related	+				−

allusions to ancestry in ritual situations. This calls for utmost caution in assuming equivalence of both genealogical and spiritual classes. The only instance in which one can safely attribute the term 'ancestor' is to a tribe or clan founder, but even he would more appropriately be called a culture hero or demiurge than an ancestor.

The final question to consider is why the tibia of a sheep – this particular bone of this particular animal – received this symbolic treatment. The fact that it is a bone does not present a problem in the light of the Mongol (and more generally, Central Asian) opposition between bone and flesh, which is used to denote opposed and complementary categories that constitute the kinship system. 'Bone' explicitly stands for patrilineal descent, and 'flesh' for matrilateral filiation. This opposition, noted in general anthropological literature (e.g. Lévi-Strauss 1949, pp. 462, 490), is well known among students of Central Asian cultures. It supports my proposition that the tibia represents patrilineal descent.

The reason for the choice of the tibia as symbol is less obvious. Imputation of phallic significance seems unwarranted, since there is no such symbolism apparent among the Mongols. However, it is not unreasonable to suggest that the symbolic power of the tibia derives from the bone's junction with the adjoining ankle bone, and the latter's customary connotation of fertility. Such an association fits in very well with the ancestors' supposed powers regarding fertility.

Why it should be a sheep bone is perhaps an irrelevant question. Sheep are the most important animals in Mongol diet, both everyday and ceremonial. The specific, practical role of sheep in ritual practices (regardless of the age and sex of the ritual animal) seems decisive. This is corroborated by the corresponding ceremonial function of equivalent cattle bones among the affinal Buryats and Yakuts, where cattle occupy the dominant position in their economy.

In the particular case of the Mongols, however, the sheep may have some intrinsic relevance. I have already mentioned *ovoo* sacrifices, basic communal rituals practised until the end of the 1930s that included immolation of a sheep. The *ovoo* is not a massive structure, and is usually described as an altar. There exist, however, *ovoo* of considerable size, comparable to towers and not associated with annual ceremonies. They are said to contain human remains, allegedly because human sacrifices were common in a remote past (noted among the Mongol Altai).

Folkloric themes contain the idea of immolated human beings mediating between society and the upper world through the *ovoo* institution. Actual *ovoo* sacrifices involve sheep in the same symbolic function, and a particular symbolic relation between sheep and man emerges. An analogy can be drawn with the Nuer ritual equation of humans and cattle (Evans-Pritchard 1956, pp. 208, 261–2). The analogy goes further in that both equations are insufficiently substantiated (cf. the critique of Evans-Pritchard's reasoning by de Heusch 1985, p. 9).

The Yakuts are more literal in this respect and use human tibia in relation to men. In their folklore a dispossessed successor to a ruling position sues the usurper, and produces a tibia of his ancestor as evidence of his claims (Ksenofontov 1977, pp. 62–3, 75, 80).

I once met a Mongol who had had his leg amputated and kept the disjointed tibia under his bed so that he could be buried 'in completeness'. Every bone is considered essential for human identity and any bone may be a substance of life, as frequently evidenced in folktale. There are many instances in Mongol epics of a dead hero being restored to life on the basis of his fragmentary bone remains (e.g. Mongol... 1982, pp. 44, 105–6, Dan'... 1986, pp. 62, 106–7).

A close relationship between human bones and human life (by no means limited to the Mongols) provides the rationale for the tibia symbolism. First, it lays the ground for symbolic identification of bone and patrilineal descent. Second, it makes it easy to adopt a sheep bone as the sign of descent, on the assumption that there is an argument for symbolic identification of sheep and man based on ritual substitution or economic dependence – the latter is evident while the former is possible.

Man is related to his ancestors by descent and symbolically by the concept of 'bone'. There is also a relation between man and sheep, both real and symbolic. The sheep's tibial bone is a material sign of the conceptual bone that symbolizes human descent, and both are linked with the mythological ancestors.

Notes

1   This chapter is a revised and extended version of a paper read at the 27th Meeting of the Permanent International Altaic Conference in Walderberg, Federal Republic of Germany, in 1984.
2   Some older women told me that they took small parts of this meat left over after meals. They did it out of curiosity when not watched and came to the conclusion that 'it was not a delicacy'.
3   The ends are hierarchically defined as the upper and lower ones; they are held respectively by the man and the woman.
4   These are morphologically indistinguishable.

References

Dan' . . . 1986. *Dan' xürel*. Alan Bator: Ulsyn Xevlel.
Evans-Pritchard, E. E. 1956. *Nuer religion*. Oxford: Clarendon Press.
de Heusch, L. 1985. *Sacrifice in Africa. A structuralist approach*. Manchester: Manchester University Press.
Kabzinska-Stawarz, I. 1985. Mongolian games of dice. Their symbolic and magic meaning. *Ethnologia Polona* **11**, 237–63.
Ksenofontov, G. V. 1977. *Elleida. Materialy po mifologii i legendarnoi istorii iakutov*. Moscow: Nauka.
Lévi-Strauss, C. 1949. *Les structures élémentaires de la parenté*. Paris: Presses Universitaires de France.
Mongol . . . 1982. *Mongol ardyn baatarlagyn tuul*. Ulan Bator: Shinzhlex Uxaany Akad.

7 Ecological community and species attributes in Yolngu religious symbolism

IAN KEEN

Introduction

Strehlow's (1970) apt expression 'geography of the totemic landscape' of an Australian Aboriginal people refers to the mapping on to land, and I would add, waters, of myths about Ancestral Spirit Beings, as well as related elements of ceremonies – songs, dances, designs, and sacred objects. Yolngu (northeast Arnhem Land Aboriginal) areas of land and water, and the related myths and elements of ceremonies are 'owned' or 'held' by patrilineal exogamous clans. These ceremony elements form a stock of programmes that can be drawn on and combined in many different ways to construct particular ritual performances (see e.g. Morphy 1984, Wild 1986). There is a close relationship of types of ceremony and their elements to topographical categories and ecological communities. This aspect of religious organization is illustrated in the first section of this chapter.

The Yolngu, like other Aboriginal peoples, draw on the attributes of species and other entities to construct worlds of Ancestral Beings with partly human attributes, and as potential analogues of events, processes, states, and relations. The second part of the chapter looks more closely at two particular ceremony elements to analyse the use of the attributes of species of living things for the construction of religious symbols.

The immediate inspiration for this kind of analysis is the work of Turner (1967), who shows how the Ndembu construct webs of analogy on the properties of natural kinds. It is Lévi-Strauss (1962) who reminds us just how crucial it is to understand the properties of natural species in order to grasp the point of a myth. I have drawn here on Rudder's (1977) studies of Yolngu ethnoclassification, as well as botanical and entomological sources, to look for attributes that are likely to be known and held relevant by the Yolngu.

Yolngu religion and social organization

Yolngu is now the generally accepted name for a population of about 3500 people living in northeast Arnhem Land, a peninsular region on the north coast of the Northern Territory of Australia. Other anthropologists have referred to these people as Murngin (Warner 1937), Wulamba (Berndt 1955) and 'Miwuyt' (Shapiro 1981). The culture of the Yolngu is somewhat distinct from that of their neighbours to the west and south; their languages form an enclave of suffixing languages in contrast to the prefixing languages of their neighbours; they employ an asymetric kinship terminology related to matrilateral cross-cousin marriage, in contrast to the Aranda-like systems of their neighbours; and the degree of polygyny is notably higher (Keen 1982). They are foragers, hunters, and fishers, their economies modified to a greater or lesser degree by life on settlements (former missions) of 700–1000 people or so, and more or less permanent smaller 'outstation' communities on traditional clan lands.

Myths and cryptic mythic statements encode beliefs about Ancestral Spirit Beings (*wangarr*), some of whom are believed to have created human groups, implanted the powers that ensure continued reproduction through spirit conception, created social institutions, and established the norms that govern them. The Beings travelled, foraged, camped, defecated or menstruated, copulated, and fought other Beings. Land and waters are conceived as redolent with the traces, substance, and powers of the Spirit Beings. The Yolngu believe that many transformed themselves into elements of the land or sea bed, such as bodies of rock or ochre; left marks such as a gully or creek; transformed their appurtenances, such as turning a digging stick into a tall tree; or live on in the deep waters, perhaps moving with the tide. Religious practices both describe and 'follow' the activities of the *wangarr*, and the objects and places associated with them, or which they created.

This religious 'law' (*rom*) is seen as a received and unchanging tradition that the older people transmit and hand on to younger people. The power of older men in particular derives from their apparent access to supernatural powers, as well as their control of secret religious knowledge to which men are gradually admitted, and from which women are largely excluded.

Yolngu ceremonies fall into three implicit sets, which I have labelled Public, Regional, and the Maḍayin revelatory ceremony (Keen 1978). Public (*garma*) ceremonies have a variety of purposes including circumcision initiation of males, disposal of the dead, purification, exchange, greetings and partings, dispute settlement, and simple entertainment. They are composed from a named series of *manikay* songs, which are classified topographically as forest, plains, saltwater, freshwater, swamp, beach and other series, as well as from related dances, painted designs, sand sculptures, and objects (see Warner 1937, Clunies Ross & Hiatt 1977, Keen 1978, Morphy 1984, Wild 1986). Each song series is related to a set of dances, designs, and objects. Each clan possesses several series, each of which it shares with several other clans of the same moiety, but the elements are distinct for each moiety. Clans of the same moiety also combine to endow the public ceremonies with proper names – the Exchange ceremonies and the Hollow Log reinterment ceremonies.

The regional ceremonies are a set of four ceremonies with proper names, belonging to Dhuwa moiety clans, related to the mythology centred on the Wa:gilak sisters, and include two circumcision ceremonies, and a revelatory ceremony. The Maḍayin ceremony is regarded as the most important revelatory ceremony, in the view of the men at least. In it, mature and old men of related clans of the same moiety make and show the *rangga* sacred objects, which represent aspects of certain *wangarr*, to younger men of their own and related clans, while men and women perform public dances that represent the reproduction of the population of the interrelated clans. Each moiety has a somewhat different Maḍayin ceremony, and each clan per-forms the ceremony in its own way.

Ceremony elements are closely related to places as well as groups. Myths describe events involving one or more of the Ancestral Spirit Beings, often with the names and attributes of nonhuman species, or entities such as water or a hollow log. The songs and ceremonies that the Ancestral Spirit Beings instituted by performing them 'follow' their precedent. Thus each song, design, and dance is related to a specific Being, the place or places where the event occurred, and the clan that possesses that country. The powers of a Being are also thought to be present in associated designs and, I believe, in names as well as places. Mythical journeys link the estates of several clans of the same moiety, which have similar ceremonies and ceremony elements, apparently as a consequence of the mythical events. Since the Beings have the attributes of species and other natural kinds, the songs and other elements that follow them are related to topographical categories and eco-logical communities, around which the categories of Beings and the cere-mony elements tend to cluster, as we shall see. Songs also describe species attributes, and dances are mimetic. The basic topographical categories with which species are associated are shown in Table 7.1. The main Yolngu categories of species according to Rudder (1977) are those shown in Table 7.2.

A Yirritja clan estate

In order to illustrate the mapping of ceremony elements on to topographical categories and ecological communities I will describe the estate and related myths of one Yirritja and one Dhuwa moiety clan.

Detjirimirri (not its real name), an area of forest, lagoons, swamps, and grass plains near the mouth of a major river, is the estate of Windbreak clan. Areas within the estate are denoted by 'big-names', each associated with a particular set of Spirit Beings and the related ceremony or ceremony elements. As Figure 7.1 indicates, the Spirit Beings cluster around particular topographical categories. Detjirimirri lagoon and its environs are related to the Djalumbu Hollow Log ceremony, including the Log itself, and Catfish (*A*) (letters refer to Figure 7.1). Nearby is a small lake (*B*) where Darter, associated with the Bullroarer dance for the Hollow Log ceremony, appears in the myth, and a little way to the south is the clearing in the forest which

Table 7.1 Yolngu topographical categories.

gapu monuk, monuk	salt water, sea
rangi, dhawaḏa	beach
barala	sand dunes
ḻarrtha, gathul	mangroves
mayang	creek, river
ṉinydjiya, dholu	tidal mud flats
milminydjarrk	freshwater springs through the salt flats and mangroves
gurrpulu	grass plains
gapu-guḻun	freshwater swamps
wayala	valley, boggy in wet season
ḏiltji	open forest, 'bush'
retja	monsoon liana forest, 'jungle'
gaykarrang	open country

Emu made in the myth. Emu is a subject of the Forest series of songs and dances, used in a variety of Public ceremonies, such as the Exchange ceremony and Wake, as well as the Hollow Log. Other subjects of the Forest songs, such as Koel, Possum, Sand Monitor, and Murayana Ghost, pertain to the forest near Detjirimirri lake. Black-headed Python is a major Spirit Being of the Windbreak clan, and is believed to lie at the creek to the south of the lake (*E*), as well as at the eastern Windbreak estate.

Snake-necked Tortoise *wangarr* 'lies inside' the area of swamp, wet-season lakes, and paperbark trees to the north of Detjirimirri (*G*). This area is also associated with the Swamp song-series, in which the Two Women, who lie beneath the camp mound by Detjirimirri lake (on which the present out-station camp stands), gathered lily bulbs.

In the northeast of the estate lies a cluster of lakes rich in fish, geese, pelican and other game, and in plant life. One of the lakes gives its name to the whole area (*I*). Two important *wangarr*, Dingo and Oxe-Eye Herring, related to sacred objects for the Maḏayin ceremony, belong to this area, which is a former ceremonial centre for both moieties. Some parts of the area consist of small Dhuwa moiety places, embedded in Yirritja estate. To the east of the lake at *I*, Rock *maḏayin* lies in a lake (*J*) where, according to tradition, Catfish *wangarr* swims round and round the Rock. Honeybee clan men perform the corresponding dance for the Hollow Log ceremony, and in circumcision ceremonies.

An area of tidal salt flats is shared with another Yirritja moiety clan whose estate lies to the north of Detjirimirri. There, according to the myth, the Dingo *wangarr* of the two clans quarrelled, and they agreed to go different ways (*K*). Dingo is the spirit ancestor of the clan, associated with the Maḏayin (or Ngairra) ceremony (see Thomson 1939).

This description shows that each Being or cluster of beings is associated with an ecologically discrete area, as well as a particular ceremony or ceremony element: the Hollow Log with Detjirimirri lagoon, the Forest

Table 7.2 Yolngu categories of plants and animals.

Plants	
mulmu	plants without a definite stem, including grasses, bulbs and some creepers
ngatha	vegetable foods, most of which are edible roots
ngatha	edible roots
mangutji ngatha	edible seeds
dharpa	plants with definite stems
dhakal	edible and inedible fruit of any of the above categories
Living creatures of the salt and fresh water	
maypal	edible invertebrates, including shellfish, crustaceans and larvae (except bee larvae)
maypal	molluscs
dhungalmirr maypal	invertebrates with hands
miyapunu	turtles, dugong and dolphins
ngarakamirr miyapunu	those with shells
balawalamirr miyapunu	those with twin-fluked tails
yinydjapana	dolphins
galanggamirr	dugong
mirinyingu	whale
maranydjalk	stingrays and sharks
guya	fish
rayinbuy guya	freshwater fish
monukbuy guya	saltwater fish
Living creatures of the land	
guku	bees and honey
warrakan	animals, birds and reptiles
warrakan butthunamirr	flying animals (including bats)
djikay	small flying animals
warrakan marrtjinyamirr	walking animals (includes the emu)
nyiknyik	small walking animals
warrakan gal'yunamirr	crawling animals
langlang	small crawling animals
warrakan djuryunamirr	slithering animals (snakes)
ba:pi	small slithering animals

Source: Rudder 1977.

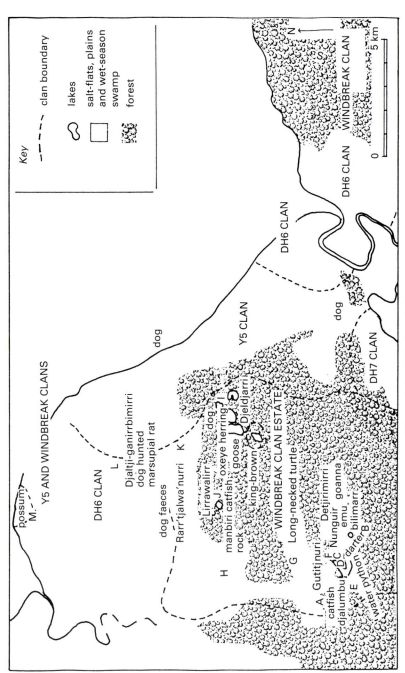

Figure 7.1 Windbreak clan estate.

Beings with the area of forest nearby, the Ancestral Snake-necked Tortoise with the swamp, and Dingo and Oxe-eye Herring with the place of the Maḍayin ceremony. The combination gives the clan access to all the major types of Yirritja moiety ceremony as well as a variety of resources. The myths about the journeys of these Beings link the estate and clan to other clans of the same moiety in a complex web.

A Dhuwa moiety clan estate

The Cloudy Water clan has estates on the mainland coast, and on an adjacent island. Its land is fringed by mangrove swamps, and includes tidal flats, freshwater swamps and grasslands, clumps of vine jungle, and extensive upland forest.

The clan's myths are about two sisters called Djang'kawu, a mature woman who has borne children (*gongman*), and a nubile girl (*wirrkul*). The clan's ceremonies centre on songs, dances, and other acts about these sisters. Its songs are of the *bilma* type, characterized by having no dronepipe accompaniment. The clan uses its songs and dances to construct Washing Purification, Wakes, Circumcisions, and the Maḍayin ceremony, to sing for the sick, and to greet. Related myths form the basis of the Maḍayin ceremony from the point of view of many clans, since all Dhuwa moiety clans with places deemed to have been created by the Sisters have rights in the ceremony.

In the myths and songs the Sisters travelled west, following the sun, along the coast of northeast Arnhem Land from an island of the dead off Gove Peninsula in the east, through the sea on a bark canoe or a raft made of a roll of paperbark (*djutu*), and on foot overland. Each woman carried two digging sticks or walking sticks (*dhona*) with which they gathered food, speared the ground to make freshwater springs, and paddled the canoe. They carried woven pandanus dilly bags, filled with *wana* ('arm') feathered cords – a species of *rangga* sacred object. As they travelled they saw and named places, animals, birds, fish and other creatures, and plants; bore the first clanspeople, named them, and gave them languages. At each clan's estate they created freshwater springs in the salt flats and mangroves, and on the beaches along the coast. The Sisters met other *wangarr* on the way, and they also met men who stole their dilly bag and sacred objects, forever depriving them and all women of the right to control the religious law. Some of their actions are believed to have resulted in or centred on permanent topographical features, especially rocks and trees (regarded as permanent, or perpetually replaced). These are equivalent to the *rangga*, implying that the *rangga* are permanent features of the land, and implying also that representations of them are permanently connected to the land. Special ḻikan names called out in ceremonies and ḻikan designs connote these connections. The word ḻikan denotes connected elements such as the branch and trunk of a tree, the limbs and torso, or the points of a crescent. They are 'connecting' names and designs.

Common to all episodes of the myth is the idea that the two sisters arrived at a clan estate, named the clan, put the sacred objects in the ground, and created a group. The central episode in the myth describes events at the Cloudy Water clan estate. In this episode *wangarr* men stole the dilly bag and sacred objects from the Sisters, with the result that men now have control of the Maḏayin ceremony and other rituals, and women became the workers, gathering food for the men. The myth thus justifies men's control of ceremonies: 'If men had not stolen the dilly bag,' the Cloudy Water clan leader remarked to me at the Maḏayin ceremony, 'the women would be dancing here, and we men would be sitting at the fire!'

The estate of the Cloudy Water clan on which its religious law centres lies adjacent to a large island, from which it is separated only by a narrow, tidal, mangrove-lined channel. The clan also possesses a small area on the adjacent island as well as the estate of an extinct clan, which is in a relation of 'mother's mother' to the Cloudy Water clan. The mainland estate, which I call here Wa:langura (a fictitious name), is centred on a dendritic pattern of mangrove-lined tidal creeks, which drain the surrounding salt flats, fresh-water plains and upland forest of the mainland and adjacent islands (Fig. 7.2). The total area of the Cloudy Water clan estate is in the region of 5000 ha. Two men, the leaders of the Cloudy Water clan and of a closely related clan, pointed out places at Wa:langura as the locations and results of events in the central episode of the Djang'kawu myth (letters refer to Fig. 7.2).

Trees are particularly significant in Yolngu symbolism, as we shall see. Several trees at Wa:langura were said to have been placed by the Djang-'kawu. Two are the 'shade' or 'image' (*mali*) of the Sisters' digging stick, and are called by any of the three names of the species *Exocarpus latifolia* (mistletoe tree), but used in this case as the proper names of a tree of a different species. An unusually tall cycad palm on the track north to the island estate of the clan is also said to be the 'shade' of the Sisters' digging/walking stick. According to the clan leader, the Sisters placed this one in the ground and carried others with them. Some trees represent the spirits of the dead: the trees near the Maḏayin ground represent the Bugunbungun (or Ma:tjarra) group, the category of all descendants of the Djang'kawu Sisters. Paperbark trees around one waterhole also represent the Ma:tjarra group, because, according to my instructors, when people die their spirits return to the water.

Certain places relate directly to the myth of the Djang'kawu Sisters. A tree called Bathi-ngal' marangala ('hung up the dilly bag') by lake G is the one in which the sisters hung up Guwilirr dilly bag, full of *maḏayin* objects (*A*). They collected crabs, shellfish, and mangrove worms at the nearby mangroves. On returning to the tree the Sisters found the bag gone, and heard the men playing the clapsticks, and performing the invocation. The Sisters realized that the men had taken the bag, but they could not get it back because they were unable to go into the men's 'inside' ceremony ground in the nearby forest (*B*); so they said: 'Never mind, we will do the work, and

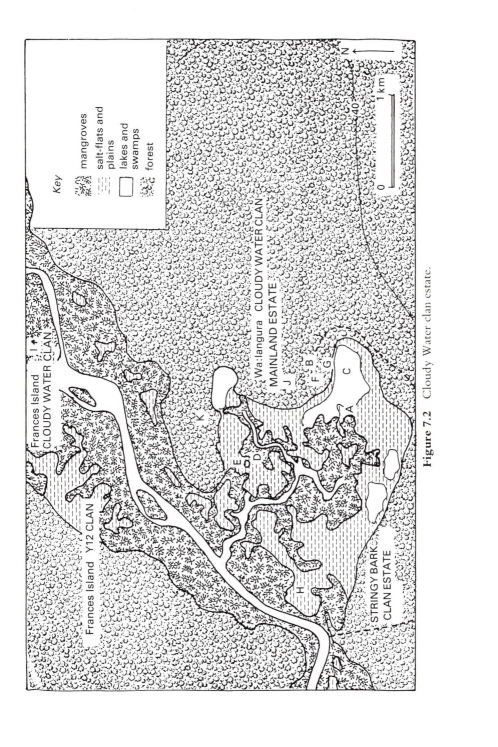

Figure 7.2 Cloudy Water clan estate.

the men can do the ceremonies.' Then the Sisters went to the lake (C) to collect longicorn beetle larvae which live in the rush corms. In the mangroves they speared springwaters with their digging/walking sticks, and made wells (E, F, and G). They menstruated into the water at G, and stones fell from their vaginas into the water. They also made a well on the west side of the estate, and said that the Stringy Bark clan could use it (H). Mudbanks and a landing – a gap in the mangroves – connect Wa:langura with the island estate. There, returning from Ambassador Island, the Djang'kawu landed, or it may have been the man Walawala, depending on the version of the myth (approximately at I on Fig. 7.2). Here the canoe sank to become a rock and a sacred object.

The clan's estate, then, is viewed as redolent with signs of the presence of the Ancestral Spirit Beings and spirits of the dead, but I must stress the apparent *immediacy* of these events in Yolngu discourse about the Beings. People will casually point out a feature and say something like 'that's where the Djang'kawu sat', as if it were sometime the year before.

Songs

The content of Cloudy Water clan songs, used during the Maḍayin and Public ceremonies, is closely related to that of the ceremonies. I recorded a song-series at a Washing Purification ceremony which the clan leader helped me to transcribe and translate, and on which he commented (Table 7.3). The series consisted of 30 songs, a number of them repeated several times, and each having about six verses or items. The order of songs varies with the type of ceremony and the performance.

People construe the songs as a journey through various topographical categories – through the sea to the mangroves, on to the salt flats and swamps, into the forest, back to the plains, swamps and lakes, and to the mangroves and sea. Table 7.3 shows the major topographical association of each song. People also conceive of the songs as a westward journey equivalent to that of the Djang'kawu from Burralku, a mythical island of the dead in the east, following the sun; or simply from Ambassador Island to the clan's mainland estate, just as in the myth. The Maḍayin ceremony, to which the songs relate, also traces a journey that partly overlaps that of the Djang'kawu from one Dhuwa clan country to another. People are thus able to construct journeys in song in ritual performances, perhaps in order to trace the route of an initiate or a deceased person to his or her clan estate (see Morphy 1984, Warner 1937).

This example indicates also that the Dhuwa Maḍayin ceremony of the Cloudy Water and other coastal clans is associated particularly with mangroves, especially where freshwater springs bubble up through the mud and saltwater at high tide, speared in Yolngu belief by the Djang'kawu with their digging sticks (see also Berndt 1955).

Table 7.3 Cloudy Water clan *bilma* song topics.

Sea	Freshwater lagoons
1 Garfish	20 Pied goose
2 Sea water	21 Pygmy goose
	22 Black-winged stilt
Mangroves	23 The Djang'kawu travel
3 Long Tom	24 Longicorn bettle larvae
4 Black butcher bird	25 Bustard
5 Little red flying fox	
6 *Gomuru* (shellfish)	Linking
	26 Black cockatoo
Linking	27 Red-collared lorikeet
7 Black cockatoo	28 Guwiḻirr dilly bag
8 The Djang'kawu travel	29 The Djang'kawu travel
Creeks and mangroves	Forest
9 Fresh and saltwater mix	30 Poison pea
10 Salmon catfish	31 The Djang'kawu travel
11 Black butcher bird	32 Honeybee (Yirritja)
12 Spangled gudgeon	33 Frilled lizard
13 Crabs and shellfish	34 Bush-bird (Yirritja)
Grass-plains	Grass-plains and lagoons
14 Longicorn bettle larvae	35 Spring waters
Lingking	Mangroves
15 The Djang'kawu travel	36 *Exocarpos latifolia* tree
	37 Black butcher bird
Salt-flats and grass-plains	38 Little red flying fox
16 Striped butterfish	39 The Ma:tjarra group
17 White ibis	
18 Masked plover	Sea
19 Brolga	40 Water – the tide comes in

Two elements of the Dhuwa Maḍayin ceremony

The Dhuwa moiety Maḍayin ceremony, like the equivalent Yirritja moiety ceremony, re-enacts the creation of closely related clans of the moiety, and represents the processes and relations necessary for their perpetuation. It depicts the creative acts of the *wangarr*, the spiritual powers and conception spirits that they left in the waters, and the relations of dependence between clans necessary for successful reproduction.

Before the ceremony begins, the Riyawarra, a small debarked tree, is planted at the camp of the organizer. This setting is a representation of the estates of all the Dhuwa moiety clans visited in the notional journey of the ceremony, especially that of the organizing clan where the journey ends.

Each clan's myth tells a similar story in which men stole the dilly bag full of sacred objects from the Djang'kawu, but centred on its own estate. The Riyawarra represents the tree in which the Sisters hung the dilly bag at each clan estate. At an 'inside' ground some hundreds of metres away from the camp, men's secret dances as well as the *rangga* sacred objects are revealed to male novices.

Each day the men paint their bodies at the Inside ground, and perform dances there in the late afternoon. They then march in dance through the camp to the Riyawarra tree, where women dance a representation of the Djang'kawu creating spring waters, creating groups, and putting sacred objects into the ground. The men chase the women away from the tree, representing the theft of the dilly bag, and then the leader climbs the tree to call the *Iikan* names of one Dhuwa clan and estate. The men dance by the tree enacting various species of fish that the Djang'kawu saw and named on their travels, and finally the men and women dance as Little Kingfisher, 'playing' by the tree. The fish dances appear to connote conception spirits implanted by the Djang'kawu. This daily sequence is repeated, with a different clan and estate called each day, thus tracing a journey from one clan estate to another, in part reproducing the journey of the Djang'kawu. The dances are varied on the final three days, introducing the themes of Fire, Thunderclouds, and finally, in the Longicorn Beetle Larvae dance, the birth of children to the participating Dhuwa clans. The ceremony ends with all the Dhuwa participants bathing in the sea, explicitly representing the unity of the groups.

Thus, in the ceremony, men dramatize their appropriation of powers from the *wangarr* as well as their control of male and female reproductive powers, enacting an ideology justifying present relations of control. Its content is adumbrated in a clan's Public ceremonies, including its songs, dances, and designs. In this way, a clan's law forms an integrated whole. This is structured so as to form a body of esoteric knowledge, encoded in songs and designs, to which only men are, by degrees, formally admitted.

The tree

The image of the tree is pervasive in the ceremony and, as we have seen, in the significance of the clan's estate. The tree signifies the permanent connection of the clan, its members, the spirits of the dead, and the *wangarr* to the country. We saw that the Djang'kawu are credited with planting trees of a variety of species at the clan estate. People insist that a tree planted by a *wangarr* stands eternally (*dha:rranhayngu*) in that place. If someone finds out that such a tree has fallen, he or she might point out a sapling and say that it is replacing the tree, an analogue of the succession of human generations. Other trees represent spirits of the dead, and one is the tree in which the Sisters hung up the lost dilly bag.

The Riyawarra tree is a public sign of trees planted by the *wangarr*, and so of the connection of the clan to the estate and the *wangarr*. The *rangga* is the esoteric sign that normally lies 'inside' the ground or the mud, its prototype also shaped and 'put in' by the *wangarr*. Regarded as tokens of transformations of the *wangarr* or of some appurtenance, such as their paperbark raft which sank, some have their equivalent in a rock in the creek, others in trees.

Rangga are modelled on the durable and less permanent parts of the remains of the human dead: bone and hair, fat and flesh. The red ochre painted wood, paperbark, stone or wax core is the 'bone' (*ngaraka*), and the string and red-breasted lorikeet feather windings are the 'flesh' (*nganak*) (see Berndt 1952, p. 7). Many represent quite specifically the bone of the *wangarr* (Warner 1937, p. 41). Moreover, the traces of some *wangarr*, such as rocks, are their 'bones', and places where the *rangga* lie are 'bone' countries. At the end of a ceremony the 'bone' of the *rangga* may be buried without its clothing of 'flesh', and some are buried with the human dead, especially *wana* cords, which are public equivalents of the *rangga*, and *likan* designs, painted on the coffin or the body, and which depict the *rangga*. The body symbolism is elaborated in the equivalence drawn between bone and tree. In the Hollow Log ceremony, the bones of the human dead are finally incorporated into a hollow version of the *rangga*, implying incorporation into the body of the *wangarr*.

We saw that the names of the tree species *Exocarpos latifolia* were applied as proper names to various trees at the clan estate. These names also apply to all the *rangga*, the Riyawarra Tree, the ritual Digging Stick representing the sticks that the Djang'kawu carried, and with which they speared the spring waters, and to the clan's Hollow Log for the reinterment ceremony. These elements are thus united by common proper names (cf. Warner 1937, p. 350, Berndt 1952, pp. 5, 50, 98, 114, 207).

The clan songs about the *Exocarpos latifolia* tree, and about Red–collared Lorikeet, Little Red Flying Fox, and Black Butcher Bird describe these animals sitting or hanging in the *E. latifolia* tree, 'noisy, full of game, feathered and fluffy'. Referring to the Little Red Flying Fox song, the Cloudy Water leader explained, 'Flying foxes hang in the tree, any tree, but whatever kind of tree it is, it is called [*E. latifolia*]'. He added that the meaning 'turns' to *E. latifolia*, and that the Djang'kawu said so; people did not make it up.

E. latifolia unites the transformations of the *wangarr*, Inside and Outside grounds, the setting and the clan country, secret and public, and all the signs of the relationship between the *wangarr*, the clan estate, the group, and the spirits of the dead. It also represents connections between the clans created by the same *wangarr*, for the Djang'kawu are said to have planted *E. latifolia* trees at each Dhuwa clan estate on their journey. Further, clans share many similar *rangga*, and unite for the *Madayin* ceremony.

Why is that particular species are chosen as the unifying proper name? *E. latifolia* is a semiparasitic shrub or small tree that flowers in the dry season, bearing an edible red fruit. The plant grows from the roots and sometimes from the branches of a wide variety of trees in a wide variety of habitats – coastal dunes, river banks, sandstone gullies, woodland, open woodland, and rainforest (Rudder 1977, Henson & George 1984, p. 24). It appears to have been chosen, then, just for its quality of attachment to a variety of trees, just as its name attaches as a proper name to a variety of types, and especially for its attachment to the roots of other trees, for roots are an analogue of the attachment of persons to land in Yolngu discourse. The semiotic use of its name follows its actual characteristics. It has been chosen for its interconnecting quality, drawing together the various habitats that might be found within a clan's estate, and the trees found in those habitats. The species is also very widely distributed across the north of the Northern Territory, so connecting groups belonging to different localities over a wide area. The red colour is appropriate to the Dhuwa moiety; Yirritja symbols are predominantly yellow. And finally it is one of the food plants utilized by several 'flying animal' species represented in the ceremony.

The concrete properties of the species are thus drawn on analogically for the application of its names as proper names to a variety of entities including trees believed to have been planted by the *wangarr*, and sacred object types believed to have been instituted by them. These and other constructs are articulated in complex analogical relations within which, among other things, the person and the body are likened to the tree, *rangga*, and Ancestral Spirit Being. *E. latifolia* is used as an 'elaborating' symbol (Ortner 1975, p. 1342) in which the connotations are overt rather than covert, explicitly constituted through a root simile or analogue. The Yolngu express this analogical relation as the 'turning' of 'meaning' (*mayali*), but consistent with a regime of traditional authority, they deny the role of the human intellect in this, and attribute origin of the device to the *wangarr*.

Birth of children to the clans

The last day's dances appear to signify the completion of the creative and reproductive processes. The men dance as the *wangarr* on their creative journey, adorned with the Kingfisher design. Two women portray the Djang'kawu Sisters at the Tree, while other women dance as Longicorn Beetles emerging as children born to the clans. Women lie on the ground under blankets or *ngaṉmarra* mats by the Riyawarra Tree. the male dancers perform the Kingfisher dance from the Inside ground to the camp, representing the Djang'kawu on their creative journey. Then the men dancers and the two women who dance as the Djang'kawu dig near recumbent women who wriggle about under the blankets or mats to represent Longicorn Beetle Larvae in the rush corms. As the leader calls the *ḻikan* names of the clans represented by the women, and the men call the *marrawinydjun* chorus, associated with the incoming tide, the women rise clan by clan to dance 'Longicorn Bettles fly', explicitly signifying the birth of children to the clans.

In the related song, the Longicorn Beetle Larvae eat powerfully from the inside of the mangrove trees to the outside. The Sisters dig out Larvae from the trees, then the songs move via the forest (Poison Pea and Little Red Flying Fox songs) to the plains and lakes where, in the Longicorn Bettle Larvae song, the Sisters dig these grubs out from rush corms in the lake. The Larvae eat the rush corms in the mud, move, grow feet and wings, and fly. In his commentary the Cloudy Water clan leader said that the Larvae are *gutharra* (DC, woman speaking, ZDC) and are people. A repetition of this song later in the series describes the Longicorn Beetles, which emerged as a 'group of brothers flying west' towards the sunset. The leader commented: 'The Larvae change their bodies and grow wings. They "turn", that is to say, they are born like children.' In this version of the song, people with the clan *likan* name Walawala collect the Larvae. What is striking in the symbolism here is the connection of analogues of children of the clan with the mud in which the *rangga* lie (in another song), as well as their emergence from within the tree, signifying the spirits of the dead, and the connection with the *wangarr* and estate.

According to Rudder (1977), the taxon *ga:murung* (cerambycids, longicorn beetle larvae) belongs to the more inclusive class of *maypal gongmirr* – 'invertebrates with hands'. The Yolngu associate *ga:murung* with a wide variety of habitats, including freshwater billabongs, timber, and termite mounds, and evaluate it as a very delicious food. Duffy (1963, p. 609) notes that the larvae of some cerambycids live in the stems of herbaceous plants, and others feed in roots.

The Longicorn Beetle dance has movements reminiscent of the Charleston and is unfailingly the object of great hilarity in participants and onlookers. It is identical to the daily Kingfisher dance at the Riyawarra Tree. Little Kingfisher represents the Ma:tjarra category of people descended from the Djang'kawu, but also has attributes that connote the Djang'kawu themselves – a tendency to forage in pairs with the larger azure kingfisher, the habit of catching fish and larvae with a beaklike digging stick. Thus, in the one dance movement are united *wangarr*, group, and children born to the group. In this way the ceremony moves through the end of the dry season, with Fire, Lightning, and Thunderclouds, to the image of the emergence of the clan's children associated with the coming of the monsoon, at a time of general fecundity.

Conclusions

In this chapter I have shown, first, how Ancestral Spirit Beings, myths, songs, and genres of ceremonies are mapped on to discrete ecological zones, and second, some of the ways in which the Yolngu draw on species attributes in their complex religious symbolism. Let me conclude by drawing these two aspects together.

Several scholars have recently drawn attention to the ubiquitous Aboriginal expression 'the same but different', which is current in North Australia (e.g. Taylor 1987). It is an expression that sums up a particular form of social relationship that is an elaboration of the relationship of similarity, difference, and interdependence that Radcliffe-Brown (1977) labelled 'opposition'. Radcliffe-Brown asked why people of southeast Australia chose the bird species of eaglehawk and crow to represent the two moieties. His answer was that the species were the same in being birds, yet were distinct species. More than that, these particular species were interdependent – the eaglehawk was a hunter, the crow a scavenger. The relationship of the birds represented the relationship of difference, homology, and interdependence between the two intermarrying matrilineal exogamous moieties that Radcliffe-Brown called opposition, 'a combination of agreement and disagreement, of solidarity and difference' (1977, p. 67). In the relation of 'same but different'; people combine into sets at once affirming their unity and asserting internal differences, but the union is contextual and relative.

Yolngu people say that several groups are all 'one' (*wanggany*) or 'conjoint' (*dha:manapanamirri*), yet each is distinct (*ga:na*). This relation of same/different characterizes both the joining together of the various parts of a clan's religious law, associated as they are with different kinds of country (and in some cases distinct subgroups hold separate estates), and the religious law of different clans with the same kind of ceremony and shared Ancestral Spirit Beings. The unity of a clan's countries and ceremonies is contextual in the sense that members of other clans may lay claim to primary rights in some part of the set, challenging the unity asserted by members of the clan in question. The relation of one clan to others is contextual in several senses. First, one clan may assert its unity with others, but some of those others deny it. Second, the set of clans is relative and open. From the point of view of B the other members are A, C, and D. But from the point of view of D, the salient members are B, C, and F. Third, in the context of one ceremony or of another concern, members of a clan may assert their membership of one set, but in another context they will stress relations with a distinct set, each associated with different *wangarr* and ceremonies. For example, the Windbreak clan's Hollow Log ceremony and Forest songs of the Emu link it to the Spear Grass, Honeybee and other clans with rights in similar myths, designs, and ceremonies. However, it is related to Dingo and Magpie Goose clans through its Dingo places and sacred objects, for these clans share similar forms.

The tree symbolism outlined in the second half of this chapter is central in both these dimensions of cohesion. Sacred objects from each genre of ceremony that a clan owns are conceived as transformations of the focal tree symbol. Not only are several varieties of tree in the Cloudy Water clan estate identified as *E. latifolia*, but, as we have seen, the various *rangga* for the Madayin ceremony, the Ancestral digging stick (*dhona*) used in public ceremonies such as purifications, the Riyawarra Tree in the public part of the Nga:rra ceremony, and the Hollow Log coffin employed in secondary burial, all are identified as the *E. latifolia* tree.

The tree symbol also unites the Cloudy Water clan to other clans at various levels of generality, while signifying its distinctiveness and its local ties. The imagery is clear. The tree is literally rooted to the spot, anchored to place. At the same time it is equivalent to the focal tree belonging to other clans with the same *wangarr*. Furthermore, the *wangarr* associated with it, including the Djang'kawu Sisters, Water Goanna, and Red-collared Lorikeet, link each clan through their travels. In the Nga:rra ceremony a conceptual journey is traced from clan country to clan country, 'visiting' each clan's estate in ceremony, in part following the journey of the Djang-'kawu Sisters. The Riyawarra Tree, a forked branch standing in the public camp as the focus of daily dances, signifies the tree at each clan's country in turn. In the ceremony, the Water Goanna visits each place from the water and climbs the tree. The ceremony re-enacts the event at each country in which the Djang'kawu Sisters hung up their dilly bag, lost the sacred objects into the possession of men, and created spring waters and people.[1]

The clans which join to perform the Madayin ceremony are ideally related in a special way which is alluded to in interpretations of the dance in which Longicorn Beetles emerge. The Dhuwa moiety clans which cooperate are ideally in a relation of mother's mother to woman's daughter's child, which is a relation not only of matrilineal descent but also of bestowal relations. A man finds his wife's mother in the clan of a mother's mother. The birth of children to the clans, which the dance celebrates, depends on these relations of reproduction within the same moiety. The dance signifies the birth of children to all the participating Dhuwa moiety clans in turn, demonstrating their interdependence while signifying their distinct identities.[2]

Acknowledgement

I am grateful to Lyndall Plant of the Queensland Forestry Department for help with the identification of beetles.

Notes

1 Whereas the species *E. latifolia* is focal also for other clans of the Dhuwa moiety with the Djang'kawu as ancestors, other sets of clans employ distinct species. For Dhuwa clans in whose mythology the Wagilak Sisters are important, the stringy bark tree (*Eucalyptus tetradonta*) is central, while for some Yirritja moiety clans a species of large paperbark takes the same role.
2 A man looks to a woman of the MMBD category as a potential wife's mother. She will be a member of a patrilineal clan which the man classifies as a 'mother's mother' clan, for it will include people who are his 'mother's mothers' and 'mother's mother's brothers' (*ma:ri*).

References

Berndt, R. M. 1952. *Djanggawuli: an Aboriginal religious cult of north-east Arnhem Land*. London: Routledge & Kegan Paul.

Berndt, R. M. 1955. 'Murngin' (Wulamba) social organization. *American Anthropologist* **57**(1), 84–106.

Clunies Ross, M. and L. R. Hiatt 1977. Sand sculptures at a Gidjingali burial rite. *Form in indigenous art*, P. J. Ucko (ed.), 131–46. Canberra: Australian Institute of Aboriginal Studies.

Duffy, E. A. J. 1963, *A monograph of the immature stages of Australian timber beetles*. London: British Museum.

Henson, H. and A. S. George 1984. *Flora of Australia*. Vol. 22. Canberra: Bureau of Flora and Fauna, Australian Government Publishing Service.

Keen, I. 1978. One ceremony, one song: an economy of religious knowledge among the Yolngu of northeast Arnhem Land. Ph.D. thesis, Australian National University.

Keen, I. 1982. How some Murngin men marry ten wives: the marital implications of cross-cousin structures. *Man* **17**, 620–42.

LeCron Foster, M. 1980. The growth of symbolism in culture. In *Symbol as sense: new approaches to the analysis of meaning*, M. LeCron Foster & S. H. Brandeis (eds).

Lévi–Strauss, C. 1962. *The savage mind*. London: Weidenfeld & Nicolson.

Morphy, H. 1984. *Journey to the crocodile's nest: an accompanying monograph to the film 'Maḏarrpa funeral at Gurka'wuy'*. Canberra: Australian Institute of Aboriginal Studies.

Ortner, S. B. 1975. On key symbols. *American Anthropologist* **75**, 1338–46.

Radcliffe-Brown, A. R. 1977. The comparative method in social anthropology. In *The social anthropology of Radcliffe-Brown*, A. Kupor (ed.), 53–69. London: Routledge & Kegan Paul.

Rudder, J. 1977. *An Introduction to Yolngu science*. Galiwinku, Northern Territory: Galiwinku Adult Education Centre.

Shapiro, W. 1981. *Miwuyt marriage: the cultural anthropology of affinity in northeast Arnhem Land*. Philadelphia: ISHI.

Strehlow, T. 1970. Geography and the totemic landscape in Central Australia: a functional study. In *Australian Aboriginal anthropology*, R. M. Berndt (ed.), 92–140. Canberra: Australian Institute of Aboriginal Studies.

Taylor, L. 1987. The same but different: social reproduction and innovation in the art of the Kunwinjku of Western Arnhem Land. Unpublished PhD thesis, Australian National University, Canberra.

Thomson, D. 1939. Proof of Indonesian influence upon the Aborigines of north Australia: the remarkable dog Ngarra of the Mildjingi clan. *Illustrated London News* **12** (August), 277–9.

Turner, V. 1967. *The forest of symbols: aspects of Ndembu ritual*. Ithaca, NY: Cornell University Press.

Warner, W. L. 1937. *A black civilization: a social study of an Australian tribe*. New York: Harper.

Wild, S. (ed.) 1986. *Rom: an Aboriginal ritual of diplomacy*. Canberra: Australian Institute of Aboriginal Studies.

8 Pictish animal symbols

ANTHONY JACKSON

In the 7th century AD a remarkable development occurred in Pictland: suddenly – just before AD 685 when the Pictish king Bridel defeated the Northumbrians at the battle of Nechtansmere – gracefully designed incised carvings appeared on some 200 standing stones (Fig. 8.1). Their similar designs indicate a common source and purpose, as does their location: almost without exception at springs, riversides, and on seashores. Yet they occurred all over Pictland – from Shetland to Fife – in a short space of time. There are no art historical precedents for these Pictish designs and there is no obvious reason why they were placed on standing stones. Nor are there any historical records that refer to their purpose.

During the 8th century there was some development of these designs. They were now sculpted in relief, with the addition of the Christian cross (Fig. 8.2). These carvings continued into the 9th century. By the time the Scots king Kenneth McAlpin took over in AD 843 the special Pictish designs had disappeared, together with the independent Pictish kingdom. Although these Pictish designs have also been found on rock faces, cave walls, and on bone, stone, and metal artefacts (Allen & Anderson 1903), these versions are in the minority. Moreover, because they only show single designs they are considered to have a different purpose to the carvings on standing stones.

By 1903 some 50 different designs attributed to the Picts had been detected on various stones (Allen & Anderson 1903). Geometric and animal designs have been distinguished (Fig. 8.3) and have been tentatively assigned, respectively, to the Northern and Southern Picts, since geometric designs are found more frequently in the north while two-thirds of the animal designs are in the south, below the Moray Firth.

In the context of 250 carved Pictish stones bearing one or more of the 50 designs, this chapter examines designs that had a special symbolic function in Pictish society. A symbol, as defined here, is a design that has a meaning over and above its physical appearance. One cannot simply equate a design with a symbol, and the criterion adopted here to distinguish them is that a Pictish *symbol* can be identified when any design combines more than once with another design to form a pair. Most of the engraved stones do in fact have such pairings. This criterion gives us a working total of 28 symbols (see Fig. 8.4) on 200 stones.[1]

The symbolic pairing of two designs may be related to the assumption that the stones were erected to commemorate a political alliance between two different Pictish lineages. Such alliances would, of course, have occurred long before AD 685 and long after the amalgamation of lineages from

Figure 8.1 Pictish standing stones, 7th century. Class 1: (a) Strathpeffer, (b) Inveravon, (c) Insch, (d) Drimmies, (e, f) Kintore.

Figure 8.2 Pictish standing stones, 8th century. Class 2: (a) Aberlemno, (b) Meigle, (c) Meigle, (d) Glamis, (e) Logierait.

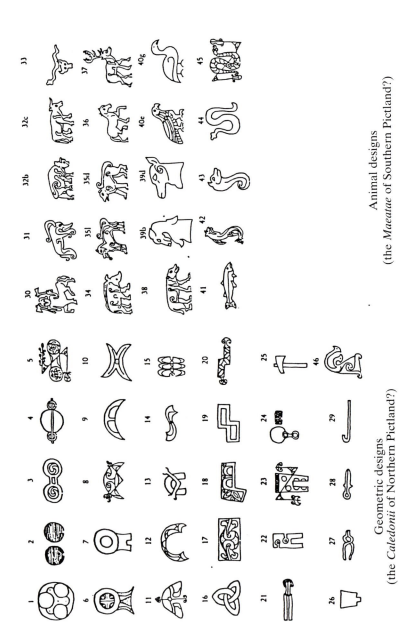

Geometric designs
(the *Caledonii* of Northern Pictland?)

Animal designs
(the *Maeatae* of Southern Pictland?)

Figure 8.3 The Pictish designs: geometric (Northern) and animal (Southern).

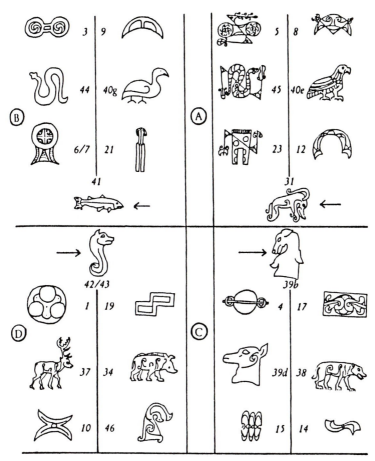

Figure 8.4   The basic 28 symbols arranged in four sets of seven.

north and south, and before stone symbols came into use. Bede suggests that the Picts were matrilineal; the Pictish king-lists strongly support this assertion and lend credence to a prescribed form of marriage. Technically, therefore, the Picts were matrilineal (descent went through the female line) and they may well have practised patrilateral cross-cousin marriage (a man married his father's sister's daughter). Symbol 24 (mirror with comb) (Fig. 8.3) is taken to denote the giving of bridewealth by chiefly families to the families of the brides (Jackson 1984, 1989). Some symbol stones have both mirror with comb while others have only a mirror. It is suggested that this could denote a difference in status between a full chief and a lesser chief. Furthermore it is postulated here that symbols were declarations of mystical powers acting as assertions of superiority by one lineage over another.

If we have four lineages *P*, *Q*, *R*, and *S* in a group and they marry correctly, where $\star$ = mirror with comb (full chief); + = mirror (lesser chief) then if *Q* and *S* are the politically leading lineages we would get:

$$\text{Superior} \qquad S+ \ Q\star$$
$$\text{Inferior} \qquad P \quad R$$

The resulting marriage arrangement between lineages would result in the generation of eight symbol stones to record these alliances and the group would have one each of the eight symbol pairs: *S/P*, *P/S*+, *S/R*, *R/S*+, *Q/P*, *P/Q*$\star$, *Q/R*, *R/Q*$\star$ inscribed on each stone. Note that *S* and *Q* do not combine; neither do *P* and *R*, since they are both equal in status. It will be seen that the + and $\star$ only occur when either the chiefly lineages *S* and *Q* are literally at the bottom of a pair of symbols. The objective in giving bride-wealth (symbol 24, i.e. mirror with comb) would be to retain the intrinsic chiefly superiority of *S* and *Q* when they receive brides from lineages *P* and *R*, who stand above them socially as wife-givers in the paired symbols. It is estimated that a total of 48 such groups could have existed and that a maximum of 364 stones might have been erected.

This chapter focuses only on animal symbols, and the first questions that arise are why animals at all, and why certain animals rather than others were chosen to represent the postulated mystical powers. In order to try to answer these questions the basic roots of Pictish thinking need to be considered. What follows is necessarily an imaginative rationale for the choice of 16 animal designs by the Picts, since there is no existing evidence to explain why animals should ever have figured in this assemblage of symbol stones. It would have been perfectly possible for the Picts to have devised a system based only on geometric symbols. What must give us pause in treating these animal symbols simply as realistic representations is the depiction of some mythical animals: the deer's head (Fig. 8.4, 39d), 'elephant' (Fig. 8.4, 31), and 'beast' (Fig. 8.4, 39b) besides the serpent and Z-rod (Fig. 8.4, 45) – frequently occurring symbols that indicate that these were no simple artistic representations of real animals with real functions. It can be assumed that the true purpose of *all* the animal symbols was the same as for the geometric symbols: a mystical one. Pictish symbols are not works of 'art', engraved for their own sake, but appear in a stereotyped form that is uniform throughout the length and breadth of Pictland. This constancy of form of each symbol is remarkable considering the distances and the short time-span involved. By subjecting the total number of 16 Pictish animal designs to various binary oppositional analyses it is clear that they fall into quite distinct clusters that cannot be purely arbitrary.

The nature–culture dimension

The Picts were a tribal society and we may assume they were dualistic in their thought, as is evidenced historically by the early division of Pictland

Table 8.1 Binary oppositions.[2]

Left	Right	
South	North	
Sun	Moon	
Heavens (sky)	Earth	Physical
Rain (clouds)	Rivers	features
Sea	Lakes	
Forest	Open arable land	
Inedible	*Edible*	
Unbounded	*Bounded*	
Nature	*Culture*	
Wild	Controlled	
Anomalous	Classified	
Odd	Even	
Bad	Good	Moral
Unlucky	Lucky	values
Illness	Health	
Sterility	Fertility	
Death	Life	
Mythical	*Profane*	
Female	Male	
Wife-receivers	Wife-givers	
Incest	Marriage (with FZD)	
Ancestors	Magic	
Witchcraft	Divination	
Mystical power	Political power	
Junior	Senior	Society
Subject	Chief	
Gift-receiver	Gift-giver	
Animal symbol	Geometric symbol	
Z-rod	V-rod	
Hunting	Cattle-keeping	

into two kingdoms and later into seven provinces each of which had double names that still persist, such as Angus and the Mearns, and Moray and Ross. Apart from the pairs of symbols on the stones, there are similarities between symbols (cf. Fig. 8.4, 3v5, 9v8, 44v45, 40gv40e). A feature of many tribal societies is that they divide their conceptual universe into two halves that may be characterized by aspects that are natural and those that are cultural or man-made. Table 8.1 is a suggested division of the Pictish world.

The important dimensions of binary opposition may be seen as follows:

    (a)   nature/culture: unbounded/bounded
    (b)   mythical/profane: inedible/edible
    (c)   wild/controlled: left/right

If the Pictish ecosystems were bounded by the four naturally occurring conditions of land, forest, water, and sky then there would be four main ecosystems that they exploited and these lay at the following boundaries:

(a) *land/forest; land/water; land/sky*
(b) (forest/water; forest/sky)
(c) *water/sky*

Note that option (b) does not constitute a viable environment for economic exploitation.

There are also some correlations between these natural conditions for social existence and ancient European views about the basic composition of matter:

(a) four basic elements: earth, air, fire, and water
(b) four ecosystem conditions: land, sky, forest, and water

The only debatable parallel is fire = forest.

From an analytical point of view, these Pictish ecosystems were framed by the fourfold boundaries: (a) open arable land/forest, (b) land/water (riverine or seashore), (c) land/sky, (d) water (loch or sea)/sky. In terms of activities these systems can be seen as providing the means for (a) hunting, (b) settlement, (c) agriculture/pastoralism, and (d) fishing. It will be argued that the 16 animal designs used by the Picts were closely associated with the four ecosystems. These associations are not simply by animal habitat alone, for cutting across these are two more dimensions: (a) a division of animals into four categories: inedible/edible, mythical/profane; (b) a dualistic division between left and right, as indicated in Table 8.2. In each of the two sets of four inedible and edible species shown in Table 8.2, each species occurs, in nature, in a different ecosystem:

forest (wolf and boar)	open land (serpent and stag)
sky (sea eagle and goose)	water (sea horse and salmon)

It is possible to distinguish between two different types of water which, in view of the known Pictish and general Celtic concern with water, may have been associated with both the mythical, and some actual, animal symbols:

(a) sky-bounded water   – *rain* – elephant (salmon)
                          – *lochs/seas* – deer's head (stag)
(b) land-bounded water   – *rivers* – beast's head (sea horse)
                          – *springs* – serpent with Z-rod (serpent)

Yet another binary opposition may be relevant to the question of why only 12 animals figure in this symbolism:

the forest	open land
hunting people	*cattle-keeping people*

Perhaps the Southern Picts had been basically hunter-gatherers while the Northerners were pastoralists. This could explain why the profane designs:

Table 8.2 Left and right dualism

		Left	Right
(a)	Inedible	wolf	serpent
		sea eagle	sea horse
(b)	Edible	boar	stag
		goose	salmon
(c)	Mythical	beast's head	elephant
		serpent with Z-rod	deer's head
(d)	Profane	dog	horse
		bull	cow

dog, horse, cow, and bull were *not* incorporated as symbols when the two symbolic systems were finally united under the aegis of the North in AD 685.

The actual 12 animal symbols fall into the following categories:

mythic	*left*	*right*	*profane*
elephant	goose	salmon	edible
deer's head	boar	serpent	edible
beast's head	sea eagle	sea horse	inedible
serpent with Z-rod	wolf	serpent	inedible

In terms of the fourfold division of the Pictish world, the mythical animals also relate to the associated pairs of animals in the following way:

elephant	*water/sky*	salmon/goose
deer's head	*open land/forest*	stag/boar
beast's head	*water/sky*	sea horse/sea eagle
serpent with Z-rod	*open land/forest*	serpent/wolf

Hence the elephant and beast's head are related to water/sky while the deer's head and serpent with Z-rod relate to open land/forest. This relationship may be clarified by considering what is meant by the term 'open'.

open water	water/sky interface
open land	land/forest interface

The interface can simply be defined as the visible boundary: where openness ends. In terms of boundedness this would be:

unbounded	*bounded*
sea	rivers/seashore
forest	clearings
nature	*culture*

These binary oppositions can be put in diagrammatic form:

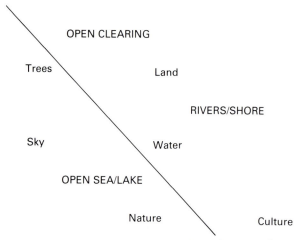

This diagrammatic division serves to reintroduce the animals since they are closely related to these binary oppositions.

forest	*open land*	*mythical*
wolf	serpent	serpent with Z-rod
boar	stag	deer's head

sky	*water*	*mythical*
sea eagle	sea horse	beast's head
goose	salmon	elephant

The mythical animals are more closely associated with open land and water animals than with those of the forest and sky. In other words, these mythical animals on the right-hand side are associated with possible human habitations at the land and water interface on agricultural clearings, along rivers, and by the seashores.

The edible species also seem to be linked to two of these mythical agencies and 'profane' species:

elephant	salmon	goose	(cow)
deer's head	stag	boar	(bull)

The inedible species are, then, linked with the other two mythical agents and 'profane' species:

beast's head	sea horse	sea eagle	(horse)
serpent with Z-rod	serpent	wolf	(dog)

The four animal designs that are *not* symbols are the profane ones, that is, domesticated animals.

Hence, the following division arises between the four mythical animals:

	nature	*culture*
water	beast's head	elephant
land	serpent with Z-rod	deer's head

Quadripartition

It can be seen that symbol designs readily fall into groups of four. In the case of the alliance groups, four lineages would have been involved. This common factor of quadripartition is readily found throughout Pictish cosmology.

If the basic 28 Pictish symbols are considered, these can be arranged in four sets of seven (Fig. 8.4). The sets A, B, C, and D represent, in decreasing order of frequency, the actual frequencies of symbols on the symbol stones. These 28 symbols represent 99 per cent of all the designs that fulfil the definition of a symbol adopted in this chapter. The symbols in sets A and B are actually present in 98 per cent of all symbol pairs, and sets C and D therefore only play a subsidiary role in symbolic combinations.

The common pattern to all four sets in Figure 8.4 is:

geometric	geometric
animal	animal
geometric	geometric

animal

It follows that with a ratio of 4:3 there will be just 16 geometric symbols to 12 animal symbols in a group of 28 symbols.

Another feature of Pictish thought is the common occurrence of sets of seven and hence this total of 28 symbols would not be surprising. To obtain parity between animal and geometric symbols it would be necessary to add four more animal symbols, but those most likely to become symbols would be the four domesticated animals – dog, horse, cow, and bull – that never combine with any other design and hence cannot be admitted to the canon.

Twelve animal symbols and 16 geometric symbols would have existed when the Northern (geometric) Picts subdued the Southern (animal) Picts in a grand alliance of just 28 symbols. This must have represented a compromise. Given the importance of the number 7, there is no way in which animal and geometric symbols could be equal in number when they are divided into four identical and corresponding sets of seven symbols (Fig. 8.4).

Other aspects of Pictish quadripartition (Jackson 1984) are: (a) the division of the calendrical year into quarters; (b) the four generations of kingly succession from four royal lineages; and (c) the four kingdoms of the Picts which are each subdivided into four pairs of alliance groups.

Quadripartition lends itself to even further subdivision and to groups of

Figure 8.5   Sixteen animal designs.

16. This is illustrated in Figure 8.5: 16 animal designs; Figure 8.6: 16 geometric symbols; Figure 8.7: 16 animal and geometric symbols; Figure 8.8: 16 divisions of the Pictish calendar. It may be no coincidence that there are just 16 animal designs and 16 geometric symbols but only 28 basic symbols. The number 28 can be connected to the lunar cycle but also to the yearly solar calendar of 28 days $\times$ 13 lunar cycles = 364 days of 4×49 days $+ 4 \times 42$ days (Fig. 8.8). It is suggested that the solar year may have been instrumental in limiting the number of Pictish symbols because the mystical powers associated with them were associated with certain rites that governed the total wellbeing of Pictish society. The various skeins of this argument are set out below, and are almost entirely speculative.

In Figure 8.5 all the animal designs have been arranged around a 16-point circle such that the four main vertical and horizontal cardinal divisors are opposite each other, yet related in the same way as already discussed for Figure 8.4. The circle's subcardinal designs are also paired likewise against their opposite numbers in Figure 8.4. In terms of the *medial* symbols in

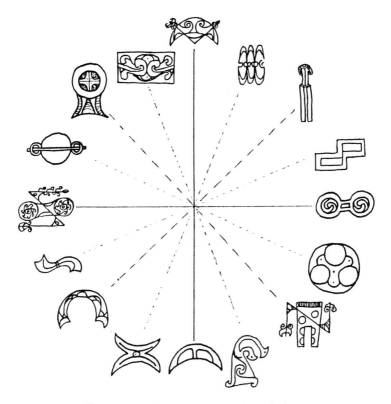

Figure 8.6 Sixteen geometrical symbols.

Figure 8.4, the four major animals are the vertical pair: elephant (31) and beast's head (39b), and the NW/SE pair sea horse (42/43) and salmon (41) (see Fig. 8.5). These four are later regrouped in the SE quadrant in Figure 8.7. It will be seen that all the *intermediate* designs in the lower semicircle beneath the NW/SE diagonal in Figure 8.5 are profane or non-symbolic designs (dog, horse, cow, bull).

In terms of the mythical agents in Figure 8.5, only the elephant is again in the same position in Figure 8.7; two others are in the SE quadrant together with the salmon. In other words, the water element has increased in importance in the final analysis when half the animal designs have had to be rejected. Those omitted are the wild and domesticated quadrupeds.

The suggested arrangement of the 16 geometric symbols is not so straightforward, as only the opposing four cardinal points (N, S, E, and W) are really similar in basic design (Fig. 8.6). There are similarities between the other opposing symbols, but they are not as clear-cut.

Thus the arrangement of eight geometric and eight animal symbols in

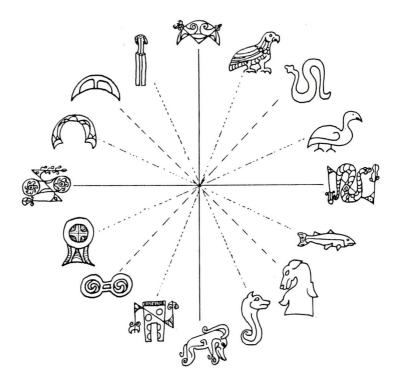

Figure 8.7   Sixteen animal and geometrical symbols.

Figure 8.7 could have been based on the notion of alternating and similar pairs: eagle/goose; serpent/serpent with Z-rod; crescent/crescent with V-rod; double disc/double disc with Z-rod, etc. They include all the 14 symbols in the statistically dominant sets A and B plus two of the main medial symbols. It is therefore suggested that these 16 symbols governed the holding of important calendrical festivals throughout the year.

In Figure 8.7 the SE quadrant is filled with the four animal mediating symbols (cf. Fig. 8.4: 41, 31, 42/3, 39b) while, correspondingly, the NW quadrant should therefore fulfil equivalent meaning(s) – *viz.* Figure 8.4: 8, 21, 9, 12, that is, all the geometric symbols *on the right hand sides* (RHS) of sets A and B. The SW quadrant has all the geometric symbols from *the left hand side* (LHS) of sets A and B (Figure 8.4: 5, 6/7, 3, 23) while the NE quadrant contains the rest of the animal symbols in sets A and B (Figure 8.4: 45, 40g, 44, 40e).

Hence, in terms of the RHS and LHS and Medial parts of sets A and B (Fig. 8.4), the symbols in Figure 8.7 fall into their respective quadrants as follows:

RHS	RHS & LHS
LHS	MEDIAL (RHS & LHS)
Geometric	Animal

The overall symmetry is thus retained from Figure 8.4 but is converted into a circular form that invites comparison with a circular calendar (Fig. 8.8). The underlying feature is the 16-fold division of the calendar since this

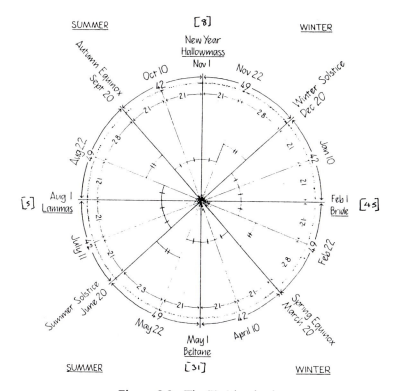

Figure 8.8 The Pictish calendar.

corresponds to the 16 animal and geometric designs. This might suggest that each symbol (lineage) had specific and equal periods of the year to celebrate their rites on behalf of the whole society. Pictish animal symbols can, of course, only be understood in terms of all the 28 symbols that were engraved on stones in the 7th and 8th centuries AD. The symbols were not single-acting but were combined in a regular way with other symbols according to a pattern that reflected marriages and political alliances. In addition, they were homologous with the physical, temporal, and cosmological environments of the Picts.

Note

1   Designs 6 and 7 (Fig. 8.3) are taken to be one and the same; designs 42 and 43 (Fig. 8.3) are taken to be one and the same. Design 24 is a special symbol with a particular function, as is explained below. Only a few of the 200 symbol stones are so grossly damaged that only one symbol remains. There are 50 stones that either have a single design or a nonsymbolic design and they are excluded here.
2   Binary oppositions are to be read horizontally. There may or may not be associations if read vertically down the columns. In a dualistic world-view there is often a consistency between elements on each side, but one cannot read these off mechanically.

References

Allen J. R. & J. Anderson 1903. *The early Christian monuments of Scotland*. Edinburgh: Society of Antiquaries of Scotland.
Jackson, A. 1984. *The symbol stones of Scotland*. Stromness: Orkney Press.
Jackson, A. 1989. *The Pictish trail*. Stromness: Orkney Press.

9 *The idea of fish: land and sea in the Icelandic world-view*

GÍSLI PÁLSSON

Introduction

This chapter discusses the place of aquatic animals in the Icelandic world-view. It explores the correspondence between human society and representations of water beings during the era of household production (from the time of settlement in the 9th century to the beginning of the 20th century), and examines how ideas about the fish world have changed during this century as Icelanders have entered into new kinds of social relationships. I take the theoretical position, following Douglas (1966), Leach (1976) and some others, that some animals, because of their anomalous position, are better to think with than others. Also, I suggest that symbolic expressions should be studied in a context of development over time. Anthropologists have overemphasized a synchronic and static analysis of symbolic systems. In reality, representations obey 'two kinds of determinisms' (Lévi-Strauss 1985, p. 104). They respond to the constraints of the present, the social relations of the people who produce them, but somehow they also reflect the traditions of the past.

It has been suggested (Hewes 1948, p. 238) that because of the special behaviour of objects in the water, aquatic environments represent a strange realm from the point of view of humans. Also, fishing is unique in the sense that the data available to the producer are quite limited. The inferences possible from them are of a 'different order' (Morrill 1967, p. 407) to those possible for terrestrial species. Likewise, it may be argued that fishing involves specific perceptual and cognitive skills. Since the prey moves in a different medium, the problem of orientation demands particular models (Pálsson 1982). As fishermen are physically separated from fish, they must make descriptive models of an environment about which they can only obtain information by indirect observation.

But cognitive models do not only address immediate and practical problems. Some are only models *for* action, whereas others transcend the material sphere as models *of* reality (Geertz 1973, p. 93). To what extent, one may ask, does the fish world serve as a vehicle of symbolic thought?

Some anthropologists suggest (see Kleivan 1984, p. 889) that fish are rarely used as metaphors of human society because there are relatively few 'obvious points of resemblance' with human beings. This kind of reasoning relates to a well-known statement of Lévi-Strauss (1966, p. 204) about the metaphorical role of birds.[1] On the one hand, birds are separated from humans by the element in which they move, but on the other hand they seem to engage in social relations with other members of their species and communicate by acoustic means resembling those of human language. Kleivan, however, claims not only that fish are further removed from humans than birds, as they are cold-blooded and live in the water, in addition he points out that they neither build nests nor communicate by acoustic means resembling articulated language.

This is contradictory to both ethology and some folk accounts. Long ago Darwin observed (1952, p. 444) that 'fishes ... make various noises, some of which are described as being musical' and that some groups of fishermen even catch fish by imitating the sounds they make. Darwin (1952, p. 443) also pointed out that 'certain fishes ... make nests, and some of them take care of their young when hatched'. Among Malay fishermen, one may note, the 'hearing' of fish is an acknowledged and important expertise (Firth 1946, p. 199). On the other hand, ethological evidence need not necessarily concern us here, as the evidence is in any case beyond the awareness or recognition of many fishermen. In Icelandic, a person who keeps quiet is said to be 'silent as a fish' (*Þögull sem fiskur*).

In several cases fish do indeed serve as mediums for the metaphorical expression of social relations (Anderson 1969, Cove 1978, Firth 1981, Knipe 1984).

Firth (1981, p. 220) argues, for instance, that among the Tikopia fish have been an 'outstanding' medium for the expression of social relations. He suggests (1981, p. 221) that the Tikopia treatment of fish may be represented as a series of asymmetrical relations. On the one hand, in their natural element, the sea, fish are superior to humans. They assume an active role, and are said to be aggressive, free, evasive, and able to manipulate humans. But on the other hand, humans are superior to fish in their strength and skills. Fish are described as pets, dependent on humans; they are exposed to a one-way ritual communication, and sometimes caught by the fisherman's devices.

In the Tikopia world-view there is a balance between the asymmetrical relations of fish and humans (Firth 1981, p. 221). In Iceland changes in social relations have been accompanied by an ideological shift, an inversion of the relationship between fish and humans in which their relative power has been reversed. The mythology during the period of household production emphasized the distinction between land and sea. A series of anomalous water beings mediated between land and sea determining the fate of humans. Humans were passive recipients of what was allotted to them. With the development of markets and capitalist fishing the ocean and its habitants were redefined. Human labour was seen to create value and the earlier mythology became redundant. Fish are no longer seen to be superior to humans, rather they are seen to be subject to human control.

Representations and social relations

From the time of settlement, fishing was an important component of the Icelandic economy. Fishing was integrated into the local subsistence economy. There were large and small landowners or farmers, but about a quarter of the population, tenants and labourers, owned no land. Fishing was not a separate economic endeavour with an elaborate role structure of its own. The crews were small and the technology was fairly simple. Hand-lines, operated by one man, were the typical fishing gear. Open boats could only exploit well-known and nearby fishing grounds.

Fish have always been economically important in Iceland. From the time of settlement fish formed a staple of the Icelandic diet, together with the milk of cattle and sheep. Soon after the union with Norway in 1262 fish replaced woollens as the island's main export and since then fish has been the mainstay of the economy. For centuries dried fish was the most important practical monetary standard. In modern Icelandic, fish is still used metaphorically to express value standards: for instance, an object or an idea is said not to 'amount to many fish' (*uppá marga fiska*) if it is of no value. Several references to fish in the Icelandic Sagas provide evidence for their economic importance. *Snorra Edda* provides the names of various species and *Gudmundar saga* (1878) describes what must have been a typical way of fishing.

The emphasis on fishing varied from time to time during the era of domestic production. There was, for instance, a substantial increase in effort during the Middle Ages, due to more adherence to duties of Christian fasting in Europe (Gelsinger 1981, p. 181). Yet the subsistence economy always put some kind of ceiling on productive targets. Because of Iceland's status as a Danish colony, foreign markets were limited. Also, landowners controlled access to the sea. People could have invested in boats, but capital accumulation was limited by colonial relations and restricted markets for fish. Furthermore, in 1783 landowners gained increased control over landless people. Law required every landless person to make an annual contract with a landowner. These legally enforced labour-service contracts (*vistarband*) gave institutional form to patron–client relationships. The labour force was guaranteed by law. Finally, during the 18th and 19th centuries, the Icelandic political elite represented the interests of the larger farmers in the colonial trade and not those of fishermen. When the terms of trade were negotiated, the elite supported higher prices for agricultural products and lower prices for fish in which they had less interest, and the price of fish remained very low. Fishing effort, then, was limited by technical and social factors. This stagnant household economy brought with it particular models of fishing. They can be discerned in old Icelandic literature, the Sagas (most of which were written during the 13th and the 14th century), and published accounts of oral traditions of the last two centuries.

Fish have always been a pervasive symbol in Icelandic folklore. The world of water beings (*sæbúar*) did not only contain fish in a strict scientific sense of the term. The Sagas provide numerous references to 'whales, seals and other fish'.[2] Nor was the ocean only peopled by real beings, as it also contained various imaginary monsters with peculiar characteristics. Davíđsson argued at the turn of the last century that the importance of fish in Icelandic folklore was simply due to their number and availability. Iceland, he suggested (Davíđsson 1900, p. 312), has very few land animals but many species of fish:

> This is reflected in the folk lore . . . There are few beliefs which relate to land animals, but the inhabitants of the deep . . . have for a long time played a great part in the popular fancy, and many a strange idea concerning them has taken hold on the ordinary mind.[3]

But just as there was a wide variety of fish, so were there many different kinds of bird and yet the bird lore was quite limited. Birds, it seems, were rarely said to have monstrous physical characteristics (see *Íslenskar Þjóðsögur og sagnir*, IV). Stefánsson agrees with Davíđsson that the beliefs connected with water beings are more numerous and 'more interesting' (Stefánsson 1906, p. 301). Apparently, birds were less 'good to think', contrary to the thesis of resemblance. Neither availability, then, nor physical resemblance account for the choice of metaphors, classes of species or types of habitats, in Icelandic folklore. Fish were important for the economy, but so were sheep, cows and horses. A functional explanation of the obsession of Icelanders with water beings does, therefore, not hold either. The choice seems to be arbitrary.

According to pre-Christian mythology (*Snorra Edda*), the oceans and the lakes were created out of the blood of a giant (*Ýmir*), and governed by the god of *Njörđur*, who was in charge of fishing and sailing (Hastrup 1985). In this cosmic order humans were merely tiny pawns, subject to supernatural forces and manipulated by aquatic animals. This is apparent in notions of 'fishiness' (*fiskni, fiskiheill*), the ability to get fish. Fishiness was a transient quality people considered to be differentially distributed among fishermen. According to an old proverb, 'no one catches another man's fish'. Most of the catch was divided by a share system, but some species were not distributed. These belonged to the individuals who caught them and were spoken of as 'fortunate draws' (*happadrættir*) (Jónsson 1945, p. 352). Some people were thought to scare fish away and were called 'fish-deterrents' (*fiskifælur*). The foreman (*formađur*) of the boat arranged his men according to their fishiness. During fishing those who lacked this quality (*ófisknir*) were seated at the oars to keep the boat in position while the others jigged with hand lines (see Jónsson 1945, p. 347). Somehow, fishiness was pre-determined. According to a proverb, 'a poor fisherman gets poor fish' (*vesælan fisk*).

The foreman did not necessarily possess fishiness, but he demanded discipline. The major qualities attributed to a good foreman were diligence, bravery, and the ability to command the crew. These were frequently mentioned in foremen's biographies and obituaries during the 19th century.

When foremen were ranked, it was according to their effort, the number of trips they made, their bravery in difficult weather conditions and their cleverness in directing the boat and crew. One of the greatest seagoers on the south coast in the 19th century is said to have made fifty trips in one winter season of a hundred days (Jónsson 1945, p. 352). The criterion for assessment was the number of trips rather than the size of the catch.

Even though fishiness was considered an individual quality, it was part of a grand design over which humans had no control. Fishing peasants spoke of their prey as a 'gift' of God (guðsgjöf) and the catch was spoken of as a 'contribution' in fish (fiskigjöf). In the folk analysis, the catch was supplied by nature and humans were just passive recipients, observers of a mysterious system of rationing.

The fate of the producers was believed to be determined by a godly design. In order to prevent failure (bad catches and accidents), prayers were read at the beginning of each season and before each fishing trip (Kristjánsson 1942). Reciting prayers was referred to as vani, which means habit, the usual. The ritual associated with fishing did not imply, though, that people thought they had any control over the fish, rather it was directed at getting supernatural forces to aid the fishermen and prevent the worst eventualities.

While humans were seen to be manipulated by fish, in mythology these relations were sometimes reversed. According to some medieval accounts, in Paradise, where presumably the constraints of earthly existence did not apply, nature obeyed human authority: 'If a man asks the water for fish, it will provide various kinds at his feet' (Matheus saga postola, 1874, p. 828).[4] But even though humans were subject to fish, and both were ultimately controlled by something else, their fates were highly interconnected. The major opposition encoded in myth and folklore was that between land and sea. One of the ocean-taboos (sævíti) implied that if a boat contained some dirt belonging to the land the catches were bound to be poor (Íslenskar Þjoðsögur og sagnir IV, p. 311). A boat had to be pure. During fishing its terrestrial nature had to be suppressed. The contrast between land and sea is also underlined in Icelandic ways of speaking, as anything that is out of place is metaphorically represented as 'fish on dry land' (eins og fiskur á Þurru landi).

Humans belonged to the land, but their fate was largely responsive to two kinds of uncertainties relating to the sea. On the one hand, there was uncertainty concerning the resource brought ashore for consumption and exchange, the size of the catch. On the other hand, expeditions at sea were always potentially dangerous, given the level of technological development and the whims of nature. One type of uncertainty was related to the other. Thus, fishing success or lack of it was thought to be an indication that a fisherman would die young. If a good fisherman caught little, or someone with very limited fishiness fished 'like crazy', he would be short-lived (Thorarensen 1945, pp. 170–1).

Numerous folktales and mythological accounts stress the mediation between the opposition of land and sea. Some water beings are simply

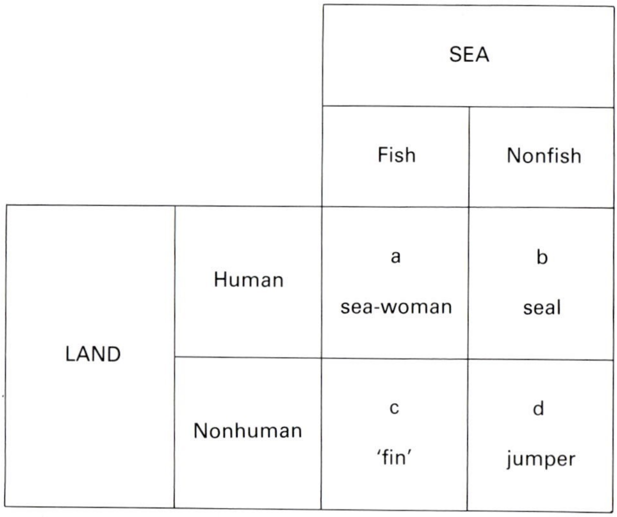

		SEA	
		Fish	Nonfish
LAND	Human	a sea-woman	b seal
	Nonhuman	c 'fin'	d jumper

Figure 9.1   The logic of opposition.

described as monsters (*skrímsli*), but most beings are either described as fish or nonfish, or human or nonhuman. Logically, there are four possibilities. Table 9.1 shows four examples, which are briefly described below.

The beings that mediate between the opposition of land and sea, whether real or imaginary, are characterized by some anomalous property. They either reduce or increase the catch, ensure safety or pose a threat to human lives (see Table 9.1).

Medieval manuscripts describe 'sea-women' that 'have the nature of fish while in the sea but look like humans while ashore' (*Flóres saga konungs og sona hans* 1927, p. 167, *Saga þiðriks af Bern* 1905, p. 46). Sea-women are sexually attractive and sometimes they have children with sailors. Their children become giants, 'not like humans'. Apparently, sea-women are protective but not dangerous. *Flóres saga konungs og sona hans* (1927) also describes a mermaid (*margýgur*) with the head of a giant woman and huge breasts, but a whale-like lower part. She sings beautifully but destroys ships and kills people.

Seals are said to have 'human figures, natures and qualities all complete, concealed beneath their coats of seal skin' (Davíðsson 1900, p. 314). According to some stories the seal ensured good catches and delivered valuable things upon the foreshore. Fishing power was embodied in the seal: if the eye of a seal caught by a successful hunter was given to a less successful one, his luck was said to be sure to change for the better. Sometimes the seal cooperated with humans by warning of danger (Kristjánsson 1980, p. 449). According to other stories the seal could be quite dangerous. *Laxdæla saga* provides an account (1934, p. 41) of a boat that gets destroyed in a storm because the crew attempted to shoot a seal.

Table 9.1 Anomaly and uncertainty.

Water beings	Logical category	Uncertainty Catch	Safety
Wicked-whale (*illhveli*)	d		−
Otter (*ottr*)	b	+	
Seal (*selur*)	b	+	−
'Fin' (*öfuguggi*)	c	−	
Hairy trout (*loðsilungur*)	c	−	
Horse-whale (*hrosshveli*)	d		−
'Jumper' (*stökkull*)	d		−
Sea-woman (*sækona*)	a		+
Mermaid (*margýgur*)	b		−
Flying fish (*flugfiskur*)	d		−
Sea-dog (*sæhundur*)	d		−
Sea-man (*hafmaður*)	b		−
Water horse (*vatnanykur*)	d	−	−
Loki (as salmon)	c	−	−

The 'fin' (*öfuguggi*) is considered to be a particular species of fish with reversed fins. When it moves about, it swims backwards. It is poisonous and has red flesh, indicating that it eats the bodies of drowned men. It is nonhuman and inedible. A particular species of trout, 'hairy-trout' (*loðsilungur*), was said to be covered with hair. It was believed to be created by giants and demons, as a punishment for some human wrongdoing. Sometimes lakes and rivers were full of fins and hairy trouts, which were considered totally useless or a kind of noncatch.

Völsunga saga (1905–8, p. 34) provides an account of a man named *Otur* (Otter) who was a great fisherman. He was like an otter during the day when he stayed in the water and caught fish, but during the night he was human and slept ashore.

Several species of whales, so-called 'wicked whales' (*illhveli*) are said to do damage to ships and men. They know their own name and appear as soon as they hear it mentioned. Fishermen take care not to use their proper name and call them 'big fish' (*stórfiskur*) instead. One of them is the 'jumper' (*stökkull*). It has flaps of skin hanging down over the eyes. The only way it can lift the flaps and see what is going on is by leaping clear of the water. When in the air it can look from under the flaps. It attempts to sink everything that it sees floating (Davíðsson 1900, pp. 318–19). The 'horse-whale' (*hrosshveli*) was one of the wicked whales. It was said to resemble a horse, to neigh like a horse, and to have a horse's tail that sent tremendous waves across the ocean and destroyed boats and men (Davíðsson 1900, p. 320).

The folklore contains numerous accounts of strange water beings that attempt to drag humans into the ocean or destroy their boats: 'sea-men' (*hafmenn*), 'water-horses' (*vatnanykrar*), 'sea-dogs' (*sæhundar*), and 'flying fish' (*flugfiskar*), to name only a few (see *Íslenskar Þjóðsögur og sagnir*, IV,

Íslenskar Þjóðsögur og ævintýri, I–VI). All these stories establish series of pairs of oppositions that relate to the contrast between the land and the ocean. The strange beings mediate between the polar opposites; their peculiar properties draw the relevant contrasts. Judging from the sample listed in Table 9.1, anomalous beings of category (a) (human:fish) reduce danger, while those of category (d) (nonhuman:nonfish) are dangerous. Those belonging to category (b) (human:nonfish) ensure good catches, even though some are dangerous, while most of those of category (c) (nonhuman:fish) represent poor catches. The association with human qualities is good for catches, but the association with nonhuman attributes is detrimental to both catches and safety. The popularity of category (d) indicates that safety was a major preoccupation.

The mythology establishes several other contrasts, for instance between gods and giants, gods and humans, the social and the wild, and male and female. *Loki*, the king of giants, is one of the major characters in *Snorra Edda* and he is frequently transformed. At one point he changes into a woman. On several occasions he changes into a salmon to escape the punishment of the gods (he is supposed to be responsible for most mischief both among gods and humans). His transformation into a salmon strongly emphasizes the distinction between land and sea. Salmon are not just fish, for they live both on land (in fresh water) and in the sea. This anomaly is underlined in the myth (*Snorra Edda* 1975, p. 86) where Loki faces 'two choices' when escaping from the gods – to head for the sea or to jump inland up the river.

In Icelandic peasant society, the world of fish and water beings provided a convenient tool for folk analysis. It offered a kind of totemic operator in terms of which Icelanders could account for events and express social realities. Big fish (*stórfiskar*) posed a threat to humans while at sea, but the same term was also applied euphemistically to refer to terrestrial danger, *valdsmenn*, or those in power. Those who are a threat to the social order are also spoken of metaphorically as anomalous water beings or *öfuguggar* (fish that have reversed fins and swim backwards). This term is used for all kinds of misfits – the eccentric, the outsider and the homosexual. The social world was represented by a natural model.

Nature was also organized culturally. Each fishing location had a permanent name, usually associated with characteristics of the sea bed or some natural feature of the landscape. The fishing grounds were seen to be a closed and stable natural domain. The natural coding of the fishing grounds, by the application of names for landmarks to individual fishing spots, reflected the idea that such spots were permanent. The peasant's cognitive map of the ocean had an immunity to history; this was a world-view of stasis in which society was mapped on to nature.

Reversal of the roles of fish and humans

Towards the end of the 19th century and during the first decades of this century, a number of the constraints associated with peasant fishing in Iceland relaxed. These brought about changes in the nature and organization of fishing. The legal obligations of landless workers to associate with landowners was lifted, markets for Icelandic fish developed, and access to the sea was increasingly made public rather than private as fishing villages formed around bays and purchased jointly the landing sites from the farmers who had controlled them in the past (Pálsson 1982, Pálsson & Durrenberger 1985).

With these constraints removed, fishing was no longer for subsistence, and productive targets became indefinite. Production was oriented to the market and, for the first time, labour power became a marketable commodity. The fishing skipper became a full-time professional, his training was institutionalized and his rights and obligations were defined by law. Motorboats became available and new offshore fishing grounds were opened up. With the new markets, both in products and factors of production, the national economy of Iceland became focused on the extraction, processing and export of fish and derived products. The resources were redefined as 'there for the taking' rather than being given up as gifts. The prey was no longer seen to be an offering *to* humans who passively received what was allotted to them, rather it was seen to be actively pursued *by* humans and extracted from the indifferent sea.

With the growth of capitalist production the world-view of stasis disappeared. The ocean is no longer considered to have some kind of power or force, and its inhabitants are no longer seen to control the fate of humans, except as passive objects of production. The peasant mythology, and its image of the cosmic order, was replaced by the notion of infinite natural resources. The uncertainties of production have changed, the relevant contrasts are different, and the earlier metaphors and mediators have become obsolete.

The new conceptual model of fishing is secular and individualistic and the modern notions of 'luck' and 'chance' have entered the vocabulary of fishing. In the previous model, no probability could be assigned to uncertain outcomes of natural events. The present model is much more attuned to the idea that the workings of nature contain an essentially random element: the idea of (calculable) risk. The change from subsistence economy to capitalist production involved a change from dependence on nature and to dependence on commodities.

During earlier centuries, of course, someone had to coordinate the activities of the crew. He was the foreman. But it was not an honorific role or title. In contrast, the present 'skipper' (*skipstjóri*) is highly respected (Pálsson & Durrenberger 1983). As fishing became a full-time occupation, the role of skipper evolved. It became a specialized role in an autonomous branch of production.

    According to modern folk accounts, the skill of the skipper is critical for
fishing success. Skippers are said to differ in their ability to locate and catch
fish. Catches are said to vary from one boat to another because skippers are
different. The ability to catch fish is supposed to be 'in the blood'. This is the
idea of the 'skipper effect'. Some skippers are said to be perceptive, to
memorize detail, and be able to get into a particular state of mind – 'fishing
mood' (*fiskistuð*). They fish 'by cleverness' (*af lagni*) while others fish 'by
force' (*af krafti*). Two skippers may be equally successful, but by different
means. Those who fish by force are said to make more trips, to use more
gear and fuel, and to destroy more gear in the process. Those who are said to
fish by dexterity or cleverness, hampered by their limited assets, small boats
or engines, are said to develop original fishing strategies to compensate for
what they lack in force.[5]
    The modern model of success is a model on which people draw to
organize their long-term experience. When fishermen talk about their
careers, they often count the number of years they have spent with particular
skippers rather than the years they have been on particular boats. After each
winter season the names of the 'top' skippers (*aflamenn*, literally, catch-men)
in the Icelandic fleet are reported in the mass media. In developing accounts
for whole seasons as well as careers, people emphasize the personal characteristics and fishing tactics of the skipper. Accounts of these and speculations about such features are popular topics of discussion throughout
Iceland.
    With the development of fishing the old system of rewards was changed.
In the present share system the skipper receives twice the share of a deck
hand. During the period of peasant production there were different share
systems at different times and places, but usually the foreman received the
same share as an ordinary crewman. A foreman boat-and-gear owner
received no more than four times as much as a fisherman-rower. The
modern skipper-owner gets about 25 times as much as a deck hand. There
are obvious reasons for the extra share allotted to the skipper. The operation
of fishing equipment such as electronic gear and modern deck technology
demands expertise and institutionalized training. Modern fishing also
requires a high degree of cooperation between crewmen. Not only must the
skipper be a skilful decision-maker and operator of equipment, he must also
be in control of the total coordination of activities.
    While changes in the nature of the process of extraction and the tech-
nology of fishing explain the increase in the share allotted to those in charge
during fishing operations, they do not account for the idea that the expertise
of the skipper is critical for his success, *relative* to that cf others. The reasons
for the notion of the 'skipper effect' must be looked for elsewhere. With the
development of capitalist production the leaders of fishing operations were
involved in new kinds of social relations. Labour was no longer guaranteed
by law, and skippers had to recruit followers. As boat technology developed, the demand for skilled crewmen further increased. Moreover, among
skipper-owners there was competition for financial support, sometimes

available from merchants and processors. Other skippers competed for access to boats. Competition became extreme. Given this competition, and the role and the economic place of the skipper as a manager of specialized means of production, the most important criterion for his success was his catch. Although all skippers seem to have been equally competent, the idea that they differ greatly in their catching potential entered the skippers' rhetoric, allowing each to enhance the demand for his expertise as a unique commodity on the labour market (Pálsson & Durrenberger 1982).

Changes in the social relations of production do not quite explain why models of fishing took the particular form they did. While differences in 'fishiness' had to be explained and new social relations limited the range of appropriate models, to account fully for the content of the models it would be necessary to refer to available cultural idioms. The explanations that emerged were consistent with the culturally plausible rhetorics available to the actors – the emphasis on individualism, and the idea of a personal fishing power. Catches are no longer seen to be allotted to humans, but differential success is still accounted for in personal terms, even more so than in the past.

When the skipper became a frontiersman, the ocean was seen to be 'opened up'. As a result the skippers' map of the fishing grounds changed. There are uncharted spaces to be explored and unknown spots to be discovered. Most fishing spots are a matter of secrecy and each skipper has his own personal naming grid. The names are usually entirely arbitrary, as they do not refer to features of the landscape. The old natural coding of the seascape has been replaced by a system of transient and euphemistic names. The names are fortuitous, they change frequently and there is no consensus. They are *in* history.

During the last decade, capitalist production in fishing has been subject to an intricate institutionalized machinery. (One of the main reasons has been the threat of overexploitation of the cod stock). This institutionalization fosters the notion of homeostatic fisheries and a 'harvesting' orientation – a scientific rationality that assumes humans are in total control of the eco-logical situation. The annual total catch of cod and the maximum catch of each boat is decided upon in advance. There is a new ceiling on production. Fishermen often complain that the new system is unfair because the 'best' skippers are allotted the same quota as the 'bad' ones. As competition between skippers is reduced a new model of fishing is likely to emerge. Already one hears the argument that it is the boat and its technology that catch fish and not the skipper or the crew.

Conclusions

I have tried to show how the rationale applied by peasants to fishing before it was industrialized reflected social and technical constraints. There was a ceiling on production. The main uncertainties of fishing related to the danger of fishing trips and the size of the catch. To these conditions corresponded a folk model that emphasized the contrast between land and water. Mysterious water beings mediated between the ocean and the domain of humans. According to the peasants' model, humans were almost passive recipients of fish. Even though 'fishiness' was an individual quality, no one was credited or blamed for the size of the catch. Humans were subject to forces over which they had no control. As the domestic economy gave way to capitalist production and the ceiling on production was lifted, the rationale applied to fishing changed. The relative power of fish and humans was reversed. Humans became active, their labour was said to create value, the resources were redefined as infinite, and the ocean was opened up. The old mythology became redundant and its metaphors obsolete. New ideologies developed concerning attitudes towards fish and other natural resources and the definition of social roles. The competitive nature of fishing encouraged the notion of the 'skipper effect' whereby the skipper was made responsible for fishing success. More recently, with the threat of overfishing, another ideology has emerged. Humans are seen to be collectively responsible for the maintenance of fish stocks.

The changes discussed suggest an inversion in the role of animals as mediators in human relations with the cosmic order. According to the peasants of earlier centuries, fish were responsible for the maintenance of humans. Now humans are considered responsible for the maintenance of fishing stocks. With the new ecological order that is being founded, changes in the Icelandic fisheries have come full circle. Now as in a primitive society, people are induced to cooperate because of a threat to nature; those who violate the new prohibitions are considered guilty of creating disorder in nature. But there is a difference: the fish are no longer a gift from the spirits. If the fish are seen as a 'gift' at all, they are a gift from humans to the new ecological order, which of course serves human ends.

Recent changes have rendered many of the earlier supernatural explanations for the behaviour of fish superficial. It is not just that increased capitalization has brought with it more knowledge. In Iceland, as I have demonstrated, representations of nature have changed as a result of a transformation of social relations. The relations Icelanders have entered into at different points in time, in the process of appropriating marine resources, are reflected in their cognitive appropriation of nature.

Acknowledgements

I thank Stefán Karlsson of the University of Iceland, and Eyvindur Eiríksson of the Arnemagnean Institute in Copenhagen, for supplying information on references to fish in the Sagas. I also thank Paul Durrenberger, University of Iowa, and Tim Ingold, University of Manchester, for their comments upon some of the ideas presented here. Finally, I thank Ingibjörg Ásta Gunnarsdóttir for her assistance in collecting some of the material used. The research on which this chapter is based was financed by the Icelandic Science Foundation, the British Council, and the University of Iceland.

Notes

1 Later Lévi-Strauss (1985, p. 104) seems to have taken the view that the choice of species for symbolic expression is entirely arbitrary:

> Each culture settles on a few distinctive features of its environment, but no one can predict which these are or to what end they will be put. Furthermore, so great is the wealth and diversity of the raw material offered by the environment for observation and reflection that the mind is capable only of apprehending a fraction of it. The mind can put it to use for elaborating one system among an infinity of other, equally conceivable ones: nothing predestines any one among them for a privileged fate.

2 The ambiguity of the category of 'fish' (*fiskur*) continues to this day. Sometimes 'fish' refers only to cod, for instance in sentences such as 'fish follow capelin'. This ambiguity is not peculiar to Icelandic. Jernudd & Thuan (1984) argue that generally there is a lack of correspondence between three fish-naming systems: the scientific, the common, and the folk naming system. Brown (1984, p. 15) argues that the category of 'fish' represents one of the largest and most diverse discontinuities found in nearly all environments.

3 Davídsson's aim was to eradicate 'erroneous' beliefs in imaginary beings. The extent to which folk beliefs are intelligent or stupid is not at issue here, but clearly Davídsson's informants sometimes got things wrong. So did the 17th-century naturalist Rumphius, who accepted the native view of Ambiona that leaves of the mangrove changed into small fish when hanging in the water (see Ellen 1985, p. 9).

4 *Matheus saga postola*, one should note, is largely a translation of a foreign text. It may therefore not be representative of Icelandic culture.

5 The admission of 'force' in the folk model of success may seem to qualify the basic claim that the size of catches is entirely due to the personal qualities of the skipper. Clearly material factors are also considered. But models of success may differ in their conceptions of technology and in where they draw the boundary between humans and the environment. As Geertz (1973, p. 9) has shown, a technical construction can be seen either as a feature of the physical landscape within which the individual is set and to which he must adapt, or as a cultural 'weapon' in his struggle against a harsh environment. Thus the boat can be seen either as a part of the fisherman's environment or as an instrumental extension of his person. According to the dominant Icelandic model of success, the boat is a culturally fashioned tool, a kind of material extension of the skipper's personality. Even though material factors are considered, these are more a matter of style than of constraint.

References

Anderson, E. N. 1969. Sacred fish. *Man* **4**, 443–9.

Brown, C. H. 1984. *Language and living things: uniformities in folk classification and naming*. Brunswick, NJ: Rutgers University Press.

Cove, J. J. 1978. Ecology, structuralism and fishing taboos. In *Adaptation and symbolism: essays on social organization*, K. A. Watson-Gegeo and S. L. Seaton (eds), pp. 143–54. University Press of Hawaii.

Darwin, C. 1952. *The descent of man and selection in relation to sex*. Chicago: Encyclopaedia Britannica.

Davíðsson, Ó. 1900. Folklore of Icelandic fishes. *Scottish Review* **36**(72), 312–32.

Douglas, M. 1966. *Purity and danger: an analysis of the ceoncepts of pollution and taboo.* London: Routledge & Kegan Paul.

Ellen, R. E. 1985. Species transformation and the expression of resemblance in Nuaulu ethnobiology. *Ethnos,* **1–2**, 5–14.

Firth, R. 1946. *Malay fishermen: their peasant economy.* London: Routledge & Kegan Paul.

Firth, R. 1981. Figuration and symbolism in Tikopia fishing and fish use. *Journal de la Société des Océanistes* **72–3**, 219–26.

Flóres saga konungs og sona hans. 1927. Hallea/S: Ake Lagerholm. [14th century].

Geertz, C. 1973. *The interpretation of cultures.* London: Hutchinson.

Gelsinger, B. E. (1981). *Icelandic enterprise: commerce and economy in the Middle Ages.* Columbia: University of South Carolina Press.

Guðmundar saga Arasonar Hólabiskups. 1878. J. Sigurðsson and G. Vigfússon (eds) Biskupa sögur **2**, 1–184. Copenhagen. [Mid-14th century].

Hastrup, K. 1985. *Culture and history in medieval Iceland: an anthropological analysis of structure and change.* London: Oxford University Press.

Jewes, G. W. 1948. The rubric 'fishing and fisheries' *American Anthropologist* **50**, 238–46.

Íslenskar Þjóðsögur og sagnir, IV. 1982. Collected by S. Sigfússon. Reykjavík: Þjóðsaga.

Íslenskar Þjóðsögur og ævintýri, I–VI 1961. Collected by J. Árnason. Reykjavík: Þjóðsaga.

Jernudd, B. H. & E. Thuan 1984. Naming fish: a problem exploration. *Language in Society* **13**(2), 235–44.

Jónsson, E. (1945). *Þjóðhættir og ævisögur frá 19. öld.* Akureyri: Bókaútg. P. H. Jónssonar.

Kleivan, I. 1984. The fish world as a metaphorical Eskimo society. In *The fishing culture of the world: studies in ethnology, cultural ecology and folklore,* B. Gunda (ed.), Vol. II, 887–91. Budapest: Akadémiae Kiadó.

Knipe, E. (1984). *Gamrie: an exploration in cultural ecology. A study of maritime adaptation in a Scottish fishing village.* New York: University Press of North America.

Kristjánsson, L. 1942. Trúarlíf íslenskra sjómanna. *Ægir,* pp. 249–60. Reykjavík.

Kristjánsson, L. 1980. *Íslenskir sjávarhættir,* 1. Reykjavík: Menningarsjóður.

Laxdæla saga. 1934. Reykjavík: Hið íslenska fornritafélag.

Leach, E. 1976. *Culture and communication: the logic by which symbols are connected.* Cambridge: Cambridge University Press.

Lévi-Strauss, C. 1972. *The savage mind.* London: Weidenfeld & Nicolson.

Lévi-Strauss, C. 1985. *The view from afar.* Oxford: Basil Blackwell.

Matheus saga postola. 1874. *Postula sögur.* Christiania: C. R. Unger. [13th century].

Morrill, W. T. 1967. Ethnoichthyology of the Cha Cha. *Ethnology* **6**, 409–16.

Pálsson, G. 1982. Representation and reality: cognitive models and social relations among the fishermen of Sandgerði, Iceland. PhD thesis, Department of Social Anthropology, University of Manchester.

Pálsson, G. & E. P. Durrenberger 1982. To dream of fish: The causes of Icelandic skippers' fishing success. *Journal of Anthropological Research* **38**(2), 227–42.

Pálsson, G. (1983). Icelandic foremen and skippers: the structure and evolution of a folk model. *American Ethnologist* **10**(3), 511–28.

Pálsson, G. (1985). Peasants, entrepreneurs and companies. *Ethnos* **1–2**, 103–22.

Saga Þiðriks af Bern, 1905–11. Copenhagen. [mid-13th century].

Snorra Edda. 1975. Reykjavík: Iđunn. [early 14th century].

Stefánsson, V. 1906. Icelandic beast and bird lore. *Journal of American Folklore* **19**, 300–8.

Thorarensen, J. 1945. *Sjósókn*. Reykjavík: Ísafoldarprentsmiđja.

Völsunga saga. 1906–8. Copenhagen: Samfund til udgivelse av gammel nordisk literatur. [13th century].

10 *Animals in Hopi duality*

MARK TOMAS BAHTI

The Hopi Indians of the American Southwest live in villages on top of and at the foot of rocky buttes known as mesas. The land around their windswept mesas is flat and arid with barely 30 cm of rainfall a year and a growing season of only 133 days. The Hopi believe that they owe their survival for over eight centuries in such a marginal, often hostile environment to the success of their religion, to *Hopitu*, which best translates as 'the Hopi way'.

Hopi religious observances are tied to celestial occurrences – the equinoxes, lunar phases, and solstices. The Hopi concept of time is cyclical and rhythmic, not linear. While Christians celebrate the anniversaries of Christ's birth, death, and resurrection, Hopis do not commemorate an ancient event during such ceremonies as the Soyala or the Powamu. Each year is new and each year requires the age-old ceremonies to continue the cycle and ensure that year's birth and renewal. Thus, Hopi religion is rooted in a meaningful, vital present rather than an ever-receding past, giving it a vitality and flexibility that has confounded missionaries and ethnologists alike.

According to the emergence story, the Hopi came through three underworlds before arriving at this, the fourth world. Their contact with spirit-beings, frequent in the three previous worlds, did not end with entry into the fourth world. Though there are somewhat different versions as to how or why it came about, Hopi spirits spend only half the year at the mesas and the other half at their home on Nuvatukyaoi, also known as the San Francisco Peaks, near what is now Flagstaff, Arizona.

Intimate coexistence

Special dances are held during the ceremonial year, between the Soyala observance of the winter solstice and Niman, a few weeks after the summer solstice, when the *katsina* spirits live among the Hopi. The dances, called *katsin tikive*, are performed by Hopi men who have been initiated into the *katsina* society. The *katsina* society is but one of a number of religious societies that have existed among the Hopi. While others have diminished in importance and even completely disappeared over the past several hundred years, the *katsina* society remains and has become the most important (cf. Dockstader 1985). During these ceremonies, the masked dancers who impersonate the *katsina* spirits are believed to tread on the threshold between the Hopi world and the world of the *katsinas*, thus enabling them the better to convey the prayers of the Hopi for renewal and maintenance of the life cycle.

This duality, this view of the two worlds, the temporal and the 'spiritual', is an integral part of traditional Hopi thinking patterns. It may also be a major factor in the survival (thus far) of Hopi religion in a world of television, cars and VCRs. By relegating such technological phenomena to the 'real' world, the modern world can be kept at bay where the 'spirit' world is concerned.

How intimately the two worlds coexist is described by a Hopi from Shungopavy, who said: 'When a bowl of *nyookwivi* (mutton stew) is set before you, the *nyookwivi* is of the world. The steam that rises is the *nyookwivi* that belongs to the other world'.[1]

The belief that the two worlds occupy the same space is further reflected in the Hopi custom of leaving a small patch of a house unplastered so that the unseen people of the spirit world might plaster it in their world with an equally unseen plaster.

'Acting human'

For its embodiment of the essence of this world, the spirit world is itself no less real. Daily acknowledgement is made by many traditional Hopi who gratefully leave bits of food on their plates at a meal's end for the *katsina* spirits. The small amount is of no import as the spirits partake of the food's essence. It is a world described by a Hopi Kikmongwi (religious leader) as a place where things are 'just the same, just the same. Only a little different'.[2]

The spirits of plants, geographic places, insects, forces of nature, animals and even other tribes can be represented as *katsinas*. The animal *katsinas* include Honau/bear, So-wing/deer, Honan/badger, Chop/antelope, Pang/mountain sheep, and Wakas/cow, a *katsina* of post-European origin. Among the third *katsinas* are Kwahu/eagle, Kisa/prairie falcon, Angwus/crow, Monswa/owl and two relatively recent introductions, the Kowaku/chicken and Takawea/rooster *katsinas*.

The animal *katsinas* represent the animal spirits. Whether one bear *katsina* or several appear, the function is still the same. Animal spirits or the animal people of the spirit world are thought of as 'acting human', for lack of a better phrase. Indeed, it is felt that they are able to doff their fur or feathers like so much clothing. In the *katsin tikive* dance, deer, antelope and mountain sheep *katsinas* dance as a prayer to increase their kind. A staff is carried to represent the forelegs of the animals, but they do not mimic animal behaviour as it is seen in the nonspirit world.

Newly introduced animals, like the horse, cow, pigs and domestic fowl, while appearing as *katsinas*, evidently have not been part of Hopi life long enough to be incorporated in Hopi thought as 'people'. Whether this perception will ever change is difficult to say, though there are two precedents to consider.

First, the *kyash* (parrot), introduced to the Hopi in pre-European contact times by Indians far to the south in what is now central Mexico, has become an integral part of Hopi religious thought and practice, from its identity as an animal associated with the direction 'south' to the use of its feathers on religious articles. There even exists a parrot clan.

The second example is that of the rooster. This domestic bird is recognized within the *katsina* world where he has a position as the pet of Tawa, the sun.

At this point it is important to note the pitfalls inherent in translating or attempting to translate concepts from the language of a culture where they exist to one where they do not. Attempts to draw parallels can be equally misleading. The great body of literature on the Hopi make references to the badger clan, the badger people, the *katsina* clan, the *katsina* people, the *katsina* society, yet the Hopi use the word *yom* for what non-Hopi somewhat arbitrarily divide into clan, society and people.

Many animals are also recognized through *yom* (clan) names, such as bear, snake, deer, and badger as well as nonanimal snow, water and sand. Hopi clans perform a number of religious and social functions, of which only a few relate to what is commonly referred to as their 'totem'. The totemic aspect of Hopi clans is, however, tenuous at best and clearly nonexistent in other instances.

Members of the Honauyomu/bear clan count themselves as descendants and relatives of that clan; in fact they are 'the bear people', but to impute a strong and clear totemic relationship with the bear would be a mistake, as they generally do not regard themselves as direct descendants of the bear itself.

That there was once a much stronger, clear totemic relationship is possible but not demonstrable. Clans are often named not so much for mythic descent from the 'totem' involved, but from association with it, as in the case of the Navak/snow and Patki water/*yom*.

Animal *yom* and animal *katsinas* do not directly link with one another in religious observances. When the Badger *katsina* appears, for example, it is not incumbent upon badger clan people to represent him, nor are members of other clan people prohibited or even discouraged from representing him.

Representation of animals in the 'Hopi way' is not limited to *katsinas* and clans. The emergence story and Hopi folktales deal extensively with animals: the birds who helped find the way into the fourth world, animals who turned the tables on coyote, and the pivotal role of spider woman in many an exploit. References are made to the antelope people, snake people and others much as one would reference other tribes or people.

The double image

A frequent sight around the Hopi mesas, Isau wuyomu/coyote figures prominently in many Hopi folktales, with an entire body of stories recorded dealing specifically with coyote, the trickster-turned-buffoon. In non-secular stories he is mentioned as the one who destroyed the order of the stars, scattering them in the random pattern that we see today. There is an Isau wuyomu/coyote clan, but he is not represented as a *katsina*, though it should be noted that because an animal is not currently represented as a *katsina*, it does not mean it never was so represented nor that it never will be. Ethnological studies among the Hopi in the past 75 years show that many *katsinas* have come and gone, some repeatedly. There are no recorded strictures against eating coyote meat, but he is not listed by Hopi as being among the meats eaten.

Kweo/wolf is a *katsina* associated with, and appearing in, *katsin tikive* with the deer, antelope and other hoofed dancers, yet he goes unmentioned in Hopi mesas, making his use as a food source moot. Other animals that historically have also dwelled at great distance from the Hopi, such as the bear, mountain sheep, even buffalo, have clan and/or *katsina* representations, appear in Hopi folktales, and were eaten.

Honan/badger, little brother of the bear, is believed to have curing abilities that come from his intimate association with roots and plants. Snakebite and arthritis and rheumatism are within his ability to cure. They are also within the ability of the badger clan/Honanyomu to cure. The Hopi who belong to the badger clan count badger as an ancestor and the badger people as relatives, but do not necessarily believe they are directly descended from the badger, who is also represented in *katsina* form.

Antelope are a source of food for the Hopi. Prior to being hunted, prayers and offerings are made to render the antelope willing to be caught. Like other large animals, after being killed they are traditionally covered with a white blanket, or *manta*, and smoke is blown over them, an act usually described as a blessing or a prayer offering of thanks. Antelope clan people, like other Hopi, may eat antelope meat when available despite the apparent 'totemic' relationship. The antelope is represented in *katsina* form and clan members are believed to be able to treat problems with urination.

Rabbits are the smallest animals to receive a similar ceremony or sign of respect. Rabbits, deer and antelope, because of their speed, lope and tendency to circle back are regarded as related. The rabbit is not represented in *katsina* form, though its place in Hopi legends and folktales is firm. The rabbit clan people were once given the position of guardians of the village to defend it against outsiders (Kabotie 1949).

The eagle is among the most important of Hopi animals. Highest-flying of all the birds, eagles are closely associated with rain-bringing clouds. Their fluffy down is prized for its cloud-like qualities and their feathers are a vital part of Hopi religious objects and clothing. The eagle is never eaten. Special expeditions to obtain eagle feathers are arranged under the direction and supervision of religious leaders. When a nest is located, it is the young that are captured. They are strapped into cradleboards that are miniatures of those used for Hopi infants. After being brought to the villages, the eaglets have their heads washed and are given presents of bows and arrows and the females are presented with baskets and *puch tihu* – small, flat *katsina* dolls.

Ethnographic literature about the Hopi speaks of full-grown eagles being 'sacrificed' by smothering after the Niman ceremony, but to the Hopi the eagles are being simply 'sent home'.[3] Prayer feathers are tied to legs, wings and necks for forgiveness or blessing, and to ensure that they return to this world from the spirit world for which they are about to depart to nest and hatch. Prayer smoke is blown over the body after skinning and the remains are interred in a special burial ground for hawks and eagles. Cornmeal is sprinkled in the burial hole, for the birds are messengers to the cloud people of the spirit world.

An oft-repeated Hopi story tells of a young man, one of the mountain lion clan people, named Tiyo, who married a woman of the Tsuayom/snake people. According to the story, the snake people, like most animal people, could remove their skin. When they did, they looked like the Hopi. The children of Tiyo and his wife included both snakes and humans, and it is from this couple that most members of the Tsuayom count their descent.

Snake messengers

Snakes are also vital messengers, able to carry prayers, a role they perform during a snake dance. The snakes are gathered without regard to whether they carry venom. They are ceremonially purified through washing and smoke, danced with, and given cornmeal during the ceremony. Afterwards, they are released by the handful and armful below the mesas to carry the prayers of the Hopi people. There is no snake *katsina* though there is a snake clan, and there are absolute strictures against eating snakes.

Pakwabi/frogs and Yonyosona/turtles, represented by *katsinas*, are not only never consumed, but also enjoy protection from being teased or molested as they are believed to be 'spirits that can help us', perhaps because of their close association with water and rain. Turtles, however, are often 'sent home' so that their shells can be used as leg rattles by the dancers in the *katsina* ceremonies. In attempting to structure or even characterize the role of animals in Hopi duality, we find that economic importance, whether direct food value, as with the antelope, or indirect economic value as with the eagles who act as intermediaries in helping to ensure the continuation of the life cycle of all things, does not bear directly, or even consistently on their role in the spirit world.

However, if we examine them from the perspective of the spirit-world first, we find a less perplexing view. All animals with a role or position of significance in the spirit world are treated with respect and ceremony in this world, regardless of their position in daily Hopi life.

This conclusion is a powerful statement in favour of the argument that the Hopi, in recognizing the coexistence of the two worlds, see the spirit-world as the more influential, more powerful and indeed more permanent of the two. Attempts to translate the 'Hopi way' into English have resulted in the unintentional but undeniable infusion of Western cosmology, with the result that the spirit-world is usually represented as being less substantial because it is more a reflection than a reality.

This examination of the role of animals in Hopi duality shows that, if we begin with the spirit-world and work towards this world, it becomes evident that the relationships between the Hopi and animals in this world are based upon their relationships in the spirit-world. Further, ceremonies or observances connected with animals in this world serve to acknowledge the spirit-world, its predominance, and serve as a kind of threshold or connection between the two worlds.

Notes

1   1983 conversation with a Hopi-Tewa woman aged 60+, first Mesa village.
2   1979 conversation with Kikmongwi, aged 80+, second Mesa village.
3   1983 conversation with the same Hopi-Tewa woman as in Note 1.

References

Dockstader, F. J. 1985. *The Kachina and the white man.* Albuquerque: University of New Mexico Press.
Kabotie, F. 1949. *Designs from the ancient Mimbrenos with a Hopi interpretation.* San Francisco: Grabhorn Press.

11 *Eat and be eaten: animals in U'wa (Tunebo) oral tradition*

ANN OSBORN*

The U'wa (known in the literature as Tunebo) once consisted of a number of clan-like groups inhabiting the eastern Andean cordillera of Venezuela and Colombia. The groups appear to have been organized into a number of feder-ations, each federation of eight groups having a central point of reference and considering themselves to be 'the people', with other federations related to them. One of these was resident around the Sierra Nevada de Cocuy (Chita, Chiscas, or Güican) in the Colombian department of Boyáca, well after the European conquest. Then as now, they inhabited three different altitudinal zones and exploited a fourth; chanted mythology was and is performed in each zone as specific activities are carried out (Osborn 1982). Of the eight groups in the Sierra Nevada de Cocuy federation, four were centred around the northeastern flanks of the Sierra Nevada (3000 m) and farmed down to a temperate zone (2000 m), while the other four groups inhabited a band of terrain stretching from the temperate zone (2000 m) to the lowlands (500 m). It will be seen below how crucial different altitudes and corresponding eco-logical zones are, since they correspond to the cosmology, and also particular foods eaten in each zone seasonally are vital fertility substances.

The information that forms the basis of this chapter was gathered inter-mittently over 14 years from members of the Kubaruwa clan, one of the last remaining traditional groups (population 500), belonging to the Sierra Nevada de Cocuy federation (Osborn 1982). Throughout this chapter I refer to the Kubaruwa clan unless stated otherwise.

In the course of a year the Kubaruwa move their place of residence several times. Within the range of altitudes they occupy (from 450 m to 2000 m above sea level), three different zones can be distinguished: lowland, foot-hills, and mountain. In a wider context these zones correspond in the Kubaruwa world-view with the major division of the whole region into plains, mountains, and highlands. Topographically these three zones are visibly different, but agricultural activities and crops are basically the same in all three. There are differences in emphasis, because of soil or climatic conditions, but only a few products are confined to particular zones.

* The author died in August 1988 and was unable to make final revisions to her chapter (see Preface).

In the lowlands and the plains the crops that do best are manioc and lowland varieties of maize. The lowlands and foothills are also used for hunting, fishing, and collecting the honey and wax of the stingless bee. The essential hallucinatory drug yopo (*akwa*; *Anadenthara macrocarpa*) is a product of the foothill zone, where the natural vegetation consists of tropical forest, cut through by unnavigable rivers.

When they are in the mountain zone, the Kubaruwa live closely together in the village of Cobaría (altitude 1300 m), made up of some 70 houses interspersed with small garden plots and surrounded by forest. Life in Cobaría is associated with the *Aya* ceremony (see below) and its maize harvest. To the southwest, and above the region inhabited and used by the Kubaruwa, lies more rugged country, the cloud forest where the mountains rise up to snow ranges, a terrain covered by forest and nearly inaccessible. The Kubaruwa say that not even animals and birds inhabit those regions, for there is no food for them. They themselves do not enter this zone, except for its fringes, where they collect cane for making baskets and for the cere- monial crowns worn by some men during Kubaruwa ceremonies. Above 3000 m is the *páramo* zone, with a few gnarled trees and alpine type plants. Although this region is unsuitable for agriculture and is not permanently inhabited, it contains sites of ritual importance for the U'wa.

The Kubaruwa move seasonally between the different altitude zones of their homeland, but this mobility cannot be explained by simple ecological determinism. The Kubaruwa pattern of sowing and harvesting maize does not seem to make the best use of the climate, nor does it provide maize throughout the year. The only way in which sense can be made of the Kubaruwa maize cycle is to juxtapose it with the ceremonial calendar. Maize is sown principally to provide crops for the main ceremonies: the *Reowa* (see below) which starts in May, and the *Aya*, which begins in August and lasts until mid-November. The maize harvests – regardless of the state of the maize, and even if the cobs are still unripe – are made to coincide with major ceremonies. The reasons why the Kubaruwa move up and down the slopes at set times of year are not so much economic nor gastronomic as religious.

This introduces the theme of Kubaruwa cosmology. Besides their physical world, the U'wa live within another universe defined by mythology and ritual. In Kubaruwa religious cosmology, the universe initially comprised two spheres, an upper world of dry heat and light, and a lower one of wet darkness and void. Then there was movement, in which the upper and lower worlds met or came together, and from their mixing the middle world, in which the U'wa live, came about. These worlds (spheres or firmaments) are identified by, and associated with, colours. The upper world is called White, the lower world is Red, and, where they mix, Blue and Yellow are created. In other words, the mixing and blending of the upper and lower worlds formed the middle world in which the U'wa live.

Whereas the upper and lower worlds are thought to be indestructible, the middle world is able to exist only by keeping the upper and lower ones separate. The relationships between these different worlds have to be maintained in balance by the U'wa. Since they are equidistant between their divine forebears of the Red and White worlds, the U'wa embody the delicate balance between the lower and upper extremes, and it is their task to maintain this balance through ritual and chants. If this balance were to be disturbed, the reverse of order would occur; Red would move upwards and invade White, which would signify the end of the universe.

The U'wa belief system is laid down in their chanted oral tradition. In it the acts of deities, the miscegenation between those of the upper and lower worlds, and the acts of shaman deities are recorded. Chanted myth links the past to the present and to the future. It is the people's repeated performance of chant, among other things, that maintains the deities in their place performing their specific activities and keeps everything in its position preserving, in principle, an ordered and harmonious universe. If the chants are not performed it is conceivable that things will 'get out of place' with the eternal manifestation of basic properties, and transformed animals, plants, and trees may return to their former states as proto-people.

The chanted myths are performed seasonally and are myths in which all people take part. They are, therefore, communal myths, as are others chanted on the occasions of individual life crises such as initiation and death. Each chanted myth belongs to one of two categories: *Reowas*, 'Blowings' (mainly concerned with cooling or purifying, and tending to deal with mortality, sickness and the coming into the middle world of properties that combat such conditions), or *Ayas*, 'Orderings' (which are performed after the *Reowas*, and tend to be about appearance and order). In *Reowas* the principal participants and chanters are from the east of the village, while *Ayas* are performed by people from the west of the village. The two groups have to cooperate and to perform each other's myths and rituals for these to be effective.

This chapter demonstrated the significance of animals in U'wa culture through analysis of some of the chanted myths. First, however, it is necessary to grasp the basic U'wa concept of mortality. Creatures of flesh and blood embody explicit mortality: given their birth from a womb, their sexuality for reproduction, death, and the need to eat a variety of foods and to defecate. People, as animals, have mortality; the deities do not. Life in the middle world of mortals was created out of materials and properties owned by the deities of the upper and lower worlds. All these elements were obtained by stealth by travelling shaman deities, mainly celestial beings, and were put by them into the middle world. Thus, all things in this middle world, having acquired the essential wherewithal of life, are composed of the same matter and, accordingly, no rigid distinction is made between the living beings that exist in this middle world.

The myths presented in this chapter are organized in terms of the seasonal cycle that governs their performance. I contend that the meaning of oral tradition varies according to the seasonal context, notwithstanding unifying features (or structures) repeated throughout the myths that are susceptible to varying interpretations. The four seasons are associated with gestation, birth, conception, and maturity. Because the U'wa believe that they, as well as animals, are composed of the foods they eat, food consumption is ordered in accordance with the development cycle.

Kubaruwa and, by extension, U'wa chanted myths are divisible into four parts, each of which contains a number of episodic cantos of unequal length. Chant procedure and accompanying ritual separates out the parts and cantos and is one of the keys to understanding them. These parts are the following:

Part 1: The description of the unsatisfactory state of the middle world, and of the initial task undertaken by deities of bringing about suitable conditions for existence. (In the actual performance this part takes place from dusk to about 11 pm.

Part 2: The arrival of essential matter from the upper world. (This part carries over the midnight hour to about 12.30 or 1.00 am).

Part 3: The arrival of complementary matter from the lower world.

Part 4: The beings celebrated in the chant return to their appropriate places. The chant ends with everything back in its place. (The performance finishes just before the sun comes up.)

Performances take place inside a ceremonial house that symbolizes the U'wa middle world, or, in some cases today, in a master shaman's domestic house.

Before describing the myths, we should note that each chant-part and the cantos often seem unrelated and today cantos may be told as separate myths. These are, however, 'interlaces' building up a thought system which cannot be perceived if the myths are separated.

The *Aya* performance

The *Aya* performance takes place over the September equinox, from August to November, with the performance punctuated by maize harvests around the upland village of Cobaría. The maize harvested during this season is grown round the houses and represents the original essence or matter, *bita*, and the embryonic female seed, *kuna*, of maize. It is human infants' nutrient since it 'nourishes' or stimulates the production of maternal milk. As with many first crops, some of the maize is eaten raw, particularly by women and children; the essences are thus taken into the body unharmed by cooking. Animals attacking the maize and other cultivated plants are trapped or hunted, for they should not eat human food. If they do this consistently, and particularly since they eat it raw (in other words without destroying its life force), the animals may return to their former state as human females. This is the wet-to-dry season and the time of many human births.

The *Aya* is performed in the *Aya* ceremonial house, which is situated in the lower central house cluster of the village. All the Kubaruwa take part in the performance, men, women and children, except for the sick and the maimed. Since the *Aya* chant is about birth and life, it must not be contaminated by unwhole people. The performance is conducted by the *Aya* master shaman, assisted by three senior chanters. The first performance of the *Aya* takes place immediately after the post-*Reowa* ceremonies have finished and when the women have harvested the *Aya* maize. After a series of complex preparations and the blowing of conch trumpets to inform the people, the ancestors, and the deities that the performance is about to begin, everyone sets off to the *Aya* house. There the *Aya* master leads the ritual, which is performed with great solemnity.

Part 1 (Cantos 1–4) of the chant describes the creation of the middle world of the U'wa in the form of a ceremonial house.

Parts 2 and 3 (Cantos 5–12) refer to gifts from the upper and lower worlds. The upper world contributes embryonic male seed (*rora*), soul breath (*oka-kambra*), seed of hair strength (*anáre*) (which subsumes coverings such as feathers and leaves woven into protective thatch and garments), weaving equipment, cotton seed, wax, menhirs, pollen (*ohíra*) and certain diseases (such as *íbara*, that of stinging and spots, and that of heat, *oka*). Gifts from the lower world are sent (out of a womb) and include *kanoba*, the germ, or sap, of life. Sap relates to life as does disease to death. Although at first sight this seems a very mixed set of gifts, the point is that all nature, including human beings, receives them, and they are planted beneath menhirs, some of which still stand on U'wa territory (Osborn 1985).

Part 4 concerns the populating of the middle world. This part consists of nine cantos, beginning with no. 13 (the first 12 having formed Parts 1–3). Although the cantos in Part 4 seem relatively simple they are, in fact, complex; comments on them by Kubaruwa are confusing and contradictory. In this chapter I have divided Part 4 into sections or episodes. For each of these I first present a summary of the content of the chant, and then an analysis.

> Rukwa (the Sun) is thinking. He must send the warmth of the sun and the water of the lakes of the upper world to the middle world for the seeds to grow. (Canto 13)

What Rukwa observes at the beginning of Part 4 is that, although everything has been created it has not yet been set in motion. To this effect he mixes sun-warmth with lake-water and thus finally triggers off life – and mortality – in the middle world.

> Master/leader of Animals (Ruáhama) and Original Earth Sun (OES, Thírbita) come into the middle world. The first clears the thorny plants and bushes, the second warms the lake-water. Master of Animals sows the essential properties of life around these lakes. Tree turkey enters the door of a mountain cave at the edge of the snow mountain. (Cantos 14, 15)

Rukwa instructs Master of Animals to put his thoughts into practice. Rukwa's orders are, in effect, to sow male and female elements throughout the middle world. Ruáhama and Thírbita are shaman deities; one clears away inedible plants and sows edible foods for animals, and the other warms the icy lakes of the Sierra Nevada sufficiently for their waters to become drinkable. The tree turkey is one of the disguises of another shaman deity, Yagshowa, who is the son of upper-world male deity and appears in a great many myth cantos under different guises. He is also capable of bewitching (*kwika*: a broad term subsuming magic or reversal of order, and including the changing of appearances, as above, and also sexual practices).

> Highland and lowland deer (*Thíkaraman* and *Rúkathira*), hare (*Wamara*) and peccary (*Theya*) emerge from the cave door. OES orders his sister's son Ancient Tree (Rémkara) to collect firewood and make a fire so that they can singe and cook his sister's daughters, the animals. OES eats each of the animals; only the bones are left. (Canto 16a)

In this canto the animals appear. It is their fate to be eaten and this is first done by Thírbita, the original Earth Sun, who does not give any meat to Rémkara.

Kinship terms, employed as metaphors of classification, are used throughout U'wa oral tradition. Mothers' brothers order sisters' sons, and both may marry sisters' daughters. Siblings and parallel cousins are termed *Raba* (their respective parents are of the same sex and therefore of the same kind). Cross-cousins are termed *Shara* (their parents are of different sex and in consequence these cousins are not of the same kind). The two sets of cousins are expected to cooperate and exchange their sisters. The mothers' brothers, in social groups and in myth, are the pivotal relationship between bilateral cross-cousins, *Shara* his son, and *Raba* (his sister's son), and his sisters' daughters. The terms also include *rúwa raba* (flesh siblings), mammals eating the same food as people, and *shara*, carnivores. Eating is a metaphor for copulation and we can assume that OES in the myth, like the sun today, is a carnivore and consumes the woman in the above canto.

> The Tree Turkey emerges from the cave door proclaiming that he is also a leader (of animals). He has testicles (therefore) he can eat meat, and proceeds to do so. OES wakes up, gets hold of Tree Turkey, and beats him over the head until his face is black and blue. (Canto 16a cont.)
>
> Turkey cries out in pain and is named Yan-kuawa (the sound of his cry). He travels from the highlands to the lowlands, builds houses, clears and sows land, harvests cotton (? of trees), spins and weaves. He does this in each lowland group's territory. He works very quickly and does all of this four times. When he has finished he travels up and over the high mountains, crossing the Sierra Nevada, and disappears into the west. (Canto 16b)

In Canto 16b Yagshowa, as Turkey, takes cotton to the middle world, as Rúwahama took animals. Turkey consumes his 'father's women' who, in addition, are of a different type, and he is punished (or is it Turkey Buzzard who does this, who should rightfully eat only carrion, as some U'wa suggest?). Turkey removes himself to the lowlands (that is, the lower world). Turkeys are still recognized today as associated with certain lowland groups. In the past, turkeys were domesticated by them and turned loose in the forest; then, as adults, the feathers were taken to be woven into ceremonial capes and girls' initiation hoods. Men belonging to a specific lowland group wore turkey-bone necklaces. In the past, and to a certain extent today, feathers were exchange items between different altitudinal zones. The shaman deity of cotton, a lowland product, is Yagshowa (who sowed it in turkey guise). Among groups of the temperate zone and the lowlands, weaving is a male occupation (today with sheep's wool brought from the highlands). However, lowland and highland groups did not intermarry, although they were indirectly related by overlapping marriage alliances. In the same sense, animals and people (which share a common origin) have their specified marriage partners.

Deer, Hare, and Peccary are talking by the side of the cave door. They must run to work up their strength; they must run in rain and wind. They run along the lakes in the highlands. Deer and Hare run faster than Peccary and the other deer, and they win. The winners say to each other: 'shall we stay or shall we not stay here?' and decide to stay. The losers say to each other: 'let us go to another lake'; so they go down the mountain, where they run round the lakes to work up their strength, and they stay in the middle country. (Canto 16c)

Four different kinds of birds with forked tails (swallows or perhaps fork-tailed kites?) appear in the east. They fly west, following the river beds and streams up the mountains. The birds fly west, and then underneath, back to the east, whence they start again. When they are underneath, Kanwara tells them that they must stop flying and must settle on the land to breed. He recompenses them by giving them distinctive markings which are their *raiya* (fertility wealth), and he also gives them the hallucinogen yopo, so that they will still be able to fly when they want to, even when they have settled on the land to breed. The swallows fly from east to west four times, higher each time, as they gain strength and their wings grow. They sing as they fly. On the fourth journey, over the high ridges, they land and eat; now they have to stay in the middle world to breed. (Canto 16d)

Old man, what are you doing? I am putting fish into the rivers. First crab, and then all the other fish. They swim up from the sea; they grow to gain strength, they swim up the rivers. The fish race up the rivers, and the large, strong ones win, so they may stay in the large rivers; the small fish, who lost the race, go up the smaller rivers and streams (Canto 16e)

The Deer, Hare and Peccary now appear in the lowlands. Thírbita tells Bibra (Monkey) to collect firewood. The plot follows that of Canto 16a, but the animals have now matured by running down into the lowland, and Bibra tries to copulate with them. Thírbita beats him over the backside so that the blood comes out and his bottom is red and black. (Canto 16f)

In Canto 16d it is Kanwara who gives hallucinogen to the birds, enabling them to fly, and in the chant they address him as *Aya*. It may, therefore, be suggested that both Yagshowa and Kanwara are deity shamans. The former acts as a medial deity between the upper and middle worlds, and the latter acts as a medial deity between the middle and lower worlds. Both cooperate by taking to the middle world goods that the denizens of the upper or lower worlds try to hoard for themselves.

Cantos 16c to 16e have a similar pattern, each one dealing with competition for females and territory. Mother's brother is a competitor as shaman deity. As a result of this competition, the animals, birds, and fish are, according to their size and speed, distributed between highland and lowlands. To the highlands go the winners: the larger and faster animals. The losers, slower animals, move to the lowlands. The fish are sown in the rivers; the large fish remain in the lowland rivers and their cross-cousins, the smaller ones, in the upland streams. The equation is, therefore, big = fast and low = small = slow, and also birds/air, animals/land, and fish/water. Breeding and eating habits are also established.

The animals whose distribution is recorded in the chant are today associated with human groups inhabiting the different altitudinal zones. The highland deer and the hare belong to highland groups. The lowland peccary is the Kubaruwa clan's specific animal. The swallow-tailed birds, being migratory, fly over and inhabit U'wa territory at all altitudes, and are given hallucinatory yopo by their mother's brother, the shaman deity Kanwara (Osborn 1985).

These cantos may be classifying things according to habitat, but another explanation is that these sections are concerned with documenting U'wa territory (Osborn 1985). As the birds, animals, and fish move, so are the places through which they travel named: mountain peaks, places on routes, and rivers. Hence place names are recorded which are those of U'wa territory in the past, and also those where the U'wa travelled in order to teach or learn from other Indians. The chants therefore serve as a recording device or mental map.

Finally, there is Canto 16f in which Tree Turkey's actions in the highlands (Canto 16b) are repeated in the lowlands by Bibra (howler monkey), who tries to cohabit and mate with Kubaruwa women (as lowland deer, hare, and peccary) instead of exchanging goods with the Kubaruwa. Monkey is a lowland animal but, nevertheless, ought to mate with his own type.

The animals (including humans) and the plants are classified according to their habitats and the foods eaten there, but, because they all have the same basic properties (sap/saliva, *kanoba*; embryonic male seed, *rora*; original essence or matter, *bita*; embryonic female seed, *kuna*) they are capable of transformation. The U'wa believe that things become what they eat, and that species change according to altitude. These concepts can be seen in the Hives chant presented below.

The Hives (Anbaya Bee Order) chant

The Hives chant and the Hallucinogen chant are performed after the *Aya* in the season spanning the December solstice. At this time of year the Kubaruwa reside in the lowlands where they have their main coca crop. There is a maize crop here as well, and other cultivated foods include roots and tubers. The accentuated activities are honey-collecting and preparing wax (the first drunk, the second exchanged), and tending the coca bushes. This is done before the December solstice, after which small groups of men travel to the lowlands to collect yopo, or to the highlands to exchange wax for rock salt. This is the dry season, when low-growing forest plants and shrubs are seeding. These are considered the proper food of animals. People copulate during this season with the aim of conceiving children. Honey and yopo are ingredients that compose male and female procreative liquids and, in the case of yopo and coca, soul stuff.

The Bee chant is performed by men after collecting honey. The Bee myth is an Order, as its name Anbaya indicates. The aims of the performance are to promote the strength and welfare of the bees. The chanting begins soon after dusk; the men sit cross-legged on leaves on the floor of the eastern half of the house, facing east. The women remain at the back of the house where the mead or beer is kept and do not chant. The chant is sung by all the men present, following a main chanter; when it treats of the bees travelling, the men walk to and fro between the east door and the middle of the house. At dawn, when the chanting has ended, the men and women drink beer and sexual intercourse may take place.

The South American stingless bee makes combs that lack geometric regularity; they are made in horizontal layers or spheres. The Kubaruwa visualize their own universe as being made up of similar spheres, as the middle world is of zones. The bees' products, honey and wax, are to the Kubaruwa the epitome of the notion of 'wealth' (*raiya*), which includes fertility, exchange goods and, nowadays, money. Honey is pure, without contamination, sickness, or mortality; it endows strength and fertility to the person who consumes it. Wax is a traditional exchange good. The bees' most celebrated attribute, however, is their chewing: the male ones are seen to chew pollen and the wood of trees, which they transform into wax; the female bees are said to chew the yellow earth of the plains and to transform it into the yellow core of the nest (*kuna*). By chewing, the bees produce their *kanoba*, or saliva, which is eaten now as honey.

Of all the properties of the environment of which the U'wa feel themselves part, it is to the bees that they compare themselves most closely, saying that they live socially, construct houses (hives), have gatherings, ceremonies and chants, particularly at swarming times, for which they make ceremonial beer in pots (*kumtas*) and consume this themselves (as beer, *kanoba*). Honey is drunk by both men and women for the maintenance of health and to vitalize and replenish the human capacity to make *kanoba*.

The Hives (Bee Order) chant has the same fourfold structure as the *Aya* chant.

> Part 1: The forests of the middle world of U'wa are dry, there is hunger and thirst. The upper and lower world deities, Rukwa and Kanwara, cooperate to produce bees' *kanoba* by each chewing and spitting into large pots.

In the beginning the world is thirsty without bees, their honey and their wax. The world is without the means of germination; it is dry, hungry, and thirsty, which are all metaphors for this condition. Bees' *kanoba* is produced asexually by chewing, and by immortal deities. The chewing by women to produce fermented drink is also called *kanoba*, as is maize chewed to bait traps to catch small rodents. Rain in certain seasons is thought to be the chewings of immortals and is called *kanoba*.

> Parts 2 and 3: Rukwa says to his children the bees that they must go down to the middle world of U'wa. Yagshowa and Ruáhama (Master of Animals) lead the bees' *kanoba* through the coloured spheres. In the 'wealth-lakes' of yellow they bathe and develop bodies. They fly over the red lake of Kanwara. Some of the bees are cheated into bathing in the red lake and are touched by Ruáhama. They develop bodies with blood, and are named Kanwara's sisters' daughters. Those bees that came through the yellow lake undergo an initiation ceremony, are given coca, peppers, ginger, and tobacco to eat. As payment for inhabiting the middle world they are given crowns, seed, covering, yellow soil, and musical instruments. The bees who touched down on the red lake fly into the middle world and settle there as flies, wasps, and other stinging winged insects, and they eat animal excreta. They fly to the cold highlands and enter the cave door, emerging as highland and lowland varieties of deer, and as hare and peccary. They are led by Ruáhama and have Kanwara's illnesses.

These sections refer to two groups of bees. For each group the original material (asexually produced *kanoba*) is the same, but it develops in divergent ways according to the different properties in the coloured lake spheres. Being able to fly, some bees avoid the red lake of menstrual blood (see below) and reproduce asexually. Their essential *kanoba*, honey, is conducive to health, longevity, and purity, and is therefore drunk by humans. The bees are also allocated their specific foods, which are U'wa medicinal plants, used by shamans as trance producers and cleansers (coca, peppers, tobacco, and ginger juice). The gift of yellow soil obliquely refers to gold. In the past, U'wa acquired gold by silent trade, leaving wax and other goods, later collecting gold objects which they say were left by bees.

In contrast, the *kanoba* that developed in the red lake was the source of harmful, illness-causing, stinging insects, the antithesis of the South American stingless bees. By eating animal excreta and travelling to the highlands, the bees who passed through the red lake are transformed into the animals whose excreta they eat (the herbivorous animals of the *Aya* chant, Part 4).

> Part 4: Yagshowa takes bees' *kanoba* from the yellow lake and sows it through the middle country where it transforms into plants: coca, peppers and ginger. The bees settle and chew the pollen of palms, trees and squash, which become wax. The male bees give their female sisters yellow earth (*kuna*) and the pollen of a hallucinogenic vine (*shebara*) to chew so that they can breed.

The stingless American bees are domesticated by the U'wa of temperate zones. In the above canto, bees are given appropriate food to produce their goods. Bees' embryonic female seed (*kuna*) is their larvae. They frequent an unidentified vine which provides a hallucinogen used by shamans to perform *kwika* (bewitching, a term also for incest). The fact that this pollen is particularly mentioned draws attention to the U'wa belief that the bees breed between opposite-sex siblings, and are therefore incestuous. The bees perform something very akin to magic in producing honey and wax and are, indeed, in a shamanic state when consuming hallucinogenic pollens. However, the most apposite manner in which to approach the position of bees in U'wa culture is to concentrate on the aspect of purity, not only because of the belief in the curative powers of honey, but also because bees feed off medicinal plants and hallucinogens. Incestuous relationships are also pure, as extraneous sexual liquids are not exchanged.

The acquisition and use of the hallucinogen yopo (*akwa*) is the theme of a *Reowa* chant performed at the same season as the Hives chant, and the two myths are interrelated.

> The Hallucinogen chant Part 1: There is no light, no thought. Rukwa, Upper World deity sits stationary in the house of the *upper* world. There is no eye of thought in the universe. Hallucinogen is in the *lower* world. Upper World deity sends his breath (*kambra*) into a female deity of the *lower* world, and embryo Kanwara comes about. He looks at the place where he was born and sees the birth blood of the *middle* world beings, who are without movement or protection and he thinks of yopo.

The U'wa make no rigid distinction between themselves and animals because they all came about by the same creative process, contain the same properties, and consume foods that are similar. All acquire hallucinogenic snuffs, but specific mixtures develop particular properties; however, excessive properties and particular abilities and attributes must be balanced out and exchanged albeit, at times, by cunning and stealth. That shaman deities associated with different spheres and abilities are benefactors of beings belonging to other spheres, and in charge of different deities, is consistent with U'wa thought processes.

With the acquisition of hallucinogenic snuffs, lower world animals are able to become carnivorous males in the middle world. Middle world mammals are able to become carnivorous birds, and birds shamans, in the upper world. Transformation of beings between altitudinal zones and universe spheres is common in U'wa beliefs, and the main vehicle for this is eating food, including hallucinogens, belonging to different zones and spheres. In the context of transformation from shamans to carnivores or vice versa, U'wa interpreters place the emphasis on the visionary power of a hallucinogen that changes vision according to the place concerned. The shaman sees himself as a jaguar, bear, or bird in the lower or upper world, and they in turn see themselves as people in their own area. The U'wa do not see carnivorous activities as viciousness or evil, but rather as a case of mistaken identity and the fault of the deities who gave hallucinogens to them. This was rather succinctly explained to me by the example of a bear who recently attacked and killed a child; it was not the animal's fault; he saw the child (a female) as maize and was hungry. The bear was killed so that it would not make the same mistake twice. The bear was then given a human burial, for in the lower world it *becomes* human.

Both honey and hallucinogen, particularly yopo as an U'wa deity, are related to each other by their consumption by both men and women, for the same reasons and to achieve similar effects. They are, however, consumed in different ways; honey is drunk, yopo is taken through the nose. Honey goes through the digestive tract and nourishes and cleanses the body like milk of tender maize; it is thought to be particularly conducive to the female reproductive cycle at a time when copulation takes place with the intention of having children. Honey is drunk by men since they play a part in this cycle, and they take yopo to strengthen their semen, and to render it potent. The yopo travels through the body via the nose, down the spinal column, and into the genitals (these and the noses are seen as being connected). Yopo is thought to produce bone and soul stuff. For this reason it should also be taken by pregnant women; although a male drug, it is not exclusively so.

The myths indicate the concern of the U'wa with disease, of which there are essentially two types that are acquired in the yellow or red world sphere. The bees' *kanoba* was contaminated by yellow disease, but also produces the disease's antidote (honey). Those bees contaminated by red disease produce poison (the red lake is equated with menstrual blood which is considered diseased because it is nonproductive, not fertile, and wasted). Hallucinogenic snuffs were given to all beings as an antidote.

The following season's chanted myth and associated activities deal with the point at which the animals became mature.

Thenakuba (male fox) and *Ruwa reowa* (animal purification) chants

The first of these chants is an *Aya* (Order) and the second a *Reowa* (Blowing myth). Both these chants are performed in the dry-to-wet season, from the end of February to the beginning of May, so spanning the March equinox. At the equinoxes, the sun is overhead, and at its closest to the U'wa world. The sun, as a carnivore, is particularly dangerous (*Aya*, Part 4) when overhead because he then counts the population and is likely to consume/copulate with fertile but nonpregnant women. In the temperate zone the *Aya* maize fields are now sown. As each field is sown the Fox chant is performed by men (in the past by women). The people then move down to the lowlands where a variety of crops is now ready for harvesting (a maize crop, avocados, and chontadura–*Guilielmo gasipaes*). The agricultural routine of harvest/mulch/sow/seed-selection and storage continues. This is the main hunting season in the lowlands, during which the Animal Purification chant used to be performed by men (for women) since, as will be seen, the animals are in fact about to mature and mature as human females.

The Fox chant

Part 1 of the Fox chant is no longer performed. I have therefore had to rely on informed comments as to its content. The first part of this chant (dealing with the unsatisfactory state of the universe) describes how the protagonists fox(es) and opossum(s) (*kwitrama*) arrive in the U'wa middle world in a potential state of maturity as humans. As such they attempt to eat people's procreative foods, in this case honey. Arriving (or 'being born') as adults is not the right way to come, and accordingly they are sent back into the inner place of the mountain in the highlands in order to emerge as infants. The entire myth is a record of 'mistakes' on the part of these animals in their endeavours to become people and parents.

> Part 2: Skin and placenta of fox emerge from the highland cave inside the mountain already provided with sight, breath, tools and wealth. They address each other as *raba* (siblings of the same sex and parallel cousins) and run down the mountain, emerging in the temperate zone and clan territory.
> The canto is repeated with the opossum in place of the fox. Foxes run round lakes and think of their *shara* (opossum) male cross-cousin and they look for honey. Opossum does the same and thinks of crab to suck.

The animals emerge with their basic abilities, which are developed by running down the mountain. The tools which are developed are teeth, claws, and male genitalia (also they address each other as men), and they intend to consume procreative foods. These are not women, nor do they symbolize women, as they intend to procreate with foods not females.

> Part 3: Fox and opossum meet. Fox remarks that opossum has no cutting tools. Opossum remarks that fox has no scraping tools. Fox climbs to get honey, opossum catches ground wasps. They meet face to face, their tools are blunt. They travel to the edge of the middle world to where the land and sky meet. They go below the foot of the mountain lakes. Fox steals tools from upper world deity of light. They return to the middle world in the lowlands and eat honey.

They eat different procreative foods, which pass through their bodies and become procreative liquids, and mix them during copulation ('face-to-face', a euphemism for copulation), but to no avail, as their genitalia, in addition to being male, are immature (blunt). They travel to the horizon and go up (via stars) to the upper world and steal new and mature genitalia from the stone house of an upper world deity (a sun?).

> Part 4: Fox eats more and becomes fat. The fox returns to the depths of the earth, to the stone base (menhirs) that support the middle world house. He sits and becomes like stone. He becomes the seventh star of the Pleiades.

The male fox becomes pregnant by eating too much honey and is banished from the middle world and becomes an immortal (asexual) deity, who, for the clans that perform the chant, is a star. Opossum is not mentioned but reappears in the following myth as a female who, with others, is about to mature physically.

The series of 'mistakes' on the part of the animals all centre around and underscore the fact that men cannot reproduce without women, and that sexual maturity produced by different foods is in addition necessary. The following myth deals with female sexual maturity, and yet another requisite for its efficacy is required: that of initiation ceremony and chant.

The Animal Purification chant

> Part 1: A message is sent from upper world deity (Rukwa) to lower world deity (Kanwara) that an initiation ceremony is needed as females as animals (*ruwa raba*, meat siblings) are maturing and will eat each other. The elders (*thakina*) of the old people (*remína*) are gathered below the middle world in Ruya; paca (*baña*), anteater (*áthora*), peccary (*bucá-*

rama), armadillo (*rúrama*), coati (*bina*), porcupine (*kánta*), deer (*rojo-kura*), sloth (*tákaja*), and turkey (*bithura*) are maturing.

The females are on the point of menstruating, and it is at this time that their female role is established. As is the case with human children, their gender is not fully established until the onset of physical maturity. They are only female initiation rites in this society. The females are potentially human and the female initiation ceremony and chant must be performed in this case to prevent them from becoming human mammals. The list in the Animal Purification chant is probably specific to the clan performing its version of the chant; all the animals are lowland mammals and the implication is that they are women of female-oriented clans.

> Kanwara, who is immobile, wills his sister's son Sheba to chant and perform an initiation ceremony for the elders. Sheba chants four times and on the fifth goes to Kanwara crying. Sheba's mother's brothers ask Sheba what is the matter and he replies that he is no longer Kanwara's sister's son but his sister's daughter. Kanwara tells him that he harmed himself as he did not chant correctly and chanted five times: 'Now you will have to eat and so die'. Sheba returns to Ruya. Ferret (*bethkura*) puts on a hood and begins to menstruate from a vagina. Opossum goes to tell Kanwara and is instructed to tell Ferret to put on a hood made of leaves. All the animals do the same and all begin to menstruate. They are now worried about eating.

The deity planned to turn his sister's son into sister's daughter. The incompetence episode is an excuse to introduce a carnivorous female among the omnivores. It is established that some animals will eat others.

> Part 2: Kanwara looks for another sister's son to perform the initiation ceremony and he locks the elders up in a house inside the mountain in a lowland group's territory. Opossum returns to Kanwara to tell him that all the elders are secreting fluid. Kanwara is pleased. 'Ha,' the thinks, 'so I am powerful. They will now have to eat and be eaten as they are. I am the one to provide food for Tabija and Kwiyora (Kanwara male ancestors) for they have no women. I have made the elders menstruate.' Kanwara wills Thunder to perform the ceremony. Thunder demands payment and is promised Ferret as a wife, for she has a splendid white blaze under her neck (*raiya*, wealth and women's necklaces of shell put on during initiation ceremonies). Thunder, as a courting male, travels through lakes to the house, followed by monkey (Bibra) who is playing a flute. Opossum, who is outside Ruya stealing from clan male ancestors, rushes in to warn that Thunder is on his way and will burn (*wanro*, toast, to warm and singe) them up. Ferret tells Opossum to shut up. Thunder arrives and performs the chant three times, giving the elders ceremonial foods. They have no *kanoba* nor

menstrual blood. At each successive blowing the elders become less smelly and bitter. Only armadillos and paca become almost edible. Thunder comes a fourth time. Ferret refuses to allow him to copulate with her and escapes; he is very angry and tries to take the elders by force and flashing his lightning-penis they are burnt. The exceptions are armadillo and paca.

The ceremonial foods today are mice or frogs, two types of small fish, ginger and a type of pepper. They are used in many purification ceremonies and jointly called *e'na ruwa* (embryonic meat) and *kanoba*, and are said to extract 'harm'. At the onset of menstruation, girls are given *e'na ruwa* to eat during ritual and chant. If available, armadillo, paca (or crab) (the Fox chant, Part 2) are given to them during the concluding ceremony (in the past a complete female initiation ceremony took four years, during which time a hood was worn, as by the mammals in the myth). These meats are said to produce and purify menstruation. It is possible that, as these animals escaped burning, their essential 'seed' and properties were not destroyed and in addition they developed into female clan ancestors. It should be mentioned that the culturally important animals, those in the myths, when caught, are given a purification ceremony to extract their potential humanity before they are eaten. Thunder, while burning the animals, also burns off his own penis, and is banished from the middle world.

Part 3: Kanwara sends a message to Rukwa the upper world deity telling him what has happened, and the two agree to cooperate and perform an initiation ceremony for the animals, for they are still bitter; in such a state copulation between them and clan male ancestors is not permissible. They perform the ceremony for four years and on each successive year the animals taste better, with the exception of armadillo and paca.

The myth states that the underworld people inside the mountain are potential women. At the onset of menstruation a first set of initiation ceremonies is performed. Instead of purifying the menstrual blood, thus making the women fit for breeding they are transformed by trickery into lowland animals. In the second set of initiation ceremonies the women now become fully fledged animals and their menstrual blood is less bitter-hot, and they are ready for breeding among themselves. Lowland ancestor people who were women are now female animals. On the other hand, those that emerge into the middle world do so as women and are marriageable.[1]

The *Reowa* (purification) chant

The seasons, as has been shown, are defined on the basis of a number of variables: climatic conditions, particularly rain, the sun's movements, and specific seasonal activities including myth-performance and ritual. In the wet season spanning the June solstice the falling rain is said to be *kanoba* of the deities who, as immortals, are sending this their 'fertility essence' to mortals. The women who are pregnant are now in the final stage of gestation, and food restrictions are observed by all. Hunting and fishing are prohibited when chanting this season's myth, and people abstain from normal foods, particularly salt and peppers (hot and dangerous substances at this stage in the development cycle, although beneficial in other stages). Instead, the people feast on *kara* (*Metteniusa edulis*) nuts and *kutha* (*Brosumum utile* H.B.K.) fruits. One of the themes of the season's myth documents the coming of the above trees as ancestors who change, in part, into trees and teach the people how to prepare their fruits. The *kara* nut is extremely bitter and the bitter liquid, its semen, has to be drained off. Clearly it should not be consumed by people unless they wish to return to another former state as fruit-bearing trees. This liquid is drained into small diverted and dammed streams in which fish and frogs are seen to spawn and feed. Both fish and frogs are consumed ceremonially during this season as part of the chant's performance. Both the chant and associated practices underline the U'wa beliefs that their ancestry derives not only from animals but also from trees and plants. The wet season is in a sense the one that joins the others together by linking the forest products to those of the river: the fruit-bearing trees to fish and frogs. It also involves birds, particularly the toucan, in the system, as people specifically leave some of the nuts to be consumed by birds which take the first crop. The nuts are left as payment for birds who are seen to be propagators of seed. The women and nature are seen to be in the final stages of gestation and the chant is in itself both an example of a purification ceremony and a means of encouraging gestating nature. The chant and ceremony banish all harm from the universe, including confused weather conditions and poisonous snakes. Animals and people as such are not mentioned. The performances are for all foetal development and safe birth.

Although the chant is performed in the temperate zone, its benefit is 'taken down' to the lowlands by the master chanter and shaman during performances, where he and another shaman perform a purification (*Reowa*) for mammals, particularly these mentioned in the Animal Purification chant.

Concluding remarks

Many of the classic themes treated by Lévi-Strauss (1966, 1970) occur in the material presented here. This study also relates to the work of many other authors writing on South American Indians. Among the recurring themes are the following: shamanisn and transformation (Reichel-Dolmatoff 1975); exogamy, incest, and animality (Reichel-Dolmatoff 1971); the position of the mother's brother (Rivière 1969); space-time and the development cycle (Hugh-Jones 1979); and the supposedly incorrect behaviour of animals

(Wilbert 1970, Taylor 1979). This chapter also brings a nonmaterialistic slant to the Andean concept of 'verticality' (Murra 1975, Salomon 1986). The central issue that unites U'wa material to those themes is the interrelationship between reproduction, consumption, and transformation.

One of the main themes of this chapter has been to show how animals are incorporated into U'wa beliefs by documenting the chanted mythology in which they occur. By placing this material in the context of performance and by relating it to present-day activities, it has been shown that U'wa exegesis continually relates the past, present, and future, which may be reversed if myth and ritual and associated practices are not performed in place, on time. That is, in the U'wa belief system it is possible for animals, plants, and humans to revert to former states. This is demonstrated by the fact that carnivores may turn into shamans and vice versa according to the place and the drugs or food consumed.

The U'wa do not make a rigid division between themselves and nature: all living things including plants are seen as being mortal, having the same wherewithal of life, and are thus interrelated. In this society there are a number of ways in which mortals and animals are classified. Birds, bees, reptiles, and aquatic species are close to immortals. The immortals are unable to reproduce sexually but do so through the medium of mortals. Mortals survive by continually reminding immortals of their debt to replenish the universe's essential properties.

Acknowledgement

This research was funded by the Wenner-Gren Foundation and the Social Science Research Council of the United Kingdom.

Note

1   Part 4 of this myth cycle was not recorded in context, but it was said to concern the coming of Kubaruwa male ancestors.

References

Hugh-Jones, C. (1979). *From the Milk River: spatial and temporal processes in northwest Amazonia*: Cambridge Studies in Social Anthropology 26. Cambridge: Cambridge University Press.

Lévi-Strauss, C. (1966). *The savage mind*. London: Weidenfeld & Nicolson.

Lévi-Strauss, C. (1970). *The raw and the cooked: introduction to a science of mythology: 1*. London: Jonathan Cape.

Murra, J. V. (1975). El control vertical de un máximo de pisos ecológicos en la economia de las sociedades andinas. In *Formaciones económicas y políticas del mundo andino*. Lima: Instituto de Estudios Peruanos.

Osborn, A. (1982). Mythology and social structure among the U'wa of Colombia. D.Phil. thesis, University of Oxford.

Osborn, A. (1985). *En vuelo de las tijeretas*. Fundación de Investigaciones Arqueólogicas Nacionales. Bogotá: Banco de la República.

Reichel-Dolmatoff, G. (1971). *Amazonian cosmos: the sexual and religious symbolism of the Tukano Indians*. Chicago: University of Chicago Press.

Reichel-Dolmatoff, G. (1975). *The shaman and the jaguar: a study of narcotic drugs among the Indians of Colombia*. Philadelphia: Temple University Press.

Rivière, P. (1969). *Marriage among the Trio: a principle of social organisations*. Oxford: Clarendon Press.

Salomon, E. (1986). *Native lords of Quito in the age of the Inca: the political economy of the north Andean chiefdoms*. Cambridge Studies in Social Anthropology **59**. Cambridge: Cambridge University Press.

Taylor, K. I. (1979). Body and spirit among the Samúma (Yanoama) of North Brazil. In *Spirits, shamans and stars: perspectives from South America*, D. L. Browman & R. A. Schwarz (eds.), 201–21. The Hague: Mouton.

Wilbert, J. (1970). *Folk literature of the Warao Indians*. Los Angeles: Latin American Centre, University of California, Los Angeles.

12 *Tezcatlipoca: jaguar metaphors and the Aztec mirror of nature*

NICHOLAS J. SAUNDERS

... the jaguar is feared because he is not an animal but a fiercely predatory man. (Goldman 1979, p. 263)

Introduction

Feline symbolism, displayed in a wealth of archaeological, ethnohistoric, and ethnographic contexts, is widespread in Central and South America. From prehistoric times to the present day, felines in general and the jaguar in particular occupied an important place in visual and verbal representations of belief and ritual. The prevalence and continuity of jaguar imagery must have been due in part at least to its potency as a metaphor signifying aggressive qualities, elite status, and perceptual abilities. From the mythology of Amazonian societies to the art of the classic Maya and Aztec civilizations of Mexico, the jaguar appears associated with shamans, rulers, warfare, and sacrifice. In this chapter the jaguar symbol is examined in terms of its origins and the appropriateness of its use as metaphor to signify and express human actions and human attitudes.

Felines are the most widespread and populous group of native American predators. By virtue of size, distribution, and type variety, felines compete with humans for all manner of animal food resources, so occupying the dominant position in the natural predatory order. Within this class of predatory carnivores the jaguar (*Panthera onca*) (Fig. 12.1) is the most important representative, competing with other felines as well as humans for the total range of available prey. Accounting for the jaguar's hunting success in human terms, Amerindians came to regard it as the supreme predator. Such notions appear, from archaeological evidence, to have originated during the precontact period (i.e. before AD 1492) when human populations, predators, and prey-species were almost certainly more numerous and interaction more frequent.

Figure 12.1 Jaguar (*Panthera onca*). (Photograph Tony Morrison.)

Amerindian attitudes to the jaguar

Within the tropical rainforest and along its margins the jaguar was the only animal to present humans with a significant threat to their livelihoods. Siskind (1973, p. 174) talking of the Peruvian Sharanahua, said that jaguars, like men, are predators; the only important predators of the tropical forest. In a real sense jaguars compete for meat, stalking game by night as men stalk by day. This threat occasionally manifested itself as a direct physical danger to individuals, as described in a 1926 incident among the Mataco of Brazil in which a jaguar attacked, killed and carried away a Mataco man from a camp fireside despite the presence of some twenty other Indians (Alvarsson 1988, p. 273).

These dangers were both real and imagined, as is apparent in the case of the Akuriyo of Suriname, reported by Kloos (1977), who states that there were three ways in which one could be killed by a jaguar: by being grabbed and killed (Fig. 12.2); by being killed and eaten; and by being 'jaguar-killed' in which an Akuriyo shaman sent a spirit in the shape of a jaguar to kill another man or woman (Kloos 1977, p. 118). Amerindians had good cause to display a variety of considered attitudes towards the jaguar and the various ways in which it could be hunted. Based on experience, attitudes reflected a reality in which the jaguar, as supreme predator, could directly and indirectly threaten individual and collective survival.

Killing a jaguar, while removing a dangerous and disruptive competitor from the physical and social environments, was recognized as a dangerous undertaking and became associated with the achievement, maintenance and display of social status. Crocker (1977, p. 139) reports that slaying a jaguar was considered by the Brazilian Bororo as the best metaphorical equivalent of taking a human life, as jaguars, like people, are carnivores. Such an equivalence is apparent also among the Paraguayan Héta who, on occasion, caught jaguars in traps baited with the corpse of a Héta who had been killed by a jaguar (Kozák, et al. 1979, p. 388).

For the Guato of the upper Paraguay River basin, individual prestige was won by killing a jaguar (Steward 1949, p. 682) and amongst the Bolivian Mojo, jaguar hunting was a major avenue to fame. In the celebrations that followed a kill, the Mojo spent the night dancing around the slain animal and ate its flesh in the belief that this act imparted the animal's fierceness to them (Metraux 1948, pp. 422–3).

Prestige, fame, strength and aggressiveness were expressed and reinforced by the visual display of jaguar symbolism in clothing and regalia. Among the Mocovi, Toba, Mboya and Pilaga tribes of the Chaco, jackets of jaguar pelt were worn as ornaments and protection, in the belief that they imparted the animal's fierceness to their owners (Metraux 1946, p. 299). Practically all male members of the Parintintin of central Brazil had a jaguar tattooed on the inside of the forearm (Nimuendaju 1948, p. 287), the Suya of the Upper Xingú commonly possessed jaguar claw necklaces (Lévi-Strauss 1948, p. 365), and the Caingang of Brazil prepared for fighting by painting

Figure 12.2 Jaguar attacking Indian woodcutter on the coast of Surinam, north-east South America. From 'Amerikaansche Voyagien', A. Van Berkel, 1695. (Photo, The Bodleian Library, Oxford.)

themselves with black spots or stripes and making war cries that sounded like the roar of the jaguar (Furst 1968, pp. 152–3).

The predatory equivalence between jaguars and human hunters was in part based on the qualities of strength and ferocity, which were perceived as defining the successful predatory nature of the jaguar and which, in turn, were ascribed to humans engaged in any generically related activity. Such activities were those of the warrior, the hunter and killer of other humans, and the shaman, the hunter and killer of souls. Each may be referred to as hunter, predator or 'jaguar'.

Conceptual equivalence is often reflected in terminology; for example among the Barasana of the Colombian Amazon, the term for predator is *yai*, the same word being used for the jaguar and powerful shamans (Hugh-Jones 1979, p. 124). The underlying correspondence between predator–prey

relationships that permeates Amerindian taxonomy and classification implicitly states that all animals have their predators to whom they appear as
prey; in this sense, as the deer is to the jaguar so the tapir is to the hunter,
weaker men to stronger warriors and the souls of 'ordinary' humans to the
shaman.

One consequence of predatory equivalence was the association of high-
ranking individuals with the jaguar and the consequent display of jaguar
symbolism in situations where status and prestige were of prime importance. Well attested in the ethnographic and the archaeological literature
(e.g. Reichel-Dolmatoff 1975, Benson 1972, respectively) the jaguar's significance ultimately related to its dominant position as supreme predator
inhabiting the natural landscape.

In 'egalitarian' Amerindian societies there is often an implicit hierarchy of
roles and relationships. The absence of any observable formal structure is
arguably less significant than the many differences between individuals in
terms of sex, age, access to knowledge and the perception that some individuals possess the ability to interpret that knowledge more meaningfully
than others. Order and hierarchy is expressed by the use of analogical associations between people and animals, predators and prey.

Within these societies it is the shaman who articulates social and ritual
activities by virtue of occupying the only recognizable role of pre-eminent
social status. His access to, and control of, the spirit-world is the basis upon
which his authority is founded. The association displayed by the shaman to
express his social pre-eminence metaphorically is often with the jaguar as
lord of animals and master of spirits.

The association of jaguar and shaman is based on the perception that both
are recognized as supreme predators within their respective realms – the
predatory 'power' ascribed to the jaguar being passed to the shaman during
initiation. Among the Mojo especially powerful shamans were recruited
from men who had survived a jaguar attack; they performed special rites
connected with jaguar spirits, with whom they 'conversed' in a hut, to
emerge bleeding with clothes torn as if attacked by the animal (Metraux
1948, p. 422). For the Cubeo of the northwest Amazon, shamans were
graded in terms of their access to power; only the most powerful were
identified with the jaguar and were believed to be able to transform into the
animal (Goldman 1979, p. 262).

The association of shaman and jaguar found its most elaborate metaphorical expression in the former's ability to transform himself into a jaguar,
where a shaman's soul might enter the body of a jaguar or might turn into a
jaguar. One of the earliest accounts of transformation was recorded by
Dobrizhoffer (1822, pp. 77–8) for the shamans of the Paraguayan Abipon:

[they] change themselves into a tiger [sic] and tear everyone of their
hordesmen to pieces. No sooner do they begin to imitate the roaring of
a tiger, than all the neighbours fly away in every direction. From a distance however, they hear the feigned sounds. 'Alas! his whole body is

beginning to be covered with tiger spots!' they cry. 'Look, his nails are growing'.

Metraux (1946, p. 365) talking of the Mbaya, relates how their shamans change themselves into jaguars so as to attack and devour people. Similarly a Desana shaman may change himself into a jaguar (*ye'e dohpa yege*/making himself like a jaguar) in order to attack an enemy (Reichel-Dolmatoff 1971, p. 133). In both situations the jaguar is engaged in activities requiring fierceness, the jaguar symbol serving as an appropriate metaphor for this purpose.

Shamans operate in the spirit world, which is entered through trance. In this domain they are acknowledged perceivers, individuals who 'see' the true nature or essence of things and consequently know and understand more about the world than others. Amongst the Akawaio of Guyana a real shaman is 'one who perceives' (Butt-Colson 1977, p. 63) and can control spirits. These abilities are often regarded as the gift of the jaguar who was the shaman's teacher and spirit helper (Furst 1968, p. 156).

In his role as 'supernatural warrior' the shaman defends against spirit attack by forest spirits or the shamans of other villages. In this sense he is defending his community in the same way as hunters protect it against starvation and warriors against physical attack. The shaman may adopt jaguar regalia in dress and mannerisms in the same way as hunters and warriors do, claiming that the jaguar represents his predatory soul-essence. In a sense, both shamans and jaguars can be regarded as nocturnal predators who need excellent night vision for their activities; the former to hunt human souls in the metaphysical realm and the latter to hunt prey in the jungle.

The shaman's identification and equivalence with the shaman in terms of the correspondence between their nocturnal activities is strengthened by the description of the shaman's perceptual abilities in terms of feline vision. The shaman's use of mirrors to perceive spirit-essence by looking into the parallel spirit world is well documented (e.g. Eliade 1974, pp. 151–4, Reichel-Dolmatoff 1975, pp. 13–14). For the Colombian Tukano the idea of mirror image is fundamental to many of the concepts that structure their cosmology. Here the jaguar is the double of the shaman, controlling a mirror-image universe beneath the hills where everything is organized as a reflection of Tukano society (Reichel-Dolmatoff 1975, p. 84).

The association between shamans, mirrors and jaguar-vision is specific, Reichel-Dolmatoff (1975, p. 200) states that the Tukano squeeze the juice from unidentified herbs into their eyes to produce a strong dilation of the pupils – the person is now described as possessing 'jaguar eyes' and being able to see in the dark. In the mythology of the Kogi of the northern Colombian Andes the culture hero Kashindukua put on a jaguar mask, was transformed into a jaguar and was able to perceive things in the way a jaguar sees them (Reichel-Dolmatoff 1975, p. 55). The correspondence is not just the equivalence between predatory jaguar and shaman, but also between the acute vision of the jaguar (which helps make it the supreme hunter) and the perceptual abilities of the shaman which, with the aid of mirrors, enables him to master spirits and maintain social cohesion.

The basis of this particular correspondence may be due to the fact that, like all felines, jaguars possess an image intensifying device behind the retina, at the rear of the eye. This light-reflecting layer is called the *tapetum lucidum* and acts like a mirror, reflecting light back to the retinal cells. Its function is to gather every particle of light to aid the cat in its nocturnal hunting activities (Saunders 1988, pp. 10–12). The jaguar possesses mirrored eyes, navigates well in the dark, is a more successful predator as a consequence and appears to carry in its eyes the image of light and fire. Amerindian notions of mirror image spirit worlds, shamans-turning-jaguar, predating souls in nocturnal trance, seeing with 'jaguar eyes' and using mirrors may be seen as an integral part of the equivalence between jaguar and shaman. As naturally reflective eyes are to the jaguar, so are mirrors to the shaman, each allowing their owners to see their prey.

Notions concerning social pre-eminence and control may lead the shaman to activate jaguar imagery in situations designed to express power relations in terms of his control over spirits and, by extension, society. The purpose of employing jaguar metaphors is that their utility and potency is based in part on widely recognized and well understood pan-Amerindian notions of predator–prey relationships. Those circumstances within which jaguar symbolism is either displayed, or displayed with greater density than at other times, are specific situations in which the ordering of relations between individuals may be implicitly or explicitly restated and reinforced.

Tezcatlipoca: jaguar nature of an Aztec deity

The visual, textual and metaphorical use of jaguar symbolism in the Pre-Columbian Mexican Aztec civilization (*c* AD 1395–1519) parallels the association between shaman, the jaguar, social pre-eminence and spirit realms in the societies of *c* AD 1800–1970 described above. For the Aztecs, feline imagery was directly associated with sorcery (Sahagún 1950–82, Book 11, p. 3), royalty (Sahagún 1950–82, Book 8, pp. 23, 25, 28) and the elite warrior cadre known as the Jaguar Warriors (e.g. Durán 1971, pp. 177–9). Aztec sorcerers, like their Amazonian counterparts, were closely associated with the jaguar. But, above all, the display of jaguar symbolism and metaphor relates to the supreme Aztec deity, Tezcatlipoca. Befitting Tezcatlipoca's omnipotence was his role as arch-sorcerer associated with darkness, the night, and the jaguar as nocturnal predator (Nicholson 1971, p. 412). The association between jaguar and sorcerer, recalling that between jaguar and shaman, is made explicit by Sahagún (1950–82, Book 11, p. 3) when he relates how:

[Sorcerers] went about carrying [a jaguar's] hide – the hide of its forehead and of its chest, and its tail, its nose, and its claws, and its

Figure 12.3 The Aztec deity Tezcatlipoca in his jaguar guise as Tepeyollotli – 'The Heart of the Mountain'. Note the smoking mirror device attached to deity's foot. (Drawing, Pauline Stringfellow from Codex Borbonicus, after Seler 1904, Fig. 28a).

    heart, and its fangs, and its snout. . . . with them they did daring deeds, that because of them they were feared . . .

Tezcatlipoca represents a complex and culture-specific manifestation of jaguar symbolism in Aztec religious thought and mythology. The deity had associations with the Aztec elite, with mirrors, and obsidian, and possessed a transformational manifestation as the jaguar. Aztec use of jaguar imagery is best understood if Tezcatlipoca is regarded as the agency through which human–animal, shaman–jaguar and deity–jaguar analogical associations found their metaphorical expression in Aztec state ideology.

The Aztec pantheon was characterized by a large number of deities but within its hierarchy it is the deity referred to in Aztec as Tezcatlipoca who is regarded as the supreme god. This is a double nuclear name, *Tez-Catl*, 'it is a mirror', and *Ih-po-ca*, 'it emits smoke' (Ruiz de Alarcón 1984, p. 235), thus the usual rendering of 'Smoking Mirror'. Tezcatlipoca possessed a transformational manifestation as the jaguar Tepeyollotl (*Tepel-tl*, 'mountain'; */yol-loh/-til*, 'heart') (Ruiz de Alarcón 1984, p. 235), usually rendered as 'Heart of the Mountain' (Figure 12.3).

Tezcatlipoca was regarded as omnipotent, omniscient and omnipresent, before whom all creatures were completely helpless (Nicholson 1971, p. 412).

In terms of his shamanic features, it is significant that Sahagún (1950–82, Book 1, p. 5) states that Tezcatlipoca was a god whose abode was everywhere, in the land of the dead, on earth, and in heaven, and, elsewhere (Sahagún 1950–82, Book 3, p. 11), that he was invisible, just like the night and the wind. As with the supernatural jaguar spirit of Amazonian belief, Tezcatlipoca bestowed wealth, heroism, valour, positions of dignity, rulership, and honour (Sahagún 1950–82, p. 5). In terms of the shaman's associations with the mirror-image spirit realm Tezcatlipoca similarly brought misfortune, illness, and death by casting his shadow on one (Sahagún 1950–82, Book 1, p. 5) and wielding his all-seeing mirror to look into people's hearts.

Tezcatlipoca was the patron of sorcerers and warriors alike, an association that was connected, in terms of shaman–jaguar beliefs, with notions of predatory activities not only in the physical world but also in the spirit realm with which sorcerers dealt, and to which warriors despatched the souls of their enemies.

Jaguar and shaman are associated by the coequivalence of their preeminent status as supreme predators in their respective realms – as controllers of particular situations. These situations are critical theatres for the visual and verbal expression of dominance of one over another. Such expressions of dominance and control must associate the user with that which he uses. For the Aztecs the jaguar was described as princely, the lord and ruler of the animals, who was cautious, wise and proud (Sahagún 1950–82, Book 11, p. 1). These are human qualities ascribed to the behaviour of a nonhuman inhabitant of the natural world. For the Aztecs it was Tezcatlipoca, who, as the major deity, possessed jaguar traits and it was Aztec royalty who possessed and utilized jaguar symbolism through their metaphorical associations with the deity.

As Townsend (1987) has recently shown, the period leading up to the coronation of a new Aztec emperor (*huey tlatoani*) included a liminal period of separation and retreat during which speeches were given and addressed to

Tezcatlipoca as the patron-deity of royalty, and identified as the life-force that animates all beings and things (Townsend 1987, p. 393). Within this sequence of speeches the emperor spoke of the sacred bonds between himself and Tezcatlipoca that revealed the correspondence between his office and the deity through the analogical associations of shaman-jaguar imagery. Appeals by the emperor for Tezcatlipoca's guidance included the following (Sahagún 1950–82, Book 6, pp. 44–5):

> Our master . . . I place myself completely in thy hands . . . for I am blind, I am darkness . . . May thou incline thy heart . . . a firefly-flash of thy torch, thy light, thy mirror, in order that, as if in dreams, as if seeing in dreams, [I endure] for a while, a day.

References to mirrors and 'seeing in dreams' find many parallels in tropical forest shamanic vision-quests, indicating a concordance of world-view between the latter and the Aztecs in terms of the perceived nature and origins of social, political and religious power. After the investiture, the emperor was considered the image of Tezcatlipoca (in the same way as the shaman became the jaguar), and other speeches were presented to him by the nobility (Sahagún 1950–82, Book 6, pp. 52–3).

> . . . thou speakest in a strange tongue to the god . . . Thou art his lips, thou art his jaw, thou art his tongue, thou art his eyes, thou art his ears. He hath given thee honour, he hath provided thy fangs, thy claws.

Tezcatlipoca was believed to have provided the Aztec emperor with some of his most significant qualities, the ability to 'speak in tongues', to hear the voice of spirits, to see or perceive spirit essence and to possess, through metaphor, the weapons of the jaguar.

The fang and claw weapons that Tezcatlipoca had provided can be seen as metaphors for the elite warrior societies over which the new emperor now exercised effective control and through which he was expected to maintain and extend the boundaries of the state. This is analogous to the way that a new shaman acquired mastery over the jaguar spirit, which provided him with supernatural power. Both shaman and Aztec emperor were charged with using their unique access to power in order to maintain the economic viability, political integrity and metaphysical well-being of their respective domains.

Jaguar symbolism was closely associated with Aztec rituals of dynastic succession, just as shamanic initiation employed jaguar imagery to reinforce its potency. An example of this is the ethnohistorical documentation concerning the coronation of the Aztec emperor Tizoc (Davies 1973, p. 152).

> He mounted a throne, decorated with eagle feathers and padded with jaguar skins, known as the Eagle and Jaguar Throne . . . Next he followed the prescribed rites of auto-sacrifice, by drawing votive blood

Figure 12.4 Moctezuma impersonating Tezcatlipoca engaged in auto-sacrificial bloodletting. The carving is inside the stone sculpture of a jaguar 'heart container'. (Drawing, Pauline Stringfellow, after Seler 1904, Fig. 111.)

from his ears and thighs with a pointed jaguar-bone, fitted with a handle of gold.

The bone of the jaguar shed the blood of the emperor, initiating him into the status of *huey tlatoani* and placing upon him the duty to sacrifice the blood of others for the physical and cosmological maintenance of both the state and the Aztec universe. Evidence for such an association of jaguar symbolism with elite ritual blood-letting has been claimed (Klein 1987, p. 338) on the basis of a 'heart container' stone jaguar sculpture that contained a carving of the emperor Moctezuma piercing his own body, and dressed as Tezcatlipoca (Figure 12.4).

Drawing blood by piercing the skin with sharpened jaguar-bone as part of initiatory ritual is directly paralleled in Amazonian societies. 'Ritual bleeding' is also referred to by Ruiz de Alarcón (1984, p. 182) for the post-contact Mexican period where the accompanying incantation refers to the lancet (the agent of bloodletting) as 'jaguar'.

The display of jaguar symbolism by those who wished to use it to metaphorically reinforce their social status is also seen in the thrones of power used by the elite. For the Aztecs, as well as other Pre-Columbian Mexican civilizations (e.g. Robicsek 1975, p. 111) this seat often took the form of a throne covered with jaguar pelt or carved in the shape of the animal. As Dibble (1971, p. 324) has pointed out, Aztec terms refer to 'the mat' and 'the chair' to express authority, rulership and government. In ethnographic societies the shaman's stool was often similarly shaped or covered (e.g. Hernandez de Alba 1948, p. 403, Roth 1915, pl. 5), allying wisdom and supreme power with the form of the jaguar. For the occupant of the Aztec throne supernatural sanction was provided by Tezcatlipoca and his jaguar associations.

Little attention has previously been paid to comprehending apparently discrete features of Tezcatlipoca within the Aztec world-view which was inspired by, constructed and reinforced in terms of the natural environment and human interaction with that environment.

Tezcatlipoca can be set against the background of the physical environment of the Central Highlands of Mexico, and, in particular, the metamorphic geology and ecosystem of the Valley of Mexico. It was this volcanic environment that generated, in part, the framework within which those metaphysical relationships that structured the Aztec world-view were created and maintained. Above all, this environment produced obsidian, widely regarded as the 'steel' of New World prehistory (Cobean et al. 1971, p. 666). There are many indications of Tezcatlipoca's associations with this dark volcanic glass. In the Aztec capital, Tenochtitlán, the deity's image was made of a lustrous black stone (Durán 1967, vol. 1, p. 37), presumably obsidian (e.g. Heyden 1988, p. 222):

> The form of this idol [of Tezcatlipoca] in the City of Mexico was the following: it was made of a shining stone, black as jet, the same stone of which sharp blades and knives are fashioned. (Durán 1971, p. 98).

Itztli, presumably obsidian, was also used for the manufacture of bloodletting implements. Some of these were probably for self-immolation: 'this one is very pointed on one end; with it one is bled' (Sahagún 1950–82, Book 11, pp. 226–7). Others, such as spears, arrow points, and knives were apparently used not only in warfare but also for sacrifice (Durán 1971).

Obsidian was also the main material worked by the Aztec to produce mirrors. Tezcatlipoca was renowned for possessing and wielding his magic mirror (*tezcatl*) which was often, but not always, made of obsidian. By virtue of this mirror he was able to see into men's hearts and foretell the future. Durán (1971, pp. 98–9), in his description of the god, relates how, in his left hand, the deity carried:

> a fan of precious feathers, blue, green, and yellow. These emerged from a round plate of gold, shining and brilliant, polished like a mirror. This [mirror] indicated that Tezcatlipoca could see all that took place in the world with that reflection. In the native language it was called *Itla-chiayaque*, which means Place From Which He Watches.

The notion of an omniscient being who possesses an all-seeing magical mirror with which he penetrates time and space to perceive spirit essence strongly allies the activities of Tezcatlipoca to those of the shaman. This association is reinforced when the *former* is found to possess an alter ego – a manifestation as a jaguar – in the same way, and, it is argued here, the same situations, as the latter.

Díaz del Castillo (1939, pp. 302–4) describes what he saw when, accompanied by Cortés and fellow conquistadores, he visited Tenochtitlán's major shrines in 1519. He reports that 'they saw a statue of Tezcatlipoca with a face like a jaguar and bright shining eyes made of obsidian mirror' (Fig. 12.5).

Tezcatlipoca, as Tepeyollotl, was the 'Heart of the Mountain' who took jaguar form and inhabited the earth's interior (Benson 1988, p. 165). Representations of this jaguar-being appear in the codices (e.g. Codex Borbonicus, Fig. 28a), and here show the deity replete with the 'smoking mirror' symbol of Tezcatlipoca at his feet, a direct iconographic association between the deity, the jaguar and mirrors. In terms of analogical association, Tezcatlipoca, Tepeyollotl and jaguars see and perceive in the world of darkness by the use of mirrors.

The sharp cutting blades of warfare and sacrifice can be viewed as analogues of jaguar fangs and claws. This analogical association is reinforced directly by Aztec warriors being referred to as *ocelotl* (jaguar), and the material from which the blades were made being the 'divine substance' of Tezcatlipoca (Heyden 1988, p. 222), who, as Bray (1968, p. 162) points out, was the protector of the *telpochcalli* schools where young warriors were trained. The association is strengthened by the fact that in Nahuatl the obsidian knife is rendered as *itztli* which was considered another manifestation of Tezcatlipoca (Ruíz de Alarcón 1984, p. 229). The association is reinforced indirectly by Tezcatlipoca's manifestation as the jaguar Tepeyollotl, who, as 'the heart of the mountain', symbolizes and embodies the geological source of obsidian.

An association between the Lord of the Smoking Mirror, obsidian and blackness is revealed by the mythological status and attributes of the deity. Tezcatlipoca was the lord of night, the master of the dark realm and conjuror of shadows, which are only seen when the light of day is obscured. Codex representations of Tezcatlipoca show him painted black with a blue eye-band. In the temples of rural areas and in lesser towns the image of

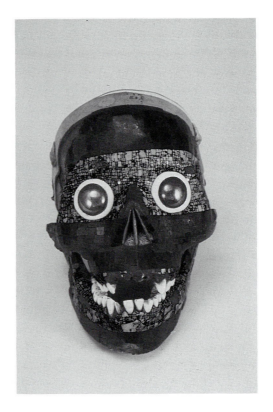

Figure 12.5   Aztec skull, decorated with jet and turquoise representing the deity Tezcatlipoca, the 'Lord of the Smoking Mirror'. (Photo, Trustees of the British Museum.)

Tezcatlipoca was made of wood and painted black. As Heyden (1988, p. 222) says:

> the bodies of priests in prehispanic Mexico were painted black. A black pitch, mixed with ground poisonous insects and certain herbs protected them from danger, especially from wild animals, made them invisible in the night, and gave them the power to communicate with the divinity. . . . this pitch, called Tezcatlipoca's 'divine food,' was the same black bitumen applied to one of the god's statues to give him a protective covering and the divine color, black.

Another possible symbolic equation may be the characteristic black colour of obsidian inasmuch as this blackness may be associated with the colour of dried and congealed blood which, according to the conquistadores, stained the walls of Aztec temples. As Díaz del Castillo (1976, p. 236) remarked, concerning the shrine in which he observed the obsidian image of Tezcatlipoca: 'the walls of that shrine were so splashed and caked with blood that they and the floor too were black'.

Bearing in mind the origin of obsidian, the use to which implements made from it were put and its black colour, shared by dried blood, this may provide another association suggesting that obsidian be regarded as the solidified blood (essence) of Tezcatlipoca/Tepeyollotl.

A possible further symbolic equation concerned Tepeyollotl as the jaguar heart of the mountain. The deity's name includes Yóllotl, heart, itself the most valuable offering the Aztecs could make to their deities. As López Austin (1973, p. 60) says of Yóllotl:

It is derived from 'ollin', movement, and in its abstract form y-óll-otl, literally signifies 'its mobility, or the reason for its movement'. The Aztecs considered the heart the dynamic organ that generated and preserved the movement of life, a vital aspect of being human. (my translation)

The importance of blackness, obsidian, and dried blood may be supported by several other considerations. When offered to the gods human hearts and blood were burnt by the Aztecs in elaborate braziers. Apart from the stench that accompanied such actions (referred to by the Spanish on several occasions) the smoke itself was black. Smoking braziers of burning hearts may have been analogically associated with smoking volcanoes as the source of obsidian – the material from which Tezcatlipoca's 'smoking mirror' was made.

The association of blackness, shadows, the underworld, Tezcatlipoca, the nocturnal activities of jaguars, and the dark colour of congealed blood and obsidian are indicative of a complex set of interrelationships that were an integral part of the Aztec world-view, possessing many shamanistic features.

Concluding remarks

Any attempt to decode the significance to a human society of an animal metaphor is inevitably fraught with difficulties, as other chapters of this book illustrate. This chapter has attempted to do so in two very different contexts: recent and present egalitarian Amerindian societies and a highly centralized ancient civilization.

The starting point has been the physical characteristics and natural behaviour of the jaguar which, it has been suggested, made it an appropriate symbol for the expression of human prowess in those areas within which it is the dominant predator. That such a relationship between signifier and signified is more than fanciful speculation is suggested by the apparent similarities in the use of jaguar symbolism across a distance of 4000 km and over a period of at least 600 years in societies with very different social and political organizations.

To suggest such a conclusion is not to assume that the symbolisms in any particular society, at any particular time, were simple or one-dimensional. As has been shown, attempts to unravel the levels of meaning of the jaguar in the societies considered above depend on an attempt to seek interconnections, however implicit or overt they may be. All cultures create and express a meaningful order but the status of meaning and the logic of connections are constantly open to change and elaboration as a result of human, nonhuman and environmental interaction.

This chapter has only identified some of the possible levels and extensions of the meanings of jaguar symbolism. Thus, for example it would be possible to extend the discussion of Aztec use of jaguar symbolism and its connotations by drawing attention to the possible associations between Tezcatlipoca, human sacrifice and smoke. In the burning of human hearts, braziers may have been associated generically with smoking mountains (e.g. Popocatepetl, literally 'smoking mountain') as sources of snow, ice, mist, water and fertility. In this instance brazier-smoke was the transformed essence of heart-blood, and mountain-smoke was the transformed essence of water; the former was an earthly offering that moved upwards to the deities whereas the latter was a heavenly offering that moved downwards, in the form of rain, to the earth.

No doubt such complex extensions of symbolic significances of animals applied equally to Amerindian societies. In these cases, the information available, despite anthropological accounts, lacks some of the richness of the material culture and early ethnohistorical accounts dealing with the Aztec civilization. This chapter has pointed to the likely complexities that Amerindian societies may adopt, and have adopted, as expressions of their forms of social control. That this may, and in some circumstances was, the case is suggested by the apparent parallels between some of the practices and conceptual formulations of the ancient Aztec civilization and the recent and present Amerindian societies.

The centrality of the jaguar metaphor in circumstances of confrontation, sorcery, status achievement, and reinforcement is an indication that Amerindian notions of predatory equivalence may have played an important part in symbolizing human relations.

Metaphorical allusions display a strong degree of specificity. Thus Amazonian warriors are described as jaguars in the same way as the elite Aztec warrior society was called Ocelotl (i.e. jaguar); shamans transform into jaguars in the same way as Aztec sorcerers disguised themselves with jaguar pelts, and the most powerful shaman, sitting on his jaguar stool, is identified as the jaguar in the same way as the Aztec emperor on his jaguar throne was regarded as the personification of Tezcatlipoca.

Tezcatlipoca, as patron of Aztec royalty, warriors, and sorcerers, possessed a magic mirror with which he pierced the boundary between the physical and metaphysical worlds in the same way as does the shaman. As jaguars are thought to see their prey through their naturally mirrored eyes, so shamans perceive spirit-essence with mirrors and so Tezcatlipoca saw into the hearts of men with his enchanted mirror.

Acknowledgements

I am grateful to the Department of Archaeology, University of Southampton and the British Academy for financial support. This allowed me to attend the 46th International Congress of Americanists, Amsterdam, 4–8 July 1988, where a previous version of this chapter was presented. I would like to express my thanks to those who have offered encouragement, comments and criticism, Elizabeth P. Benson, Roy Willis, Jane Hubert and Peter J. Ucko.

References

Alvarsson, J.-A. 1988. *The Mataco of the Gran Chaco*. Uppsala Studies in Cultural Anthropology 11. Uppsala: Acta Universitatis Upsaliensis.

Benson, E. P. (ed.). 1972. *The cult of the feline*. Washington, DC: Dumbarton Oaks.

Benson, E. P. 1988. The eagle and the jaguar: notes for a bestiary. In *Smoke and mist: Mesoamerican studies in memory of Thelma D. Sullivan*. J. K. Josserand & K. Dakin (eds), 161–72. BAR International Series 402. Oxford: British Archaeological Reports.

Bray, W. 1968. *Everyday life of the Aztecs*. London: Batsford.

Broda, J. 1987. The provenience of the offerings: tribute and *cosmovisión*. In *The Aztec Templo Mayor*, E. E. Boone (ed.), 211–56. Washington: Dumbarton Oaks.

Butt-Colson, A. 1977. The Akawaio shaman. In *Carib-speaking Indians: culture, society and language*, E. Basso (ed.), 43–65. Tucson: Anthropological Papers of the University of Arizona 28.

Cobean, R. H. *et al.* 1971. Obsidian trade at San Lorenzo Tenochtitlan, Mexico. *Science* **174**, 666–71.

Crocker, J. C. 1977. The mirrored self: identity and ritual inversion among the Eastern Bororo. *Ethnology* **16**, 129–45.

Davies, N. 1973. *The Aztecs*. London: Macmillan.

Díaz del Castillo, B. 1939. *The discovery and conquest of Mexico, 1517–1521*, G. García (ed.), P. Maudslay (transl). London: Routledge.

Díaz del Castillo, B. 1976. *The conquest of New Spain*. Harmondsworth: Penguin.

Dibble, C. E. 1971. Writing in Central Mexico. In *Handbook of Middle American Indians* Vol. 10. R. Wauchope, G. Eckholm & I. Bernal (eds), 322–48. Austin: University of Texas Press.

Dobrizhoffer, M. 1822. *An account of the Abipones, an equestrian people of Paraguay*. (Transl. S. Coleridge from the Latin edn of 1784.) 3 vols. London.

Durán, D. 1967. *Historia de las Indias de Nueva España e Islas de la Tierra Firme* 2 vols, A. M. Garibay (ed.), Mexico DF: Editorial Porrúa.

Durán, D. 1971. *Book of the gods and rites and the ancient calendar*. F. Horcasitas & D. Heyden (trans. & eds.). Norman: University of Oklahoma Press.

Eliade, M. 1974. *Shamanism: archaic techniques of ecstasy*. Princeton: Princeton University Press.

Furst, P. T. 1968. The Olmec Were-Jaguar motif in the light of ethnographic reality. In *Dumbarton Oaks Conference on the Olmec*, E. P. Benson (ed.), 143–78. Washington, DC: Dumbarton Oaks.

Goldman, I. 1979. *The Cubeo*. Urbana: University of Illinois Press.

Hernandez de Alba, G. 1948. Sub-Andean tribes of the Cauca Valley. In *Handbook of South American Indians* Vol. 4, J. H. Steward (ed.). Bulletin 143, 297–327. Washington: Smithsonian Institution Bureau of American Ethnology.

Heyden, D. 1988. Black magic: obsidian in symbolism & metaphor. In *Smoke and mist: Mesoamerican studies in memory of Thelma D. Sullivan*, J. K. Josserand and K. Dakin (eds), 217–36. BAR International Series 402. Oxford: British Archaeological Reports.

Hugh-Jones, S. 1979. *The palm and the Pleiades*. Cambridge: Cambridge University Press.

Klein, C. F. 1987. The ideology of autosacrifice at the Templo Mayor. In *The Aztec Templo Mayor*, E. H. Boone (ed.), 293–370. Washington: Dumbarton Oaks.

Kloos, P. 1977. The Akuriyo way of death. In *Cario-speaking Indians*, E. B. Basso (ed.), 114–22. Tucson: Anthropological Papers of the University of Arizona 26.

Kozák, V., D. Baxter., L. Williamson & R. L. Carneiro. 1979. *The Héta Indians: fish in a dry pond*. New York: Anthropological Papers of the American Museum of Natural History. **55**(6).

Lévi-Strauss, C. 1948. The Nambicuara. In *Handbook of South American Indians* Vol. 3, J. H. Steward (ed.), 361–70. Washington, DC: Smithsonian Institution.

Lopez-Austin, A. 1973. *Cuerpo Humano e Ideología* 2 vols, Mexico D.F: National Autonomous University of Mexico.

Metraux, A. 1946. Ethnography of the Chaco. In *Handbook of South American Indians* Vol. 1, J. H. Steward (ed.), 197–371. Washington, DC: Smithsonian Institution.

Metraux, A. 1948. Tribes of eastern Bolivia and the Madeira Headwaters. In *Handbook of South American Indians* Vol. 3, J. H. Steward (ed.), 381–454. Washington, DC: Smithsonian Institution.

Nicholson, H. B. 1971. Religion in Pre-Hispanic Central Mexico. In *Handbook of Middle American Indians* Vol. 10, *Archaeology of Northern Mesoamerica*, G. F. Eckholm & I. Bernal (eds), pt. 1, 395–446. Austin: University of Texas Press.

Nimuendaju, C. 1948. The Cawahíb, Parintintin, and their neighbours. In *Handbook of South American Indians* Vol. 3, 283–99. J. H. Steward (ed.), Washington, DC: Smithsonian Institution.

Reichel-Dolmatoff, G. 1971. *Amazonian Cosmos*. Chicago. University of Chicago Press.

Reichel-Dolmatoff, G. 1975. *The shaman and the jaguar*. Philadelphia: Temple University Press.

Robicsek, F. 1975. *A study in Maya art and history: the mat symbol*. New York: Museum of the American Indian, Heye Foundation.

Roth, W. E. 1915. *An inquiry into the animism and folklore of the Guiana Indians.* 30th Annual Report of the Bureau of American Ethnology, 103–386, Washington, DC: Smithsonian Institution.

Ruiz de Alarcón, H. 1984. *Treatise on the heathen superstitions that live among the Indians native to this New Spain, 1629.* J. R. Andrews & R. Hassig (trans. and eds). Norman: University of Oklahoma Press.

Sahagún, B. de. 1950–82. *Florentine Codex: general history of the things of New Spain*. A. O. Anderson & C. E. Dibble (trans. and eds). 12 books in 13 vols. Santa Fe: School of American Research and the University of Utah Press.

Santley, R. S. 1983. Obsidian trade and Teotihuacan influence in Mesoamerica. In

Highland–lowland interaction in Mesoamerica: interdisciplinary approaches, A. G. Miller (ed.), 69–124. Washington, DC: Dumbarton Oaks.

Saunders, N. J. 1988. *Chatoyer*: Anthropological reflections on archaeological mirrors. In *Recent Studies in pre-columbian archaeology*, N. J. Saunders & O. de Montmollin (eds), 1–40. BAR International Series 421. Oxford: British Archaeological Reports.

Seler, E. 1904. Veber Steinkisten, Tepetlacalli, mit Opferdarstellungen und andere ähnliche Monumente. *Gesammelte Abhandlungen zur Amerikanischen Sprach-und Altertumskunde*, Vol. 2, 717–66. Berlin. (1961 edition, Graz: Akademische Druck-u. Verlagsanstalt).

Siskind, J. 1973. *To hunt in the morning*. Oxford: Oxford University Press.

Steward, J. H.: 1949. South American cultures: An interpretative summary. In J. H. Steward (ed.) *Handbook of South American Indians* Vol. 5, 669–783. Washington, DC: Smithsonian Institution.

Townsend, R. F. 1987. Coronation at Tenochtitlan. In E. H. Boone (ed.), *The Aztec Templo Mayor*, 371–410. Washington, DC: Dumbarton Oaks.

13 Nanook, super-male: the polar bear in the imaginary space and social time of the Inuit of the Canadian Arctic

BERNARD SALADIN D'ANGLURE

(translated by Roy Willis)

Contrary to Western scientific thought which, particularly in the social sciences, has become accustomed to making explicit what it considers important, whether principles or facts, and all too often overestimates the explicit in what is observed, the *pensée 'sauvage'* of hunter-gatherers such as the Inuit prefers to conceal what is valued, keeping it implicit or expressed only in certain signs or outlines.

This fact, which doubtless gives to this *pensée 'sauvage'* a greater room for manoeuvre, would seem to explain the manifest inability of traditional anthropology to make it comprehensible. The obscurity surrounding the figure of the polar bear in Inuit ethnography illustrates the difficulty. This image or its representations are of course to be found in classic monographs such as those of Boas (1888, 1907) and Rasmussen (1929, 1931) and in comparative studies such as those of Hallowell (1926), Weyer (1932), Lot-Falck (1953) and Søby (1970), to name only a few. But the image is fragmented, diffused, and evanescent, and absent from the majority of descriptions and analyses. These typically concentrate on the manifest aspects of the culture, whether they be ceremonial activities, major myths, or the salient figures of the Inuit pantheon.[1]

With the help of data drawn on by these authorities and material collected by me in the central Canadian Arctic between 1971 and 1980.[2] I shall try to show how the polar bear is a dominating figure in the imaginary space and social time of the Inuit. This is because of its omnipresence in Inuit culture, from the very beginning of the cosmogonic ('world-making') myths to the limits of the powers of the shaman, as well as in everyday life. It is also significant as an instrumental and symbolic support of male authority.

The polar bear in Inuit mythical space

According to the Inuit, at the beginning of time animals and human beings lived together in total promiscuity. It was easy then to change from one kind

Figure 13.1 During the mythological Creation period, animls and humans lived together and easily metamorphosed into each other. The picture shows a polar bear, dressed in Inuit style, cordially greeting a male Inuit. (From an original drawing by Davidialuk Alasuaq, in the possession of the author.)

to another (Figure 13.1). The animal species, who shared terrestrial life with the first human beings, were relatively few and in their metamorphoses all assumed the same human appearance, speaking the same language as the Inuit, living in the same kind of habitation, and hunting in the same manner. There were, however, certain differences of physical or psychological traits. These meant that marriages between humans and animals, while possible, were nonetheless precarious.[3]

There were predatory and scavenger species such as the polar bear, wolf, fox, crow, snowy owl, eagle, ermine, and weasel. They had as prey certain rare species such as the arctic hare, the ptarmigan and the lemming. When food was lacking, which happened quite often, human beings ate earth, which in those far-off times was edible. The polar bear was the closest to man of all the animals: when it metamorphosed it was recognizable by the size of its canine teeth and its pronounced liking for fat.[4]

The perpetual darkness was the main obstacle to the expansion of terrestrial life. But when the sun was created through the magical words of a man, in spite of feminine opposition which managed to preserve a portion of nocturnal time, there was rapid development of productive forces, knowledge of the territory, and new techniques of hunting. Terrestrial life then saw an unparalleled demographic expansion. This happened despite a heightened level of sterility among women which was compensated for by gathering babies that came out of the ground which were brought up like people's own children, or by adopting the offspring of animals such as the polar bear.[5]

During these times when boundaries between species could be crossed, as could those between sexes – it was thought that men could change into women and vice versa – and when the field of marriage alliance, like that of reproduction, enjoyed the contribution of the animal world, the earth played a regulatory role through its nutritive and procreative capacities (Saladin d'Anglure 1977a, 1977b).

For a long time human being lived without knowing death: people were periodically rejuvenated. But little by little the population became dangerously large on its unstable ground, which was in fact a floating island. One day it began to tip under the excessive weight of its human load. Seeing the danger, an old woman used her magical words to summon death and war, so as to lighten the world. And, despite masculine opposition, she succeeded in rescuing humanity through the reduction in its numbers brought by death and the dispersion caused by war. From that time onwards the earth ceased to provide directly for human needs. Woman took on procreation, and animals provided food (Saladin d'Anglure 1978, 1980a). It was the end of metamorphoses, of transsexuality and the mixing of kinds. Human beings married among themselves and hunted the animals. From being equals, potential marriage partners and comrades, the primordial animals turned into game, a source of food and other useful products. Some, however, became competitors and adversaries. With the polar bear, who was so close to man, the new relation was one of tension and ambiguity. The animal retained a special status as game, but also became a source of fear, of hunger or sexual desire as well as a source of prestige and power.

Humanity thus had to reconcile itself with death, with war and with women. This was the price of survival. From the point of view of the men, this was self-evident.

If specific and stable forms now differentiated living beings, another differentiating factor, which crosscut that of the species, posed a problem: degrees of size. There were three principal gradations which partially overlapped: the human, subhuman, and superhuman scales. There were ordinary humans (*Inuk*), dwarfs (*Inugagulliq*) and giants (*Inukpaq*).

There were animals of human scale and others of inferior and superior sizes. The beings of one scale had their homologues in the others. The humans of different sizes pursued their activities in parallel and pacific ways as long as they did not meet and their territories and hunting grounds did not overlap. Otherwise, grave misunderstandings could arise because of the incompatibility of their different points of view, each wishing to claim normality and impose his own solution to conflicts in accordance with his own scale of reality. Each thought that the humans of the other scales were either dwarfs or giants. Thus the dwarfs took the Inuit for giants and the foxes for polar bears; and conversely the giants took the Inuit for dwarfs and the polar bears for foxes (Saladin d'Anglure 1978, 1980b).

The disequilibrium resulting from the differences of scale was compensated for by two properties belonging to the inferior scales: cunning, for the humans in face of the giants and, for the dwarfs, the ability to increase in stature to the scale of their adversaries.[6]

Hunting, matrimony and perpetuation of life were rather complicated when they brought beings of different scale into relation, as the myths recount:

> An Inuk went off one day to check his fox traps and, while he extricated a fox caught in one of them the animal was claimed by a dwarf as his 'polar bear' . . . He had in fact seen the animal first and long followed its tracks . . .

Each was right from his own point of view because the fox belonged to the owner of the trap and the polar bear to whoever had seen or wounded it first.[7]

Other myths illustrate the trouble the Inuit had in adapting to the giants:

> Two Inuit were hunting a whale in kajak when they saw a giant advancing into the sea, walking on the bottom. He was also hunting the whale but for him it was a sea scorpion. The giant was so big that the sea barely reached his waist. Suddenly, thinking that he saw before him the head of a sea scorpion (a whale), he struck it a blow with his club and he himself fell lifeless into the sea. He had struck his erect penis which had broken the surface of the sea.[8]

Matrimony posed corresponding problems:

> An Inuit man and woman married giants one day but the man became lost in his wife's vulva while the woman was impaled on her husband's penis.[9]

And the adoption of Inuit by giants led to as many problems as the adoption of animals by humans:

> A giant, who had adopted an Inuk, wanted one day to have a sleep; and he told his adopted son to wake him as soon as he saw a polar bear. When a large male bear appeared, the man awoke him by throwing stones, because the giant's slumber was deep. The giant looked in vain for the bear and saw only a 'fox' which he crushed with his foot; then he went back to sleep telling his adopted son to wake him only for a 'bear'. Shortly afterwards, there appeared an enormous giant bear (Nanurluk) which was so huge that it darkened the sky. Awoken, the giant then killed his prey in front of his terrified adopted son.[10]

The mythical history of the Inuit saw other developments: new kinds of game were created to meet a demand for food which the primordial prey were insufficient to supply: caribou, walrus, seal, white whale and salmon were thus added to the original species.

There was also the transformation into spirits of humans who transgressed the new rules, threatening the delicate balance established between the Inuit and the natural world. These spirits populated the sky, the earth and the sea and became the guardians of the cosmic order.

> When they were hunting a bear, some Inuit violated a taboo and immediately hunters, equipment and prey rose into the sky and formed the constellation of the Pleiades (Nanurjuk).[11]

Another narrative brings out the relation that exists between the bear and a dominant figure in Inuit beliefs, the Moon-Man:

> A young boy, suffering from snow blindness, was dispossessed by an unworthy mother of the first polar bear which he had just killed. Discovering the theft, he revenged himself by throwing her into the waves ... Later, becoming guilty of incest with his sister, he rose into the sky in pursuit of her and became the moon while she became the sun.[12]

The relation between the deprived adolescent, the Moon-Man and the bear is expressed in another myth:

> Kaujjajjuk, a little orphan suffering from bad treatment by his fellows, was reduced by them to sleeping with the dogs in the porch when he was visited by the Moon-Man. This personage gave the boy superhuman size and strength and sent him three polar bears which he used as whips to kill his oppressors.[13]

Another deprived orphan, Kiviuq, was given as protector a polar bear that he could summon to his assistance by a magical prayer. He used the bear one day to frighten off a 'sorceress' who tried to threaten his life.[14]

The rules regulating relations between humans and the natural and supernatural environments soon became too complex and the consequences of their violation too grave for humanity. So an Inuk, wishing to help his fellows during a severe famine, sought a means to intervene with the spirits ordering the world and the animals. He invented shamanism and discovered the techniques of exploring space and time and visiting the celestial, terrestrial and aquatic spirits, so discovering the hidden causes of events: thus the mythical period came to an end.

While the last mythical heroes discovered and exploited the resources and territories accessible to human beings, the new shamans visited the Moon-Man in the sky and in the depths of the sea they visited the mistress of the marine animals, Kannaaluk, whose father, wrapped in the skin of a polar bear, kept watch beside her over the observation of taboos.

Thus we find the bear's presence in the depths of the ocean as well as in the heavens, in all the realms of sea, land and air, in association with life and the powers of the greatest spirits as well as the weakest of humans (the orphans).

The polar bear in the social time of the Inuit

The special status of the polar bear among the animal species is clearly apparent if we consider, on the one hand, the parallel drawn by the Inuit between their way of life and that of the bear and, on the other, the numerous rituals devoted to the bear during the growing up of an Inuit boy.

The ability to stand erect on its two hindlegs, which the bear shares with man and with certain small animals such as the weasel, ermine, lemming, otter, and groundhog has led the Inuit to attribute to these animals magical qualities that are doubtless linked with their anthropomorphism. The predatory nature of the bear, which largely subsists on marine mammals and fish, also makes it closer to man, particularly having regard to the size and strength of the beast, which distinguishes it from the other animal predators in being superior to man's. Two hunting techniques employed by the bear have particularly caught the Inuit imagination. One is the bear's ability to catch seal by waiting by the animal's breathing hole in the ice and luring the seal to its death by scratching with its claws on the ice to arouse its curiosity: the animal is then dispatched with a blow of the bear's paw. The Inuit hunters appear to imitate this technique, but instead of claws they use a small implement that produces the same effect, and instead of a paw they use a harpoon. This technique is one of the most frequently employed in the Inuit Arctic. The second technique consists of killing walrus with a piece of ice or stone while they lie asleep in the sun on the ice floes. Several explorers and ethnographers have borne witness to this practice by the bear, and it has been described by many Inuit informants.

But apart from the hunt, the peculiarity of the bear that seems most human is its construction of a winter shelter. This is made in a large mass of snow on the lee side of a hill, away from the wind. Here the pregnant females hibernate from the end of autumn, bringing forth their young in the spring before emerging into the open. The form of these shelters is strangely like the Inuit igloo.[15]

A further characteristic shared by man and bear is their ability to travel over both land and sea: we shall see below how belonging to two environments makes the bear a privileged vehicle of shamanic mediation.

When it was abundant the bear was much sought after as a game animal. It was hunted for its pelt, which gave excellent protection against the cold when stretched across the platform of the igloo, or was cut up and sewn into trousers or hunting boots. It was also much appreciated for its meat, for its fat which fuelled the oil lamps, and for its bones, claws, and fangs which served as tools, amulets, or ornaments.

Use of these materials was regulated by numerous prescriptions and prohibitions for, according to our informants, 'the bear is the ancestor of man and its flesh much resembles that of human beings in colour, texture and taste'. It was forbidden to those who had already eaten human flesh. If a bear was killed the same restrictions on work and play were observed as if someone had died in the camp. It was said that the soul of a bear was dangerous, that it should be treated like that of a kinsperson, and so all work had to be stopped for three days. The person who had killed the bear had to remove all his outer garments before entering his home and for a month could not eat the bear's meat or fat.

If it was a male bear the bladder, penis, spleen, and part of the tongue were removed and hung up in the igloo together with the harpoon and other weapons that had been used to kill it. If the animal was female the bladder, spleen, and gall bladder were removed and hung up with the feminine tools of thread, needle, and knife, so that the bear's soul would feel at home. After three days, the instruments thus suspended were cast into the porch by the beast's killer and the children of the household competed as to who could retrieve them first.

Pieces of bear meat were then thrown to the young boys, who struggled with each other to obtain them: thus, it is said, they became good bear hunters. The bear's soul was then considered to have left its body. But as long as the bear's fat was burning in the lamp, it was necessary to avoid eating caribou bone marrow. There was felt to be a deep-rooted antagonism between these two animals, which meant they had to be kept separate. The same antagonism existed between woman, identified with the earth, and the bear, a marine hunter. Women were therefore forbidden to eat bear or walrus meat in midwinter, when the sun no longer appeared above the horizon. It was also forbidden to play bilboquet (an Inuit boardgame), the board of which was frequently sculpted to represent a bear, during this period.

This was the moment in the annual cycle when the social reproduction of the group was most threatened, when the principal animal species were experiencing gestation or had migrated far to the south. The whole cosmic order was in danger, hence the need for care and strict observance of taboos. The feeding of the group was dependent at this time on the marine mammals, and all efforts, both technical and symbolic, were directed towards securing their uncertain reproduction.

Inuit women were taught from an early age to fear the bear. Many stories told how women were attacked, mutilated, and devoured by hungry bears that unexpectedly appeared in camp when the men were away hunting, or which intercepted solitary and defenceless women along the paths (Fig. 13.2). That the relation of woman and bear is deeply ambiguous is apparent from the existence of other myths on the theme of the bear-spouse, the bear as adoptive child, and the bear-father, without forgetting its alimentary valuation in daily life as bear-food.

When a recently delivered mother ends her period of retreat and returns to the family home with a male newborn she cooks – or makes believe she is

Figure 13.2 The picture shows a polar bear attacking a defenceless woman – a recurring theme of womens' stories and dreams. (From an original drawing by Davidialuk Alasuaq, in the possession of the author.)

cooking – a dog's head. Then she takes a poker or a fork, places it in the infant's hand and causes it to strike the dog's head while telling her son that this is his *Idluq*, his cross-cousin, and his 'adversary in game and song'.[16] This is said to enable the child to be victorious later over his opponents in games, particularly in boxing; it makes him a great hunter of bears. It also enables his dogs to overcome the bear because, it is said, the bear and the dog are 'cross-cousins'.[17] This belief should be related to the principal Inuit technique of bear hunting, which consists in unleashing dogs on the bear to impede its progress, harass, immobilize and tire it so that the hunter can bring it down in close combat.

The young boy sleeps against his father's back so that later he can approach his prey without being seen and easily attack bears with spear or knife, as testified by Ujaraq:

I slept against my father's back and became able to approach game animals; Thus I was able to kill three polar bears I took by surprise, and three others with a knife attached to a wooden shaft. When the bear

Figure 13.3   The picture shows a hunter about to kill his first polar bear, and thus gain recognition as an adult.

attacked my dogs I concealed myself beside them and, being invisible, was able to run the creature through.[18]

It was necessary to prepare the young boy both physically and psychologically for the rigours of the bear hunt. Not only was it one of the most perilous of activities, it was also the one that would give him his adult status (Fig. 13.3). In this boy's experience would be the converse of that of the Moon-Man, who had been deprived of such status by a cruel mother while he was blind, whereas the boy was to be made invisible to his prey, the better to capture them.

The first whip a boy received had to be equipped with a handle made from the penile bone of a polar bear. It was necessary to know how to drive the dogs in order to approach the bear: to that end the whip, as both tool and weapon of precision, served as a fine training implement. A phallic symbol, like most masculine tools and weapons, combining tension and relaxation, aggression and play, the whip had enabled the Moon-Man to build up the stature of the little orphan Kaujjajjuk and harden him to adversity, just as it enabled the man to train his dogs for productive purposes. In the same way, the polar bear was like a dog in relation to the Moon-Man, the instrument of his power. Let us recall how Kaujjajjuk had made use of the bears sent by the Moon-Man to overcome his oppressors. It was also held that a first whip fitted with such a handle had the power to chase away evil spirits when cracked.

When the boy finally came to kill or wound his first bear numerous precautions had again to be taken so as to establish a positive relation between the hunter and his prey:

> When the young Inuksuk succeeded in wounding his first bear it was necessary for Ilupaalik, his father, to finish off and cut up the animal. But beforehand the old man knelt down and recited a long prayer, interspersed with songs, to make sure that in the future his son would have to do with bears which would not see him and would let themselves be easily killed.[19]

There was considerable ambiguity in the relationship between hunter and prey. The bear, a hunter like the man, whose ancestor he was, the kinsperson and the equal, was a feared and respected adversary, but also a much sought after victim who was killed with passion, butchered with care, and eaten with delight. According to some informants, it could even happen that the hunter, confronted with the still-warm body of a female bear that he had killed, was overcome with an irresistible sexual desire and violated his victim:

> Ungalaq had sexual relations with a female bear he had killed; in revenge, the animal caused one of his eyes to become infected, resulting in his death, despite the efforts to save him of five shamans.[20]

This confusion of kinds, which has echoes of the mythical period, was a threat to the cosmic equilibrium that the shamans saw it as their duty to preserve.

Nanook, super-male

Several myths demonstrate the close relationship between the bear and the Moon-Man. Examples include the myth of origin of the sun and moon which begins with a bear-hunt, or the story of the orphan Kaujjajjuk which

ends with the hero employing bears to wreak a deadly revenge. But the
Moon-Man, who was the patron of young boys and hunters, and protector
of orphans and the disinherited, also had the power to fertilize barren
women. This was a power he shared, according to the Inuit of Ammassalik,
with the bear, whose penis these women consumed (Gessain 1978, p. 208).
According to these same Inuit, the Moon-Man himself is clad from head to
foot in the pelt of a bear (Gessain 1978, p. 211).

In this same region the Moon-Man is held to be the principal source of
shamanic power: the power to 'see' and understand the hidden causes of
things present, past and future, the secret thoughts of people. Paradoxically
this old blind man, deprived by his mother of his first bear and of his
masculinity, the incestuous lover rejected by his sister, and master of an
extinguished celestial body (it is held that the feeble light of the moon is due
to the burning out of his master's torch), has become the source of the 'new
light' which, in the hands of certain privileged persons, is used to prevent
abuses and rectify the mistakes of humankind. The bear is present here too:
according to the people at Igloolik, he also can dispense shamanic power
and, metamorphosed into a man, become the best helper of the shamans.

However, before he can perform his function, the future shaman has to be
filled with an interior illumination so bright that he is able to see his own
skeleton, bone by bone. Next he has to call on one or more auxiliary spirits
who, according to some Inuit, fill him with supernatural power or, according to others, devour him and crush up all his bones in order to vomit him
whole, invested with all his powers.

In Québec-Labrador where this last belief was collected, it was held that
the auxiliary spirits had as master a giant bear called Tuurngasuk.[21] It was
necessary that the apprentice shaman endure a symbolic death if he wished
to acquire shamanic powers. This 'death' was sometimes experienced at
birth, as in the case of Ava, who was born dead, having been strangled by
his umbilical cord, and who was restored to life by a shaman who also
predicted a shamanic destiny for the child. Or he would be given the name
of the orphan Kaujjajjuk which earned him – in addition to the tutelary
protection of this being – the help of the bear. It was, according to Ava's son
Ujaraq, as if he had been clothed in the skin of a bear:

> It was as if the shaman wore the skin of his auxiliary spirit, because he
> owned it . . . the auxiliary spirit of Ava was a bear and when Ava acted
> like this he was no longer himself, he feared no one . . .[22]

Qinngaq, the last of the Sadlirmiut, who lived and died at Igloolik, had
been buried alive soon after his birth, in his mother's grave. He owed his life
to a merciful traveller who rescued and adopted him. An orphan, socially
and nearly physically dead, Qinngaq later became a powerful shaman when
he received, along with the shamanic light, a giant bear (Nanurluk) as a
spirit ally.

Another Inuk called Nanook (polar bear) living in the Chesterfield region, lost his name when the old woman he had been named after died: their identity was so close that it was as though he had died also.[23] He became a shaman and in so doing regained the power of his name when the bear became his spirit ally. But his name is no longer uttered except in the metaphoric form of the shamanic language used in the region, which is *Pisukti* ('The Walker'). A term with the same root designates the fox and the lemming for the shamans of Iglooik who, however, employ the term *Uqsuralik* ('Fat One') to refer to the bear and the ermine.

The analogical scales described earlier provide the key to understanding these apparently arbitrary usages. On the cosmic scale, that of spirits and giants, the word 'bear' is used of the giant bear (Nanurluk) and the astral bear (Nanurjuk) which are pursued by the hunters of the Pleiades. Otherwise there are only foxes, ermines and lemmings. On the minuscule scale, that of the dwarfs, the fox, lemming or ermine is called a 'bear' according to the size of the dwarfs and the local tradition. The real bear belongs to the human scale. The ermine is often compared to the bear because of its anatomical characteristics and predatory habits. This analogy is particularly prominent in children's games. In current usage the ermine and the fox are denoted by terms with a common root (*Tiriaq* and *Tirigaaniaq*, respectively).

We are thus dealing with a series of homological and substitutable concepts employed in the transformations of scale so frequent in Inuit symbolic thought.

I now recapitulate the main components of the image of the polar bear as conveyed in the relationship attributed to it with the human environment (social, technical, religious), its animal environment, and cosmic forces.

An initial relationship between the bear and masculine sexual power appears with the killing of the first bear, which is the proof of adult virility, and with the eating of the bear's penis by sterile women. The bear, like the hunter, was valued for his predatory and reproductive qualities, that is, his powers of vision, rapid movement and force that are also associated with sexual potency.[24]

A second relationship has been described, between the bear and the dog, imaginary 'cross-cousins' and 'sporting opponents' and real adversaries in the bear-hunt. On the cosmic scale of the Moon-Man, which is also the scale of the shaman, the bear was like a dog: one of the Moon-Man's dogs was called Tiriattiaq, meaning 'beautiful ermine' which was an animal assimilated to the bear in shamanic language. Iqallijuq confirms this hypothesis with the following description of a shamanic seance attended in his youth:

It was my uncle Makkiq who officiated; he had been carefully bound with a long strap so that he could effect a celestial journey and cure a sick person . . . At the end of the seance we heard the noise of the strap which had fallen from a great height to the ground. When the lamps were rekindled we saw on the ground the appearance of a sled with a passenger and towed by a bear, it was the buckles of the strap which had assumed this form . . .[25]

The bear was thus a sleigh-dog for the shaman. Moreover, it was forbidden for the shaman to whip his dogs during the year following his initiation.[26]

A third relationship, between the bear and the whip, is embodied in the myth of Kaujjajjuk in which the hero, having endured the ordeal of the whip as inflicted by the Moon-Man (which enables him to grow), uses the bears sent by his protector to whip his former oppressors.

A fourth relationship, between the bear and the Moon-Man, has been clearly established through the origin myth of the sun and the moon; through the myth of Kaujjajjuk; and also through the Ammassalik tradition concerning the Moon-Man wearing the pelt of a bear. It is also held in Igloolik that the Moon-Man could send bears from the moon to humans and conversely that an amulet made from a bear's molar tooth had the power to convey humans directly to the Moon-Man after death, without passing through the underworld. This presence of the bear in the celestial sphere is interesting because normally only terrestrial game are found there, marine game being confined to the spirit world beneath the sea. This is confirmation of the mediatory role of this amphibious beast, a role pre-eminently belonging to the Moon-Man who fed the celestial dead with marine game and the dead of the underworld with terrestrial game.

A fifth relationship, between the bear and the shaman, has been examined in the light of mythical history and the new human needs to which shamanism was a response. Here the bear plays a preponderant role as the main source of shamanic power, after the Moon-Man. This relationship completes the circle, bringing us back to our point of departure where sexual power is associated with visual acuity, as in the myth of the blind hunter of bears who became the Moon-Man, source of light, of bears and of fecundity.

I have tried to show elsewhere (Saladin d'Anglure 1977b, 1978a) how Inuit shamanism employs certain feminine characteristics and representations, such as the ritual use of the left hand, high-pitched cries, and rites resembling female pregnancy and delivery; and it is interesting to note here that the polar bear has the reputation, in both eastern and western Arctic regions, of being 'left-handed', a supposed characteristic that hunters take into account when stalking the animal.

Shamanism thus appears to reinforce the masculine power already elaborated around the concept of predation. But before showing that the image of the bear is another expression of such power we must allude to another analogy often found at Igloolik, even though the bear is not obviously implicated in it, and that is the metaphor of the dog as 'penis' of the man. This idea is present in myths, in traditional narratives and in many everyday sayings. The image first appears from the point of view of the human foetus, which is on the minuscule scale, where there intrudes a 'nourishing dog' with a vertical 'mouth' at the entrance of the uterine 'house'.[27] The image also occurs on the cosmic scale from the point of view of Kannaaluk, the submarine goddess, who married her dog and brings forth the various races of humankind. This analogy vividly illuminates the image of the bear because it confirms the crystallization around that image of a constellation of phalloeconomic themes that pervade various domains of Inuit life. Beginning in the domain of the reproduction of the human workforce (procreation), this constellation of themes integrates the tools of masculine labour as represented by the penile whip, the quiver of arrows, the knife, the bow, and the harpoon; then there is the domain of canine labour, the double meaning of which has just been outlined; then the object of labour, that is nature as represented by the polar bear, which is also eminently ambiguous, being at once the most dangerous competitor and adversary of man as hunter and his principal associate in shamanism. Finally there is the cosmos, with its most active agent in the social reproduction of human beings, the Moon–Man.

This thematic constellation, which makes sense only if we shed the dogmas of economic and psychoanalytic interpretations,[28] confronts us with representations where production and reproduction, and alimentary and sexual activities are always aspects of the same reality, the social reproduction of human life and its prolongation in cosmic life.[29]

Certainly these two aspects, which join and mutually reinforce each other, give rise to many confusions where the distinctions between the body of the self and that of the other, of human and animal, of game animal and spouse, etc., tend to be obscured. The polar bear becomes a multidimensional configuration; a potent ideological tool in the hands of men. They use it to consolidate their domination of women by subtly investing the foundations of their power in the materiality of the bear, an animal they otherwise manage to control. The polar bear is perhaps the most dangerous of beasts, but it is killable, edible, and thinkable.[30] It is also well placed to serve as support, instrument, and symbol of male power.[31]

Acknowledgements

I would like to thank the CRNS, the Conseil des Arts du Canada, the Musée National de l'Homme (Ottawa), the Ministère de l'Education (programme de subvention d'équipe) of Québec, the Canadian Ministry of Communications, the Canadian Foundation Killam and the Québec Ministry of Cultural Affairs, Ethnological and Archaeological Division for their help, and also our colleagues in the Association Inuksiutiit (Québec).

Notes

1 I am no less indebted to certain pioneering works that constitute interesting sources of regional and comparative information or stimulate interesting theoretical reflections, such as those of Thalbitzer (1930), Gessain (1978), and Kleivan (1976) to name only a few.
2 In the course of annual expeditions to Igloolik Territory carried out under the auspicies of the CRNS and the Laboratoire d'Anthropologie sociale of Professor C. Lévi-Strauss, then through the Department of Anthropology of Université Laval.

3   The facts relating to Inuit cosmogony are mainly taken from our data as well as from the invaluable works of Rasmussen, who inspired my research at Igloolik (cf. Rasmussen 1929, 1931; see also B. Saladin d'Anglure 1977b).

4   These two characteristics distinguish the bear in the esoteric language of shamanism: Tulurialik, 'Who Has Fangs', and Uqsuralik, 'Who Has Fat', at Igloolik.

5   A myth told at Igloolik describes how an old woman adopted a bear cub and made it a hunter of bears (cf. Rasmussen 1929, pp. 267–8).

6   This ability to increase in size is also found in the miniature replica of each living creature, contained in its vital soul in the form of a packet of air; also with maltreated children (cf. Saladin d'Anglure 1980b).

7   This myth was collected from David Alasuaq at Povungnituk in the Québec Arctic. At Igloolik it is he who first wounds the bear who owns it, but in several other regions such as Hudson Bay it is he who sees it first.

8   This myth is known in many regions of the Arctic, including Igloolik. It illustrates the relation between hunting and sexual potency; it also illustrates the weakness of the giants when facing the Inuit, a frequent mythological theme.

9   Myth collected at Igloolik (cf. Saladin d'Anglure 1971–9; also Rasmussen 1929, p. 214).

10 Myth collected at Igloolik (Saladin d'Anglure 1971–9) and also at Inujjuaq (Saladin d'Anglure 1968); see also Rasmussen 1929, pp. 215–16. In another myth an Inuk helps rescue a giant from his enemies (Saladin d'Anglure 1980b).

11 The generic name of the constellation at Igloolik is Udlaaktut, 'The Bear Hunters'; Nanurjuk, constructed with the root Nanuq (Nanook), 'Polar Bear', represents the bear in particular (cf. Jenness 1922, p. 179; and also Rasmussen 1929, p. 263 and Saladin d'Anglure 1971–9). We encounter there also the term Nanurjuk as designating the image of the bear in the Inuit string game (cf. Mary-Rousselière 1969, pp. 12–13).

12 This is one of the best-known Inuit myths and is the subject of an interesting study by Savard (1966, pp. 103–18); see also Rasmussen (1929, p. 77) and Saladin d'Anglure 1971–9.

13 There are numerous version of this myth: this version was collected at Povungnitik, Québec Arctic, in 1968.

14 According to a well-known narrative collected at Igloolik (cf. Rasmussen 1929, p. 287 and Saladin d'Anglure 1971–9).

15 See the description by Mary-Rousselière (1957, pp. 16–19). See also Van der Velde (1957, pp. 8–15) for interesting details of bear hunting in the Igloolik region.

16 At Igloolik the term idluriik denotes two cross-cousins of the same sex; it also denotes opponents in game and song who confront each other in public. This second meaning is found much more extensively than the first in the Inuit Arctic (cf. Damas 1972, Burch 1972).

17 These Inuit statements suggest an analogy between four types of relation between 'cousin-adversaries': man and dog; dog and bear; bear and man; and man and man.

18 Information collected at Igloolik in 1971 (cf. Saladin d'Anglure 1971–9).

19 Information collected at Igloolik (cf. Saladin d'Anglure 1971–9).

20 This relation between becoming blind and sexual abuse does not seem to be accidental, since it confirms the connection between sexual and visual power encountered already in this paper (cf. also Savard 1966). Cases of bestiality were far from uncommon and also involved seal and caribou.

21 This giant bear is said to live in a cave on the east coast of Ungava Bay; the same image is found at Ammassalik (Gessain 1978, p. 217), which brings us back to

the giant bear already mentioned in relation to the various scales of being. The high value attributed to this bear in certain regions of the Arctic corresponds to a transposition to the cosmic scale of the value given to the bear on the human scale.

22 Information collected at Igloolik (Saladin d'Anglure 1971–9).

23 Cf. Frederiksen (1964, pp. 109–12). Frederiksen was one of the first to attempt a theoretical analysis of Inuit shamanism. Denigrated during his life and ignored after his death, we consider the insights of this researcher to have been greatly underestimated and to have reflected a deep knowledge of Inuit thought.

24 The development of these faculties was much emphasized in the education of Inuit boys.

25 This narrative was recorded at Igloolik (Saladin d'Anglure 1971–9) and is similar to descriptions of shamanic seances in Rasmussen (1929, pp. 129–31).

26 According to Boas (1907, p. 510) cited by Weyer (1932, p. 430) for the Inuit to the west of Hudson Bay.

27 See the representation of this scene by the Inuit artist Leah Idlaut d'Argencourt (cf. Saladin d'Anglure 1977a).

28 This criticism relates, of course, to the ethnocentric use of these disciplines.

29 I have outlined elsewhere (Saladin d'Anglure 1980b) a preliminary treatment of this theme; it ends in a refusal to permit the reduction of a reality as rich as that of Inuit representations, which express the reproduction of life, to one or other of its components; to privilege an explanation through the economic would be as misleading as explanation through a theory of sexuality. In Inuit thought, as in their experience, these two aspects of life are not dissociated.

30 At this point in our presentation of the bear image among the Inuit I share the perspectives opened by Lévi-Strauss (1962) in relation to totemism, on the symbolic relations established by humans with animals.

31 All my recent work, since 1977, has explored the field of traditional Inuit representations with a view to clarifying at this level the problem of the relation between the sexes. It is interesting to compare these studies with the works of Briggs (in particular 1974) who, based on a thorough ethnography of Inuit family life carried out in a more recent context, questions the idea of masculine domination among the Inuit and posits the existence of a male and Western bias among Inuit ethnographers. In the same context I draw attention here to my own recent paper on the image of the polar bear where, while remaining 'super-male', he is also a symbol of the 'third social sex', a category I apply, in particular, to the shaman (cf. Saladin d'Anglure 1986).

References

Boas, F. 1888. The Central Eskimo. In *Sixth Annual Report of the Bureau of Ethnography*. Washington, DC: Smithsonian Institution. (Reprinted in 1964, University of Nebraska Press).

Boas, F. 1907. *The Eskimo of Baffin Land and Hudson Bay*. American Museum of Natural History, Bulletin 15.

Briggs, J. 1974. Eskimo women: makers of men. In *Many sisters: women in cross-cultural perspective*, C. J. Matthiasson (ed.), New York: The Free Press.

Burch, E. 1972. Alliance and conflict: inter-regional relations in North Alaska. In *Alliance in Eskimo Society*, L. Guemple (ed.), Proceedings of the American Ethnological Society 1971 Supplement.

Damas, D. 1972. The structure of Central Eskimo associations. In *Alliance in Eskimo*

Society, L. Guemple (ed.), Proceedings of the American Ethnological Society 1971 Supplement.

Frederiksen, S. 1964. Some preliminaries on the soul complex in Eskimo shamanistic belief. *Journal of the Washington Academy of Sciences*, **54**, 109–12.

Gessain, R. 1978. L'homme-lune dans la mythologie des Ammassalimiut (côte est de Groenland). In *Systèmes de signes: hommage à Germaine Dieterlen*. Paris: Hermann.

Guemple, L. (ed.) 1972. *Alliance in Eskimo Society*. Proceedings of the American Ethnological Society 1971, Supplement.

Hallowell, A. I. 1926. Bear ceremonialism in the Northern Hemisphere. *American Anthropologist* **28**, 1–175.

Jenness, D. 1922. *Life of the Copper Eskimos*. Report of the Canadian Arctic Expedition, 1913–18.

Kleivan, I. 1976. Status and role of men and women as reflected in West Greenland petting songs to infants. *Folk* **18**, 5–22.

Lévi-Strauss, C. 1962. *Le totemisme aujourd'hui*. Paris: Plon.

Lot-Falck, E. 1953. *Les rites de chasse chez les peuples sibériens*. Paris: Gallimard.

Maertens, T. 1978. *Ritologiques 4: la peau des autres*. Paris: Aubier.

Malaurie, J. 1975. *Les derniers rois du Thule*. Paris: Plon.

Mary-Rousselière, G. 1957. Une chasse à l'ours sur la péninsule de Simpson. Eskimo **45** 16–19.

Mary-Rousselière, G. 1969. *Les jeux de ficelles des Arviliqjuarmuit*. Ottawa: Musée Nationaux du Canada, Bulletin 233, série Anthr., No. 88.

Mauss, M. & M. H. Beuchat 1906. Essai sur les variations saisonnières des sociétés eskimos. In *L'Année sociologique*, 9° année (1904–5).

Rainey, F. G. 1947. The whale hunters of Tigara. Anthropological Papers of the American Museum of Natural History 41.

Rasmussen, K. 1929. Intellectual culture of the Iglulik Eskimos. Copenhagen: Report of the Fifth Thule Expedition, VII, 1.

Rasmussen, K. 1931. The Netsilik Eskimos, social life and spiritual culture. Copenhagen: Report of the Fifth Thule Expedition 1921–4, vol. 7, No. 2.

Saladin d'Anglure, B. 1968. Enquête réalisée dans le Québec arctique. Manuscript.

Saladin d'Anglure, B. 1971–9. Transcription en langue inuit des entrevues réalisées dès 1971 à 1979 à Igloolik, Territoire du Nord-Ouest, Canada, sur les mythes, les tabous, le vocabulaire et les pratiques chamaniques.

Saladin d'Anglure, B. 1977a. Iqallijuq ou les reminiscences d'une âme-nom inuit. Québec: *Etudes Inuit/Studies* **1**, (1), 33–63.

Saladin d'Anglure, B. 1977b. Mythe de la femme et pouvoir de l'homme chez les Inuit de l'arctique centrale canadien. *Anthropologie et Sociétés* **1** (3) 79–98.

Saladin d'Anglure, B. 1978a. L'homme (angut), le fils (irniq) et la lumière (qau) ou le cercle du pouvoir masculin chez les Inuit de l'arctique central. *Anthropologica*, **20** (1–2), 101–44.

Saladin d'Anglure, B. 1978b. La parole changée en pierre, vie et ouvre de Davidialuk Alasuaq, artiste inuit du Québec arctique. *Les cahiers du patrimoine* **11**. Ministère des Affaires Culturelles, Québec.

Saladin d'Anglure, B. 1980a. L'idéologie de Malthus, les sauvages d'Amérique et la démographie mythique des Inuit d'Igloolik. Communication présentée au colloque *Malthus hier et aujourd'hui*, Unesco, Paris. 27–30 May 1980.

Saladin d'Anglure, B. 1980b. 'Petit-ventre', l'enfant géant du cosmos inuit. *L'Homme*, **20** (1), 7–46.

Saladin d'Anglure, B. 1986. Du foetus au chamane, la construction d'un *troisième sexe* inuit. *Etudes/Inuit/Studies* **10** (1–2), 25–113.

Savard, R. 1966. Mythologie esquimaude: analyse de mythes groenlandais. Québec: Centre d'Etudes Nordiques, Travaux divers, 14.

Søby, R. M. 1970. The Eskimo animal cult. *Folk* (1960–70) **11–12**, 43–78.

Spencer, R. 1959. *The North Alaskan Eskimo, a study in ecology and society*. Washington, DC: Smithsonian Institution, Bureau of American Ethnology, Bulletin 171.

Thalbitzer, W. 1930. Les magicines esquimaux, leurs conceptions du monde, de l'âme et de la vie. *Journal de la Société des Américanistes* **22**, 73–106.

Van de Velde, F. 1957. Chasse à l'ours blanc dans le bassin de Foxe. *Eskimo* **45**, 8–15.

Weyer, E. M. 1932. *The Eskimos, their environment and folkways*. New Haven, Conn.: Yale University Press.

14 *Antelope as self-image among the Uduk*

WENDY JAMES

We *'kwanim pa* [Uduk] don't have guns, we don't know how to fight, we ask for security from the government, and the government attacks us. So we just run into the bush like wild animals.

(Elderly man, displaced to Khartoum, August 1988)

This chapter is about a relatively inconspicuous African animal. Unlike many animals that are the epitome of the rough and the wild, the antelope even for 'us' – and more especially for the Uduk-speakers of the south-eastern Sudan – it is a quiet, gentle, and familiar creature. 'African animals' is a phrase in lay English conjuring up the externality, the otherness, of the world of nonhuman beings. It evokes the notion of alien, powerful, and dangerous species, the lion, snake, scorpion, rhinoceros, and elephant; and whether or not they are inherently more aggressive than others, it is their aggressive and fearsome aspect that comes to mind. 'African animals' of a gentle or subtle disposition rarely enter the imagination of the West, or that of China, India, or the Middle East for that matter. But in the vernacular languages and imaginative discourse of African peoples, not only are the representations of power and danger in animal form themselves more differentiated, but the animal world as a whole is not necessarily opposed as a wild and dangerous realm quite antagonistic to the human and domestic sector. Nonaggressive species and a range of muted qualities fill out any 'ethnozoological' account and figure prominently in myth, stories, art, dance, and ritual.

Consider the recurring appearance in these contexts, for example, of the hare, the spider, the mouse, the lizard and chameleon, the tortoise, the frog, the birds, as well as the antelopes. These relatively pacific creatures do not provoke the explorer's or tourist's attention, but representing internalities as much as, or more than, external character they figure commonly in indigenous imagery. Lienhardt's (1985) essay on aspects of the self in Africa draws attention to the way the tortoise has been used to suggest the hidden, inner self. Most of the species in my brief list appear mainly in the verbal contexts of story, riddle, and song; while the ante-lopes, though remarkably silent in 'oral literature', are prominent in some areas of African art. The use of the antelope horn as a generalized image of dynamism and growth in the sculpture and mask-making traditions of West and Central Africa has become well known through the work of

Fagg (1958, p. 23, 1973 for example; see particularly the captions to illustrations in the latter).

It is in the context of rock art, perhaps particularly pertinent to my present theme, that the dominance of antelope images in Africa is most conspicuous, dramatic and evocative. Vinnicombe's (1976) detailed study of Bushman rock painting revealed how a single antelope species there has long provided a focal image (see especially chapters 6 and 7 on animal forms, and the representation of animal connections in human forms). Leakey (1983) suggests that in Tanzania too antelopes dominate the range of characteristic motifs in rock art, though a greater variety of their species is present. Both these authors point out that the dominance of antelopes in rock paintings cannot necessarily be accounted for by a simple utilitarian explanation in terms of hunting. Even though some 77 per cent of Bushmen paintings are of antelopes, especially the eland, and there are many practical uses to which the carcase of the animal is put, the artistic emphasis on the eland was likely to have been prompted more by its social and metaphysical importance than its economic use; and the same is likely to have been true of former East African cultures (Leakey 1983, 117).

We do not have to hand any very detailed account of the place of antelopes in the symbolism and ritual of any particular African people, and even if we did, this would not necessarily throw any light on specific questions of prehistoric art. But as there is so little in this field it seems perhaps useful to offer some notes on the representation of the antelopes as found today among the Uduk-speaking people of the Sudan–Ethiopia border. By analogy these may suggest, in general, the kinds of questions that could be asked elsewhere. The Uduk language belongs to the Koman grouping of tongues and, according to Christopher Ehret (pers. comm.), itself represents that descendant preserving most closely the consonantal system of proto-Nilo-Saharan. As with the other Koman-speaking peoples the cultural tradition of the Uduk draws very heavily on a hunting and gathering idiom, an idiom that strongly suggests a hunting background in the historical sense, and pervades their expression of selfhood and distinctive identity today (James 1988).

The Uduk case is worth consideration, I believe, against the background of current shifts in the perspective of moral philosophers on the question of our relationship, as human beings, with the world of the (other) animals. This was until recently seen as an oppositional one, a confrontation of different kinds. Moral philosophy in the West took for granted, along with theology and most of zoology for that matter, that a primary elemental difference sets us apart from the rest of the creatures, and on the whole justifies our dominion over them, some would say our exploitation of them. Thomas (1983) has illustrated how our own Western European attitudes to nature have been formed since the Renaissance, and reminds us of the recency of our notions of dominion. But some philosophical writing has begun to challenge the assumption of essential, and justifying, difference. The formerly sharp watershed between humankind and the rest of bodily life has been eroded, and philosophers have begun to suggest that on the ultimate basis of bodily kinship with the rest of the animal world our moral recognitions should extend beyond our own species boundary (Clark 1977, 1984, Midgley 1979, Regan 1984, Ingold 1988).

In ethnographic description and anthropological analysis, we have tended in the past to impose rigid structures of dichotomy, of separation and classifying distinctions, and even of confrontation, on the animal world as supposedly understood by African peoples. Man transcending nature and imposing control through formal principles of separation and classification tends to be the dominant theme (e.g., Douglas 1966). But this kind of approach, based on an almost naturalistic assumption of a creation structured by hierarchy, can be seen more clearly today as only one particular view, even a particular view rooted in our recent history and imperial experience, that may not conform generally to human understandings of the natural world. As a tool for ethnographic analysis it may miss indigenous themes of continuity, of integration, and of interaction between the various species of the living world, including ourselves. Willis (1974) contrasts the worlds of the Nuer, the Lele and the Fipa, the latter emerging as more conscious of the interdependence and complex balance of human and animal, while the two former cases appear to be patterned by rigid structural separations of one kind or another. However, Willis's interesting discussion may actually tell us more about the changing sensibilities of Western ethnographers than about the inherent differences between the Nuer, Lele and Fipa.

The newer philosophical approaches to the problem of our position in the wider biological world should encourage us to reconsider the way we ask questions of the ethnography of 'animal symbolism'. The Uduk evidence is very suggestive here, for in several different contexts, and a variety of ways, they see themselves as set firmly within the animal world. In particular, they see themselves implicitly, and sometimes explicitly, as members of the great family of hoofed creatures, and kin to the wild antelopes.

The antelope as intimate other

Uduk see all living, moving creatures, including human beings, as having a common bodily nature. All are kept alive and active through the inner vitality of *arum*, a life force carried in the blood and in the breath. In warm-blooded, breathing creatures this force is focused in the liver. From this organic centre of bodily life stem the spontaneous experiences of feeling and of spiritual sensitivity. Beyond this common heritage that human beings share with the animals, humans have the extra capacities of controlled 'reason', the processes of which go on in the stomach, and of psychic receptivity signalled by the evidence of dreams. Whereas these specifically human capacities cease with the death of the body, the *arum* of human beings, like that of animals, can outlast death.

In the world of mythical stories, there was at the start of things no separate 'god' or encompassing divinity. *Arum* was present in the living creatures as the grounds of their existence, and in as far as there was no final death (people died and rose again) there was no separate realm of *arum*. However, when circumstances led to the breaking of the cycle of death and rebirth, the *arum* of people became finally separate, and the *arum* of all those who have died now exist in a parallel world underground. These may sometimes be met with, as may various loose *arum* in the bush, including those of animals that have been killed.

Important links are made on different levels between the community of animals, specifically of antelopes, and that of human beings. The major classes of animals are differentiated according to their feet and style of locomotion: there are for example the clawed animals, the hoofed animals, the creeping earth creatures, the feathered creatures, and the water creatures. It is quite explicit that before the emergence of human beings in the physical form we now know, and before the great split between domestic and wild that divided the world, we belonged to the same bodily kind as the hoofed creatures (*tonycuk*).

In the southeastern Sudan there occur, in recent historical times a range of bovid types (Kingdon 1982): buffalo, bushbuck, greater kudu, klipspringer, dik-dik, bush duiker, bohor reedbuck, kob, waterbuck, Thomson's gazelle, Grant's gazelle, gerenuk, hartebeest, tiang, roan antelope, and possibly oryx. Although the wild forebears of sheep and goats do not occur in northern Africa but in the Middle East, it seems likely, according to modern research, that cattle were first domesticated from a new extinct wild species more than 8000 years ago, in a relatively wet phase of the Holocene (Gowlett 1988). This interpretation is of great interest in view of the known cultural evaluations of cattle by the pastoralist peoples of northeastern Africa, and also for the lesser-known evaluations of wild bovids by people like the Uduk with an evident ancient bias towards hunting.

From within the general class of 'hoofed creatures', in the Uduk view, several domesticated species emerged. For example, goats developed from the *cish*, a term applied to the small gazelles, sheep from the *yul*, glossed in the typescript dictionary produced by the Sudan Interior Mission as reedbuck or kob, and cattle from the roan antelope, *she̱t*. Among other species of bovid distinguished in Uduk are *almaŋa'th* (buffalo), *shwa'ti'de* (kudu), *uwiy* (dik-dik), for which I do not know of any domestic partner; and *bothoŋ* (hartebeest), *golga* (tiang), and *ko̱p* (waterbuck), all of which I have heard represented as direct bodily associates of human beings. In particular, the Uduk speak of themselves as hartebeest, a species that seems to have been common in the region in former times. The term *bothoŋ* (hartebeest) is sometimes used in a generic sense for antelopes as a broad class (this does not include the buffalo). According to Uduk we human beings were also a form of antelope early in our evolutionary history, and went on all fours with hoofed feet. An elderly man called Bu̱k̲ko told me that his group in particular were the ones who had been hartebeest, while other groups in the neighbourhood had developed from other hoofed species, such as waterbuck and tiang.

Again according to various Uduk sources, the emergence of these proto-human hoofed beings coincided with the appearance of sheep, goat, and cow; a domestic variety of several other wild species appeared, some warthog becoming pig, some francolin chicken, some giraffe camel. Most significantly, as one change triggered the others, the fox became dog. The personified Dog brought the hoofed humans fire, taught them language, and provided them with spears to defend themselves. At that point they were able to stand upright, their hands and feet changed, they could hold and use spears, and they organized through language. The other newly domesticated species joined them, on the same side against the remaining wild animals that they now hunt. (The monkeys, rather than being original ancestors, are degenerate human beings derived from a brother and sister who ran off into the bush and grew tails).

I have given a more coherent picture of these events than is contained in any one account I have heard; detailed evidence, and its circumstantial emergence, is recorded elsewhere (James 1979, 1988). But there is coherence behind the metaphors, allusions, and fragmentary exegesis, a coherent view of our intimacy with the rest of the living creatures. Our difference from the animal world is not based on inherent distinction of substance or a separate creation. We are of one origin with the other creatures. The differentiation that came about was not even exclusive to ourselves; the separation was rather between those from almost every major class of animal who associated themselves with us, and those who remained wild. Our superiority was not one of God-given dominion over nature, nor was it a qualitative bodily change that set us completely apart. The change was not even exclusive to us; we learned from the fox/dog, who had taken the initiative. Our success then, as perhaps up to the present, lay in our superior organization, with the use of language (which is understood today by the dog as by no other animal), sexual division of labour, cross-species cooperation, and technology. It is not man alone who faces an alien wild as hunter: it is man in concert with woman, assisted by dog, together with the use of fire and weapons, who is able to engage and overcome the wild because of his affinity with it. Like the antelope, humankind has few bodily defences or natural weapons; without their animal allies, their social organization, and their technology, human beings would be prey, rather than hunters, in the forest. At home, they are able to use the defenceless domestic forms of the hoofed family for their own survival without having to fight the wild directly at all. Human beings protect them while limiting their freedom (cattle are sometimes known as 'tied-up animals', *tonyok*, and small stock as 'fenced animals', *tonkal*).

We are often used to referring to 'man' as a hunter confronting his prey, the 'man' being thus understood as a male carnivore facing, typically, the grass-eating antelope, unmarked for gender. The masculine image seems to fall naturally into place, in the Uduk context as in English. But this antagonism is not given in the man's bodily nature; take away his dog, his weapons, and his collective organization, and you are left with a being much less obviously carnivorous, much less obviously masculine, much less fit to confront the antelope. Without these added trappings, the human being unadorned and unarmed is more like the prey than like the hunter. It is interesting that the contexts in which antelope–human associations are evoked in metaphor or ritual are those of the defenceless person, the inner person, the woman, or the nonhunter. The human being is in his or her nature rather like an antelope; but dressed up for the hunt (or trained as a diviner as described below), the male becomes more like one of the naturally endowed hunters, one of the clawed species.).

Let me give some examples of metaphor and image. The litheness of a young girl's body may be compard to a roan antelope, and the softness of her skin to that of a gazelle. In music and movement, the antelopes are celebrated in many ways; their horns (especially roan and kudu) are used as instruments, both blown by hunters and by diviners, and beaten with soft wood sticks in the percussion music of the diviners' dance. Dancers may hold aloft forked twigs, to signify the horns of antelope, birds, or more recently the large Fulani cattle. Young men at the diviners' dance may leap forward in long strides, stretching the head forward and back as they go; this step is known as the 'roan antelope'. The image of the hartebeest, in the form of a line drawing, may be used in ornamental scarification, particularly by girls (and I think particularly amng the southern Uduk). The recurring image of defenceless antelopes running wild in the bush runs through accounts of the disturbances of the turn of the century. Robbed of home, fire, and supportive kin, refugees are no more than antelopes wandering in the forest. A man who had been killed in the cultivations was described to me once by an eyewitness as lying there all flowing with blood like a great hartebeest.

The world of the antelope herds is never too far away. Hunting stories are a favourite entertainment in the Uduk villages, and hunting rituals are very elaborate. Some people dream about the game, especially those who specialize in leading the hunt and their immediate matrilineal kin. These people, of both sexes, may 'herd the animals by night' as ordinary people herd them by day; but the former are herding antelope, the latter cattle. In a dream they may call out to their charges; they may milk them, and let them out of their enclosure. If they all rush out at once, the person may have some teeth knocked out; or their eyes may be hurt by the swishing of an antelope's tail, and their sight may suffer. These people know how to treat each other for these problems, usually by such techniques as burning the tail hairs of an antelope as a fumigating medicine. They know where the herds are so that they can direct ordinary hunters to them by day. Sometimes these animals look thin and weak as though they have 'just come out of a hole'. That other world in which they seem to participate is sometimes accessible to one who has just died, and on the occasion of the final beer to mark the end of mourning and the settling of the deceased's grave, the people may go to hunt, expecting that their deceased kinsman will cooperate in sending the animals to them. This close affinity between the *arum* of a man who has died and the world of the wild, itself a testimony to the timeless connections of humankind with the sources of life, evokes for us and I think for the Uduk the notion of ancient connection and commonality of being.

Notions of the bodily and 'spiritual' connection with the antelopes is more than representation, more than rhetoric. Certain communities deemed to be descended through matrilineal substance from a part of the Lake, the largest and historically most central birth-group of the Uduk, are thought to embody still a connection with the *golga*, the Uduk term applied to the tiang (a Nilotic word; the creature is known in East Africa as topi or, very suggestively, bastard hartebeest). Sometimes named as Laken Golga, they may claim (or it may be claimed for them) that an inherited priestly quality has come to them from long ago, from their original ancestress who gave birth to a tiang as well as to human offspring. Sometimes others are thought to suffer from their vulnerability to this power; one of the ways in which this may find expression is through the unexpected irruption of abnormality within their birth-line. The birth of twins, along with what we would regard as pathological deformities, is interpreted in these terms. To give birth to two is termed *wol*, a word used otherwise only of hoofed animals that have multiple births, such as goats and cattle. It is seen perhaps to some extent as a reversion to a purely animal state, after all defences have been lost and the uniquely human capacities have gone. From such a person, that is the woman in whom the abnormality appears, the twins and any subsequent births in the female line for some generations, the raw emotions well up from the liver. Such is their contaminating power that these *dhathu* may grow up to cause sickness and death around them. For a period of decades in the middle of the present century, it was assumed that only physical elimination could rid the community of this scourge; not only were individual twins eliminated, but the Uduk became notorious for murders of adults based on this diagnosis.

In the course of the present century, partly perhaps in response to the claims made by both Christianity and Islam upon the Uduk, there has been a remarkable growth in the numbers and activities of diviners. A good proportion of the population has joined, in particular, a movement I have called the Order of Ebony Diviners (after their main oracular technique of consulting burning ebony wood). In many contexts the diviners represent and act out the drama of the hunting scene; there are, for example, five branches of the Order, named respectively after the dik-dik (these are said to be shy and quiet), the throwing stick (a standard hunting weapon), the weasel (a sharp-witted chicken-thief among other things), the elephant, and the monkey. But in other, more generalized contexts, the diviners as a body are represented as clawed animals, and modelled on the image of the hunter. After the death of a diviner, and the final mourning ceremony, people would not go hunting; they might encounter a leopard or a lion. After the conclusion of mourning for a layman, however, the hunters are safe; the antelopes may even come freely, gently guided by the *arum* of the deceased, almost to surrender themselves.

I have suggested that the new philosophical ideas about ourselves as members of the animal world have implications for the way we do ethnography. I do not mean that the Uduk see nature with a modern European, perhaps essentially Romantic, sensibility – that they are basically vegetarian and Quakerly in their attitudes to animals. They are far from being 'kind' to animals in this sense. But they do place their own existence, as moral beings, in a universe oriented to other living creatures. Their actions towards those creatures impinge upon themselves, and upon their relations with each other. To use modern jargon, they could not properly be accused of 'speciesism'. The human being's position in the world may occasionally be triumphant, but it is at root a vulnerable and variable one, like that of the shy antelope in the forest.

References

Clark, S. R. L. 1977. *The moral status of animals*. London: Oxford University Press.

Clark, S. R. L. 1984. *The nature of the beast*. London: Oxford University Press.

Douglas, M. 1966. *Purity and danger*. London: Routledge & Kegan Paul.

Fagg, W. 1958. (with E. Elisofon) *African sculpture*. London: Thames & Hudson.

Fagg, W. 1973. In search of meaning in African art. In *Primitive art and society*, A. Forge (ed.), 151–68. London/New York: O.U.P.

Gowlett, A. J. 1988. Human adaptation and long-term climatic change in North East Africa: an archaeological perspective. In *The ecology of survival: case studies from north east African history*, H. Johnson & D. M. Anderson (eds), 27–45. London: Lester Crook Academic Publishing.

Ingold, T. (ed.) 1988. *What is an animal?* London: Unwin Hyman.

James, W. 1977. *'Kwanim Pa: the making of the Uduk people: an ethnographic study of survival in the Sudan–Ethiopian borderlands*. Oxford: Clarendon Press

James, W. 1988. *The listening ebony: moral knowledge, religion and power among the Uduk of Sudan*. Oxford: Clarendon Press.

Kingdon, J. 1982. *East African mammals: an atlas of evolution in Africa, Vols IIIC and IIID (Bovids)*. London: Academic Press.

Leakey, M. 1983. *Africa's vanishing art: the rock paintings of Tanzania*. London: Hamish Hamilton.

Lienhardt, R. G. 1985. Self: public, private. some African representations. In *The category of the person: anthropology, philosophy, history*, M. Carrithers, S. Collins & S. Lukes (eds) 141–55. Cambridge: Cambridge University Press.

Midgley, M. 1979. *Beast and man: the roots of human nature*. Brighton: Harvester Press.

Regan, T. 1984. *The case for animal rights*. London: Routledge & Kegan Paul.

Thomas, K. 1983. *Man and the natural world: changing attitudes in England 1500–1800*, London: Allen Lane.

Vinnicombe, P. 1976. *People of the eland*. Pietermaritzburg: University of Natal Press.

Willis, R. 1974. *Man and beast*. London: Hart-Davis, MacGibbon.

15 *The track of the python: a West African origin story*

EUGENIA SHANKLIN

Introduction

The Kom people of Cameroon's Grassfields believe they were led to the area they now occupy by a python (*ngvim*).[1] The python that led the Kom is said to have been an incarnation of their late ruler, who hanged himself after falling victim to a trick played by the ruler of Bamessi. The lake that formed from the body fluids of the late Kom ruler exploded, killing most of the Bamessi people.

My purpose here is to analyse and decipher a few elements of this African origin story. I will consider a functional analysis of the sociopolitical elements, and a symbolic-structural analysis of the symbol of the python. I will also mention briefly the evidence for the lake explosion and I will use Wagner's (1978) obviation model to unpack the symbol of the python. My own conviction is that Wagner's obviation model explains the story's internal thought processes in a way that no other model is able to, but that a combination of social, historical, and symbolic techniques is necessary for a full understanding of this very complex story.

History of the Kom people

The Kom (Nkom, Bikom, Bekom) are a matrilineal group, of about 100 000, who live by horticulture and coffee cash-cropping in the Bamenda Grassfields of Cameroon's Northwest Province. At the time (1889) of first contact with whites, Kom was expanding its territorial boundaries under the military leadership of Fon Yuh (reigned 1865–1912).

The kingdom of Kom was headed by a *Fon* (in the Kom language, *Foyn*, hereafter Fon), a semi-divine king whose position was hereditary and who governed with the aid of the *Kwifoyn* (literally, the voice of the Fon), a governing body similar in many ways to a parliament. The *Kwifoyn* advised the Fon and enforced his decrees; some of their duties, for example, execution of traitors, were carried out by secret societies, subgroups made up of members of the *Kwifoyn*. As a whole, the *Kwifoyn* consisted of men from all parts of Kom; they were recruited as children, and after several years training in politics and diplomacy at the Fon's palace at Laikom, they either became members of the *Kwifoyn* or were returned, somewhat ignominiously, to their parents.

The reign of Fon Yuh was a time of centralization in Kom; under Yuh's leadership, Kom successfully incorporated several neighbouring non-Kom, non-matrilineal groups within its political jurisdiction and expelled others that refused the required political allegiance. Late in the 19th century a number of groups under attack by Fulani raiders also pledged allegiance to the Kom Fon in order to gain protection.

After the short-lived German occupation of the Cameroons, Kom had to come to terms with British colonial rule, and Fon Yuh's successor, Ngam (reigned 1912–26), was forced to abandon his expansionist policies. The British administrators followed the policy of indirect rule and had little visible effect on existing political institutions, but the missionaries who accompanied them to set up schools and hospitals were more successful in their attempts to undermine indigenous practices. Young men who in previous eras would have gone to the palace to become members of *Kwifoyn* or to secret society groups for instruction in Kom tradition were instead sent to Christian schools. During the reign of the next-to-last Fon, Nsom reigned 1966–74), the position of members of *Kwifoyn*, formerly gained by merit, was made hereditary to counteract the decline in the numbers of palace retainers.

At independence in 1960 a religious schism in Kom between Baptists and Catholics found a new application as a decision-making device in dealing with national political matters. Presently religious affiliation in Kom seems less a matter of faith than a means of getting jobs and positions in the national government. The numbers of people affiliated with each Church in Kom are difficult to specify accurately but the churches estimate that about 12 per cent are Catholic, 12 per cent Baptist, and 76 per cent pagan, with far more practising pagans apparent than these percentages would suggest.

Whether on religious, economic, or political grounds, there are many bases for factionalism in Kom. There are also bases for integration, for example, the major ritual of the death celebration in which matrilineage members with varying religious affiliations come together to carry out the appropriate Kom activities. Another aspect of Kom culture, and an important component of ethnic identity that most Kom people would adhere to, is that they are the people of the snake, the descendants of those who followed the snake on the journey by which the Kom reached the territory they now occupy.

The origin story

In Kom it is said that the ancestors arrived at Laikom, the site of the Fon's palace, after following the track of a python. Most of those who tell the story say they are uncertain about where the Kom originally came from – perhaps from Tikari or Ndobo, in the west – but all agree that the Kom were settled for a time in Bamessi on the Ndop Plain and that they left there because of a trick played by the Bamessi Fon.

The Kom people flourished and the wily Fon of Bamessi began to worry about the growing numbers of Kom. One day he suggested to the Kom Fon that some of their people were becoming too headstrong and might cause a war between their two groups; he proposed that they each build a house, invite in the troublemakers and set the houses afire.

The Kom Fon, whose name was Muni,[2] agreed to the plan and the houses were duly built. The Fon of Bamessi, however, had his house built with two doors, while the guileless Muni built his according to instructions, with only one door. When the doors at the front of each house were locked, the houses were burned. The Bamessi people escaped through the second door and the Kom people were destroyed.

When Muni discovered the trick that had been played on him, he was so angry that he struck the Bamessi Fon on the head with the harp on which he had been playing laments for his lost people. Muni struck with such force that the harp remained embedded in the Bamessi Fon's head for the rest of his life.

Muni went to his sister, Nandong, and told her that she should be preparing to leave Bamessi, for he was planning to hang himself. Saying, 'I want revenge', he told her that he would go to the forest and commit suicide. When his body rotted, a lake would form (from the fluid that came from the rotting corpse) and the maggots that dropped from the body would become fish.

'Then,' he told his sister, 'you remain where you are until you hear that they have found fish there in the big water; but you do not go to the place because anyone who goes there will die. When you hear that the place has sunk and disappeared,[3] begin to go closer each day. Soon you will see the track of a python; you then collect your people and begin to follow that track. The people of Bamessi will ever after be a small population, but you should not worry.'

All happened as Muni had predicted. When his sister saw the track of the python, she and her people began to follow it. Nandong knew that wherever the track disappeared, she should stop. The first place it was lost was at Nkal. Three people from Nkal (usually said to be people of the Ndotitichia clan) followed, too, when the track reappeared and they went from Nkal to Ba Djottin, then to Idien, near Akay. Nandong the sister of Muni, had delivered a female child, who was near the age of maturity.

When the Fon of Idien, whose name was Kuboh, saw Nandong's daughter, Bih, he took her as his wife. Bih stayed in Kuboh's compound and bore a son named Jinabo. Later Bih delivered another son, Kumambong Boh, and then three daughters: Nangay Boh, Nakunta Boh, and Nyangha Boh. When the track of the python reappeared, Nandong and Bih decided to leave Jinabo at Idien and follow the snake. They came to Ajung, and Nandong stayed there to cook castor oil for Bih to rub the children with.

From there, Nandong went back to Idien and Jinabo, who was about ten or eleven years old at this time, wanted to leave with Nandong. When

Nandong returned to Ajung, the python track had reappeared, so they left and followed the snake once again, leaving Jinabo at Ajung. Then they went to Ijum, where they were near what would be the palace at Laikom.

Kuboh, the Fon of Idien, was angry that his wife and son had left, so he turned himself into a leopard and came to Ijum, to eat Jinabo. After Nandong collected Bih, Kuboh came to Ijum but Bih discovered in a dream that he was coming. She spent three days struggling with the leopard, having already hidden the children in the ceiling.

On the fourth day, with the leopard still worrying her and trying to come into the house, Bih had a dream in which she saw Muni. The leopard was then digging into the foundations, trying to dig a hole to come into the house. Muni asked her to warm potash in the fire and throw the hot potash into the leopard's face. When the leopard was killed, the snake road reappeared and led them to Laikom. Muni had said that wherever the road was lost, they should remain, so they stayed at Laikom.

Jinabo, however, was still at Ajung. When the Kom had been at Laikom a short time, they decided to go and get Jinabo. He put up the circle of stones in the centre of the palace. By then Nakunta had founded the Itinala clan and Nyangha the Achaf. Only Nangay Boh stayed with the Ekwu people. When Jinabo died, Kumambong was his successor; Kumambong died and Nkuo, a nephew, was taken. Three compounds were built: AbeEkwu, up; AbeItinala, down; and AbeAchaf, mud. One son decided to build down, another in the mud; the one who stayed at Laikom was the first son, Jinabo. All were (grand)sons of Nandong.

Functional analyses

The version of the Kom origin story I have just presented is a shortened, flattened composite of the story as it is told in Kom. Further, it is what I came to think of as the 'standard' version of the story. Most Kom people are convinced that one could understand nothing about the Kom people unless one knew how they came to the territory they now occupy.

It is important to know that everyone 'believes' the story, at least on some level, and that people think a python actually did lead their ancestors to Laikom. Even those whose ancestors came in more recently, that is, within the last two or three generations, describe themselves as the people of the snake, though their particular ancestors were not part of the migration. With some few exceptions, those who told me the story were nonliterate, but among my Kom acquaintances there are several well-educated people (English, Canadian, and American degree-holders living outside Kom) who had never considered questioning the origin story. There is an active political dimension (Shanklin 1981) to this belief as well: over the last 80 years various colonial administrations have tried to get the Kom to move their capital, Laikom, down from the highest mountain peak in the kingdom to the valley beneath so that administrators could work closely with the Fon. This request has always been refused, politely but firmly, because 'the snake stopped here.'

I was told this story more than fifty times in the course of 17 months' fieldwork. Once I was sufficiently familiar and bored with the story, I began to ask questions about the events: Why was the Kom Fon so stupid? How does a lake explode? What does the harp mean? Was anyone else here when the Kom people came? What would you do if the python came back? The answers varied, but what was of more interest to me was that about a third of the versions varied so much as to be at odds with any standard version or any functional anthropological interpretation of myth, for example, by allowing the Kom to pass through the Baptist Mission (built after 1900) at Banso; or by asserting that Jinabo, the first Kom Fon, was succeeded by his son; or by suggesting that the Kom, contrary to the snake's wishes, decided to move down from Ijum to Laikom 'because Ijum was too cold.'

Another kind of evidence of belief can be adduced from ethnographic data: first, when a woman sees a snake[4] in the yard of a large compound where many people are buried, she takes it as a representative of the ancestors and sprinkles it with camwood as a blessing. Second, a good number of Kom medicines contain dried snake. Both suggest that snakes are intermediaries between the ancestral world and that of the living; the taking of medicine involves a kind of communion, because illness is often attributed to ancestral anger. This interpretation is further supported by the fact that the Fon of Kom, who is the intermediary between the worlds of the living and the dead, cannot eat python in any form after he has undergone the rites that transform him into a semi-divine, immortal being (Shanklin 1985).

Using the functional hypotheses drawn from social anthropology, there are many other kinds of evidence that can be evaluated, such as the active political use of the story to avoid moving the palace, with the claim that Laikom is where the snake stopped and is therefore the place where the Fon must remain.

Following Malinowski, the sociopolitical-functional hypothesis would read: if an origin story exists, then it should serve as a 'charter' for existing social and political practices and customs, and should underline aspects of current practice. To analyse other sociopolitical elements of the origin story, I will deal only with the social elements and relationships that may be teased out.

The Kom are matrilineal, polygynous and patrilocal; after marriage a woman goes to live with her husband, in the compound he has built as a precondition for marriage. When she produces children he must build her a house of her own, separate from the house of the cowife (or sometimes husband's mother) with whom she will have been living until the delivery of her first child. Her children are members of her matrilineage, not her husband's, and though the husband has certain rights and responsibilities toward them, the sons cannot inherit property from the father after his death.

During his lifetime, the father will give land to his sons and they will build compounds near him. Later in their lives the sons will succeed to their mother's brothers' compounds and pass on the compounds they have built to their younger brothers. The husband has rights with respect to his sons: he can claim their support if he is ill or if he needs money. In principle, a man's sons are supposed to be his allies but this does not always work out in practice; their allegiance may be claimed by others who have building land to offer them or by their matrilineage.

Social relationships are determined by membership in four groups: the compound; the matrilineage, which is part of a clan; the quarter, a residential unit; and the secret societies. Both compound and quarter are spatially defined, but compound membership is ephemeral because compounds are based on fragile marriage ties. Disputes among cowives, divorce, or succession disputes may affect compound membership adversely.

Quarters are territorial units with a given head, BoNteh, who hopes to attract members of his own clan to his quarter; many quarters also have subquarters, with subquarterheads, under their supervision. In the past, the quarterheads were the local administrators who governed with the aid of at least one and often several (male) secret societies, to whom they were as 'fathers'.

The other two groups have no necessary spatial loci, except for the secret societies that are sometimes associated with a particular quarter and quarter-head's compound.

The matrilineage, which consists of an individual's maternal kin traced back usually to a great-grandmother, is a group without a spatial locus (because of patrilocal residence) though it may have certain foci, for example, the lineage head's compound from which a young man is free to beg land should his father not give to him. The questions of giving of land and succession are the major preoccupations of lineage groups; the other main concern is with death celebrations, the most important ritual events in Kom social life.

Matrilineages are the socially active component of clans: matrilineages are exogamous, but clans are not. There are 25 to 30 clans in Kom, each of which acknowledges common ancestry in the distant past. However, not one of these can trace these genealogical links through to all living clan members. In the past, clan membership (versus matrilineage membership) was effective largely for claiming land, or, in the case of quarterheads, offering land in return for political allegiance.

I will now decipher the elements in the origin story according to what they say about social elements of Kom life. The first and most important relationship in the story is that between Muni and his sister, Nandong. In Kom, brother–sister relationships are important and enduring; a promise made to a sibling must be taken very seriously. In the story, Muni, the Fon who hangs himself, entrusts his sister, Nandong, with the mission of leading the Kom people to their final destination. As Fon, Muni was presumably married to several wives but in not one of the versions I collected was a wife of Muni mentioned. Indeed, it was often said that Nandong was the only woman among the original migrants, and this may be the basis of the claim that the Kom were already matrilineal when they arrived.

Male–female relationships and complimentarity or interchangeability of roles are also commented on in the story; males always lead, even after death, though the visible leader may seem to be the female. Husband–wife relationships are tenuous, as in the case of Bih, who decides for unstated reasons to leave her husband, the Fon of Idien, and to take along her children. In Kom tradition a wife who leaves her husband must also leave her children behind but Bih violates this rule and follows her mother (and the python) to Ijum, thence to Laikom. Husbands or wives may be capricious but matrilineage members are dependable and it is to them that one must look for help in difficulties. When the Fon of Idien turns himself into a leopard and comes to devour his children, it is the dead Fon, Muni, who appears to his niece (sister's daughter) in a dream, to advise her on how to kill the leopard and protect her children.

Father–son ties are often stressed in Kom ideology, but this story specifically denies them or denies their reliability in two ways. The first way is that Muni allows both his fictive children (Kom people) and presumably his real children to be burned alive. Secondly, Jinabo's father decides, apparently out of pique at his wife's having left him, to devour his children. The question of father–son relations is never directly discussed in the story, though a powerful statement about the dangers of patriliny is made in the episode about the father's attempt to devour his children. Here one is also struck by the fact that it is Bih, Jinabo's mother, who kills her husband to protect her children. This is a statement that Kom people often make in other contexts, too, especially in answer to questions about the uncle–nephew inheritance pattern. They believe that if sons inherited from fathers, mothers would kill their husbands in order that the son might inherit. Mother–son ties are 'obvious' to Kom people and never appear in ideological form, that is, they are seldom discussed.

However, if husband–wife relationships are problematic and father–son relationships are tricky, the most difficult relationship of all is that between uncles and nephews. In some instances, uncles and nephews merely avoid one another whenever possible; in a few (widely admired) instances, an uncle selects the nephew he wishes to be his heir and instructs the nephew as to his posthumous wishes. This is said to be the way things were in the past, though from historical data I collected on compound inheritance this does not seem to have been the case. And in the story it is noteworthy that Muni is safely dead when he helps Bih to save her children and thus to ensure Jinabo's succession.

In summary, then, a number of elements in the origin story do serve as charter for existing social or political practice, or can be (somewhat loosely, I believe) attributed to it. But there are other elements that are not mentioned in the story, such as land problems or succession disputes within

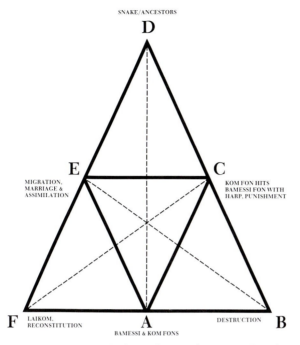

Figure 15.1 Events and relationships in the Kom migration story.

matrilineages, that is, between nephews. The functional interpretation is, however, a shallow one and while such hypotheses are useful for a limited understanding of how the story works within Kom society and, more particularly, how some sophisticated Kom people might account for the origins of their social system, I believe that they do not advance that understanding beyond the bounds of Kom society.

Unexpected vindication of the claim that the lake exploded before it sank came in the tragic deaths of 1746 people following the explosion of Lake Nyos in August 1986. When I first collected this story in 1981–2 and asked the question, How does a lake sink?, several people responded that it first 'exploded' (*se bvi*), then sank and disappeared. Descriptions of this mythical event are very similar to that of an eyewitness to the Lake Nyos explosion. Sinking or exploding lakes are not common folklore motifs, but similar episodes do occur in Grassfields stories (Shanklin forthcoming), though Kom people are reluctant to suggest that such an episode might account for their own migration. They remain firmly convinced that the python trail was the important factor, not the 'incidental' explosion and sinking of the lake.

In Figure 15.1 which is based on Wagner (1978), the letters A–F refer to the succession of events in the story. The external triangle (DFB) represents the story as it is told, while the internal triangle (EAC) represents an inversion of the pattern of relations set up by the story, the dialectical and creative thought process that Wagner says is inherent in all storytelling, a process he calls 'symbolic obviation'. The dotted lines (DA, FC, EB) link contrasting pairs of ideas that form the structure of the story.

To understand how this model works, it is necessary to go through it point by point:

Point A   Two Fons, Bamessi and Kom, are talking, one makes a suggestion about getting rid of their people.

Point B   The Kom people are destroyed by fire in a house with one door.

Point C   The Kom Fon is playing his harp when he discovers the trick that has been played on him, and he punishes the Bamessi Fon by hitting him on the head with the harp; the harp sticks fast.

Point D   The Kom Fon announces his intention to his sister, then hangs himself and his body fluids form a pool, maggots become fish. The pool collapses when the Bamessi people enter and the Bamessi Fon is left in the same situation he had plotted for the Kom Fon, with few people.

Point E   The Fon, incarnate as python, leads the Kom people through a series of places, where they acquire new members by 'adoption' or birth, including the son or grandson of the Fon's sister. Jinabo's father is the Fon of Ajung/Idien (patrilineal peoples) and his wife, the Fon's sister or niece, leaves him to rejoin her people at Laikom, the place where the snake stopped.

Point F   The angry Fon of Ajung/Idien comes to Laikom in the form of a leopard to devour his children and punish his wife; the python-Fon appears to his niece in a dream and tells her to kill the leopard with potash (wood ash leached with water). She kills the leopard but refuses to return its pelt to the people of Ajung; instead she puts her foot on it, cuts off its whiskers and sprinkles them on Jinabo's head, thus crowning him Fon of Kom.

Now let us look at some of the points as they relate to each other internally.

A, C, E: A, verbal communication (between the Bamessi and Kom Fons); C, musical communication; E, mystical communication with the ancestors. This internal triangle deals with various modes of shared communication, two of which have disastrous consequences and end in death. There is also a sort of 'wheels-within-wheels' point, as Wagner called it: At E, when the Kom people are wandering around looking for their home, not only do they collect people, they also collect obligations to other groups. So they get bamboos from Djottin (which could be a mnemonic for a previous salt trade, as salt is carried in bamboos) and other substances from other places. I believe this relates to the obligations the Fon of Kom owes to the other Fons of the area, to the other groups in the area.

B, D, F: B, destruction; D, incarnation; F, reconstitution. The external triangle deals with right/wrong leadership; the Kom Fon's mistaken notion, his eventual self-sacrifice that enables him to lead his people to a place where they will be reconstituted.

D & A, E & B, F & C should all serve as cross-checks to this model. D is the point at which the Kom Fon becomes a python, i.e., a 'right' or wise leader, having been at point A a 'wrong' leader, i.e., a gullible and foolish human. E is the point at which the Kom people are gaining members, having lost almost all their members at point B. F is the point at which the Kom people are established as matrilineal people, having prevented the leopard from devouring his children, and C is the point at which the Kom Fon, still in his human form, strikes the Bamessi Fon with the harp for having 'devoured' the Kom people.

One can also read this as A, B, C – thesis; C, D, E – antithesis; E, F, A – synthesis.

Although there are doubtless several other aspects of this narrative that would repay closer analysis, I contend that Wagner's 'obviation' model as employed here affords the best framework for exploring the internal thought processes in what could be called a 'continuing dialogue' within the story.

Notes

1   The Pidgin word for python is 'boa,' but this word, like Pidgin English itself, is an American import; there are no boas in West Africa. Pythons in the Old World, like boa constrictors and anacondas in the New World, kill their prey by constriction. There is also some confusion about the 'leopard', which is often called a tiger in Pidgin. Like boas, tigers do not live in Africa. There are two words in the Kom language: *nyamabo* means leopard, and *egvu binkem* means lion. Most informants referred to a leopard, while others maintained that the creature was a lion.

2   Nkwi (1976, p. 20 n.) says of the name Muni that 'many aged informants . . . referred to the leader as Muni by name.'

3   Most Kom say merely that the lake sank and disappeared.

4   The snake in this case is not a python, for these are seldom found in Kom. It is called in the literature a 'glow-worm', and the two ends of it seem to be the same. These are killed if found in the farm; a woman who kills one will give it to a man to dry and its head is used in a particular kind of anti-snakebite remedy called *fu'yuo*. This is ofen used as a protective device, to prevent snakes from entering a compound.

Another medicine that contains snake is *ndzi*; it also uses things that are from the ground. This medicine is a protective one, carried by women in calabashes and by men in phallic-shaped containers decorated with cowries. If someone tries to bewitch another who has this medicine, the medicine protects by 'absorbing' the witchcraft.

References

Chilver, E. M. & P. M. Kaberry. 1967. The kingdom of Kom in West Cameroon. In *West African kingdoms in the nineteenth century*, D. Forde & P. Kaberry (eds), 123–51. London: Oxford University Press.

Evans, G. V. 1927. An assessment report on the Kom (Bikom) clan, Bamenda. Mimeo.

Nkwi, P. N. 1976. *Traditional government and social change: a study of the political institutions among the Kom of the Cameroon Grassfields*. Fribourg, Switzerland: University Press.

Nkwi, P. N. & J.-P. Warnier 1982. *Elements for a history of the western Grassfields*. Yaoundé: Department of Sociology, University of Yaoundé.

Shanklin, E. 1981. Two meanings and uses of tradition. *Journal of Anthropological Research* **37** (1), 71–89.

Shanklin, E. 1985. The path to Laikom: Kom royal court architecture. *Paideuma* **31** 111–50.

Shanklin, E. forthcoming, *Exploding lakes in myth and reality*.

Vansina, J. 1973. *Oral tradition*. Harmondsworth: Penguin.

Wagner, R. 1978. *Lethal speech*. Ithaca, NY: Cornell University Press.

16 *Nigerian cultural attitudes to the dog*

J. OLOWO OJOADE

A dish of dog meat cooked in medicine could revitalise a weak husband thereby saving his marriage. (Yelwa 1985, p. 8)

The role of the dog in Nigerian culture is considerable when compared with its European counterpart (cf. Krappe 1964, p. 252). Explaining the poverty of dog lore in European culture, Krappe says it is 'because the animal has been man's constant and familiar friend for thousands of years'. But this is precisely the reason why the role of the dog in Nigerian folklore is so considerable.

The dog in myth

How the dog became a domestic animal and has since been staying with man is related in a Nigerian folktale (Umeasiegbu 1977, p. 45). When the dog was living with his colleagues in the forest he was very ferocious, and even wilder than the lion. While all the animals lived together, men also lived together. Men however began to hunt and kill the animals. The king of the human society one day invited the king of the animals to a meeting which he held with his subjects. They promised to stop killing the animals on condition that the latter give them one of their members. Votes were cast by 105 animals to decide which of them was to be handed over to men. The dog was chosen by 63 of the animals, the lion by 21, the antelope by 13, and the fox by 8.

The dog therefore had to go, but within a short period he mastered the customs in his new abode. He discarded his crude ways and became a domestic animal. He endeared himself to his human neighbours to such an extent that even when there was a shortage of fish in the human community and the only solution seemed to be to turn to the dog, the humans stoutly resisted the temptation and instead hunted the other animals in spite of the treaty between the two societies. The animals complained through their king, believing that the human action was instigated by the dog. Their king pleaded with the humans to give the dog to him and promised to give them other animals in his place. The dog refused, saying, 'I am happy in my new abode'. The two societies have been at loggerheads since then.

A notable characteristic of the dog is its sexual life. In some Nigerian stories we read about dogs transforming into men and vice versa. When they take human form the objective is usually to gratify their sexual lust through women. It is in this connection that we hear about cities of dog-husbands (Tremearne 1914, p. 83). Many Nigerians therefore use the dog as a symbol of sexuality. Thus when a man is sexually promiscuous he is likened to a dog.

Dogs in the household, the hunt, and war

Dogs are generally guards for Nigerian households. In this role they are unfriendly to strangers, whether of their own people or not. It is also in this role as a guard that the dog is credited in Nigerian folklore with the power to drive away evil spirits, witches and bogeys.

Among some Nigerians, dogs are also commonly employed as nurse-maids to small children. Their main assignment here is to lick the anuses of babies after defecation and clean the ground in the same way. Thus in some Nigerian carvings dogs are depicted eating excreta. We have a proverb to the effect that 'one does not have one's own dog and then remove the child's excreta with one's hand', which is used in the sense of 'why keep a dog and bark yourself?' Exceptionally, some also eat the excreta of older people. This is confirmed by the following episode:

> When they came to the meeting at Abu ise, the (newly appointed) King suffered diarrhoea. A dog came from the street, went beneath his clothes, and licked up all the excrement. When the meeting was over he got up and said, all the kingmakers must regard the dogs as sacred. No kingmaker may ever eat dog. (Isichei 1977, pp. 149–50)

One of the most important roles of the dog is to help in farming and hunting. In this role the dog helps to retrieve animals killed by the farmer or hunter. A Nigerian tale tells how the dog started to accompany the hunter to the forest:

> The dog was said to have been chased out of the forest by other animals because of its habit of barking every night. Then it was captured by man and taken home. There it was fed and it began to help its owner by keeping watch over the compound at night. When at last it became the friend of its keeper, it began to take vengeance on its former neighbours (i.e. other animals) by leading people who came to hunt them into their dens. (Isichei 1977, p. 48)

A Nigerian folktale also explains why the dog hunts in particular for the porcupine any time he goes into the bush, whether alone or with his master. One day the Ennying (francolin) was sitting on her eggs. She grew very hungry and went out to find some food. While she was away, Njaw (dog) ate her eggs. Then he went off, stole some feathers and covered himself with them, so that he should not be found. When inquiry was made about the egg-thief, Porcupine said, 'It is Njaw who is guilty'. The dog therefore thought, 'From today Porcupine is my enemy'. He ran after her, but she got to her home and hid within it. Njaw got nets and hung them round the hole. Then he waited, and after a while she tried to come out, and was caught. That is the reason why, when a hunting dog goes into the bush, he always seeks out the place where Porcupine lives. They have been enemies for many years.

Normally a hunter shows appreciation to the dog that has killed or retrieved animals for him. For example, the Kagoro hunter gives the bones of the animals to the dog, the Igbo hunter gives the head and intestines, while the Amo hunter gives the heart and intestines. In parts of Ogoja the head of the animal killed is cooked with hot pepper and other ingredients and presented to the dog.

Nigerian folklore abounds in tales of hunting dogs that have saved the lives of their masters. One example is a Yoruba story about Orisa Oko the hunter and his dog. Orisa Oko, Johnson (1899, p. 37) records, 'kept a dog and a fife, and on several occasions when lost in the bush his whereabouts were discovered by his dog at the sound of the fife'.

But more striking is the story of Awsang Atikwat, the famous hunter, and Ada Etim Agbo Etum, the terrible Forest Woman. She had arranged to cut down the tree on top of which Atikwat had climbed when he escaped from her wrath. The following passage recorded by Talbot (1912, p. 254) contains the rest of the story:

> At the moment when this tree also came crashing down, the dogs reached the spot. Now one of them was called Oro Njaw. He was the fiercest of them all, and at once darted on the Forest Woman, while the other attacked her men and put them to flight. Many of these were killed, but some escaped. Ada herself was torn in pieces.
>
>   Thus ends the story of Awsang Atikwat, the famous hunter, and Ada Etim Agbo Etum, the terrible Forest Woman, who had within her belly all the music of all the world, and also all weapons which have ever been made.

It is in appreciation of this type of service that hunters generally honour their dogs. For example, it is not uncommon for a dog to be given an elaborate burial as if he were a human being, especially if he dies bravely during a hunting expedition.

Dogs also used to accompany warriors to the battlefield, where they actually participated. Some dogs are reported to have performed actions that caused their army to defeat its enemy. A good example is Tungbe's dog called Lekewogbe (he who drives liars into the bush). About this dog a citation was composed, part of which reads (Beier 1959, p. 32):

The dog who brought the luck of War with him when he came to this world from heaven. No day is as sweet as the day when Lekewogbe followed his master to war . . .

Dog on the menu

An appreciable number of Nigerians eat dogs, including the Amo, the Angas, the Berom, the Efik, the Ibibio, the Igara, the Igbo, the Kagoro, the Magazawa, and the Yoruba.

Even among these groups it is not everyone who eats dog's flesh, but among those Nigerians who do, the meat is considered a great delicacy. On all occasions when I visited Kugiya (near Jos), the focal point of my local investigations, I discovered that the sellers of dog's meat attracted more customers than the sellers of other types of meat.

Dog-eaters do not call the parts desired by their common names, but give them special names. Thus while the dog itself is called '404 station wagon' (because of its supposed resemblance to the Peugeot 404 station wagon) (Fig. 16.1), the head is called 'gearbox' or 'loudspeaker', the legs are known as '404 wheels', the tail is referred to as 'telephone', the intestine 'round-about' and the feet are called 'tyres'. The ears are called 'headlamps', and the water with which the dog is cooked is called 'penicillin'.

Those who wonder about the penchant of dog-eaters for the meat must

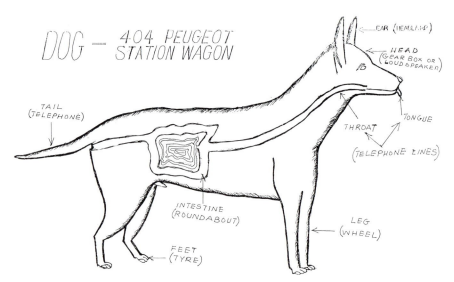

Figure 16.1   The naming of the parts. The edible dog as a Peugeot 404 station wagon. (Drawn by Peter U. Idika, Nigerian National Museum, Jos.)

remember that the dog contains more protein than many other animals, including humans (Stone and Cozens 1977, p. 227).

The dog in therapy and magic

The dog is also said to possess therapeutic properties. Thus many people eat dog's meat because of its magical value. For example, some eat the fat of the dog together with some concoctions against fever and syphilis. In northern Nigeria it is believed that one remedy for boils is to kneel to a dog. It is also believed that if girls desirous of marriage eat puppies, they will get suitors. Dogs are also eaten as a protection against *juju* (harmful magic). A dog's eyes roasted or fried and ground together with some other ingredients and made into powder will enable the user to see more clearly. Fearful people, everyone agrees, must not attempt this because the effect is immediate: the user will begin to see exactly as the dog sees and in fear may even begin to bark like a dog. Many Nigerian clairvoyants use this preparation, as also many nightwatchmen who are thereby enabled to see thieves at a long distance.

Barren women also approach medicine men who prepare concoctions for them containing parts of a female dog. Some parts of the dog are used to make love philtres: 'Dog meat dynamizes potency,' one informant said.

It is strongly believed by the Yoruba that the head of a dog put in a container over which some incantations have been uttered will produce a wide range of good things for the user. In a similar way the head of a dog can be used as a medicinal soap. To this must be added tobacco, and water from an indigo dye. The head of the dog will be ground together with the tobacco, all of which will be mixed with the soap. This is prepared for persons who desire money to start trading. If such traders wash with such soap, people will approach them and sympathize with them, giving them money with which to start their businesses. The following is the incantation which the trader must utter as he baths with the soap:

> Help me to dye, help me to soak does not stop at the dyer's house, I am sniffing, I am wanting does not stop at the tobacconist's house. It is come-and-get-come-and-get that we call dog. Men and women, may you (similarly) be calling me.

Dogs are believed to be associated with spirits, and when they see spirits they naturally bark at them. Should a dog howl or bay in front of a person's house early in the morning, it is a sign that a member of that household will die because the dog has seen the spirit of that person.

My Kagoro source described an incident which she had witnessed herself. A young man had bought about seven dogs for slaughter. It was then noon, which is the hour when the spirits are supposed to be active.

One of the dogs started barking furiously, as if it had seen a spirit. Still, he slaughtered this animal, together with the others, and put the remains in a bag which he carried on the back of his bicycle. On the way home he saw what appeared to be the same barking dog that he had just killed. The experience unnerved him, but he managed to reach home and to cook the dog meat.

After he had sold all the meat his condition worsened. His parents finally took him to a native doctor. The young man described his experience and the doctor concluded that it was the barking dog that had sent him mad. The young man is still afflicted.

Because of the various superstitions woven around the dog, various taboos also have to be observed. For example, among the Yoruba, a person must not use the bare hand to beat a dog otherwise the hand will swell up.

The dog and sacrifice

Among the Zuru people dogs are sacrificed in order to appease the gods. The Efik tie the dog and throw it into the sea to appease their river gods and goddesses in the hope that they will catch plenty of fish. Among the Yoruba the dog is a favourite sacrificial animal for a number of gods, notably Ogun, god of hunters and warriors; Erinle, a river god; Eshu, the god of fate; and Shango, god of thunder.

Why the dog, and not other animals? This question has been answered already: the dog has now taken the place of human beings as a sacrificial victim because he is the next best victim after man. Thus some gods particularly demand dogs for sacrifice. But in the case of Ogun, who especially desires a dog's sacrifice, an additional reason is offered. On a certain occasion, according to a Yoruba myth, a dog bit off the god's penis. Immediately Ogun cut off the dog's head to stop it from swallowing the organ. That is one reason why the dog's head must be severed by a stroke of the sword whenever the animal is to be sacrificed to Ogun.

The ceremony of the killing of a dog for sacrifice varies from place to place even among a homogeneous group like the Yoruba. I take the Ilesha Ibegun festival as an example. The people of Ilesha (a subsection of the Yoruba) observe the festival yearly. Ibegun or Ibeja means the cutting of the dog. Worshippers of Ogun gather together in a large square in front of the palace of the chief of the Ijeshas, at Ilesha. A priest appointed for the ceremony holds the dog, which is:

> stretched out at full length by having its front legs tightly drawn forward and its hind legs similarly drawn backwards. When the dog has been stretched almost to breaking point, the Owa (that is the chief) or a priest cuts the dog asunder by a stroke of the sword, the crowd immediately raising a tumultuous shout. (Lucas 1948, p. 108)

In some part of Yorubaland the dog is worshipped. A notable example is the town of Ara in Oyo State where an animal is sacrificed to the dog during a festival known as Mobo. Also among the Yoruba there is a deity called Aroni, a god of the forest which has the head and tail of a dog. Another group, called Tokuoje, also in Oyo State, 'were born of the dog'. Members of the Tokuoje clan are called 'children of Lamishe', the word Lamishe meaning 'dog' (Beier 1959, p. 34).

The dog as pet

In view of all that has been said so far, it seems paradoxical to learn that, as among Europeans, the dog is also used as a pet. This attitude is fascinatingly manifested in the names that owners give to their dogs. Many such names are determined by prevailing sociocultural factors (cf. Ojoade 1980, pp. 195–214). But Nigerian doggy names are more fanciful and varied than their European counterparts. As among Europeans, however, Nigerian dogs may also bear human names, though this is not common.

Some examples are the Yoruba *Lekewogbe* ('He who drives away liars into the bush') and the Igbo *Dike Ogu* ('Great man of war'), *Omeihe Usu* ('Troubleshooter'), and *Obagidere Agu* ('Conqueror of lion'). Other names may refer to the owner rather than to the dog, such as the Yoruba dog-name *Tanifekani* ('Who wants us to be rich?') and *Tanitolorun* ('Who can claim equality with God?'), while yet others invoke proverbs (Ojoade 1980) or refer to deities.

Whatever one's opinion about the Nigerian attitude to this animal, one need not be sentimental about it. Dog-eaters and dog-lovers alike should accept that the dog's flesh is one man's meat and another man's poison.

References

Beier, U. 1959. The Yoruba attitude to dogs. *Odu* **7**, 31–7.
Isichei, E. 1977. *Igbo worlds*. London: Macmillan.
Johnson, J. 1899. *Yoruba heathenism*. Lagos: Government Printer.
Krappe, A. H. 1964. *The science of folklore*. New York: Norton.
Ojoade, J. O. 1980. African proverbial names: 101 Ilaje examples. *Journal of the American Names Society* **28**(3), 195–214.
Stone, R. H. & A. B. Cozens. 1977. *New biology for West African schools*. London: Longman.
Talbot, P. A. 1912. *In the shadow of the bush*. London: Heinemann.
Tremearne, A. J. N. 1914. *The Ban of the Bori*. London: Heath, Cranton & Ouseley.
Umeasiegbu, R. N. 1977. *The way we lived*. London: Heinemann.
Yelwa, A. 1985. 404: one man's delicacy. *Sunday New Nigerian*, 17 November.

17 Rodeo Horses: the wild and the tame

ELIZABETH A. LAWRENCE

Rodeo, a legacy from the days of the American trail and range cowboy, is extremely popular throughout the western United States. Rodeo is an integral part of traditional life for many people in the Great Plains, where there is historical continuity between the cattle frontier and ranching, and the modern 'cowboy sport' that developed from them. The origins of rodeo can be traced to the Wild West show as well as to the sports and contests that were first held by early working cowboys for their own amusement (Lawrence 1982, pp. 44–82). Rivalry between cowhands as to who could ride the wildest bronc for the longest time or rope the liveliest calf or biggest steer led to riding and roping matches. Ultimately these events became popular with spectators and developed into full-scale rodeo, in which the utilitarian skills of cowboys became intensified as the sport of cattle country, comprising both performance and contest.

In its particular social and cultural context, rodeo is an important ritual event, participated in and sponsored by the ranching population as well as others who share that group's ethos. My research reveals that the sport serves to express, reaffirm, and perpetuate certain values and attitudes characteristic of the cattle herders' way of life. Rodeo picks up on the main themes from the work of the cowboy, identifies and magnifies them, and makes them explicit through patterned performances, almost all of which involve interactions with horses. Just as the cowboys' horses, their essential helpers in all tasks, were and are of prime importance to them, so these horses also play a pre-eminent role in contemporary rodeo. Horses are involved in virtually all standard professional rodeo events, with the exception of bull-riding. Various classes of equine animals take the role of the rodeo participants' antagonists in bronc-riding events, and of their partners in the various mounted contests in which cattle are chased and roped or subdued.

Symbolic conquest

Findings from my long-term field studies of the Great Plains ranch and rodeo complex indicate that by means of the range and diversity of equine contests and performances included in rodeo, information is communicated about people's perceptions of, and interactions with, the species of animal whose subjugation and use was vital in the 'winning of the West.' On a deep level, human–horse interactions, in the various forms in which they are presented in rodeo, have come to symbolize that conquest itself, the subduing of the wilderness, the transforming of nature to culture through the process of taming that which was wild and controlling that which was free, as it was enacted upon the American frontier.

The equine animal is remarkably well suited to re-enact and represent symbolically the wild–tame transition, for within a single species it encompasses the extreme polarities of wild and tame and embodies the varying degrees between them. In their differing categories within the structure of the sport, horses exhibit characteristics ranging between the oppositions of wild and tame. The balance between the amount of control over the horse that the rider demonstrates and the amount of wildness and rebellion or tameness and obedience that the horse displays varies with each event, and both control and wildness are determinants of the contestant's success or failure. The dramatic countering of forces makes the process of exerting human dominance over animals particularly evident.

To become useful for human purposes each individual horse must first be transformed by taming, even though its species is domesticated. Though in many cultures the schooling of a colt is a gradual process, a Western range horse may come to its first day of training with little or no past experience with people and no knowledge of being subject to their domination. Thus there is a sudden and intense human–animal contest in which a person opposes the brute strength of the horse with his own type weapons – whip, spur, and bit, the instruments of culture – because he is inferior to the animal in physical strength and power. The resulting dramatic process, characteristically abrupt and violent, known to cowboys as 'breaking a bronc', becomes universally symbolic for the act of conquering. Working cowboys are by necessity intimately concerned with this process because the maintenance of their way of life depends on mounts that do their bidding. Further training beyond the 'broke' status refines the horse's repertoire, making it into a reliable working partner.

As perceived and used by the Western ranch and rodeo complex, the equine species includes many gradations. These, I propose, may be conceptualized as a continuum between wild and tame. At the wild pole are the feral animals, known as mustangs, which are descendants of horses reintroduced to the New World by the Spanish, and presumably have never been handled. Next in progression are the broncs, which can usually be handled to some degree and may be halter broken, but cannot easily be ridden. Nearer to the tame pole of the continuum are the trained saddle horses – dependable, safe, and obedient to the rider. Then there are the horses that go further, to learn the skills of cattle roping, which requires still more co-operation between mount and man. Advancing beyond this even closer to tame, in the direction away from nature towards culture, are the highly schooled animals such as dressage horses that perform intricate feats. In rodeo, novelty acts involving clowns and their trained horses are in this category.

Thus through the complex nature of the equine that allows it to assume many roles, different stages in the wild–tame transition are dramatized and their meanings explored within the context of rodeo. Traditionally, contests are divided into two categories: bucking, or rough stock events, and timed or cattle ranch oriented events. Special events like the wild horse race are often added to the programme.

Archetype of the wild

From the earliest days of the American West wild horses have been objects of fascination and have represented the epitome of freedom. The transformations of the process of taming these animals drew the attention of perceptive frontier chroniclers like Gregg (1966, p. 208) and Irving (1971, p. 122), who expressed empathetic identification with their transition from freedom to slavery. The facility with which the horse can reverse this process, that is the capacity to revert from tame to wild, was also noted by Gregg. This theme is elaborated upon by other observers, who assert that the formerly subservient animal becomes the wildest of all horses if its freedom is obtained (Steele 1941, p. 188; Amaral 1969, p. 38).

It must be remembered that it was the fully trained and obedient mounts brought from Spain to America that were able to resume a feral state on the New World plains and evolve into what was to become the American mustang. Since the horse that regains its liberty is often considered wilder than one that never knew captivity, it is clear that the American mustang is a perfect symbol for freedom. Ryden, an authority on wild horses, in summing up the mustang's history and its many contributions to New World development, concludes that 'the most interesting thing this horse ever did in America he did for himself when he took his freedom' (Serven 1972, p. 17).

In conquering the powerful and beautiful mustangs, frontiersmen found expression for the sense of mastery that was paramount in the conquest of the Western wilderness. The wild horse remains as the archetypal representation of the wild spirit of the Old West and of the excitement of taming it. There was, and is, however, an inherent contradiction, for at the same time that men wished to subdue and dominate the mustangs, they also admired their freedom and indomitability. This ambivalence is a characteristic of the contemporary debate over the fate of the remaining American wild horses. In exploring the mustang controversy with informants, I learnt that ranch and rodeo people, though not always motivated by purely economic factors (which, admittedly, can be important), generally show a strong imperative to bring these animals under control. Yet counterbalancing this, especially among rodeo participants, there is also a less potent, but nevertheless real, strain of feeling that if all the mustangs were to be subjugated or destroyed, an element that is of value in the frontier heritage would be lost.

In discussion, many ranch and rodeo people expressed a certainty that there has been genetic deterioration among wild horses, with both physical and mental effects. Horses that have gone feral are described by informants as having become progressively 'smaller and weaker', with poor body conformation, and possessing 'low mentality', making them 'nearly impossible to train', and hence 'good for nothing'. This is universally attributed to 'inbreeding'. In these attitudes I can identify a prime example of the use of the nature–culture opposition: people are expressing the belief that without the influence of man – that is, of culture – exerted upon it, the wild horse became totally useless. Left to itself – that is, purely to nature – the animal degenerated in body and mind. The whole complex of domestication comes into play here – the intervention of man through selective breeding to 'improve' livestock, to alter its characteristics in order to make it more useful for human needs. According to these informants, the imposition of culture over the natural animal not only moulds the species to human needs, but also leads to greater mental capacity and increased physical prowess. Scientists disagree, asserting that a wild species generally possesses more intelligence and vigour than its domesticated counterpart. As an authority on mustangs explains it, 'the common idea that wild horses gradually degenerated through uncontrolled breeding is contrary to fact . . . Until the white man interfered, mustang stock did not degenerate any more than deer, antelopes, buffaloes and other wild species left to themselves degenerate' (Dobie 1952, p. 139). But rodeo people's contrary perceptions are especially illuminating because they assert the idea that what is domesticated through the imposition of the will of mankind is in so many ways improved. Such concepts are the reflections of an ethos that generally places human beings, and all that results from human manipulatory power, on a level of greater value than that which is natural, or wild.

The wild horse race

The human conquest of nature through domination over animals is dramatically expressed in the wildest of rodeo's equine events, the wild horse race. When included on the programme, this spectacle forms a fitting grande finale. Animals used are required to come to the arena with little or no previous contact with people, and they demonstrate great fear at the unnatural situation into which they have been so abruptly thrust. The result is a spectacle of confusion consisting of a melée of plunging hooves and rearing bodies, dust, and whinnying. Groups of men pulling and straining on ropes attached to the horses' halters forcefully oppose the balking animals. Every action of the horses expresses rebellion against the men who work against time in teams of three to subdue, saddle, and eventually ride them. Announcers call attention to 'the stored-up cussedness of these wild, vicious, and defiant mustangs'.

This violent event is the quintessential representation of cowboy bronc-busting, as practised on feral horses, and is often referred to as 'a rodeo unto itself'. It holds great appeal for audiences, especially when biting the animal's ear is part of the process. Observers consciously relive the taming of the wild, as expressed by an older ranchman who said:

> I won the wild horse race at Whitehall in 1938. I liked doing it; it was no different from what I had done all my life as a cowboy. We rode horses that way all our lives. I still train all my own horses, and wouldn't let nobody break a horse for me yet. Maybe I will at seventy. We break 'em as three- or four-year-olds, and they're wild till that time. We don't raise 'em like in the East, around a barn and in a small pasture. It's a different life for a horse.

Rodeo's central symbol

The broncs of rodeo are wild, yet slightly less so than the mustangs. As rodeo people phrase it, 'they have the wild edge taken off them'. They can be handled to some extent, but will rebel by bucking when an attempt is made to ride them. Unlike those used in the wild horse race, broncs are mounted by contestants while being confined in chutes before being released into the arena. By virtue of their wildness, bucking broncs are a long way from trained riding mounts. Broncs are at the very heart of rodeo, and are the central symbol of the sport. Riding a bucking horse serves to express a basic concern with the phenomenon of subduing that which is free, taming that which is wild, and measuring humankind's role in the process. The bareback and saddle bronc-bucking events pit the wildness and rebellion of the horse against the skill and control of the rider, thus counterbalancing the forces of beast and man, wild and tame, dominance and resistance. The spirit of these oppositions is reflected in the oft-repeated rodeo verse:

> There isn't a bronc
> That can't be rode;
> There isn't a cowboy
> That can't be throwed.

All broncs wear a bucking strap and are spurred by their riders. Through differences in the structure and order of the two bucking events, however, rodeo manipulates the amount of apparent control exerted on the horses. In bareback riding the rigging consists of only the minimum of equipment: a leather strap with a handhold on top encircles the horse's body, and no halter or rein is used. Thus the unrestrained head of the horse gives it leeway for resistance to the rider, who has no equipment with which to control it. Standard rodeo tradition dictates that bareback riding is the opening event. Thus the programme is neatly framed by the two wildest events – bareback riding as the keynote and the wild horse race (or in its absence bull-riding) as the finale – representing contests in which human control is minimized.

In the saddle-bronc event a halter and attached rope gives the rider some apparent measure of control of his mount's head. A simplified saddle with stirrups provides more apparatus to signify control. Significantly, points are deducted from the contestant's score for losing his stirrups (indicating failure to maintain control) as well as for touching the animal or equipment (denoting too much control). Saddle-bronc riding is considered 'the corner-stone of rodeo'. It was born out of the cowboy's basic need for tractable mounts, and represents a familiar range task exaggerated for the sake of contest and performance. Rodeo people say that this classic event 'shows the process of making a bronc into a partner'. Bareback riding is a variant of saddle-bronc riding that was added to the programme more recently. The variations that were thereby introduced into the sport to differentiate two relatively similar contests serve to allow further exploration of the range of the man–horse struggle, which becomes metaphoric for taming and conquest.

Broncs are perceived as mean, tough, violent outlaws, 'mavericks who delight in tossing the cowboy to the ground'. Rodeo people say 'broncs are crazy, they don't want to cooperate with society. You couldn't use them on a ranch; they would keep bucking'. A strong belief is that 'it's got to be in them to buck; only about one in a thousand will keep it up. Broncs are ornery, and they've got to have a fighting heart'. Rodeo people say 'the bronc has an inbred resentment for man'. Rodeo publicity releases assert that 'power, violence, and rebellion are terms of pride when applied to bucking horses'. As rebels, broncs cannot be relied upon for useful tasks. Their image is one of unpredictability: 'bucking broncs are not trained, just mean, and you can never tell what one will do'. Informants insist that 'it's not possible to cue or teach a horse the bucking motion'.

Breeding for wildness

The trait of bucking, then, is believed to be inherent to a particular bronc and without exception genetically determined. It is nature, not culture, that produces the bucking action so essential to the equine athletes. The concept that broncs are wild solely because of innate predisposition has practical as well as symbolic implications for the sport. For now that broncs are much in demand due to the increasing popularity of rodeo, attempts are being made to produce them through organized programmes of selective breeding for this trait. A fascinating point emerges here, for in essence such efforts are an attempt to reverse techniques that have been directed over centuries towards breeding the buck out of the horse. Human progress has been associated with the production of a tame horse, obedient to the rider's will. Now, in order to ensure the continuance of rodeo and to preserve the spirit of the American frontier past that the sport exemplifies, people are conversely trying to breed the buck back into the horse. The hopeful director of one such breeding project says that 'so long as we produce horses with the will to resist by bucking, we'll continue to have rodeo'. The efforts being made are remarkable testament to the strength of the frontier ethos as expressed in rodeo and the importance attached to keeping it alive.

Presently, the greatest percentage of bucking horses are 'spoiled saddle horses' or 'kids' horses or riding mounts that go sour'. Rodeo people say such animals are the commonest sources of broncs, since breeding farms as suppliers are still in the future. A riding horse 'goes bad', becomes 'an outlaw', starts bucking riders off, learns he can do it, and is henceforth unsafe to ride. No special event or cause initiates this change; the bucking trait is believed to be just 'in' this particular animal, and presumably was previously held in check. The wild–tame dichotomy is well exemplified here, as it exists in the horse's dual nature. The animal has the capacity to be in either realm; it can shuck off the restraints of culture that have been imposed on it by human training, and revert to the wild – its true nature in the case of the bronc. The belief that 'the best broncs' are obtained in this way is indicative of the concept that a former state of domesticity means an increased degree of wildness in the animal. Relevant to this idea is the frequently related story about a pack horse in Glacier National Park that started bucking off his packs. The animal was, of course, sold because of this habit, and eventually became one of rodeo's most celebrated broncs.

Experiences of ranch and rodeo people support the notion often encountered in frontier reminiscences, as mentioned previously, that horses can go in either direction between wild and tame, and often do. A rancher told me 'I once got a horse from a bucking string and it was one of the best saddle horses I ever had. I had to educate it a bit. It didn't buck very often; it only piled me a couple of times. After I treated him gentle, he quit this. But he was always a one-man horse, though; I was the only one who could ride him. A stranger might make him buck'. Thus he indicated that a conversion between wild and tame was made, but it was a fragile and quickly reversible one, and did not essentially change the horse; the animal was transformed only in relation to a particular rider. This data again demonstrates the duality of the horse which enables it symbolically to enter and re-enter the domains of culture and nature, in both directions.

By means of the bronc events rodeo recapitulates the taming of the wild in a ritual glorification of the process that has been structured into the sport. Each contestant longs to be the conqueror, the winner, the man who can ride the unridable, who can defeat the rankest animal. Participants say 'there is no feeling on earth as good as the satisfaction that comes from knowing you have done it, you have made a good ride'. Yet at the same time they want the wildness of the animal preserved so they can continue to pit themselves against it. Significantly, broncs are not demonstrably changed by the events of modern rodeo; they are not 'broken' in the arena, and still appear wild when they leave it after each performance. In very early rodeo, horse and rider were turned loose and the contest was continued until the animal stopped bucking or the rider was thrown off. Today the eight-second buzzer abruptly halts the contest, and the broncs are not literally 'conquered' (though the word is used) even in a high-scoring ride. Thus wildness as an ongoing value is preserved.

Contestants show the same sort of ambivalence towards broncs demonstrated by frontiersmen and their present-day counterparts with regard to wild horses. Bucking horses are viewed as enemies to be conquered, yet they are admired as fellow athletes whose performance in opposition to their own enables riders to be victorious. Rodeo people identify strongly with the indomitable spirit of the broncs, which makes them the outlaws of society, a role that contestants often perceive as analogous to their own. Ultimately, there is a dilemma in their desire to have wildness perpetuated so that the taming process may continue.

The acceptance of 'culture'

In contrast to the unpredictable bronc, which occupies a position near the wild extreme of the wild–tame dichotomy, is the timed event horse, which is well along the continuum towards the tame end. Unlike the bronc, the enemy of society that men admire yet strive to defeat, the dependable roping or steer wrestler's horse is the counterpart of the range cowboy's mount, his highly trained and obedient partner. Within the context of standard rodeo events the calf-roper's horse stands nearest to the tame pole. Indeed, this concept is structured into the sport. For if a rodeo logo or motif includes a second equine figure as well as a bronc, it is always that of a calf-roping horse – his motionless, subdued, and controlled pose contrasting sharply with the leaping, kicking, rebellious bucking bronc. As 'the horseman's sport', calf-roping is said to represent the clearest example in rodeo of cooperation between horse and man, and a large share of a contestant's success is credited to his horse.

Ropers claim that not every horse has the potential to become a calf horse: 'You can't make a calf roper out of a horse if it's against their nature to do it. You have to stop and get another horse to try with. You go through dozens and ruin several before you know how to do it'. Here it is noteworthy that in spite of the great amount of training given to a calf horse, there is still something innate within the individual, a capacity or potential, that is a prime requisite. With the calf horse this is its ability to accept – not resist as the bronc would – the superimposition of culture (in the form of training) over its animal instincts (nature).

Contestants assert 'there is more to calf-roping and training a calf horse than is true of any other rodeo event. The things they must do are unnatural. They have to move backwards, pull back against the rope, and stand firm without moving. What the calf roping horse does is completely against nature. The rider is not on him while he pulls back against the calf rope; he has to do it on his own'. Making the horse move backwards is uppermost in many ropers' minds, representing the force of schooling that can, with difficulty, overcome natural instincts.

Calf-roping horses are expected to do the bidding of man, and represent the fulfilment of the obedient role society views as proper for the horse. Rodeo people stress the partner image, and often describe calf-roping as 'the marriage of horse and man'. The ability of a roping horse to concentrate on the task at hand, not becoming 'unglued' by mishaps or events occurring outside the arena, is admired. By implication, the horse's animal nature has been overcome, and he is in the realm of superdomestication – predictable. This is especially true since horses as a species tend to 'spook' or shy, a characteristic that has never been successfully bred out of domestic mounts.

Horses that fail to perform perfectly in their role are harshly criticized by audiences, who let it be known that their sympathy is with the contestant, not the animal, when his horse misbehaves. The image of the bronc as unpredictable has been reversed, for dependability is the paramount quality of the roping horse. Man and mount must 'know what each other is going to do, what is expected of one another,' rodeo people claim, and great advantage is said to accrue to the contestant whose horse gives a consistent performance. Ropers say 'you can't treat a rodeo horse like a dog. If you pet him, he won't work well; he must have discipline to perform'. There is a precedent among range cowboys, who felt that 'the meanest, most unreliable object in cattle country was a "pet horse"' (Rollins 1973, p. 268). Obviously, a pet horse would not display the machine-like precision required of the calf horse, which should have no input of its own and should be constrained at all times by the rider's will.

The 'level-headed' horse

The most significant thing about the horse's role in the calf-roping operation is that it performs its most essential function while not being directly controlled by the contestant. For the animal is not mounted during the critical time of tying the calf. This places it near the tame end of the continuum. Its status is dramatically emphasized: being free from the physical domination of a rider, it could bolt and run away, or refuse to pull the rope, but rarely does.

Other ranch-oriented events involving cattle as the quarry also demand highly schooled horses. The steer-roping event, in which the contestant ropes, knocks down ('trips' or 'jerks'), and ties a large bovine animal, is called 'the thinking man's part of rodeo' because it requires not only skill but also planned precision. The horse shares in that image. The event, with its intricate manoeuvres and the weight of the steer is, contestants admit, 'very demanding on the horse; there's a lot to learn'. They feel horses have to be 'level-headed' and have a 'steady disposition' to qualify.

In team roping the factor of two horses and two riders working in conjunction adds a dimension of camaraderie between the men and demands an extra measure of cooperation from the two horses. Each mount must manoeuvre his rider into position according to whether he is the header (who ropes the head of the steer) or the heeler (who ropes the hind leg or legs), coordinating their movements.

In the steer-wrestling event the contestant leaps from his horse and throws the steer to the ground. Even though the steer wrestler is on foot for the major accomplishment in this event, his horse plays a significant part in the contestant's success. The mount must be carefully trained to gallop up next to the running steer, enabling the rider to jump off at just the right time and place.

Thus in all the timed events of rodeo, man–horse relationships show important differences from those involving the rough stock used in bronc riding. The roping animals are far along the continuum near the tame end, and as servants and adjuncts to their riders their training and dependability serve to highlight the contestants' skills.

The horse as 'friend'

Appearing in the arena during much of rodeo performance are two other classes of equines – the stock contractor's horse and the pickup men's horses. The stock contractor's mount must be a quiet, responsive, adaptable, and tireless animal, in which he places a great deal of confidence; he rides it continually while directing the operation of the rodeo. The horse used by the pickup man, whose task is to rescue the bronc riders as soon as their rides are over, has to be fearless, willing, and dependable, for it must come in close contact with wildly bucking and kicking broncs. It should be agile enough to avoid the hooves of the broncs, and at the same time stay near enough to allow a contestant to jump off the still-plunging animal and onto its back behind the pickup man. It must also allow its rider to release the flank strap of the bronc. These two types of horses, both significantly characterized by the quality of predictability, are categorized as friends, totally dependable coworkers. They appear to share the symbolic, as well as the physical, realm of their riders. The stock contractor's and pickup men's horses are near the tame polarity. Partnership is concomitant with their riders' mastery, and they are counterparts of working cowboys' mounts. Going beyond merely carrying out their riders' wills, they seem, through reciprocal communication and interaction, to have been accepted into the human circle of domestication. In a sense, by occupying such a role the horse has become part of its rider's cultural sphere, and the man in turn has extended something of himself into the animal by close contact and mutual dependence.

The horse in the bar

In connection with rodeos in some towns a traditional cowboy prank is carried out by contestants in which a versatile and even-tempered pickup horse is ridden into a building, virtually always a barroom. There, in keeping with a spirit of Wild West camaraderie, two drinks are ordered – one for the man and one for his equine pal. It is a commonly occurring motif in the folklore of the American West, and the rodeo version has become part of the annual routine at Cheyenne Frontier Days and in certain other areas. While it occurs infrequently, due to practical limitations, the possibility of doing it is constantly considered, joked about, and discussed.

The procedure is that 'rodeo hands who are whooping it up – often on a dare – will steal a pickup horse and ride it into a bar'. Significantly, participants assured me 'a pickup horse will go anywhere'. This adaptable mount is thereby made to seem at home in both worlds – the animal and the human. It then becomes an agent transcending its usual role in society, violating order and propriety, and extending itself into a 'higher' realm. In their concern with this act, rodeo participants seem to be imposing culture on the horse to a degree that is the ultimate possibility – taking the animal into a strictly human sphere. The whiskey-drinking horse of the old Western folk narratives and tall tales does not merely express the cowboys philosophy of 'what's good enough for me is good enough for my horse'. In addition, by partaking of liquor, the equine animal shares in the consumption of an unnatural substance that has undergone a 'raw to cooked' (Lévi-Strauss 1975) or nature–culture transition, becoming a substance with power to affect the mind. This act therefore thrusts the horse further into an artificial and incongruous realm.

A bar in the Old West served as a centre of male social activity, a gathering place for men from outlying areas to exchange news and share conviviality. Bars in today's ranch society have retained some of the same functions, and often serve as places of business for the cattle trade. By bringing his horse into this setting, in reality or in a tale, the cowboy made a statement about this animal's inclusion in an important aspect of his life. The horse can be accepted into the circle of intimacy shared by male comrades in the atmosphere of the bar. Today's rodeo hand, with a strong sense of identification with his cowboy predecessor, is motivated to recreate this scene with his equine partner. By overcoming its own fear and resistance, as well as in breaking a strong social and spatial taboo by entering a building, the horse becomes, at least momentarily, a humanized animal, having undergone a symbolic nature–culture transition.

Horse and clown

Trick horses that perform in novelty acts and special exhibitions of rodeo generally occupy a position even further along the continuum from wild to tame than roping horses and pickup men's mounts. Horses that appear in special acts and exhibitions often serve to provide a contrast to animals appearing in standard events. Horses in these performance contexts defy the traditional roles rodeo assigns to them, and provide another way in which the sport further explores and comments upon the range and dilemma of human–horse relationships. Themes expounded in novelty acts contrast to rodeo's overall message concerning the urgency of human domination of animals and the conception of nature as an inimical force to be conquered. The acts seem to belong to an ethos alien to rodeo. They are real, but temporary, counterpoints to it.

Almost all the specially trained horses in rodeo novelty acts appear with a clown. As the classic figure of ineptitude, the clown serves as a foil for the horse with which it is paired, making the animal appear more intelligent. Often this status is portrayed by means of a routine in which the blundering harlequin tries unsuccessfully to keep a saddle blanket and saddle on the horse, who deftly removes them when the clown looks away. Not only is the horse shown to be superior in intelligence by outwitting the man in this act, but it has also defined the traditional role of equine subservience by refusing to accept the symbols of human domination. Of course in rodeo this evokes much laughter; the general belief holds firm that such a situation can only occur in a mythic universe – the carnival world momentarily created by buffoonery. It is soon over; the broncs are in the chutes, and the roping horse is ready to aid his master in tying up the calf; things will return to normal as order is restored.

There are several typical varieties of clown and horse acts, and the animal does not always end up in a position of control, though he may reach it during part of the sequence. Sometimes a scene is staged in which the horse brings the clown home safely after he gets drunk on Saturday night. In this act, the horse will push the clown out of the arena with his nose, as the clown staggers forward. Or the horse may come up behind the clown, lower its head between the clown's legs, and cleverly appear to put the man on its back, carrying him from the arena in a mounted position. Here there is a temporary symbolic reversal of roles – the horse is wiser, and is the 'keeper' of the man. Nature is thus seen to triumph over culture, especially when 'culture' has included getting drunk. It is significant that at some point during a typical clown and horse performance, the horse usually rolls over on its back and the clown will sit on its recumbent body, re-emphasizing human control and dominance. Then the animal will rise and again become the 'superior' of the clown. The animal at a certain moment is made to seem temporarily in control of the man, thereby allowing the expression of a concept that is a counterpoint to the main theme of rodeo – the assertion of human superiority to and rightful domination of nature. Needless to say, such an act is in reality the product of arduous training and mastery over the horse, but it is made to appear otherwise to the spectator. Cues are disguised by comic gestures and are seldom evident to the amused audience.

Humanization

Frequently at the end of such a repertoire the horse is 'dressed' by putting a hat and a pair of spectacles on its head and placing a pipe in its mouth. Here is found the ultimate extreme in representing culture over nature – the horse is humanized to the furthest extent possible. As a finale, the announcer typically gives a name to the caricatured horse, saying 'there you have it, folks, that is Hubert Elton' (some well-known figure who is disliked). Rodeo parades, as integral parts of the bigger celebrations, also display the prominent themes of the sport. Near the beginning of the Cheyenne Frontier Days parade, for example, this motif of culture over nature was keynoted. A famous rodeo clown walked beside his faithful companion, a horse dressed in a pair of trousers – undeniable evidence of the humanization of the equine species.

A pertinent rodeo variation on the theme of performing horses is an act heralded by trumpet fanfare and a proclamation by the announcer that the audience would now be treated to a display of the equine brilliance of the world-famous Lipizzaner stallions. 'Here, direct from Austria, you will see high-schooled horses perform difficult feats like the capriole'. At this point, having built up the audience's anticipation, he is interrupted by the entrance of a clown who rides two mules 'Roman style' – in a standing position with one foot on the back of each. With mock seriousness, the announcer calls for a 'reverse' and each mule goes in the opposite direction, confounding the clown. Here the lowly and ungainly mules provide an ironic contrast to the vision conjured up in the minds of observers of the precise and intricate manoeuvres exhibited by the Lipizzaners. For the celebrated horses are paragons of equine expertise, and as such symbolize a high degree of human culture being extended over the natural realm. The Lipizzaners, of course, would be as out of place at a rodeo as a cowboy in a tuxedo. The message in the act just described is that such sophisticated performances are all right for urbanites and Easterners, but, as for Westerners, give us the simple life. Let us cling to rural values, lowly creatures, and down-to-earth attitudes. The anti-intellectual, anti-aesthetic strain of the frontier is clearly framed in the language ranch and rodeo people understand – through the use of horses.

Exhibitions of mounted drill teams also typcially occur in rodeos. These demonstrate the cumulative skill of riders and horses working in unison in various routines, symbolically stressing conformity. Unity of motion is the overall effect, with individual uniformed riders being submerged in the visual pattern. Such displays of mounted teamwork in rodeo suggest the collective power and force implicit in the conquest of the West and seem to represent the traditional social order which endorses the taming and domi-nation of nature. Stressing conformity, they provide a striking contrast to the individualism that is constantly extolled in rodeo as a vital frontier trait, one that the sport generally emphasizes and ranch and rodeo poeple value highly. Thus the cowboy sport expresses through horse–human interactions both its emphasis on individualism – as with the lone bronc rider or roper who demonstrates and expresses attitudes regarding the wild and the tame – and its regard for conformity to cultural values, as represented by group displays.

References

Amaral, A. 1969. The wild stallion: comments on his natural history. In *Brand Book no. 13*. Los Angeles: Westerners.

Dobie, J. 1952. *The mustangs*. Boston: Little, Brown.

Greeg, J. 1966. *Commerce of the prairies*. 2 vols. New York: Readex.

Irving, W. 1971. *A tour on the prairies*. Norman: University of Oklahoma Press.

Lawrence, E. A. 1982. *Rodeo: an anthropologist looks at the wild and the tame*. Knoxville: University of Tennessee Press.

Lévi-Strauss, C. 1975. *The raw and the cooked*. New York: Harper.

Rollins, P. A. 1973. *The cowboy: an unconventional history of civilization on the old-time cattle range*. New York: Ballantine.

Serven, J. 1972. Horses of the West. *Arizona Highways* 48, 14–39.

Steele, R. 1941. *The mustangs of the mesas*. Hollywood, Calif.: Murray & Gee.

18 *The beast without: the moa as a colonial frontier myth in New Zealand*

ATHOLL ANDERSON

From the earliest days of 18th-century exploration, Europeans found it difficult to come to terms with the scarcity of large animals in New Zealand. In a temperate land the size of Britain, and more various in its topography and vegetation, there were plenty of small birds but almost no terrestrial mammals; only tiny bats that were rarely seen, a small introduced rat, and the domestic dog of the Maori. In particular the vast forests struck Europeans as uncannily deserted.

The sailors at once put their imaginations to work and came up with sightings of various small quadrupeds, a polar bear, a kangaroo 10 m tall, a merman, and a number of water monsters. Their speculations were propelled, in part, by Maori tales of *taniwha* – dragon-like or saurian water monsters – and other mythological beings, but none of these, nor the early European monsters, were taken seriously by the colonists who began to arrive from Britain in the 1830s. It was only about ten years later that a believable monster captured the public imagination. The giant ostrich-like birds known by the Maori name of moa (*Dinornithiformes*), which were undeniably evidenced by enormous bones which often lay upon the ground, became the subject of intense speculation, not least about whether they might still survive in the forests and mountains of the interior. The Maori view was that moa had been extinct for some centuries,[1] but that discouragement notwithstanding, and despite the lack of any Maori claims to moa sightings after 1840, Europeans began to report encounters with giant birds from this time onward.

This chapter assumes that no real moa were involved in these incidents. In my view the evidence, extensively reviewed elsewhere (Anderson n.d.) is plain: moa were extinct by the 16th or 17th centuries. One argument will suffice here. There are no reports of moa dating to the first 60 years of European contact after 1780, and no alleged sightings until after the osteological evidence of moa and its implications had been widely disseminated in New Zealand. Most sightings date, in fact, to the later 19th century (1850–80). The issue here, then, is the significance of moa *visions*, or reports of such manifestations. Nonetheless, for the sake of simplicity I shall refer to the observations as being of moa, although I propose the class 'colonial moa', more or less in the analogical sense conveyed by 'colonial goose'.[2]

Table 18.1 Alleged sightings of moa by Europeans.

Date of sighting	Observer(s)	Locality	Source
1830s	Robert Clark	unlocalized	Field 1893, p. 562
1830s	George Pauley	inland Otago	Taylor 1855, p. 238
1842	two Americans	Kaikoura range	Colenso 1879, p. 69
1840s	E. Jessop	Dun Mountain	Beattie n.d.
1850	men with Lt Impey	Kaikoura range	Buick 1931, p. 275
1850s	anon. prospectors	Oroua Valley	Field 1893, p. 567
1858	anon. prospectors	Mt Arthur	OW 2 October 1858
1859	anon. prospectors	Takaka range	Field 1893, p. 564
1860	James Cameron	Waiau Valley	Beattie 1958, p. 38
1863	Walker and Smith	Harris range	ODT 21 January 1863
1863	Cottier	Mohikinui R.	*Nelson Examiner* 12 May 1863
1863	anon. prospector	Southern Alps	ODT 23 July 1863
1867	anon. prospector	North Otago	Beattie 1938, p. 44
1870	prospectors/ Sutherland	Rangitikei V.	Field 1893, p. 565
1873	anon. shepherd	Waiau Valley	OW 12 April 1873
1876	Slight and Hunt	Rangitikei V.	Haast 1948, p. 804
1870s	anon. boy	Whangaehu V.	Beattie 1958, p. 34
1870s	McDonald	Waiau Valley	Beattie n.d.
1896	Charles Port	Lake Hauroko	Overton
1896	anon. boy	Brunner	Beattie 1958, p. 41
1940	Miss Chell	Wanganui	ODT 18 September 1958

Note: ODT – *Otago Daily Times*; OW – *Otago Witness*.

European claims of contemporary moa survival can be divided into three groups (Anderson n.d.). Of 44 cases, 3 are admitted hoaxes and several are simple mistakes of transcription between one reference and another. Many of the remainder refer to carefully described encounters with real birds that could not have been moa, or to other phenomena such as loud cries, tracks, feathers, crashing noises in the forest and so on that might fit with a variety of explanations. Eliminating these leaves 21 claims of direct sightings spread over the century from the late 1830s to 1940 (Fig. 18.1, Table 18.1). Fourteen of these encounters, and the best described, occurred between 1850 and 1880 and there is only one from later than 1900. To appreciate what claimants reported it is useful to outline a selection of cases.

(a) In 1842 William Colenso was told by a 'mechanic' who had recently come from Cloudy Bay that the moa existed in the Kaikoura ranges. One night two Americans and a Maori guide took weapons, he said, and 'ascended the mountain to the place where these birds resort, where, at the native's request, they hid themselves behind some bushes. Presently they saw the monster majestically stalking down in search of

Figure 18.1 A map of New Zealand showing the main areas of colonial moa
sightings and places mentioned in the text.

food; they were, however, so petrified with horror at the sight as to be
utterly unable to fire . . . they observed him for near an hour . . . They
described this animal as being fourteen or sixteen feet in height'
(Colenso 1879, p. 69).

(b) One evening in 1858, in the goldfields district about Mount Arthur, a
moa 14 ft tall was chased into a cave by miners. The next morning the
miners returned and found a young bird like a goose, covered in yellow
down, which they exhibited to others at a shilling a head (*Otago Witness*
2 October 1858).

(c) In 1859 'Four English migrants . . . farm labourers . . . proceeded to
Golden Gully [Takaka Hill range] looking for work, and shortly after
went some miles further on prospecting, I presume. They returned in

great alarm one day stating that they had come suddenly upon an enormous bird standing at the entrance to a cave or hollow on the hillside. They described the bird as standing about 8 ft. or 9 ft., of a brown colour, with a red mark around the eye. With the greatest difficulty we persuaded them to show us the spot . . . and we examined the cave and other places for the period of two or three days . . . these countrymen were thoroughly frightened . . . [and] . . . had never heard of a moa . . . I do not think they could ever have been twenty miles from their home.' (Major Locket to H. C. Field, in Field 1893, p. 564).

(d) In 1860 a shepherd called James Cameron, who had just arrived from Scotland, took up a job on the Manapouri Run. One day he came to the eastern bank of the Waiau River and 'To his great surprise he saw a huge bird emerge from the scrub on the opposite side of the river, walk along the sandy river bank, and finally disappear. At the time he had not heard of the Moa.' (Beattie 1958, p. 38).

(e) In 1863 two miners camped in the mountains about twenty miles beyond the Arrow River goldfield looked up at a dusk to the edge of a terrace about 300–400 m. away and saw 'a large bird apparently seven or eight feet high . . . The bird sat down for about ten minutes . . . it had a long head as large apparently as that of a horse. The bird then walked away.' The next morning the miners followed its tracks and saw where it had ripped the edible hearts from cabbage trees along its route (*Otago Daily Times* 21 January 1863).

(f) In 1863 a recently arrived immigrant named Cottier was walking beside a creek that flowed into the Mohikinui River on the West Coast. It was early morning and he suddenly noticed a bird like a giant woodhen (*Gallirallus australis*) about 200 m. away. 'Its head was hard looking, dark coloured, and flat at the top, with a semi-circle of red below the eyes. The head of the bird was as large as that of a calf, and standing about eight feet from the ground.' Cottier observed the bird for some time and then returned to his camp for a gun. When he came back the bird was gone (*Nelson Examiner* 12 May 1863).

(g) A party of miners, also in 1863, undertook an expedition through the Southern Alps in western Otago. One night a bird, about 3 m tall 'thrust its head over the [camp] fire but only remained a very short time; the dogs gave chase and they heard it for some time making its way through the timber.' The miners made a trap from logs and laid about it some large, baited eel hooks. In the morning the fishing lines were broken and the logs overturned (*Otago Daily Times* 23 July 1863).

(h) In 1870 a group of twelve to fourteen prospectors about 100 km. up the Rangitikei River saw a moa. It was during a cold winter with heavy snow on the ground and the sighting 'frightened the life out of the lot of them. They cleared for their bare lives . . . [when the moa came out of the bush and stalked across a clearing]'. Later a sheepfarmer called Sutherland said that he saw the moa. 'It must have stood 16 ft. or 17 ft.

high, and the body a tremendous size ... it was speckle or greyish colour, with a woolly look.' (Olsen to H. C. Field, in Field 1893, p. 565).

(i)   In 1873 a shepherd's dog flushed a moa from a patch of scrub near the Waiau River. 'The moa ran from the dog until it reached the brow of a terrace above him, and some thirty or forty yards off, when it turned on the dog ... The moa stood for fully ten minutes ... bending its long neck up and down exactly as the black swan does when disturbed. It is described as being very much higher than any emu ... and as standing very much more erect on its legs. The colour of its feathers is described as a sort of silvery grey, with greenish streaks through it.' (*Otago Witness* 5 April 1873).

(j)   'In November 1876, according to the *Rangitikei Advocate*, Mr George Slight, working on the Paraekaretu block, saw a young bird about four and a half ft. high, with a long hooked bill and very small wings. He and a Mr Hunt gave chase, but the bird ran away from them very swiftly.' Next morning their employer measured the bird's footprints and found that they were larger than his own and showed evidence of partial webbing. The weather atthe time was intensely hot according to Haast (1948, p. 804), who records this odd tale.

There are a number of points about these stories and others like them that ought to be noticed. First, the moa are generally very tall: up to twice as tall as the tallest species of Dinornithidae (ostrich). The emphasis upon height is, however, seldom accompanied by much interest in bulk. A tall, rather slim creature more like an ostrich than a moa seems to be what the observers generally had in mind (Fig. 18.2).[3] In addition, the imposing size is sometimes underlined by other potentially threatening features such as a very large, hard-looking head, red rims about the eyes, very large feet, or a hooked bill. Second, the behaviour of the moa is audacious and somewhat mysterious. They never attack the observers, no matter how close, but neither do they flee in fright. They often stand in conspicuous positions for lengthy periods of time before disappearing unhurriedly. They are also silent, despite an insistence on blood-curdling cries in contemporary stories about unseen moa.

Of equal importance are the circumstances in which colonial moa were seen. In most instances they appeared in the early morning or at dusk, sometimes at night. They were usually seen towards the limits of observation, for example, in the light of a fire, on the skyline, or on the edge of a forest.[4] Most importantly, whenever the information is recorded, it is almost invariably the case that these moa were seen by recent immigrants. Established settlers, surveyors, scientists and so on never reported sightings of moa, despite their frequent speculations on the subject and their reports of other phenomena that they attributed to surviving moa.

What, then, are we to make of colonial moa? My hypothesis begins with the common suggestion that people who see visions, or simply report

Figure 18.2 19th-century man and moa: Richard Owen beside a moa skeleton assembled in the unnaturally elongated style of the times. At right is a modern drawing of a reconstructed moa (after McCulloch 1982).

having seen them, are likely to be under some sort of unusual stress. The stress in the present case arises from the fact of migration. Mid-19th-century European immigrants to New Zealand were faced with a variety of challenges, and all at once. On top of the business of making a living in difficult circumstances they had to adapt to an unfamiliar landscape and climate, a new social milieu, and the anxieties and loneliness of finding a psychological accommodation to the loss of family and friends and the imposition of new standards of social and moral behaviour. There is a good deal of particular evidence of these problems in the diaries and letters written by migrants, but as yet no broader synthesis of the New Zealand material. Studies of voluntary migrants from Europe in other situations, however, have revealed a significant increase in feelings of helplessness, frustration and aggression, as well as in that intense longing for the familiar we generally call homesickness but which can reach the proportions of 'migrant psychosis' (Malmberg 1980, pp. 112–14).

These anxieties are likely to be experienced most strongly by recent immigrants, of course, and I argue that they are also likely to be strongest amongst the poorer or less educated. Lacking much practical experience of geographical or social diversity, the latter had most to learn and the fewest resources to assist them.

In one particular respect the balance between colonial opportunities and perils was, for such people, a fine one. In the socially simplified and somewhat egalitarian settler societies that characterized 19th-century European migration in rural districts, they also had the opportunity of significant social advancement (Wynn 1983, pp. 358–9). But there was a ticklish corollary. If the way up had been shortened and eased, the way down was equally facilitated and it led right off the end of the social scale. For small subsistence farmers, shepherds or prospectors far from settlements, and whose only social intercourse was of the most rudimentary kind, the distance between their unsocial existence and that of a savage, as they conceived it, was uncomfortably short.

The problem was exacerbated by the desire to push across the frontier and farther still from civilization. For the poorer or less clever colonist who was the loser in the brisk competition of colonial life, almost all the potential satisfaction of material aspirations had to lie in the wilderness across the frontier. But dreams of what this far and future state might hold were accompanied by fear of the dangers of the unknown. Often this resulted in ambivalent beliefs about the wilderness, such as the idea, amongst some colonists in the northern part of the South Island, that a great inland plain lay beyond the mountains, across which stalked giant birds that might kick a man to death.[5] Materially attractive but socially repugnant, the wilderness was thus a source of considerable anxiety to the recent colonist. In this context it is possible, I think, to understand something about the symbolism of colonial moa sightings.

The colonist's dilemma may be restated in this way: released from a familiar landscape, society and social order he is confronted with increasing unfamiliarity and disorder as he moves closer to the wilderness, but he is compelled towards that goal by the aspirations, or desperation, that prompted his migration in the first place. His fear is that geographical and social disorder will upset his own moral and psychological order (cf. Douglas 1970, p. 114), and that the wilderness will induce in him the appropriate moral degeneracy of a disordered world and thus reduce him to the status of a savage or wild man.

The Wild Man has been, of course, a long-standing and powerful image of individual moral and material dissolution in European civilization (White 1978, pp. 150–81, Thomas 1983, p. 134). It is an image of personal rather than group decline and the intimacy of the threat has been translated into a spatial conception of the Wild Man as 'inhabiting the immediate confines of the community. He is just out of sight, over the horizon, in the nearby forest . . . [he] . . . is conceived to be covered in hair and to be black and deformed . . . [and he] . . . almost always represents the image of the man released from social control' (White 1978, p. 166). The Wild Man could thus come to the mind's eye as a grotesque human or human-like monster whose manifestation marked the edge of the wilderness. In this marginal position his relationship to the observer had an element of ambiguity. The threat represented by the Wild Man might be plain enough, but the fate was not inevitable and his appearance on the frontier served as a territorial warning that a prudent traveller would heed.

In the present case, however, it was moa that were seen, and not wild men or other human forms. Furthermore there existed appropriate models for an indigenous Wild Man image, had one been sought. The Maori feared a race of wild humans, known as *maero*, who were entirely covered in hair except upon the forehead and who skewered their prey by means of their long, sharp fingernails. There was some initial interest shown in *maero* by early European travellers in the South Island interior, but the myth seems to have been overtaken on several fronts before it could gain a hold on the European imagination.[6] The testimony of moa bones, which proved that these giant beasts had existed, and not long before, rapidly promoted moa to pre-eminence in the public mind during the 1840s. At the same time the *maero* myth became entangled with Maori stories of the 'Lost Tribe' and was thus ensnared by the Noble Savage image, which is the obverse of the Wild Man coin (cf. White 1978, p. 191).

But apart from anything else, colonial moa were really a quite sufficient model for the Wild Man image to inhabit. Conceived as tall, upright, rather slim, bipedal creatures that were conspicuously covered in feathers (sometimes of a woolly appearance), and occasionally having large heads and eyes, they were at once ambiguously human, as suited their degenerate status, and almost believable to a morphologically adequate extent as moa.

One proposition may be added to conclude this argument. If fear of our own capacity for uninhibited behaviour, especially violence, is metaphorically designated the Beast Within (e.g. Midgley 1980, pp. 36–44, 1988), then fear of what we might become in situations beyond our present experience may be regarded as the Beast Without. But as soon as one creates this juxtaposition it becomes evident that these fears are essentially the same: the loss of civilized standards of social and moral behaviour. The Beast Without is also the Beast Within, or to put it another way, the colonists at the frontier feared themselves and sometimes projected their fears into warning visions of quasihuman moa.

It is not difficult to see that an interesting comparison might be made between this explanatory model and other cases of similar frontier myths, which stem, in the European literature at any rate, from 19th-century colonial observations. The human-like Sasquatch, Yeti, and Almasti are obvious examples (Shackley 1982). More broadly, this study suggests that further analysis of the nature imagery of 19th-century European settler societies may contribute to our understanding of other aspects of the anthropology of migration and colonisation.[7]

Notes

1   Of 34 references to this question by Maori, only five considered moa survived beyond 1840, and then only by vague speculation about survival in remote areas. The few prosaic recollections of moa stood alongside an elaborate mythological tradition of moa as giant birds with human faces and other odd characteristics (Anderson n.d.).

2   Actually a dish of rolled, stuffed mutton flap – gooselike but no goose.
3   One immediate origin of this conception was possibly the moa skeletons in museums which were frequently set up in an unnaturally elongated fashion in the mid-19th century (Fig. 18.2). There were no reconstructed moa to demonstrate body bulk until the end of the century.
4   If any actual thing was seen in the Central Otago cases it might have been a feral horse or bovine beast, since these were sparsely distributed throughout the district before the arrival of prospectors in the 1860s.
5   These tales also belong, of course, to the universal class of stories about a flawed utopia.
6   In the Coromandel district of the northern North Island well away from areas of colonial moa sightings, the miners did, in fact, take up a *maero* myth. It still persists as the so-called 'Moehau Monster'.
7   As Thomas (1983, p. 40) argues, animal symbols were also useful in the continuous process of human self-definition (see also Rowland 1973, p. xv).

References

Anderson, A. J. n.d. *Prodigous birds: moas and moahunting in prehistoric New Zealand.* Cambridge: Cambridge University Press, in press.

Beattie, H. 1958. *The Moa: when did it become extinct?* Dunedin: *Otago Daily Times and Witness.*

Beattie, H. n.d. Information mainly about moas. Unpublished manuscript. Dunedin: Hocken Library.

Buick, T. L. 1931. *The mystery of the moa.* Wellington: Board of Maori Ethnological Research.

Colenso, W. 1879. On the moa. *Transactions of the New Zealand Institute* **12**, 63–108.

Douglas, M. 1970. *Purity and danger: an analysis of concepts of pollution and taboo.* Harmondsworth: Penguin.

Field, H. C. 1893. The date of the extinction of the moa. *Transactions of the New Zealand Institute* **26**, 560–8.

Haast, H. F. 1948. *The Life and times of Sir Julius von Haast.* Wellington: The Author.

Malmberg, T. 1980. *Human territoriality: survey of behavioural territories in man with preliminary analysis and discussion of meaning.* The Hague: Mouton.

McCulloch, B. 1982. *No moa.* Christchurch: Canterbury Museum.

Midgley, M. 1980. *Beast and man: the roots of human nature.* London: Methuen.

Midgley, M. 1988. Beasts, brutes and monsters. In *What is an animal?* T. Ingold, (ed.), 35–46. London: Unwin Hyman.

Rowland, B. 1973. *Animals with human faces: a guide to animal symbolism.* Knoxville: University of Tennessee Press.

Shackley, M. 1982. The case for Neanderthal survival: fact, fiction or faction. *Antiquity* **56**, 31–41.

Taylor, R. 1855. *Te Ika a Maui: New Zealand and its inhabitants.* London: Wertheim MacIntosh.

Thomas, K. 1983. *Man and the natural world: changing attitudes in England 1500–1800.* London: Allen Lane.

White, H. 1978. *Tropics of discourse: essays in cultural criticism.* Baltimore: Johns Hopkins University Press.

Wynn, G. 1983. Settler societies in geographical focus. *Historical Studies* **20**, 353–66.

Newspapers: *Nelson Examiner*, *Otago Daily Times*, *Otago Witness*.
Letters: Overton, C. F. to Skinner, H. D. (Otago Museum), March 1951.

19 *The meaning of the snake*

ROY WILLIS

> Science and the humanities, biology and culture, are bridged in a
> dramatic manner by the phenomenon of the serpent. (Wilson 1984,
> p. 83)

The inspiration for this chapter was a reading of Mundkur's path-breaking
survey of ophidian symbolism worldwide, *The cult of the serpent* (1983, and
see 1988). In this powerful work, Mundkur, a biologist, brings together
evidence from ethnology, psychology, ethology, and biology to support his
thesis that the snake has a special significance for *Homo sapiens* and probably
all the primate species, a significance that is genetically inscribed in these
species' physiology. In human beings this special meaning takes the form of
an attitude polarized between the emotions of fear and awe – hence, according to Mundkur, the near ubiquity of serpentine cults in human cultures,
both past and present, around the globe. This massive body of cross-
disciplinary evidence strongly suggests that the snake was the first, and
remains the most fundamental, of all animal symbols.

Mundkur's scholarly *tour de force* has had remarkably little impact on
sociocultural anthropology, even though his findings are manifestly relevant to our understanding of human nature, of the relation between humanity and nonhuman animality, and the origins of human religious experience.
All of these are problems that might reasonably be supposed to be of general
and perennial concern to archaeology and anthropology. To understand the
reasons for anthropology's current neglect of Mundkur's important argument requires a digression into the modern history, and prehistory of our
subject.

A little more than a century ago Tylor, who is quite properly regarded as
the 'father' of British anthropology, announced in his Introduction to
Primitive culture (Tylor 1871 p. 2) the inauguration of a new social science
that would consider itself 'a branch of natural science' and would deliber-
ately follow the methods and approach of the natural scientists in their
recognition of 'the unity of nature, the fixity of its laws, the definite
sequence of cause and effect through which every fact depends on what has
gone before it, and acts upon what is to come after it'. In advocating this role
for anthropology, Tylor was explicitly aligning himself with the contention
of Mill who, in *A system of logic* (1843), had maintained the necessary identity
of the methods of natural and social science.

Such statements imply a certain view of the world, what social anthropologists nowadays call a cosmology. In most so-called 'primitive' (i.e. non-

literate) societies, such socially accepted views of 'reality' are embodied in the symbolic form of myth. Cross-culturally, Western culture is relatively unusual in possessing a recorded history from which it is possible to identify one individual as primarily responsible for the construction of the currently dominant cosmology. That individual was the 17th-century French philosopher Descartes.

Descartes, who is generally regarded as the founder of modern philosophy, wrote at a time of what today would be called 'paradigm shift'. The then conventional but disintegrating medieval cosmology featured a flat earth with its centre in the Holy Land, and a graded continuum from pure spirit to gross matter mediated through a hierarchy of invisible and visible beings with man in the middle, lording it over the lower animals. That cosmology had been shattered by the triple blows of the discovery of the New World, Copernicus's demolition of geocentric astronomy, and Galileo's demonstration that certain abstract and immutable laws governed the behaviour of material objects. In constructing wht was to become a new and resoundingly successful cosmological paradigm, Descartes took as his fundamental principles the common and probably universal polar categories of spirit and mind (more conveniently denoted in French by one word, *esprit*) and matter. What was novel in the cosmology proposed in Descartes' *Discours de la méthode* (1637) is that instead of seeing these two principles as complementary, as in the case of all cosmologies, both literate and tribal, so far described, Descartes posited both a fixed hierarchy of mind over matter and an absolute separation between them.

In Descartes' cosmology *Res cogitans*, 'the thinking thing' was entirely different in its mode of being and in the methods by which that mode of being could be investigated, from *Res extensa*, the realm of material reality. Spirit and mind were as alien from the world of nature as the natural world was devoid of consciousness. Where the world of spirit and mind was to be investigated by the methods of introspection and logical inference, the inherently mindless world of nature was to be investigated, and progressively understood and dominated, by the dual method of isolating the most fundamental components of material reality and studying the interactions and causal relations between them. This new cosmological vision, bizarre as it might seem to a naïve observer, was, as we know from the record of history, hugely successful in forming men's (the masculine noun is intentional) view of the universe and the world they lived in, and in enabling Western civilization to achieve an unparalleled domination of the Earth and nature.

As Thomas, a social historian, observes in *Man and the natural world* (1983, pp. 34–5):

> Descartes' explicit aim had been to make men 'lords and possessors of nature' ... he [Descartes] portrayed other species as inert and lacking any spiritual dimension. In so doing he created an absolute break between man and the rest of nature, thus clearing the way very satisfactorily for the uninhibited exercise of human rule.

The Cartesian vision was subsequently developed through analogical reasoning. As nonhuman animals were unfeeling machines ('automata'), so the human body was also to be understood as a machine, though mysteriously inhabited by an immortal spirit. In due course the English mathematician and astronomer Newton was to extend the 'machine' metaphor to the entire physical universe. The Cartesian cosmology legitimized the British Industrial Revolution in the later eighteenth and nineteenth centuries, and, by extending the analogy with inert matter to preindustrial and tribal societies and cultures, inspired the development of what Leclerc (1972) has called 'the first scientific colonialism' in which non-European peoples and their cultures were assimilated to the world of objects, to be controlled and manipulated at will. The Cartesian methodology and cosmology made possible the development of modern science and technology, including modern medicine and, finally, social science and anthropology. In turn these various social achievements served to reinforce the Cartesian world-view and to make it seem increasingly self-evident, an unquestioned assumption.

Such was the situation in the Western world in 1871, when Tylor saw in 'the sciences of inorganic nature', or what today would be called physics, the exemplars of what a true social science should become. As Tylor (1871, p. 3) saw it, the only real obstacles to making the study of human social behaviour as thoroughly 'scientific' as physics were 'the practical ones of enormous complexity of evidence, and imperfection of methods of observation'. It was the task of a scientific anthropology to remedy these 'practical' deficiencies.

More than a century later we find anthropology in a very different situation. Even before the end of the 19th century, growing awareness of the enormous variety of human cultural arrangements, as well as their internal complexity, was diverting attention from the Tylorian search for general laws of human society to the in-depth study of particular societies. This change in perspective, pioneered in the United States by Boas, was later developed by Malinowski in Britain into the now characteristic anthropological method of problem-oriented field research. A parallel development in psychology was the rise of behaviourism. This theoretical school, founded in the United States by Watson, reformulated the Cartesian dichotomy as one between a formative and dominating culture and a human being who was pictured as an automaton devoid of 'mind' or 'consciousness' (Watson 1914).

Watsonian behaviourism, the doctrine crystallized in the famous phrase that 'human beings have no nature' was understandably welcomed by social scientists, including anthropologists, with a professional interest in the supremacy of cultural over physiological factors in human behaviour. According to the philosopher Midgley (1979, p. 20), 'there seems to be nobody who studied any sort of social science in English-speaking countries between the wars who was not taught it [Watson's doctrine] as gospel'.

Meanwhile physics, the major scientific support of Cartesian dualism in the mid-19th century, had dramatically rejected that cosmology in 1927.

This was the year in which physicists, by accepting Heisenberg's uncertainty principle, broke with the Cartesian idea of an objective world of nature divorced from the consciousness of human beings. Since then, Capra argues (1982, p. 77):

> the sharp Cartesian division between mind and matter, between the observer and the observed, can no longer be maintained. We can never speak about nature without, at the same time, speaking about ourselves.[1]

Scientists of this persuasion have abandoned the concept of nature as a machine, the workings of which are to be understood by studying the behaviour of its smallest component parts; on the contrary for them it is the whole that determines the behaviour of the parts. And this interconnected web of cosmic relations is no longer inert, as in the models of Descartes and Newton, but alive (Capra 1982, pp. 76–8).

This 'scandalous' development in physics has not, so far, been followed in other branches of Western science, which has thus lost the monolithic unity of a century ago. In this century biology, particularly molecular biology, has emerged as the standard-bearer of Cartesian dualism. Biology's achievements have recently inspired some scientists, including certain anthropologists, to project the construction of a new branch of knowledge to be called sociobiology (and see Shennan, in press) after Wilson (1975), its founder. According to one of its philosophical proponents, Rosenberg (1980, p. x):

> closer attention to methods and concepts drawn from the natural sciences, especially biology, will lead to successes where conventional social science has hitherto failed. The premises of my explanation of the failures of the social sciences are at the same time premises in an argument that they be replaced, superseded, preempted, by sociobiology.

Rosenberg is advancing exactly the same argument about the nature of a true science of human society and culture as that proposed by Mill and Tylor, but with the difference that for Rosenberg, as for Wilson and his followers, biology rather than physics has become the paradigm of scientific theory and practice. It is against this background of competing cosmologies in Western science, of Cartesian certainties and post-Cartesian uncertainties, that Mundkur has set his thesis on the snake and its seemingly primordial role as a focus for human cultic behaviour.

In his massively documented study of serpent symbolism all over the world and through vast periods of history and prehistory, Mundkur (1983) seeks to show that for the whole human species, and possibly all primates, the snake has a special significance that sets it apart from all other animate objects. It appears that virtually all human cultures, including, surprisingly, those associated with parts of the globe like Lappland, where snakes are unknown, accord a particular prominence to the serpent symbol. Why should this be so? That is the pressing question posed by *The cult of the serpent*. Mundkur has little trouble in demonstrating the inadequacy or probable falsity of a number of current theories of serpent symbolism, particularly the widely accepted ideas of Freud and Jung, which are shown to be what anthropologists would call ethnocentric and culture-bound.

If, with Mundkur, we survey the prodigious variety of symbolic meanings associated with the serpent in different cultures it has to be conceded, I think, that no other animal is so rich in meaning for the whole human species. What is also noticeable is the common *polarization* of the serpent symbol into opposed but complementary images. Prominent in creation myths worldwide, it is also commonly associated with death and chaos. The anthropologist Drummond (1981, p. 644) notes how the famous Ouroborous image of the self-devouring serpent shows it as at once phallus and vagina, male and female, and thus as 'a perfect and naturally occurring image of androgyny'.

In Australia the rainbow snake is associated with both sky and earth, and in Central Africa the mythical serpent Nkongolo (also called 'rainbow') mediates between heaven and earth, between wet and dry seasons (Warner 1957, de Heusch 1972).

In *Biophilia* (1984) Wilson, the founder of sociobiology, cites Mundkur's survey and offers his own experience of the potency of the snake symbol. First, he recounts a recurrent dream in which he is intensely aware of a powerful serpentine being that is both 'life-promising and life-threatening, seductive and treacherous'. Then he tells of a frightening incident involving a large and lethal water mocassin encountered in the swampland of Florida. Impelled by what afterwards seemed an irrational urge, Wilson attempted to capture this creature, found it was too strong for him and was lucky to escape unharmed. He asked himself: 'What is there in snakes anyway that makes them so repellent and fascinating?' (Wilson 1984, pp. 83–4, 91–3).

I met my own serpent during field research in southwest Tanzania among the Bantu-speaking Fipa people. I had been staying in a remote hamlet on the Fipa plateau, in the home of a renowned indigenous doctor or *sing'aanga* ('father of knowledge') called Matiya Isaamba Msangawale. The doctor had invited me to stay with him and learn about his art and practice after observing my interest in his work. One evening, after a tiring day watching my host interview his clients, go into trance, and prescribe 'medicines', I went off alone into the surrounding bush in an attempt to 'unwind'. Some distance from the hamlet I heard a rustling in the long grass to my right, and was surprised to see a large snake, about five feet long and several inches in girth, cross my path only a few yards away and disappear into the grass to my left. The creature was jet black and its scales were shining in the light of the setting sun. What was equally as striking as its appearance was the way it was moving, in slow undulations that raised its body in rhythmic loops to a foot or so above the ground.[2]

This sight had an extraordinary effect on me. I recognized the snake as

Nalwiiko, the Fipa word for the spitting cobra. I also knew that its beauty was so compelling that I had to follow it, which I did, turning into the long grass where, after what may have been only a few steps, I encountered the animal again. This time it was coiled, its head drawn into the centre of the coil and gazing up at me. Again, the overwhelming emotion was awe at its strange beauty, the delicately sculpted head, the brilliant eyes, the glistening scales of its lithe body.[3] Throughout this dream-like encounter I felt as though it was happening to someone else. I viewed it with detached curiosity such as I had once before experienced in hospital, close to death (as I learned later), watching a doctor struggling, rather comically as it seemed, to attach a saline drip to an obstinately elusive vein in my ankle. I felt a similarly uninvolved curiosity about the outcome of this incident with the snake, noting with some surprise the total absence in me of any sensation of fear. Gazing with interest into the eyes of Nalwiiko, I saw no anger there, but yet a warning that said: Come no closer! Still I was close enough to sense the snake saw no less clearly into my own mind, that it registered my passionate admiration and awe.

Regrettably, I recall no more of what, if anything, passed on that singular occasion between man and beast. The next thing I remember is being back in my Fipa host's tiny village, drinking millet beer, and physically unharmed. Whether I told Matiya or anyone of my strange encounter I do not recall either, but I suspect not: it was far too intensely private for that. And if I can tell it now, it is probably because it happened a long time ago.

Notes

1 As Heisenberg (1958, p. 75) later commented: 'Natural science does not simply describe and explain nature; it is a part of the interplay between nature and ourselves; it describes nature as exposed to our method of questioning. This was a possibility of which Descartes could not have thought, but it makes the sharp distinction between the world and the I impossible'.

2 Tomas Håkannson, a knowledgeable Swedish colleague, tells me that such a mode of locomotion would be abnormal for a snake. Possibly; but I record what I seemed to see.

3 It may be relevant that, according to Wilson (1978, p. 102), 'when a rattlesnake ... is confronted by an animal large enough to threaten its safety, it coils [and] pulls its head forward to the center of the coil in striking position'.

References

Capra, F. 1982. *The turning point: science, society and the rising culture.* London: Fontana.

Drummond, L. 1981. The serpent's children: semiotics of cultural genesis in Arawak and Trobriand myth. *American Ethnologist*, 633–60.

Heisenberg, W. K. 1958. *Physics and philosophy: the revolution in modern science.* London: Allen & Unwin.

de Heusch, L. 1972. *Le roi ivre, ou l'origine de l'état.* Paris: Gallimard.

Leclerc, G. 1972. *Anthropologie et colonialisme: essai sur l'histoire de l'africanisme*. Paris: Fayard.

Midgley, M. 1979. *Beast and man: the roots of human nature*. Brighton: Harvester Press.

Mill, J. S. 1843. *A system of logic*. London: John Murray.

Mundkur, B. 1983. *The cult of the serpent: an interdisciplinary survey of its manifestations and origins*. Albany: State University of New York Press.

Mundkur, B. 1988. Human animality, the mental imagery of fear, and religiosity. In *What is an animal?* T. Ingold (ed.) 141–84. London: Unwin Hyman.

Rosenberg, A. 1980. *Sociobiology and the preemption of social science*. New Haven: Yale University Press.

Shennan, S. 1989. Cultural transmission and cultural change. In *What's new? A closer look at the process of innovation*, S. E. van der Leeuw & R. Torrence (eds), Ch. 16. London: Unwin Hyman.

Thomas, K. 1983. *Man and the natural world: a history of the modern sensibility*. New York: Pantheon Books.

Tylor, E. B. 1871. *Primitive culture*. 2 vols. London: John Murray.

Warner, W. L. 1957. *A black civilization: a social study of an Australian tribe*. New York: Harper.

Watson, J. B. 1914. *Behavior: an introduction to comparative psychology*. Cambridge, Mass.: Harvard University Press.

Wilson, E. O. 1975. *Sociobiology: the new synthesis*. Cambridge, Mass.: Harvard University Press.

Wilson, E. O. 1978. *On human nature*. Cambridge, Mass.: Harvard University Press.

Wilson, E. O. 1984. *Biophilia*. Cambridge, Mass.: Harvard University Press.

Index